Business Innovation and Growth: Tax Incentives and Sources of Funding

Business Innovation and Growth: Tax Incentives and Sources of Funding

Andrew Bourg and Derek Henry

CHARTERED
ACCOUNTANTS
IRELAND

Published in 2018 by
Chartered Accountants Ireland
Chartered Accountants House
47–49 Pearse Street
Dublin 2
www.charteredaccountants.ie

ISBN 978-1-912350-18-6

Typeset by Datapage
Printed by Turner's Printing Company, Longford, Ireland

To Brenda, our three wonderful children, Sophie, Abby and Andy, and to my parents, Antoinette and Andy, to whom I owe everything.

Andrew Bourg

To my mother and father, Mary and Martin, for everything they have done for me, and with love to Niamh, Mary, Róisín and Matthew.

Derek Henry

Contents

PART III: GETTING INVESTOR-READY

Introduction

The purpose of this book is to provide an overview of the direct taxation supports available to companies (at all stages of their development) undertaking and planning innovation and growth strategies in Ireland. It outlines and summarises the sources of funding for both innovation and growth available as a result of the changed company-funding landscape that has emerged in recent years, in terms of equity and debt finance options, government funding and supports, and other, relevantly new funding sources, such as peer-to-peer and crowdfunding.

This book is designed to help companies and their advisors plan and maximise the return on investment from their innovation endeavours, as well as highlighting the funding options available to fund a company's innovation and growth journey. Additionally, the book outlines how companies can get 'investor-ready' by preparing to plan, apply for and secure investment be it equity, debt or otherwise. In this regard, it is primarily aimed at business owners or the finance team within companies that are seeking to ensure all relevant reliefs, funding sources and supports are availed of or considered.

The book is in three parts:
- Part I – Taxation Supports for Innovation and Growth;
- Part II – Sources of Funding for Innovation and Growth; and
- Part III – Getting Investor-Ready.

Overview of Part I – Taxation Supports for Innovation and Growth

Part I deals with the direct taxation supports that are available, mapping these supports to the various stages of 'the innovation lifecycle' a company would typically undertake and follow.

The Innovation Lifecycle

The figure below illustrates a typical innovation lifecycle and is a derivation of the innovation model used by Osawa and Miyazaki.[1] It traces the innovative process (for a product or a service) from conception through to exploitation, i.e. from idea to commercialisation. The x axis of the figure represents profit/loss and the y axis represents time.

---

[1] Osawa, Y. and Miyazaki, K., "An empirical analysis of the valley of death: Large-scale R&D project performance in a Japanese diversified company (2006) *Asian Journal of Technology Innovation*, Vol. 14 No. 2, 93–116.

THE INNOVATION LIFECYCLE

Investigation	Feasibility	Development	Introduction	Growth	Maturity

Proof of concept   Pre-seed ⟶ Seed and start-up   ⟶   Early   First, second, etc.

PROFIT

LOSS

First revenues

Valley of death

TIME

Outlined horizontally across the top of the figure are the stages of the innovation process. These innovation stages can be related and translated to business phases as follows:

Innovation Phase	Business Phase
1. Investigation 2. Feasibility	Research
3. Development	Development
4. Introduction 5. Growth	Growth
6. Maturity	Realisation and Exit

The 'valley of death' (for innovation) is a well-known concept used in the start-up world or for innovation projects. It refers to the challenge faced by nascent companies/projects that are attempting to finance the cash-flow negative early stage of the process, i.e. the pre-revenue/commercialisation phase.

Mapping Tax Reliefs to the Innovation Lifecycle

Part I of the book maps the taxation supports available to companies to the various stage of the 'innovation lifecycle'. In Part I, these are presented in three phases:

- Phase A – Starting the Business (**Chapters 1** and **2**);
- Phase B – Development and Growth (**Chapters 3** to **6**); and
- Phase C – Realisation/Exit (**Chapters 7** to **9**).

These phases can be summarised as follows:
- Phase A introduces, at a high level, the tax reliefs that are available generally to assist companies in the raising of investment funding.
- Phase B deals in detail with tax reliefs that support a company's activities in creating (**Chapter 3**) and commercially exploiting (**Chapters 4, 5** and **6**) innovation.
- Phase C introduces, at a high level, the strategies that should be considered when investors exit a company, either through a sale to a third party or transfer to the next generation in a family company situation.

The full map of these tax relief/incentives and how they relate to the innovation lifecycle is represented below.

THE INNOVATION LIFECYCLE

TIME

Note: The book does not cover VAT or stamp duty that may be relevant.

Overview of Part II – Sources of Funding for Innovation and Growth

Part II of the book provides an overview of the possible sources of funding for innovation and growth. **Chapter 10** details how, following the 2007–2008 global financial crisis and an over-reliance on bank funding by a high proportion of Irish SMEs, a new funding landscape has emerged in which SMEs can diversify their funding sources, thereby avoiding an over-reliance on one particular funding source (i.e. bank funding) from happening again. This book distinguishes four funding pillars, discussed in detail in **Chapters 11 to 14**:
- **Chapter 11** focuses on equity finance (Funding Pillar 1) – how all businesses require a level of equity finance, the unique characteristics of equity, key terms to understand when raising equity, valuing an equity stake, the advantages of equity and the types and sources of equity finance.

- **Chapter 12** reviews debt finance (Funding Pillar 2) – how the aftermath of the financial crisis led to a reduction in active bank lenders and a reduced appetite for risk, and how part of this SME lending gap has been filled by an increase in alternative debt lenders along with the Strategic Banking Corporation of Ireland (SBCI), which offers a range of flexible credit facilities to SMEs.
- **Chapter 13** looks at the range of government funding and supports (Funding Pillar 3) available to SMEs through their lifecycle, which can consist of both financial and non-financial supports. These include supports from specific government organisations like Enterprise Ireland and Local Enterprise Offices, as well as industry-specific supports from organisations such as An Bord Bia, Fáilte Ireland, etc.
- **Chapter 14** examines other possible funding sources (Funding Pillar 4), including peer-to-peer lending and crowdfunding.
- **Chapter 15** considers whether there is an ideal debt-to-equity funding mix, and includes the thoughts and views of an SME founder (Justin Keatinge, co-founder of IT services company, Version 1), a banker, (Andrew Graham, Director, Corporate Banking, Bank of Ireland) and a later-stage funder (Oral O'Gorman, Head of Equity Listing Ireland at Euronext).

Overview of Part III – Getting Investor-Ready

Part III looks at how SMEs can become investor-ready, with **Chapter 16** setting out what prospective investors expect to see in a business plan. **Chapter 17** reviews pitching to investors and what they seek and assess when considering a lending/investment opportunity. **Chapter 18** contains a summary key take aways' of the dos and don'ts of fund raising.

Up-to-date to 30 September 2018, we hope that readers find this book useful in their innovation endeavours.

(**Note:** At the time of publication (November 2018) there are a number of changes proposed to the Employment Incentive and Investment Scheme (EII Scheme) under Finance Bill 2018 which, if approved, will be enacted into legislation in late 2018. These proposed changes primarily deal with the administration of the scheme and the self-certification by SMEs and investors that they qualify. As these changes had not yet been approved at the time of publication, they have not been reflected here in **Chapters 2** or **11**.)

Acknowledgements

Andrew Bourg

To the publishing team at Chartered Accountants Ireland, especially Michael Diviney: many thanks for your support, guidance and constructive suggestions throughout the planning and editing of the book.

Thank you to my co-author, Derek Henry, for your encouragement and assistance throughout. It has been a pleasure working with you.

To my fellow Partners at BDO with a special call out to Sinead Heaney and Michael Costello, thank you for your continuous encouragement and assistance.

I am sincerely grateful to my esteemed colleagues who provided me with valuable input as well as the proofing of specific chapters of the book, namely Stuart Mellon, Ashley Dixon, Anthony O'Driscoll, John Flynn, Terry McGrenaghan and Robert Rumley – thank you all.

Sincere thanks to the business leaders who were kind enough to be interviewed for the book: Justin Keatinge (co-founder of Version 1), Andrew Graham (Director, Corporate Banking, Bank of Ireland) and Orla O'Gorman (Head of Equity Listing Ireland at Euronext). Thank you for sharing your invaluable experiences and insights on funding SMEs, allowing these useful experiences and suggestions to be recorded – they will be very useful to all SMEs undertaking the funding journey.

To my wonderful children, Sophie, Abby and Andy, your patience and support while Daddy became an 'author' has earned significant brownie points! To my mother Antoinette and late father Andy, thank you for your support and encouragement, no matter what.

Above all, I would like to thank my wife Brenda for her love, guidance and understanding while I undertook this project.

Derek Henry

I would like to acknowledge the support I received from my fellow partners and colleagues in BDO, particularly, Mark O'Sullivan for his assistance in drafting Chapter 3 and Cian O'Sullivan (no relation!) for his assistance in the drafting of Appendix 3.4 to Chapter 3. Thank you also to Ciara Treacy for her extensive proof-reading of the initial drafts of all chapters, and to Alan Kirby, Philip Slattery and Mark Kilduff for their input on the project. I very much appreciate the input of Kevin Doyle, John Gilmor-Gavin, David Giles, Eddie Doyle and Angela Fleming in their technical review of various chapters, and that of Teresa Morahan and Stephen McCallion on the accounting aspects of the book. I would also like to thank Ciaran Medlar, Head of Tax and Michael Costello, Managing Partner, for their support.

Thank you to my co-author, Andrew Bourg, who has been an enthusiastic pleasure to work with on this project.

Thank you also Áine Hollingsworth in the Revenue Commissioners for her input on a number of aspects of the book, particularly Chapter 5.

I would like to thank our editor, Michael Diviney, for his guidance and patience.

I would like to thank all my clients with whom I have had the pleasure of working with over the years. Without the trust of such excellent clients, I would not have developed the experience that I have tried to reflect in this book.

Thank you to my family for their support during the writing process and their acceptance of the time contributed to compiling this book. I would like to acknowledge the support my father, mother-in-law and father-in-law has given through extended childcare duties.

I want to thank my three beautiful children, Mary, Róisín and Matthew for their patience.

Most importantly, I want to thank my wife, Niamh, for the love and support she has given me through this process. Thank you, I love you.

PART I

TAXATION SUPPORTS FOR INNOVATION AND GROWTH

Phase A: Starting the Business
1. Startup Refunds for Entrepreneurs
2. The Employment and Investment Incentive Scheme

Phase B: Development and Growth
3. The Research and Development Tax Credit
4. Start-up Companies Relief
5. The Knowledge Development Box
6. Specified Intangible Asset Allowances

Phase C: Realisation/Exit
7. The Holding Company Regime
8. Revised Entrepreneur Relief
9. Retirement Relief

Part I outlines all of the tax incentives and reliefs that can be used by companies that are carrying on innovation in Ireland. This includes both tax reliefs that specifically target innovating companies and general tax reliefs of which any company within the charge to Irish corporation tax can avail. As the focus of this book is on innovation, detailed analysis is provided of the tax reliefs aimed at companies carrying out innovation, while a more high-level introduction to the general tax reliefs is included.

As discussed in the main **Introduction**, the taxation supports available to companies at the various stages of the 'innovation lifecycle' are presented in Part I in three phases:
- Phase A – Starting the Business (Chapters 1 and 2);
- Phase B – Development and Growth (Chapters 3 to 6); and
- Phase C – Realisation/Exit (Chapters 7 to 9).

These phases can be summarised as follows:
- Phase A introduces, at a high level, the tax reliefs that are available generally to assist unlisted companies in the raising of investment funding.
- Phase B deals in detail with tax reliefs that support a company's activities in creating (Chapter 3) and commercially exploiting (Chapters 4, 5 and 6) innovation.
- Phase C introduces the strategies that should be considered when investors exit the unlisted company either through a sale to a third party or transfer to the next generation in a family company situation.

The tax reliefs discussed in Phases A and C are generally available to all companies and investors, i.e. they are not specific to companies carrying out innovation. In this regard, the chapters dealing with these phases provide overviews intended to help the reader consider whether the reliefs discussed may apply to their situation. However, detailed examinations of these topics are beyond the scope of this book and, where possible within the chapters, references are made to sources of more extensive information.

The taxation supports covered in Phase B (with the exception of Chapter 4, The Start-up Companies Relief) were specifically designed and introduced to encourage activities resulting in the creation and/or exploitation of intellectual property by companies in Ireland, i.e. innovation and innovation-related activities. Thus, the chapters in Phase B provide more detailed analysis.

Part I is structured to help you identify what tax reliefs you should be considering, depending on the current position of your business or project on the innovation lifecycle. While we have tried to reflect the typical chronological order in which a company would encounter the various tax reliefs, there are, however, always exceptions and variations. Of particular note is that the R&D tax credit (Phase B, Chapter 3) may need to be considered very early in a company's lifecycle, and sometimes before any funds are raised that would attract relief under either Startup Refunds for Entrepreneurs (SURE) or the Employment Investment Incentive Scheme (EII Scheme) (Phase A, Chapters 1 and 2).

CHAPTER 1

STARTUP REFUNDS FOR ENTREPRENEURS

1.1 Introduction

As all ideas begin with individuals, this first chapter discusses the Startup Refunds for Entrepreneurs (SURE), which is a tax relief that focuses on certain types of entrepreneurs and is particularly relevant to helping relieve cash-flow pressures during the earlier phases of the innovation lifecycle.

SURE is intended to encourage people to start up their own businesses, in particular where a person was previously in receipt of income which was subject to PAYE, e.g. employees. The relief allows the entrepreneur a refund of income tax paid in the prior six years under the PAYE up to 40% of the capital that the entrepreneur invests in their new business. SURE can provide entrepreneurs with a level of cash flow during the early phases of the innovation lifecycle (as illustrated in the figure below) before any non-founder investors have committed funding to the new enterprise. This can be crucial to allow the entrepreneur to carry out early research and validate their idea.

RELEVANT STAGE(S) IN THE INNOVATION LIFECYCLE: SURE

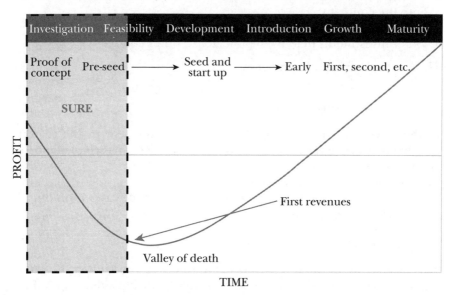

Because SURE is aimed at new companies, it is therefore only relevant to companies at the earlier phases of the innovation lifecycle.

1.2 The Relief

To qualify for SURE, the entrepreneur, who is someone who has had mainly PAYE income for the prior four years, must set up a new company which carries on qualifying trading activities, into which they invest cash by way of purchase of new shares and they must become a full-time working director or employee of the company.

Most investment tax reliefs are focused on the types of companies into which the investment is being made, rather than the type of investor. SURE relief, while having criteria relating to the type of company that can be invested in, gives more emphasis to the type of investor that can avail of the relief. In this regard, we will first look at the types of entrepreneurs who are regarded as 'eligible investors' and then look at the types of companies into which a qualifying investment can be made.

1.2.1 Eligible Investor

To be eligible for tax relief for making an investment under the SURE relief, the entrepreneur who makes the investment must satisfy certain criteria to be regarded as an 'eligible investor'. Section 495 of the Taxes Consolidation Act 1997 (TCA 1997) provides the conditions for an individual to be a 'specified individual' and therefore an eligible investor for the purposes of SURE. In summary, to be an eligible investor there are a number of criteria that need to be met in relation to:
1. prior income sources;
2. the type of investment (a 'relevant investment') that needs to be made into the company;
3. the investor's future role in the company; and
4. other investments held by the investor in other companies.

These criteria are discussed below.

1.2.1.1 Prior Income Sources

In the three years preceeding the year before the year of the relevant investment, the eligible individual must not have been in receipt of income chargeable to tax otherwise than:
(a) income subject to Irish PAYE, or
(b) income that arose from an employment or office carried on outside the State, in excess of the lesser of:
    (i) the aggregate of (a) and (b), and
    (ii) €50,000.

This means that in the three years before the year preceeding the investment, to be regarded as an eligible investor an individual must have mainly[1] earned their income from sources that are taxed under PAYE or sources that would have been so taxed but the activities were carried on outside the State, i.e. foreign employment income. The amount that can be earned from non-PAYE-type income is the lower of the PAYE-type income earned or €50,000. Thus, an eligible investor cannot earn more than €50,000 from non-PAYE-type sources even if their PAYE-type income is greater than €50,000. If their non-PAYE income is less than €50,000, it cannot be more than their PAYE-type income. For example, if the individual has €60,000 PAYE-type income, they can earn up to €50,000 non-PAYE-type income. If the individual earns €40,000 PAYE-type income, they can only earn up to €40,000 non-PAYE-type income.

Note: This restriction only applies to the three years preceding the year before the year of the relevant investment. The individual can earn income from any source in the year immediately preceding the year of the relevant investment.

1.2.1.2 Relevant Investment

To be eligible for SURE, an investor must own a minimum of 15% of the issued ordinary share capital of the company from the date of the investment and they must hold at least this amount for at least four years after the investment. The investor must subscribe for eligible shares, which are new ordinary shares in the company that carry no present or future preferential rights to dividends, assets on winding up or a right to redemption.

1.2.1.3 Role in the Company

An eligible investor must enter full-time employment with the company, either as an employee or director, for a period of 12 months commencing either within the year of the date of the investment or, if later, within six months of when the share issue is made.

The individual must not receive any payment from the company other than a reasonable remuneration and expenses in the three years after the investment.

1.2.1.4 Other Investments

In the 12-month period prior to the first investment, an eligible investor must not have owned more than a 15% interest in any other company, unless:
(a) the other company is dormant, i.e. it has had no turnover for the last three years prior to the initial investment; or
(b) the company was a trading company and has not had annual turnover exceeding €127,000 in any of the last three accounting periods prior to the initial investment.

---

[1] The legislation requires that prior income derives mainly from PAYE as the relief is trying to encourage former PAYE employees to become self-employed – see **Section 1.1**.

1.2.1.5 Follow-on Investment

It is possible for an eligible investor to make two relevant investments in the company for which SURE relief can be granted. The second investment must take place within two years of the end of the first year in which the first investment was made.

Note: An investment can be made over a number of months in a calendar year and all the investments made in the calendar year will be regarded as one relevant investment.

1.2.2 Qualifying Company

As discussed above in **Section 1.2**, while the SURE legislation has a significant focus on the types of entrepreneurs, i.e. eligible investors, that can avail of the relief, it does also specify the types of companies, 'qualifying companies', into which the eligible investor can make a qualifying investment. The concept of a 'qualifying company' is considered in this section.

Section 494 TCA 1997 provides detailed conditions that need to be satisfied if a company is to qualify for SURE, which are summarised as follows:
1. The company must be incorporated in Ireland or in another European Economic Area (EEA) Member State.
2. The company must be a new company (incorporated within two years) and must not be taking over an existing trade.
3. The share capital of the company must be fully paid up.
4. The company must, throughout the relevant period, be an unquoted company resident in Ireland or, if resident in an EEA Member State, carrying on business in Ireland through a branch or agency.
5. The company must either:
   (a) exist wholly for the purpose of carrying on 'relevant trading activities' (see below) that are being carried on through a fixed place of business in the State; or
   (b) carry on the business of holding shares or securities in a qualifying company.
6. The company must be a micro, small or medium-sized enterprise within the meaning of Annex 1 to Commission Regulation (EU) No. 651/2014 (the General Block Exemption Regulation (GBER)).[2]

1.2.2.1 'Relevant Trading Activities'

As discussed above, to be a qualifying company, the company (or its subsidiary) must be carrying on relevant trading activities. 'Relevant trading activities' are those activities carried on in the course of a trade, the profits

---

[2] Commission Regulation (EU) No. 651/2014 of 17 June 2014 declaring certain categories of aid compatible with the internal market in application of Articles 107 and 108 of the Treaty, OJ L 187, 26.6.2014, pp. 1–78.

or gains of which are charged to tax under Case I of Schedule D, i.e. normal trading activities, **excluding** activities related to the following:

(a) adventures or concerns in the nature of trade (typically, types of transactions covered by these terms include once-off or speculative transactions);

(b) dealing in commodities or futures or in shares, securities or other financial assets;

(c) financing activities;

(d) the provision of services that would result in a close company providing those services being treated as a service company for the purposes of section 441 TCA 1997 if that close company has no other source of income (examples of the types of companies excluded by this definition are standard professional services companies including, *inter alia*, accountancy practices);

(e) dealing in or developing land;

(f) the occupation of woodlands within the meaning of section 232 TCA 1997;

(g) operating or managing hotels, guest houses, self-catering accommodation or comparable establishments or managing property used as a hotel, guest house, self-catering accommodation or comparable establishment (except where such operation is a tourist traffic undertaking[3]);

(h) operating or managing nursing homes or residential care homes or managing property used as a nursing home or residential care home;

(i) operations carried on in the coal industry or in the steel and ship-building sectors; and

(j) the production of a film,

but including tourist traffic undertakings.

Finance Act 2014 removed item (h) from this excluded activities list. It also provided that internationally traded financial services[4] are to be considered a relevant trading activity subject to certification by Enterprise Ireland.

Finance Act 2015 introduced a provision allowing for monies raised under SURE to be used to expand the capacity of nursing homes or residential care units.

---

[3] Operating or managing hotels, guest houses, self-catering accommodation or comparable establishments or managing property used as a hotel, guest house, self-catering accommodation or comparable establishment will be regarded as a tourist traffic undertaking where: (a) it is registered with the National Tourism Development Authority; (b) is approved for the purpose of the relief by the Minister for Finance; or (c) promotes outside the State facilities covered by (a) or (b).

[4] 'International traded financial services' means services specified by the Industrial Development (Service Industries) Order 2010 (S.I. No. 81 of 2010) other than those covered by items (b) and (c) in the list.

1.2.2.2 Companies that Have Not Commenced to Trade

A company that has not commenced to trade and therefore has not met the relevant trading activities test may still qualify for SURE where it:

(a) commenced relevant trading activities within two years after the eligible shares (see **Section 1.2.1.2** above) were issued and expended all of the money subscribed for eligible shares on either of those relevant trading activities or research and development (R&D) activities before the end of a four-year period; or

(b) expended all of the money subscribed for eligible shares on R&D activities within a period ending one month before the end of a four-year period and disposed of a specified intangible asset within the meaning of section 291A TCA 1997 (see **Chapter 6**), which is connected with and arises directly from those R&D activities, to a person for the purposes of a trade carried on by that person.

In summary, it is essential that the company uses the money raised from relevant investments to fund trading or R&D activities within four years of the date of the relevant investment.

1.2.3 Claims for Relief

Where an eligible investor makes a relevant investment they are due a tax deduction for the amount invested from their total income for any one or more of the six tax years immediately before the tax year in which the eligible shares were issued. The investor nominates the years within this time period in which they chose to take the tax deduction. Outlined below is an example of how this relief would be claimed and the effect of the relief on an eligible investor's various tax liabilities.

EXAMPLE 1.1: SURE IN OPERATION

Michael was made reduntant in November 2017. In December 2017, he invests €100,000 in a new company that he has set up to develop and manufacture efficient light bulbs. Over the last seven years, Michael has earned all his income from his employment, which was subject to PAYE as set out below.

Year	Salary	PAYE (excluding PRSI and USC/income levy)
2017	€75,000	€21,590
2016	€90,000	€27,590
2015	€80,000	€23,590
2014	€80,000	€24,262
2013	€75,000	€22,212

2012	€55,000	€14,012
2011	€45,000	€9,912
2010	€35,000	€4,876

Michael decides to offset €90,000 of his investment against his 2016 income and receives a tax refund of €27,590. He sets the remaining €10,000 of his investment off against his 2015 income and receives a further refund of €4,000.

1.2.4 Limits on the Relief

The minimum investment eligible for SURE is €250. The maximum investment under the scheme that may qualify for income tax relief is €100,000 in any one year. This means that eligible investors can invest up to €700,000 as they can get up to €100,000 in tax relief in each of the six years prior to the investment and €100,000 in tax relief in the year of investment.

A company can raise a maximum amount of funding through the combination of the EII Scheme (see **Chapter 2**) and SURE of €5,000,000 in any one year and €15,000,000 over the company's lifetime.

1.2.5 Withdrawal/Withholding of Relief

SURE relief may be withdrawn if the conditions attached to it relating to the qualifying company (see **Section 1.2.2**) cease to be satisfied within four years of the investment being made or, if later, of the commencement of trading.

Relief may also be wholly or partly withdrawn if the investor receives value from the qualifying investee company or disposes of the shares within four years of subscribing for same. Value can be received from the investee company if, for example, it redeems shares or makes the investor a loan or provides a benefit or facility to the investor.

Disposals between spouses will generally not result in a loss of SURE relief.

The receipt of reasonable and necessary remuneration and/or normal return on investment does not constitute the 'receipt of value' from the investee company, i.e. the eligible investor is entitled to earn a normal salary or return on investment without triggering a withdrawal of the relief.

Relief will not be given where there is an agreement, arrangement or understanding which could reasonably be considered to have eliminated the risk that the person owning the shares might at any time specified or any time thereafter, be unable to realise, directly or indirectly, in money or monies worth, an amount so specified or implied, other than a distribution in respect of those shares.

In summary, for the investment to be a relevant investment for SURE, the eligible investor's investment must be an at-risk investment. Provisions or legal mechanisms cannot be put in place to protect the eligible investor's investment should the venture fail, e.g. a legal mechanism such as some sort of call option whereby the investor is guaranteed return of their investment even in the event of the company liquidation.

1.2.6 Anti Tax Avoidance

SURE relief is not available unless shares (the relevant investment) are subscribed for and issued for bona fide commercial purposes and not as part of a scheme or arrangement, the main purpose, or one of the main purposes of which, is the avoidance of tax. As outlined above in **Section 1.2.5**, investments in shares that are subject to any agreement, arrangement or understanding which could eliminate the risk for the investors do not qualify for relief.

1.3 State Aid Disclosures

In 2014, the EU introduced new transparency requirements concerning state aid granted by Member States to undertakings. As a result of these new requirements, certain previously private, confidential and potentially commercially sensitive information will now be made publicly available. The disclosure of this information may cause concern for both eligible investors and qualifying companies. In accordance with Article 9 and Annex III of the GBER, EU Member States are required to publish details of certain state aid granted to individual beneficiaries from 1 July 2016. Section 507 TCA 1997 now provides tax relief granted to eligible investors under the SURE scheme above a cumulative threshold of €500,000, subject to these transparency requirements.

Member States are required to publish the information on a central website and the information should include the identity of the beneficiary, the amount and type of aid granted and the date on which it was granted. For aid in the form of a tax relief, the information is to be published within 12 months from the date on which the relevant tax return for the relevant tax year is due, e.g. an eligible investor's tax return will be due in October/November following the end of the year and the information should be published within 12 months from this date.

As just discussed, publication will be based on the date on which the relevant tax return for the relevant tax year is due. However, aid that has been granted before 1 July 2016 does not fall under the transparency obligation, even if the tax return in which the relief is claimed is due after that date. The 12-months deadline for publishing the information starts from the due date of the tax return that pushes the beneficiary over the threshold.

1.4 Conclusion

SURE provides eligible investors an opportunity to recover tax paid through PAYE over the six years prior to the investment. The purpose of the relief is to encourage former PAYE employees to become entrepreneurs and set up their own businesses. There are a number of quite technical concepts and criteria that need to be satisfied for an entrepreneur to be regarded as an eligible investor; however, if the investor qualifies for the relief, substantial cash flow can be made available by virtue of the recovered PAYE, which can help support the development of the new business. SURE is availed of usually by founders of new business and, therefore, is the subject of our first chapter in 'Phase A – Starting the Business'.

As discussed in this chapter, SURE focuses on the status of the entrepreneur. In the next chapter, we will look at a related investor tax relief, the Employment and Investment Scheme, which has less onerous criteria for the investor to meet to avail of the relief, albeit in circumstances not as potentially valuable to the investor.

As a reminder of its key features and requirements, we include below an 'At a Glance' summary of the SURE relief.

At a Glance: Startup Refunds for Entrepreneurs (SURE)

What is the relief?	The relief provides an opportunity for eligible investors to set off investment amounts against their PAYE tax liability of the six years prior to the investment.
This relief is potentially of value if:	1. the investors had mainly PAYE income in the four years prior to making an investment; 2. the investor invests cash in a new company through the purchase of new shares; 3. the company carries out qualifying trading activities; 4. the investor enters full-time employment with the company as an employee or director.
This relief is likely to be of benefit to:	Entrepreneurs who, in the four years prior to making the investment, were earning significant amounts of income subject to PAYE.
Interactions with other reliefs:	SURE is complementary to the Employment and Investment Scheme (see **Chapter 2**). However, there are cumulative limits on the amount of investments that can be raised under both schemes over the lifetime of the company.

CHAPTER 2

THE EMPLOYMENT AND INVESTMENT INCENTIVE SCHEME

2.1 Introduction

The Employment and Investment Incentive Scheme (EII Scheme) is a tax relief incentive scheme (previously called the Business Expansion Scheme (BES)) which provides all-income tax relief to eligible investors for investments in certain qualifying small and medium-sized trading companies (SMEs).[1]

The EII Scheme offers one of the few remaining income tax reliefs for investors and one of the few sources of all-income tax relief (which includes, e.g. rental income).

The benefit for a company availing of the EII Scheme is that it can secure investment that is committed to the company for at least a medium-term period (four years minimum) at a fixed cost of capital.[2] As the investment is an equity investment (see **Chapter 11**), the balance sheet of the company is improved, which can, for example, increase the opportunity to raise additional investment by way of bank borrowings or, indeed, other potential investors including, e.g. Enterprise Ireland. Additionally, the company achieves a cash-flow benefit due to the investment type and the rules of the EII Scheme as there are no repayments until after the four-year investment period.

From an investor's perspective, the EII Scheme allows the investor to reduce the risk of their investment by giving the investor all-income tax relief, which in effect reduces the investor's cost of investment.

---

[1] The qualifying company must be a micro, small or medium-sized enterprise within the meaning of Annex 1 to Commission Regulation (EU) No 651/2014 of 17 June 2014 (generally known as the General Block Exemption Regulation (GBER)) declaring certain categories of aid compatible with the internal market in application of Articles 107 and 108 of the Treaty, OJ L 187, 26.6.2014, pp. 1–78).

[2] Generally, structured EII Scheme investments have a capped rate of return; however, some higher-risk, earlier-stage investments can have an uncapped rate of return.

RELEVANT STAGE(S) IN THE INNOVATION LIFECYCLE: THE EII SCHEME

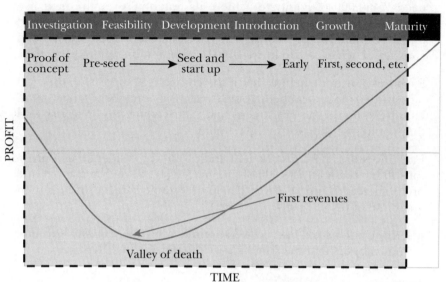

While the above figure shows how the EII Scheme is available at many of the stages of the innovation lifecycle, it is important to remember that the EII Scheme is designed to help earlier-stage SMEs raise finance, meaning that the above is not relevant to larger companies that do not meet the SME criteria.

While traditionally the EII Scheme (and its predecessor, the BES) was available to most trading companies irrespective of where they were in the innovation lifecycle, the introduction of the new general block exemption rules (see below at **Section 2.2.4.1**) has made it more difficult in certain cases for companies achieving their first commercial sales more than seven years before the investment to claim the relief and, therefore, has pushed the EII Scheme in most cases towards the earlier phases of the innovation lifecycle. However, given that companies can reach maturity stages within seven years from establishment, the representation of the EII Scheme spanning the above stages is appropriate.

The following example illustrates the benefits from the company's and the investor's perspective of undertaking an EII Scheme and demonstrates how the EII Scheme can be used through the middle stages of the innovation lifecycle, i.e. the growth stage.

EXAMPLE 2.1: USING THE EII SCHEME TO HELP FINANCE
THE GROWTH STAGE

Debbie has a software development company, EIIS Innovations Ltd, which she successfully started three years ago. She has decided to undertake an ambitious growth plan and believes that the company needs €400,000 of equity to achieve its potential over the next five years. She identifies four potential investors among her friends and unconnected business contacts who have the resources to invest in the company. Each agrees to invest €100,000 for a minimum of four years.

Each investor understands that if the company is successful, they will be entitled to a capped return of 10% on their investment. However, should the investment fail, their capital will be at risk and they could lose their entire investment.

Each investor is Irish tax resident and ordinarily resident. Each investor will have at least €75,000 of income subject to their marginal rate of tax in Year 1 and at least €25,000 of income subject to their marginal rate of tax in Year 4.

EIIS Innovations Ltd has received outline approval from the Revenue Commissioners that the company will qualify for the EII Scheme.

Year 1

Each of the investors subscribes for €100,000 in capped ordinary shares in EIIS Innovations Ltd and in their Year 1 income tax return receive an income tax deduction in relation to 30/40ths of the amount invested, reducing their tax liability by €30,000 (i.e. €100,000 × 30/40 = €75,000 × marginal income tax rate 40% = €30,000).

Year 4

EIIS Innovations Ltd has satisfied the conditions in relation to employment levels or expenditure on research and development to facilitate investors claiming the second tranche of income tax relief (see **Section 2.2** below).

Therefore, each of the investors, in their Year 4 income tax return, can receive a deduction from income tax in relation to 10/40ths of the amount invested, reducing their tax liability by €10,000 (i.e. €100,000 × 10/40 = €25,000 × marginal income tax rate 40% = €10,000).

Year 5

Debbie would like to further expand the company and would like to exit the EII Scheme investors such that she regains 100% of the shares in the company. Therefore, she buys each investor out for their original €100,000 investment plus 10%.

Chargeable gains are subject to capital gains tax (CGT) at 33% and it is assumed that the investors each have available the full amount of the €1,270 annual CGT exemption for an individual.

Investment Analysis for Each Investor

Economic Gain

Sale proceeds	€110,000
Net cost of investment (see (A) below)	(€60,000)
Gross gain	€50,000
CGT (see (B) below)	(€2,881)
Net gain	€47,119

(A) Net Cost of Investment		(B) CGT	
Amount invested	€100,000	Sale proceeds	€110,000
Less Year 1 tranche of EII Scheme income tax relief	(€30,000)	Amount invested	(€100,000)
Less Year 4 tranche of EII Scheme income tax relief	(€10,000)	Capital gain	€10,000
Net cost of investment	€60,000	Annual exemption	(€1,270)
		Chargeable gain	€8,730
		CGT at 33%	(€2,881)

Cost of Capital for EIIS Innovations Ltd

Amount raised	€400,000
Amount repaid after five years	€440,000
Cost of funds	€40,000
IRR	2.41%

2.2 The Relief

The EII Scheme was introduced in Finance Act 2011 (amended in 2014 and 2015) and is set out in Part 16 of and Schedule 10 to the Taxes Consolidation Act 1997 (TCA 1997), as amended.

The relief on an investment in a qualifying company is available to the investor in two tranches as detailed below:
1. the relief enables investors to deduct 30/40ths of the amount subscribed ('first tranche of income tax relief') to the qualifying company from their total income for income tax purposes for the year in which they make the investment; and

2. the relief will enable investors to deduct 10/40ths of the amount subscribed ('second tranche of income tax relief') to the qualifying company from their total income for income tax purposes for the year of assessment following the end of the four-year investment period, subject to the fulfilment of the conditions set out below:

    (a) staff numbers of the qualifying company have increased by a minimum of one member of staff and the total wage levels have increased by a minimum of the wage of one member of staff in the year of assessment preceding the end of the four-year investment period compared to the staff numbers and the total wage levels in the year of assessment prior to the year of assessment in which the subscription for eligible shares (see **Section 2.2.2** below) was made; **or**

    (b) the amount of research and development (R&D) expenditure (as defined by section 766 TCA 1997 (see **Chapter 3**)) incurred by the qualifying company in the year of assessment preceding the end of the four-year investment period exceeds the amount of R&D expenditure incurred by the qualifying company in the year of assessment prior to the issue of the eligible shares.

The maximum amount of EII Scheme relief an investor can claim in one year is €150,000. If an investor subscribes for eligible shares of more than €150,000 in one year, the relief will not apply to the amount invested above €150,000 in the year of investment. However, in such cases, the excess relief above €150,000 can be claimed in future years of assessment. (Further detail is set out in **Section 2.2.6** below.)

2.2.1 Basic Rules

Relief may only be claimed by an eligible investor who subscribes for new eligible shares in a qualifying company where those shares are issued for the purpose of raising money, which was used, is being used or is intended to be used by the qualifying company as follows:

1. for the purposes of carrying on 'relevant trading activities' (see **Section 2.2.4.5** below) which are, or will be, carried on within a specified period (normally two years) by such a qualifying company, or by a qualifying subsidiary of a holding company, as defined by section 494(3)(ii); or

2. in the case of a company that has not commenced to trade, in incurring expenditure on R&D; and

3. the use of the money as set out in 1 and 2 above will contribute directly to the creation or maintenance of employment in the company.

2.2.2 Eligible Shares

Eligible shares are new ordinary fully paid-up shares which, throughout the holding period beginning on the date on which they are issued, carry no present or future preferential rights to dividends, to assets on a winding up, or to be redeemed. No relief is available to an investor in relation to eligible shares where such shares are subject to any agreement, option or understanding which:

(a) would or could require a person to purchase or otherwise acquire the investor's shares at a price other than a price equal to the market value of the shares at the time of purchase or acquisition; or

(b) would or could require the investor to dispose of their shares at a price other than a price equal to the market value of the shares at the time of the disposal.

2.2.3 Eligible Investor

To be an eligible investor, the individual must be tax resident in Ireland and must not be connected with the investee company at any time in the period two years before or four years after the issue of the eligible shares.

The main rules relating to 'connection' with a company ('connected parties') are that:

(a) an investor or their associate must not be in partnership with the company or an employee or director of the company (except employees or directors who receive payments that are reasonable and necessary remuneration for services to the company); or

(b) a qualifying investor, or their associate, must not control the company, possess more than 30% in aggregate of the ordinary share capital or the aggregate of the loan capital and issued share capital or the voting power in the company.

For this purpose, an 'associate' includes a partner and certain persons with whom the individual has connections through a trust, will or estate. An investor will be an associate (for the purpose of (a) and (b) above) with another person if they are partners, i.e. are in partnership together.

2.2.4 Qualifying Company

To be a qualifying company, the company will, throughout the relevant period (i.e. four-year period from the date of investment) be an unquoted company that is resident in Ireland, or another European Economic Area Member State other than Ireland, provided it carries on business in the State through a branch or an agency.

The qualifying company must exist wholly for the purpose of carrying on relevant trading activities where those activities are principally carried on in the State and/or be a holding company of a subsidiary which carries on a relevant trading activity. During the relevant period, the company's share capital must be fully paid up.

2.2.4.1 General Block Exemption Regulation

The qualifying company must be a micro, small or medium-sized enterprise within the meaning of Annex 1 to the GBER.

A qualifying company must also meet the requirements of paragraphs 5 and 6 of Article 21 of the GBER.

Paragraph 5 of Article 21 of the Regulation states that eligible undertakings are undertakings that, at the time of the initial risk finance investment, are unlisted SMEs and fulfil at least one of the following conditions:
1. they have not been operating in any market;
2. they have been operating in any market for less than seven years following their first commercial sale; or
3. they require an initial risk finance investment which, based on a business plan prepared in view of entering a new product or geographical market, is higher than 50% of their average annual turnover in the preceding five years.

Paragraph 6 of Article 21 states that the risk finance aid may also cover follow-on investments made in eligible undertakings including, after the seven-year period mentioned at item 2 above, if the following **cumulative** conditions are fulfilled, i.e. all three conditions are met:
(a) the total amount of risk finance mentioned in paragraph 9 of Article 21[3] is not exceeded;
(b) the possibility of follow-on investments was foreseen in the original business plan; and
(c) the undertaking receiving follow-on investments has not become linked, within the meaning of Article 3(3) of Annex I of the GBER with another undertaking other than the financial intermediary or the independent private investor providing risk finance under the measure, unless the new entity fulfills the conditions of the SME definition.

A further condition of being regarded as a qualifying company for the purposes of the EII Scheme is that to comply with the EU rules on the cumulation of state aids, a company that has raised capital under the EII Scheme is obliged to reduce the maximum level of any other state aids[4]:
- by 50% for companies located in non-assisted areas; and
- by 20% for companies located in assisted areas.

---

[3] Paragraph 9 of Article 21 of the GBER states that the total amount of risk finance shall not exceed €15 million per eligible undertaking under any risk finance measure.

[4] With the exception of schemes approved under the R&D and Innovation State-aid Framework. The EU Regional Aid Guidelines (RAGs) allow each Member State to provide enhanced rates of state aid in the least economically developed areas of each country, i.e. 'assisted areas'. Areas falling outside these regions are regarded as 'non-assisted areas'. All counties in Ireland have been designated as 'assisted' with the exception of Dublin, Cork, Kildare (except Athy), Meath (except Kells) and Wicklow (except Arklow).

2.2.4.2 Companies that Are Members of Groups

Save for a holding company structure (as detailed below), a qualifying company cannot be a subsidiary of or be controlled by any other company. While a qualifying company may have subsidiaries itself, each subsidiary must be carrying on a 'relevant trading activity' (see **Section 2.2.4.5**) or the subsidiary's trade must consist of one or more of the purchase, sale or provision of services to, or on behalf of, the qualifying company. (An example of a qualifying subsidiary is a sales office located in a foreign country that sells or buys products on behalf of the qualifying company.) The qualifying company must hold at least 51% of the shares of the subsidiary and control it.

2.2.4.3 Companies in Financial Difficulty

A company will cease to be a qualifying company if before the end of the relevant period a resolution is passed, or an order is made, for the winding up of the company or the company is dissolved without winding up, other than for bona fide commercial reasons.

A company will not qualify while it is regarded as being in difficulty for the purposes of the Community Guidelines on State Aid for Rescuing and Restructuring Firms in Difficulty.[5]

2.2.4.4 Funding Limits

The maximum relief available under the EII Scheme in the lifetime of a qualifying company and its associates[6] is an investment of €15 million subject to a limit of €5 million in any 12-month period.

2.2.4.5 Relevant Trading Activities

Relevant trading activities are those activities carried on in the course of a trade, the profits or gains of which are charged to tax under Case I of Schedule D, excluding activities related to the following:
(a) adventures or concerns in the nature of trade;
(b) dealing in commodities or futures or in shares, securities or other financial assets;
(c) financing activities;

---

[5] Commission Communication 2004/C 244/02, OJ C 288 of 9.10.99, p. 2 and OJ C 244 of 1.10.2004, p.2. The European Commission regards a firm as being in difficulty where it is unable, whether through its own resources or with the funds it is able to obtain from its owner/shareholders or creditors, to stem losses which, without outside intervention by the public authorities, will almost certainly condemn it to go out of business in the short or medium term.
[6] See definition of 'associate' as provided by section 433(3) TCA 1997 as amended by section 488(1) TCA 1997.

(d) the provision of services that would result in a close company that provides those services being treated as a service company for the purposes of section 441 TCA 1997 if that close company had no other source of income;

(e) dealing in or developing land;

(f) the occupation of woodlands within the meaning of section 232 TCA 1997;

(g) operations carried on in the coal industry or in the steel and ship-building sectors; and

(h) the production of a film (except where such activity involves a tourist traffic undertaking).

Where the relevant trading activity is a tourist traffic undertaking, e.g. a hotel or guest house, the company undertaking the activities will not be a qualifying company unless prior approval of Fáilte Ireland is received.

Finance Act 2014 provided that internationally traded financial services can be considered a relevant trading activity subject to certification by Enterprise Ireland.

Finance Act 2015 introduced a provision allowing for monies raised under the EII Scheme to be used to expand the capacity of nursing homes or residential care units.

2.2.5 Claims for Relief

Claims for income tax relief under the EII Scheme may be made when the qualifying company has carried on a relevant trading activity for at least four months and must be made:

1. within two years of that date (i.e. the fourth month of carrying on relevant trading activities) or, if later, two years from the end of the year of assessment in which the EII Scheme eligible shares are issued; or

2. when the qualifying company expends not less than 30% of the money subscribed for the shares on R&D activities which are connected with and undertaken with a view to the carrying on of the company's relevant trading activities.

In this regard, an eligible investor must claim the tax relief on their investment within two years from the date the company has been trading for four months or, if later, the date the eligible shares have been issued. The second option is relevant for companies that have been trading for longer than four months. If the qualifying company is carrying on R&D activities and, therefore, may not have commenced to trade, then the eligible investor can claim the tax relief once 30% of the money raised by the company under the EII Scheme has been spent on R&D activities.

A qualifying company must qualify for a tax clearance certificate at the time the claim is made under the EII Scheme.

2.2.6 Limits on the Relief for the Investor

The maximum investment in all EII Scheme investments in any one year that may qualify for income tax relief (in two tranches) is €150,000. The first tranche of income tax relief is available in the tax year of subscription to the qualifying company. In the case of a husband and wife, each is entitled to subscribe up to €150,000 to the extent that each spouse has income in their own right. Unused amounts of relief may not be transferred between spouses. Relief is not given to an investor for an investment of less than €250 in one company in any tax year where the claimant invests directly.

Investors who subscribe for shares in a qualifying company in excess of €150,000 in any one tax year may carry forward the relief to the following year. Investors who have insufficient total income to claim full relief for their investment in the year of issue can claim relief for the balance of the investment in the following years subject to each investor's particular tax circumstances.

2.2.7 Withdrawal/Withholding of Relief

Relief under the EII Scheme may be withdrawn if the conditions attached to it relating to the qualifying company (see **Section 2.2.2.4**) cease to be satisfied within four years of the investment being made or, if later, of the commencement of trading.

Relief may also be wholly or partly withdrawn if the investor receives value from the investee company or disposes of the shares within four years of subscribing for same. Value can be received from the investee company if, for example, it redeems shares or makes the investor a loan or provides a benefit or facility to an investor. Disposals between spouses will generally not result in a loss of relief. For employees, the receipt of reasonable and necessary remuneration and/or normal return on investment does not constitute the 'receipt of value' from the investee company.

Relief shall not be given where there exists an agreement, arrangement or understanding that could reasonably be considered to have eliminated the risk that the person owning the shares might at any time specified or any time thereafter, be unable to realise, directly or indirectly, in money or monies worth, an amount so specified or implied, other than a distribution in respect of those shares. For example, these provisions prevent situations in which eligible investors enter into agreements with the company or the company's founders whereby the eligible investors' risk of investment is reduced or eliminated. Legal mechanisms such as fixed-price puts and call option agreements, which could be used to guarantee the eligible investor the return of their money, are not permitted by these provisions.

The second tranche of income tax relief will not be given unless the conditions, i.e. increases in employment numbers or R&D expenditure, set out in the second paragraph of **Section 2.2** above are fulfilled by the qualifying company.

There are additional rules whereby an investor may suffer a withdrawal of some or all of the relief by reason of other non-qualifying shareholders receiving value from the company (i.e. section 497 TCA 1997).

2.2.8 Exit of EII Scheme Eligible Investors

2.2.8.1 Share Disposal

Commonly, EII Scheme eligible investors are not long-term investors in companies in Ireland. They tend to invest for a defined period of time, claim their tax relief, receive any return that can be achieved (and often agreed) over the period and then divest from the company. Discussed below is the common manner in which they divest from the company.

Generally, when eligible shares are disposed of, the transaction falls to be taxable under CGT rules with any gain subject to the CGT rate, currently 33%. However, in certain circumstances, Revenue can seek to apply an income tax treatment to the disposal of shares under a number of specific and general provisions of legislation. This would mean that any gain would be subject to the taxpayers' marginal rate of income tax, as well as Universal Social Charge (USC) and Pay-related Social Insurance (PRSI). Based on current rates, this could be up to 55%. For the purpose of illustration, it is assumed that CGT treatment will apply.

Where CGT treatment applies on the disposal of eligible shares, the full acquisition cost can be deducted from the proceeds in an arm's length sale (i.e. third-party sale) in order to calculate the gain, if any, for CGT purposes. However, if they are disposed of at a loss, no allowable loss for CGT purposes will be recognised.

2.2.8.2 Share Redemption

Where a shareholder divests their investment by a redemption of the shares, i.e. the company uses its distributable reserves to buy back the shares from a particular investor, the excess returned to the investor above the capital that they originally invested in the company is regarded as a distribution/dividend. This classification means that the company is obliged to operate dividend withholding tax (DWT) at the rate of 20% and pay the net proceeds to the investor. The distribution element of the return is then subject to income tax in the hands of the investors and the marginal rate of income tax applies (currently up to 55%) with a credit for the DWT suffered.

However, section 176 TCA 1997 does allow CGT treatment to apply where all of the following summarised conditions are met:
1. the redemption of shares is made wholly or mainly for the purpose of benefiting the trade of the company;

2. the redemption does not form part of a scheme or arrangement the main purpose, or one of the main purposes, of which is to enable the owner of the shares to participate in the profits of the company without receiving a dividend;
3. the shareholder has held the share for at least five years;
4. the shareholder has substantially reduced their shareholding in the company (i.e. the percentage of the company that they own after the redemption does not exceed 75% of the percentage of the company they owned before the redemption);
5. the shareholder must not be connected[7] with the company after the redemption; and
6. the shareholder must be resident and ordinarily resident in the State.

2.2.9 Anti Tax Avoidance

Relief is not available under the EII Scheme unless the eligible shares are subscribed for and issued for bona fide commercial purposes and not as part of a scheme or arrangement, the main purpose, or one of the main purposes of which, is the avoidance of tax. Investments in shares that are subject to any agreement, arrangement or understanding which could eliminate the risk for the investors who do not qualify for relief, as discussed at **Section 2.2.7** above.

2.3 State Aid Disclosures

In accordance with Article 9 to and Annex III of the GBER, EU Member States are required to publish details of certain state aids granted to individual beneficiaries from 1 July 2016. Tax relief granted to eligible investors under the EII Scheme above a cumulative threshold of €500,000 are subject to these transparency requirements.

Member States are required to publish the information on a central website,[8] including the identity of the beneficiary, the amount and type of aid granted and the date on which it was granted. For aid in the form of a tax relief, the information should be published within 12 months from the date on which the relevant tax return for the relevant tax year is due, e.g. for an income tax relief for the year 2018 a return would be filed in October 2019 and the disclosure would need to be made by Revenue by October 2020.

---

[7] As provided by section 180 TCA 1997 (see section 10 TCA 1997 for specific definition of 'connected' in this context).
[8] At the time of writing, this website is not available. The Revenue Manual in relation to this issue is located at https://www.revenue.ie/en/tax-professionals/tdm/income-tax-capital-gains-tax-corporation-tax/part-37/37-00-39.pdf. Once the website is available, this Manual is likely to be updated to include a link to the new website.

However, aid that has been granted before 1 July 2016 does not fall under the transparency obligation even if the tax return in which the relief is claimed is due after that date. The 12-months deadline for publishing the information starts from the due date of the tax return that pushes the beneficiary over the threshold.

2.4 Interactions with the Startup Refunds for Entrepreneurs

The EII Scheme is provided for by the same legislation as the Startup Refunds for Entrepreneurs (SURE) (see **Chapter 1**). The funding limits discussed above at **Section 2.2.4.4**, i.e. €5 million in any one year and €15 million over the company's lifetime, are applied to both schemes cumulatively under the EU state aid rules. This means if a qualifying company raises €1 million through SURE in one year, the maximum the company can raise through the EII Scheme is €4 million.

2.5 Conclusion

Early stage SMEs can find it more difficult than established companies with proven track records to raise external investment. The EII Scheme offers SMEs the opportunity to attract equity investment from external investors by giving the eligible investors an income tax relief, which to a degree de-risks the investment from the perspective of the eligible investor. The EII Scheme (and its precursor, the Business Expansion Scheme (BES)) has been an essential source of funding assistance for SMEs in Ireland for many years.

In **Chapters 1** and **2** (Phase A), we have dealt with tax reliefs available to individuals making investments in companies. For 'Phase B – Development and Growth' (**Chapters 3** to **6**), we will now change the focus to tax reliefs available to those companies that incur expenditure on innovation.

As a reminder of its key features and requirements, we include below an 'At a Glance' summary of the EII Scheme relief.

AT A GLANCE: THE EMPLOYMENT AND
INVESTMENT INCENTIVE SCHEME

What is the relief?	The relief is an all income tax relief for investors who make an equity investment in qualifying companies.
This relief is potentially of value:	If the company: • is an SME; • carries on qualifying activities; and • is seeking to raise equity finance.

This relief is likely to be of benefit to:	• SMEs that are trying to attract equity investment and do not have the track record or scale to raise institutional investment. • Eligible investors who can commit funds to a company for at least a four-year period and would like to shelter income tax liabilities.
Interactions with other reliefs:	While the EII Scheme and the Startup Relief for Entrepreneurs (SURE) can be claimed together, amounts raised by companies under both schemes are combined for the purpose of the maximum investment limits that can be raised under the various state aid rules.

CHAPTER 3

THE RESEARCH AND DEVELOPMENT TAX CREDIT

3.1 Introduction

The company, or members of the company, may have commenced activities seeking to develop new, or improve on existing, materials, products, devices, processes, systems or services. (This can be undertaken for the benefit of the company or as a project for an external or third party.)

The company believes that these activities will act to provide a benefit above and beyond what is currently available either (a) on the market, or (b) internally, to the extent that existing solutions on the market are proprietary in nature, i.e. are protected as intellectual property (e.g. a patent).

In such circumstances, it is likely that the company is in a position to claim the Research and Development (R&D) Tax Credit, which could allow the company to reduce the cost of its R&D activities by up to 37.5% in total, i.e. 25% cost reduction as a result of the R&D Tax Credit available, in addition to the 12.5% corporation tax deduction available for such activities.

The R&D Tax Credit was introduced by Finance Act 2004, amending section 766 of the Taxes Consolidation Act 1997 (TCA 1997) to encourage companies to take the risk of carrying out R&D activities that may lead to commercially successful outcomes. The purpose of the tax credit[1] is to incentivise both indigenous and multinational companies to commit to carrying on R&D activities in the European Economic Area (EEA), and particularly in Ireland, thus promoting the creation of highly skilled jobs and further strengthening Ireland's position as an innovation hub.

When originally introduced in 2004, the regime was to be an incremental scheme, i.e. it aimed to incentivise companies to increase their spending on R&D year on year. In this regard, 2003 was set as the base year and any incremental spend on R&D activities above this base was incentivised with a 20% tax credit that could be utilised against the corporation tax liabilities of the company.

However, over the years, the regime has been amended with changes that have made the tax credit more valuable and better fit for purpose. Thus, the tax credit that is currently in place under section 766 TCA 1997 gives companies a 25% tax credit (increased from 20%) on all qualifying R&D

---

[1] For clarity, a tax 'credit' is an amount that reduces a tax liability. A tax 'relief' is an amount that is allowed as a deduction in calculating the income/profits that are subject to tax.

expenditure incurred in the accounting period (i.e. the incremental system has been replaced with a full-volume system[2]) and that credit can be used to reduce corporation tax payable. Where there are no corporation tax liabilities, the tax credit can be claimed as a cash refund, subject to requirements (see **Section 3.4.2** below). With the introduction of the cash refund option for the R&D Tax Credit, the credit became, from an accounting perspective, more akin to a government grant rather than a tax relief, as getting a benefit from the credit is now more dependent on the company incurring expenditure rather than having a tax liability. This changed how the credit could be treated in the accounts, significantly allowing companies to recognise the credit before the profit figure in the income statement, thereby increasing the profit before tax. This can be important for companies and the treatment and benefits are covered in **Appendix 3.4** to this chapter.

There are a number of key criteria that companies need to meet to avail of this tax credit, namely:
1. the applicant must be a company;
2. the company must be within the charge to Irish tax (i.e. subject to corporation tax in Ireland);
3. the company must undertake qualifying R&D activities within the EEA;
4. in the case of an Irish tax-resident company, the expenditure must not qualify for a tax deduction under the law of another territory;
5. the activities carried on must represent R&D activities as defined in section 766 TCA 1997.

RELEVANT STAGE(S) IN THE INNOVATION LIFECYCLE: THE R&D TAX CREDIT

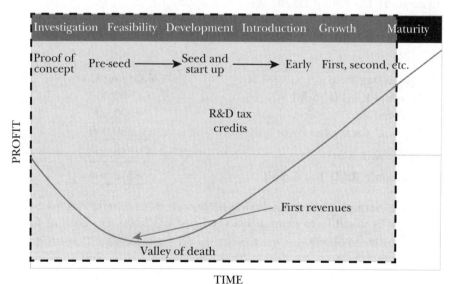

TIME

___

[2] A system whereby every €1 spent on qualifying R&D activities can qualify for the tax credit without reference to a base spend.

The R&D Tax Credit is available during the R&D stage of the innovation lifecycle and generally after the project/product definition stage, which typically arises in the investigation phase in the above figure and before the project/product introduction/growth stage. Importantly, and as mentioned above, because the tax credit is available as a cash refund, where no corporation tax liability exists, it is possible to consider making a claim for this relief regardless of whether there are taxable profits within the company (see **Section 3.4.2**).

3.2 The Relief

As referred to above, section 766 TCA 1997 provides that where a company incurs qualifying expenditure in the carrying on of qualifying R&D activities, a tax credit of 25% of the qualifying expenditure will be granted to the company. This credit can be used to reduce the company's corporation tax liabilities or, where there is not sufficient corporation tax capacity to utilise some or all of the credit, there is the option to claim the credit as a cash refund subject to certain conditions.

The qualifying expenditure of a company incurred in the carrying on of qualifying R&D activities for the purpose of the R&D Tax Credit typically includes salary costs, capital expenditure on plant and machinery, material costs incurred, certain overhead expenditure items, subcontracted expenditure to unconnected third parties and universities/institutes of higher education, and building costs related to R&D. Included below is a simplified example of the typical expenditure items that would be included in an R&D Tax Credit claim.

EXAMPLE 3.1: A SIMPLIFIED R&D TAX CREDIT CALCULATION

Qualifying Item	Qualifying Costs
Internal R&D labour costs	€1,000,000
Internal R&D material costs	€200,000
Internal R&D capital equipment	€50,000
Qualifying R&D costs	€1,250,000
Allowable R&D Tax Credit	**€312,500**

In this example, where qualifying R&D costs of €1,250,000 are identified, it is possible to claim a tax credit of €312,500, i.e. 25% of the qualifying R&D costs.

3.3 Groups

Unusually, in Irish tax, the R&D Tax Credit is calculated on a group-wide basis; it is then assigned to each company within the group as opposed to being calculated on an entity-by-entity basis and then rolled up to group level, i.e. one R&D Tax Credit figure is calculated at a group level by combining the qualifying R&D expenditure of the individual group companies. In this regard, for the purpose of this chapter, the word 'company' is used for the sake of convenience, but in most instances it is interchangeable with 'group' where a group situation arises, i.e. a group carrying on R&D activities can be substituted for a company carrying on R&D activities where appropriate. (The specifics of how a group scenario is treated is dealt with below at **Section 3.4.4**.)

3.4 Utilising the Tax Credit

There are generally three ways in which R&D Tax Credits can be utilised by a company:
1. to reduce certain corporation tax liabilities of the company;
2. as a refundable cash amount due from the Revenue Commissioners; or
3. they are awarded to key employees to allow them to reduce their personal tax liability.

3.4.1 Reducing Corporation Tax Liabilities

The R&D Tax Credit is a corporation tax relief. In this regard, R&D Tax Credits are used to offset corporation tax liabilities in the first instance. Under section 766(4) TCA 1997, the company first uses the R&D Tax Credit in relation to an accounting period against any corporation tax liability of the company for that accounting period and then carries any unutilised tax credit forward against any future corporation tax liabilities of the company. The following example illustrates how the R&D Tax Credit can be used to reduce a current year corporation tax liability.

EXAMPLE 3.2(A): USING THE R&D TAX CREDIT AGAINST A CURRENT YEAR CORPORATION TAX LIABILITY

	Current Year
Qualifying R&D expenditure in the period	€160,000
Corporation tax liability	€100,000
R&D Tax Credit amount (€160,000 at 25%)	€40,000
Resulting corporation tax liability	€60,000

However, section 766(4A)(a) further provides that if a company does not have a corporation tax liability in the current accounting period or if the R&D Tax Credit is greater than the corporation tax liability of the current accounting period, the company can carry the current year R&D Tax Credit back to the preceding accounting period and reduce any corporation tax liability for the prior year. **Example 3.2(B)** below illustrates how the R&D Tax Credit would be used if the current year corporation tax liability of the company was €20,000 rather than €100,000, meaning that the R&D Tax Credit was greater than the current year corporation tax liability and, therefore, could be brought back to the prior year.

EXAMPLE 3.2(B): USING THE R&D TAX CREDIT AGAINST A CURRENT YEAR AND A PRIOR YEAR CORPORATION TAX LIABILITY

	Preceding Year	Current Year
Corporation tax liability	€30,000	€20,000
R&D Tax Credit amount	€0	€40,000
R&D Tax Credit brought back	€20,000	
Resulting corporation tax liability	€10,000	€0
R&D Tax Credit available for carry back		€20,000

3.4.2 Cash Refund

Where a claimant company has excess R&D Tax Credits remaining after all corporation tax liabilities for the current and preceding accounting periods are considered, then it is possible to make a claim for a cash refund of the excess R&D Tax Credit (section 766(4B) TCA 1997). Generally, such a cash refund is paid in three instalments as follows:

1. 33% of the relevant repayable amount in Year 1;
2. 50% of the balance of the repayable amount in Year 2; and
3. the remaining balance of the repayable amount in Year 3.

Example 3.3 below shows the manner in which a refundable R&D Tax Credit amount of €100,000 in the accounting period ending 31 December 2016 would be claimed, assuming that there are no corporation tax liabilities for any of the periods ended 31 December 2015, 2016, 2017 or 2018.

EXAMPLE 3.3: RECEIVING THE R&D TAX CREDIT THROUGH THE CASH REFUND METHOD

31 December 2016	Cash Refundable R&D Tax Credit	€100,000
CT1 return for period ended 31 December 2016	1st instalment	€33,000
CT1 return for period ended 31 December 2017	2nd instalment	€33,500
CT1 return for period ended 31 December 2018	3rd instalment	€33,500

An alternative format in which to present this is as follows:

	2016	2017	2018
31 December 2016 cash refundable R&D Tax Credit	€100,000		
CT1 return for period 31 December 2016 1st instalment	(€33,000)		
CT1 return for period 31 December 2017 2nd instalment		(€33,500)	
CT1 return for period 31 December 2018 3rd instalment			(€33,500)
Balance brought forward of 2016 tax credit to be utilised	€67,000	€33,500	€0

The above example illustrates how a company would receive a cash refund of the R&D Tax Credit where the company has no corporation tax liability over the four-year period specified. However, if the company had corporation tax liabilities in any of the periods, any excess R&D Tax Credit carried forward must be used against such corporation tax liabilities in the first instance. If there is still an excess after all such liabilities have been eliminated, then a claim for further cash instalments should be made. In summary, this means that the benefits of an R&D Tax Credit will be fully received by a company over a maximum of three years, either through a reduction in its corporation liabilities for the four-year period (preceding period plus Years 1 to 3) or through a cash refund over the three years, or a combination of both.

3.4.2.1 Limit on Cash Refund Amounts

Section 766B TCA 1997 sets out limits on the level of R&D Tax Credits that can be claimed under the cash-refund mechanism described above. These limits are the higher of:
- the total corporation tax paid by the company in the previous 10 years; or
- the company's total payroll liabilities of the accounting period to which the claim relates plus the total payroll liabilities of the prior accounting period.

'Payroll liabilities' for this purpose includes all PAYE withheld by the employer including income tax, Pay-related Social Insurance (PRSI), Universal Social Charge (USC) and income levy (abolished since 2011), together with employers' PRSI.

3.4.3 Key Employees

The third way in which the R&D Tax Credit can be utilised is by using the credit to reward key employees involved in R&D activities.

Section 472D TCA 1997 allows a company to surrender a portion of its R&D Tax Credit to employees engaged in R&D within the company.

The employee can then use the surrendered credit to reduce their income tax on relevant emoluments. In order for an employee to be eligible for the relief they must be regarded as a 'key employee', which is defined in section 472D(1) as an individual:

"(a) who:

    (i) is not, and has not been, a director of his or her employer or an associated company or is connected to such a director,

    (ii) does not, or did not, have a material interest in his or her employer or an associated company or is connected to a person who has a material interest, and

    (iii) in the accounting period for which his or her employer was entitled to claim relief under section 766(2), has performed 50% or more of the duties of their employment in the conception or creation of new knowledge, products, processes, methods and systems; and

(b) 50 per cent or more of the cost of whose emoluments that arise from his or her employment with that relevant employer qualify as expenditure on research and development under section 766(1)(a) in the accounting period referred to in paragraph (a)(iii)."

In summary, to be a key employee the individual must not be a director of the company, nor have a material interest in the shares of the company, i.e. must own less than 5% of the shares of the company, and must spend 50% of their time carrying out qualifying R&D activities.

In addition to the 'key employee' test, the following conditions must also be met:

1. The aggregate amount surrendered to employees must not exceed the company's corporation tax liability for the period. Therefore, the relief is only available if the company has a corporation tax liability.
2. In order to be entitled to surrender any R&D Tax Credit, the company must not have any outstanding liability to corporation tax for any prior accounting period.

3.4.3.1 Utilisation of the R&D Tax Credit by an Employee

Where all of the above criteria have been met, the eligible employee will be entitled to reduce their income tax liability on relevant emoluments received from the company for the tax year following the tax year in which the accounting period for which the tax credit accrued to the company ends. (For example, where a company receives an R&D Tax Credit in its accounting year ended 31 December 2018 and surrenders it to a key employee, the key employee can use the credit to reduce their income tax liability in the following tax year, i.e. the 2019 income tax year.) It is important to note that an employee can reduce their income tax liability only, not their USC or PRSI liability.

Section 472D(3)(a) TCA 1997 provides that an employee may only benefit from the tax credit to the extent that the amount of the income tax payable on the employee's total income for the tax year to which the claim relates is not less than 23%.

Furthermore, under the relevant legislation, the onus is on the employee to make the claim and this will mean that they will have to file a personal income tax return. The following example illustrates how the surrender of the R&D Tax Credit to a key employee works and the interaction of the R&D Tax Credit with the effective rate of income tax.

EXAMPLE 3.4: SURRENDERING THE R&D TAX CREDIT TO A KEY EMPLOYEE

Company A employs an unmarried engineer on €80,000 per annum who is eligible for the relief. The company would like to give the key employee a net-of-tax bonus of 10% and surrender some of the company's R&D Tax Credit to achieve this. However, a surrender of €8,000 of the tax credit would mean that the employee's effective tax rate would be circa 18% (assuming standard personal tax credits with no other deductions). Therefore, the amount of the credit available in that year would be restricted to €3,540 in the current year, which would result in an effective tax rate of 23%; the balance would be carried forward by the employee to the following year. The back up to the above rates of tax is included in the below calculation.

Calculation of Key Employees Income Tax Liability

	Excluding R&D Tax Credit	Including Unrestricted R&D Tax Credit	Including Restricted R&D Tax Credit
Employment income	€80,000	€80,000	€80,000
Income tax @ 20%	€6,760	€6,760	€6,760
Income tax @ 40%	€18,480	€18,480	€18,480
	€25,240	€25,240	€25,240
Personal Tax Credit	€1,650	€1,650	€1,650
PAYE Tax Credit	€1,650	€1,650	€1,650
R&D Tax Credit	€0	€8,000	€3,540
	€3,300	€11,300	€6,840
Income tax payable	€21,940	€13,940	€18,400
Effective tax rate	27.4%	17.4%	23.00%
R&D credit carried forward to future periods	N/A	N/A	€4,460

However, assuming all other information remains the same but the employee had other tax-deductible amounts such as medical expenses, etc., the amount of the restriction could be much higher. The employer would have to assess the overall tax position of the employee to ascertain whether surrendering the tax credit would be of benefit to the employee. (If the employee was married, this assessment by the employer would be further complicated as the employee's spouse's tax position may need to be considered also.) An employee may be sensitive about sharing information about their personal tax situation with their employer than would otherwise be necessary. All such considerations tend to make availing of the relief extremely cumbersome.

Under section 472D(4) TCA 1997, if unused in a particular year, the R&D Tax Credit can be carried forward until such time as it is used or the employee ceases to be an employee of the company that surrendered the R&D Tax Credit. If the employee changes employment, any unused portion of the credit will be lost. (It seems a little incongruous that a tax relief intended to be a reward for past services, perhaps in lieu of a bonus, is somehow dependent on the continued future employment of the employee.)

3.4.3.2 Tax Credit Clawback

Finally, section 766(2B) and (2C) TCA 1997 contains a clawback provision: should the company's claim for the R&D Tax Credit be found to be in some way defective such that the amount of the credit claimable is less than that previously claimed, Revenue has the option to claw back the benefit from both the company and the employee.

Under section 766(2B), any clawback will be attributable to the company's claim in the first instance and as such it is unlikely that a clawback on the employee benefit would be pursued. However, as a clawback on the employee benefit can be made by Revenue, if the company claim amount is not sufficient to cover the clawback amount sought by Revenue, it is important to be aware of this provision and how it operates.

It seems that overall the 'key employee' allowance is restrictive and convoluted to such an extent that it is likely only to apply in very particular circumstances. In practice, there has been minimal uptake of this allowance to date.

In summary, even if a qualifying company has an employee who meets all of the various criteria to qualify for the relief and who has sufficient income, will the employee want the risks and burden of availing of the credit?

3.4.4 Group Expenditure

As discussed briefly in **Section 3.3**, the R&D Tax Credit is calculated on a group basis. This section provides further detail in relation to the manner in which the calculation of the R&D Tax Credit is completed in a group situation.

3.4.4.1 Calculating the R&D Tax Credit in a Group Situation

Section 766(1)(b) TCA 1997 sets out that companies shall be considered to be members of a group in the following cases:

"(i) 2 companies shall be deemed to be members of a group if one company is a 51 per cent subsidiary of the other company or both companies are 51 per cent subsidiaries of a third company: but in determining whether one company is a 51 per cent subsidiary of another company, the other company shall be treated as not being the owner of–

    (I) any share capital which it owns directly in a company if a profit on a sale of the shares would be treated as a trading receipt of its trade, or

    (II) any share capital which it owns indirectly, and which is owned directly by a company for which a profit on a sale of the shares would be a trading receipt;

(ii) sections 412 to 418 shall apply for the purposes of this paragraph as they would apply for the purposes of Chapter 5 of Part 12 if–

    (I) '51 per cent subsidiary' were substituted for '75 per cent subsidiary' in each place where it occurs in that Chapter, and

    (II) paragraph (c) of section 411(1) were deleted;

(iii) a company and all its 51 per cent subsidiaries shall form a group and, where that company is a member of a group as being itself a 51 per cent subsidiary, that group shall comprise all its 51 per cent subsidiaries and the first-mentioned group shall be deemed not to be a group: but a company which is not a member of a group shall be treated as if it were a member of a group which consists of that company".

In summary, this means that companies shall be considered to be in the same group if one is a 51% subsidiary of the other or if both are 51% subsidiaries of a third company.

Section 766(3)(a) provides that it is possible for a company to surrender its available R&D Tax Credits to another company within the same group, to the extent that formal notification is made jointly by both companies to Revenue.

Under section 766(3)(a), where no formal notice is given regarding surrendering of the R&D Tax Credits, then the attributable R&D expenditure for each company within a group is calculated as follows:

$$Q \times \frac{C}{G}$$

where:
Q is the qualifying group expenditure on R&D in the period under consideration;
C is the amount of expenditure on R&D incurred by a given company within the group in the period under consideration; and
G is the qualifying group expenditure on R&D in the period under consideration.

EXAMPLE 3.5: ALLOCATING GROUP EXPENDITURE TO A COMPANY
WHERE NO SURRENDER NOTICE IS MADE

Company ABC Ltd had qualifying expenditure on R&D of €50,000.
The group expenditure on R&D in the period was €100,000.
Therefore:

$$\text{Company ABC Ltd expenditure on R\&D} = €100,000 \times \frac{€50,000}{€100,000} = €50,000$$

This option to surrender R&D Tax Credits can be useful in situations
where the claimant company has no corporation tax liability but another
company in the group does have corporation tax liabilities, as the benefit
of the tax credit can potentially be utilised by the group in Year 1 instead
of having to wait up to three years for full utilisation of the tax credit
through the cash-refund mechanism (see **Section 3.4.2**).

3.4.4.2 Cessation of Trade by a Company within a Group

Section 766(4C) TCA 1997 provides that where one group company
ceases to trade, to the extent that another company within the group commences to carry on that trade then the successor company can claim any
R&D Tax Credits not utilised by the predecessor company going forward.
However, the use of these credits is restricted: they can only be used to
reduce corporation tax liabilities and cannot be claimed as a cash refund.
Furthermore, there is a requirement that the successor company carries
on the qualifying R&D activity for a period of two years after the transfer
of the trade.

Despite the unavailability of cash refunds for R&D Tax Credits in such a
scenario, this is still a useful provision as it allows for the potential utilisation of the tax credits over time despite a company having ceased to trade.

3.5 Qualifying Criteria

Section 766(1)(a) TCA 1997 provides:
   "'Expenditure on research and development', in relation to a company,
   means expenditure, other than expenditure on a building or structure,
   incurred by the company wholly and exclusively in the carrying on by
   it of research and development activities in a relevant Member State".

This is the fundamental legislative provision underpinning the R&D Tax
Credit regime. While this is a relatively short definition, it is supported by
a substantial number of detailed concepts that are underpinned by further, detailed legislation, which makes this definition quite technical and
cumbersome.

In outline, to claim R&D Tax Credit under section 766 TCA 1997 the criteria that a claimant company must satisfy can be broken down into three main areas:
1. fundamental criteria;
2. scientific/technological criteria; and
3. accounting criteria.

Having established that the fundamental criteria are met and in advance of making a claim, a company should satisfy itself that it will be in a position to pass the remaining tests, the key ones being demonstrating that the scientific/technological and the accounting criteria are met. The 'science test' seeks to establish whether the company is carrying out qualifying R&D activities and whether there are records to support this. The 'accounting test' is intended to ensure that the appropriate qualifying costs are appropriately allocated to any qualifying activities within a qualifying company and that there is evidence to support this. Both of these tests are discussed in more detail below.

3.5.1 The Fundamental Criteria

3.5.1.1 The Company's Tax Status

The company must be within the charge to Irish corporation tax, meaning that the company must be an Irish resident company or a foreign resident company with a taxable presence in Ireland, e.g. a UK company trading in Ireland through an Irish branch. A simple way of ascertaining if a company is within the charge to Irish corporation tax is to ask whether it has an obligation to file an Irish corporation tax return. If the company has such an obligation, it is within the charge to Irish corporation tax.

3.5.1.2 The Company Is Trading

In order for a company to make a claim under section 766 TCA 1997, it must be carrying on a trade throughout the period for which the claim is being made or be a 51% subsidiary of a company which does carry on a trade. Section 766(1)(a) TCA 1997 provides as follows:

"'qualified company', in relation to a relevant period, means a company which–

(i) throughout the relevant period–
   (I) carries on a trade,
   (II) is a 51 per cent subsidiary of a company which carries on a trade, or
   (III) is a 51 per cent subsidiary of a company whose business consists wholly or mainly of the holding of stocks, shares or securities of a company which carries on a trade or more than one such company,

> (ii) carries out research and development activities in the relevant period,
>
> (iii) maintains a record of expenditure incurred by it in the carrying out by it of those activities, and
>
> (iv) in the case of a company which is a member of a group of companies that carries on research and development activities in separate geographical locations, maintains separate records of expenditure incurred in respect of the activities carried on at each location".

In situations where a company has incurred qualifying expenditure on R&D prior to its commencing to trade, for the purpose of claiming the R&D Tax Credit, section 766(1)(b)(vi) deems such expenditure to have been incurred in the period in which the company had commenced to trade[3] (see **Example 3.6** below). This provision is important because if a company does not commence to trade in the first number of years of carrying out R&D activities, it would not be eligible to claim the R&D Tax Credit as it is not trading. Without the above deeming provision, when it commences to trade later and becomes eligible to claim the R&D Tax Credit, the qualifying R&D expenditure incurred in the earlier periods would not be claimable at that stage as they would not have been claimed within the 12-month deadline from the end of the accounting period in which the expenditure is incurred (see **Section 3.6.1**). This would mean that such a company would be time-barred from claiming R&D Tax Credits on the qualifying expenditure incurred in the pre-trading periods. The following example illustrates how pre-trading qualifying expenditure incurred on R&D activities can be claimed on the commencement of trade.

EXAMPLE 3.6: QUALIFYING R&D EXPENDITURE INCURRED
BEFORE THE COMMENCEMENT OF TRADE

Startup Co Ltd has commenced R&D activities on 1 January 2016 on the development of a new medical device. The company is a newly incorporated entity with a December year end and is not carrying out any commercial business, e.g. sales or commercial production and therefore, it could not be argued that the company has commenced to trade. It is expected that the R&D activities will cost €100,000 per annum and take three years to complete. The company will commence to trade in the year ended 31 December 2019. In the year of commencement to trade the company will only incur €50,000 on R&D activities.

---

[3] The commencement to trade rules are a complex topic and beyond the scope of this book.

In the accounting periods 31 December 2016 to 2018, Startup Co Ltd will incur qualifying costs of €300,000 on qualifying R&D activities, but it will not be eligible for the R&D Tax Credit as the company has not commenced to trade and, therefore, is not trading. When the company commences to trade in the year ended 31 December 2019, it will incur €50,000 on qualifying R&D activities. However, for the purpose of the R&D Tax Credit, the company is deemed to have incurred all the pre-trading R&D costs in this period. Therefore, it can make a claim for the R&D Tax Credit on all of the qualifying expenditure of €350,000 in relation to the accounting period ended 31 December 2019.

3.5.1.3 Location of the R&D Activities

The qualifying R&D activities must be carried out by the qualifying company within the EEA (section 766(1)(a)). Where employees of the Irish company carry out R&D activities outside the EEA, such activities and associated costs would not be considered by Revenue as qualifying.

3.5.1.4 Tax Relieved Elsewhere

Section 766(1)(a)(II) TCA 1997 provides that where the claimant company is Irish tax-resident, the company must not have received any form of relief for the purpose of tax in a territory other than the State. This provision makes it very unlikely that any significant R&D activities carried on outside Ireland by an Irish tax-resident company will qualify for the R&D Tax Credit.

EXAMPLE 3.7: IRISH COMPANY CARRYING OUT R&D ACTIVITIES
OUTSIDE IRELAND

Irish R&D Co Ltd is an ICT company carrying out qualifying R&D activities. The team is located both in Ireland and in Poland. The Polish operation has 50 employees located in the company's Polish office, which is regarded as a permanent establishment under the Ireland/Poland tax treaty and therefore constitutes a taxable presence in Poland. The Polish branch establishes that its taxable profits are subject to Polish corporation tax on a cost-plus-transfer-pricing basis. Under this arrangement, the Polish company is considered to have received a tax deduction for the cost of the employees located in the branch. As the Irish company, through its Polish branch, has received tax relief, i.e. a deduction, for the purpose of tax in a territory other than the State, the costs of the R&D activities carried out by the Polish branch will not qualify for the Irish R&D Tax Credit.

3.5.2 The Accounting Criteria

3.5.2.1 Qualifying Costs

Expenditure on R&D is defined in section 766(1)(a) TCA 1997 as expenditure incurred wholly and exclusively by the company in the carrying on by it of R&D activities in a relevant EEA Member State. This seems to be quite a broad definition and one might think that the normal cost-accounting rules would result in an acceptable costing.

However, over the past number of years there has been a fundamental shift in Revenue's interpretation of the legislation with respect to what is considered to be allowable expenditure from an R&D Tax Credit perspective. This shift in interpretation can be seen clearly when reviewing the evolving Revenue guidelines in this area from February 2011 to April 2015, which, in essence, can be described as adopting a narrow reading of the legislation.

For example, where a company incurs costs for support functions such as finance, HR, marketing or sales, Revenue currently would seek to disallow such costs on the basis that these functions are not directly involved in the carrying on of R&D activities. This is contrary to the guidelines issued by Revenue in February 2011 where such costs were explicitly specified as qualifying costs.

It can be argued that such costs should still be considered as eligible on the basis that the legislation is not clear and applying the principle that where legislation is ambiguous it should be read in favour of the taxpayer. This ambiguity is demonstrated by Revenue's change in interpretation and noting that there has been no change in relevant legislation since the February 2011 guidelines were issued. However, the purpose of this book is to give the reader a practical guide rather than detailing at length theoretical arguments about the legislation; therefore, the following sections focus on presenting advice that should assist potential claimants in ensuring that they are in line with current Revenue-accepted positions.

3.5.2.2 Staff Costs

In many respects the staff costs are the key element of any R&D Tax Credit claim because:
- the qualifying R&D activities are likely to be driven and carried out by employees;
- the employees carrying out the R&D must be competent experts in their scientific or technological field and thus typically among the higher paid staff in the company;
- the R&D Tax Credit is designed to encourage companies to employ staff to carry out R&D activities within the EEA.

All company personnel directly involved in the carrying on of qualifying R&D activities should be considered for inclusion in an R&D Tax Credit claim on the basis of their time spent in R&D activities.

Given that staff costs are typically the key element of any claim, it is generally the case that Revenue will heavily scrutinise the methodology and rationale used to calculate these costs. In this respect, Revenue expects that companies should maintain detailed contemporaneous timesheets for all individuals who are carrying out qualifying R&D activities. While there is no legislative requirement to maintain timesheets, doing so will help expedite any Revenue review. Maintaining timesheets will also act to expedite the claim compilation process as the relevant time per person per project should be readily available to the finance team, which can then apply the appropriate allocation of cost to the identified qualifying time. Where timesheets are not maintained, it can be more difficult and far more time-consuming to justify the methodologies/rationale used for apportioning each individual's time to any given claim.

While the use of timesheets for all staff is advised, where there are staff tasked with the direct management of R&D personnel and projects (e.g. an R&D group manager) we have seen Revenue accept an apportionment of their costs to an R&D Tax Credit claim on a just and reasonable basis where such staff have not maintained timesheets. Where such staff are identified, the fully loaded salary costs should be considered as potentially claimable, i.e. gross salary including benefits in kind and bonuses, employer PRSI payments and employer pension payments.[4]

3.5.2.3 Costs of Materials

Where a company incurs costs on materials purchased wholly and exclusively for the purposes of carrying out R&D activities, in accordance with section 766 TCA 1997 it is possible to include the full cost of these materials in an R&D Tax Credit claim.

However, where materials are purchased for the purposes of both R&D and commercial activities then only the element of the material cost incurred wholly and exclusively for the purposes of the R&D activities should be considered for inclusion in an R&D Tax Credit claim.

Revenue guidance provides the following commentary on this matter:
"Materials used in qualifying research and development activities may be of further commercial value after their research use has concluded.

---

[4] Where pension contributions are not standard contributions, it is likely that Revenue will seek to explore whether such contributions are reasonable to include in a claim for an R&D Tax Credit. Holiday entitlements and public holidays should also be taken in to account when considering the allowable salary cost (i.e. it should be considered reasonable to apportion holiday entitlements to the claim by reference to the amount of time spent on the carrying on of R&D activities by relevant staff).

In this situation, the lower of cost, or net realisable value of any materials or other saleable product which remain after the R&D activity should be deducted from the expenditure claimed."[5]

The following example illustrates how the recovery of material costs impacts on qualifying R&D expenditure.

EXAMPLE 3.8: SALE OF MATERIALS USED IN THE R&D ACTIVITIES OF THE COMPANY

A company is seeking to develop a new manufacturing process. While the process to be developed is new, the end product produced will remain the same. As part of this R&D effort, it is expected that some of the end product produced may not be of commercial value given the proposed redevelopment efforts to be carried out. However, it is expected that a large amount of the end product produced should be saleable, either at full price or at a reduced cost.

Ultimately, the company spends €1,000,000 on purchasing of materials and managed to sell €750,000 of the material post processing.

In this scenario above, where the material is bought for a 'dual purpose' the amount of material cost included in an R&D Tax Credit claim should be €250,000 (i.e. €1,000,000 – €750,000).

3.5.2.4 Capital Expenditure

Where a company incurs costs on either the construction, repair or refurbishment of a building, or on the purchase of plant and machinery (P&M) it is possible to consider such costs for inclusion in an R&D Tax Credit claim. Building costs are provided for under section 766A TCA 1997 and P&M costs are provided for under section 766(1)(a)(ii) and 766(1A)(a).

Additionally, revenue costs that are capitalised for accounting purposes are not precluded from being claimed, once the item of expenditure would have been allowable as a deduction in calculating the profits of the trade for the purposes of tax if the expenditure had not been capitalised in the accounts, e.g. salary costs that are captalised are still allowable because the salary costs are revenue expenditure that would have been tax deductible if they were not capitalised.

3.5.2.4.1 Plant and Machinery

Section 766(1)(a)(ii) TCA 1997 provides that in order for P&M costs to qualify for the R&D Tax Credit, the P&M must also qualify for capital

[5] Revenue Commissioners, *Research & Development: Tax Credit Guidelines* (updated April 2015), paragraph 4.6, p. 24. Available at https://www.revenue. ie/en/companies-and-charities/documents/research-and-development-tax-credit-guidelines.pdf

allowances under Part 9 or Part 29, Chapter 2[6] TCA 1997. In summary, to qualify for capital allowances under Part 9, the capital expenditure must be incurred on P&M, the company must own the asset and the P&M must be in use wholly and exclusively for the purpose of the trade at the end of the accounting period in which the claim for capital allowance is made.

Therefore, when considering whether expenditure on the provision of P&M should be included in an R&D Tax Credit claim, two points should be confirmed:
1. that the item of P&M qualifies for capital allowances; and
2. that the item of P&M is used wholly and exclusively in the carrying on of qualifying R&D activities.

Where the asset is used in both qualifying R&D activities and non-qualifying activities, section 766(1A)(a) TCA 1997 provides:
> "Where expenditure is incurred by a company on machinery or plant which qualifies for any allowance under Part 9 or this Chapter and the machinery or plant will not be used by the company wholly and exclusively for the purposes of research and development, the amount of the expenditure attributable to research and development shall be such portion of that expenditure as is just and reasonable, and such portion of the expenditure shall be treated for the purposes of subsection (1) (a) as incurred by the company wholly and exclusively in carrying on research and development activities."

Therefore, where the P&M does qualify for capital allowances and is used in qualifying R&D activities, a claimant must then consider how much of the cost associated with the P&M can be reasonably allocated to an R&D Tax Credit claim. To do this, one must consider the anticipated use of the P&M over the total useful life of the P&M. **Example 3.9** below illustrates how the inclusion of an item of P&M into an R&D Tax Credit claim might be calculated in practice.

EXAMPLE 3.9: APPORTIONING AN ITEM OF P&M TO R&D BY REFERENCE TO ITS USEFUL ECONOMIC LIFE

A company purchases a new piece of equipment, which qualifies for capital allowances. The cost of this equipment is €100,000. The company plans to use the equipment for R&D purposes for two years and then transfer it to commercial use for the remainder of its useful life, the useful life being 10 years in total. In this scenario, it would be reasonable to include €20,000 (i.e. €100,000 × 2/10) of this equipment cost in an R&D Tax Credit claim.

---

[6] Section 765 is a provision in Part 29, Chapter 2 TCA 1997 that gives companies an allowance for capital expenditure on scientific research. As it is a very rarely used provision, it is not covered in detail in this book.

Unlike capital allowances, for the purposes of the R&D Tax Credit regime the calculated attributable R&D cost for P&M is claimed fully in the year in which the expenditure is incurred or the year the asset is brought into use, as opposed to over a number of years. The following example illustrates this timing mismatch between getting an R&D Tax Credit and capital allowances on a piece of P&M.

EXAMPLE 3.10: CLAIMING R&D TAX CREDITS ON
P&M ELIGIBLE FOR CAPITAL ALLOWANCES

A company purchases a specific computer and server for exclusive use by its R&D team for €30,000 in the year ended 31 December 2018. The equipment is put into use in this period also and it is intended that it will not be used in any non-qualifying activities. While the company will claim capital allowances for the equipment over an eight-year period, i.e. 12.5% of the costs will be deductible each year from 31 December 2018 to 31 December 2025, the full costs of the equipment will be included in the R&D Tax Credit claim for the year ended 31 December 2018.

Relevant P&M expenditure should be considered for inclusion in an R&D Tax Credit claim in the accounting period within which the P&M is first brought in to use for the purposes of the trade. However, if the asset is not immediately put into use, by Revenue concession,[7] it is possible to include the P&M in the R&D Tax Credit claim of the accounting period within which the cost becomes payable, even though the asset does not yet qualify for capital allowances as it is not in use. It is important to note that there will be a clawback of the R&D Tax Credit in relation to such expenditure if the item of P&M is not brought in to use for the purposes of the trade within two years from the date of the expenditure becoming payable.

Given that P&M costs are generally estimated and included in an R&D Tax Credit claim in the early years of the P&M's useful life, it is expected that claimants review any apportionments made on a yearly basis and ensure that future claims are amended if needed to reflect any changes in P&M utilisation.

---

[7] See Revenue Commissioners, *Research & Development Tax Credit Guidelines* (updated April 2015) p. 28 and *Tax Briefing* Issue 59 – April 2005 (available at http://www.revenue.ie/en/tax-professionals/historic-material/tax-briefing/2005/tax-briefing-59-april-2005.pdf).

EXAMPLE 3.11: ADJUSTING THE ESTIMATED AMOUNT OF TIME AN ITEM OF P&M IS USED IN R&D ACTIVITIES

A company purchases a new piece of equipment, which qualifies for capital allowances. The cost of this equipment is €100,000 and the equipment is brought in to use in the 31 December 2015 claim period. It is intended that the piece of equipment will be used for R&D purposes for two years and will subsequently be transferred to commercial use for the remainder of its useful life, the useful life being 10 years in total.

An R&D Tax Credit claim is made in relation to the expenditure incurred in the 31 December 2015 corporation tax return within which €20,000 is included for this equipment (i.e. €100,000 × 2/10).

In 2016, after the equipment had been in use for one year in R&D, significant difficulties were encountered in the R&D activities. It was thus determined that the piece of equipment would need to remain in R&D for a further three years in order to enable the R&D effort to be completed. This would result in the equipment now being in use for four years in R&D (i.e. one year already completed and three more years proposed). On this basis it is expected and allowable for a claimant to amend their 31 December 2016 claim to reflect such a change.

An R&D Tax Credit claim is made in the 31 December 2016 corporation tax return within which an additional €20,000 is included for this equipment to reflect that the total proposed use in R&D is now four years, and not the two years estimated in the 31 December 2015 claim (i.e. (€100,000 × 4/10) - €20,000).

If the R&D applicable use of P&M decreased from what is stated in a given R&D Tax Credit claim, in a similar manner to the above example, future claims should be amended to reflect such a change.

3.5.2.4.2 Buildings or Structures

Expenditure on buildings, structures or refurbishments to same (hereafter collectively referred to as 'buildings'), is dealt with under section 766A TCA 1997. This provides a 25% tax credit, in line with section 766. Similar to P&M, it is important to understand that in order to qualify under section 766A, a building must also qualify for industrial building capital allowances under Part 9 TCA 1997. Where this is the case, a claimant must consider the R&D activity that is to be carried out in the building as a percentage of the total amount of activity carried out in the building. There are two reasons for this:

1. section 766A(1)(a) TCA 1997 requires that at least 35% of the portion of use of the building on which the expenditure was incurred

relates to R&D activity over a period of four years from the date on which the building is first brought in to use for the purposes of the trade; and

2. subject to point 1 above being met, it is required that the cost of the overall building is apportioned to the R&D Tax Credit claim on the basis of the portion of the building that relates to R&D over the total building space.

This means that where relevant industrial building capital allowances are being claimed on a building that is being used/partly used for R&D activities, there is an R&D usage threshold of 35% that must be met to make the building a qualifying building for the purpose of section 766A TCA 1997. If 35% or more of the building is used for qualifying R&D activities, that portion of the building cost is qualifying expenditure for the purpose of the R&D Tax Credit. If less than 35% of the building is used for qualifying R&D activities, then none of the building cost is regarded as qualifying expenditure for the purpose of the R&D Tax Credit. **Example 3.12** below illustrates this point.

EXAMPLE 3.12: QUALIFYING BUILDING MEETING THE THRESHOLD

A company incurs expenditure on a building, which qualifies for industrial building capital allowances. The cost of this building is €10 million. The company's plan is that 50% of the activities to be carried out in the building will be qualifying R&D activities going forward.

It would be reasonable to include €5 million (i.e. €10 million × 50%) of this building cost in an R&D Tax Credit claim. However, if the company only anticipated that 34% of the activities to be carried out in building will be qualifying R&D activities, then it would not be entitled to include any of the expenditure in the R&D Tax Credit claim.

Similar to the P&M provisions, section 766A(6)(b) TCA 1997 provides that if the R&D applicable use of a building changes from what is stated in an initial R&D Tax Credit claim, future claims should be amended to reflect this change, e.g. if it is initially anticipated that 50% of the activities in the building will be qualifying and in future periods the quantum of qualifying activities drops to 40%, an amendment should be made to the R&D Tax Credit claim in the period that the company becomes aware of the drop in R&D usage of the building.

Furthermore, section 766A(3)(c) TCA 1997 provides that, if within 10 years of the accounting period within which a claim is made under this section, the building included in the claim ceases to be used for either (a) R&D-related activity, (b) trade-related activities, or (c) if the building is sold, then the claimant will be subject to a Revenue clawback of the credit received/ receivable.

Revenue's guidelines provide that the costs associated with buildings can be claimed in the period within which the costs are incurred or the date the building is first brought in to use for the purposes of a trade.[8]

Costs associated with the acquisition or rights to land are considered as non-qualifying under section 766A(1)(b)(ii).

3.5.2.5 Royalty Payments

Section 766(1)(a)(iii)(I) provides that royalty payments, or similar, intended for use in R&D activities can be considered for inclusion in an R&D Tax Credit claim as long as such payments are incurred wholly and exclusively in the carrying on of qualifying R&D activities and are not made to connected parties, in whose hands form part of the overall income from a qualifying patent within the meaning of section 234 TCA 1997, i.e. the royalty payment is not made to a connected party who is exempt from tax on the royalty income by virtue of the patent income exemption.

3.5.2.6 Outsourced Costs

Under the R&D Tax Credit regime, it is possible to include an element of costs related to the outsourcing of R&D activities to other parties. This is provided for under section 766(1)(b)(vii) and (viii). These deal with two types of outsourced cost: section 766(1)(b)(viii) deals with the cost of R&D activities outsourced to third parties that are not an institution of third-level education; and section 766(1)(b)(viii) deals with the cost of R&D activities outsourced to an institution of third-level education.

3.5.2.6.1 Third-party Costs

Section 766(1)(b)(viii) provides:
  "Where in any period a company—
  (I)   incurs expenditure on research and development, and
  (II) pays a sum (not being a sum referred to in clause (II) of subpara-
        graph (vii)) to a person, other than to a person who is connected
        (within the meaning of section 10) with the company, in order
        for that person to carry on research and development activities,
        and notifies that person in writing that the payment is a payment
        to which this clause applies and that the person may not make a
        claim under this section in respect of such research and develop-
        ment activities,

---

[8] See Revenue Commissioners, *Research & Development Tax Credit Guidelines* (updated April 2015) p. 25.

then, so much of the sum so paid as does not exceed the greater of 15 per cent of that expenditure or €100,000, shall, to the extent that it does not exceed the expenditure referred to in clause (I), be treated as if it were expenditure incurred by the company in the carrying on by it of research and development activities and expenditure incurred by that other person in connection with the activities referred to in clause (II) shall not be expenditure on research and development".

In considering the inclusion of third-party costs in an R&D Tax Credit claim, it is important to understand that the third party must be unconnected to the company making the claim. The services provided by the third party must constitute R&D in its own right in accordance with section 766 TCA 1997, as opposed to maintenance services, cleaning services, etc. The third-party activities can be carried out anywhere in the world and are not restricted to being carried out in the EEA.

As can be seen in the legislative definition above, prior to making a claim, notification must be given to the relevant third parties, informing them that they are not entitled to make a claim for the same costs. Thus, it is important that potential claimants consider the nature of their contracts and where conflicts may arise between themselves and unconnected third parties in relation to who should be entitled to benefit from the R&D Tax Credit regime.

Where it is determined that the third-party activity is R&D in nature and that the third party is unconnected, it is possible to include relevant third-party outsourced expenditure amounting to the greater of 15% of the total qualifying internal spend or €100,000. The €100,000 limit is subject to the claimant having matching internal spend, e.g. employee costs, etc., incurred directly by the claimant. The following examples illustrate these provisions.

EXAMPLE 3.13: OUTSOURCED R&D COST RESTRICTED TO 15% OF INTERNAL COSTS

A company incurs qualifying internal expenditure of €4 million. It also incurs qualifying third-party costs of €800,000.

The third-party expenditure represents 20% of the qualifying internal expenditure. As this is over the 15% threshold, the outsourced expenditure of €800,000 must be restricted to €600,000 (i.e. €4 million × 15%). Thus, the total expenditure that could be included in an R&D Tax Credit claim above would be €4.6 million (i.e. €4 million internal + €600,000 external).

EXAMPLE 3.14: OUTSOURCED R&D COSTS RESTRICTED TO INTERNAL R&D COSTS

A company incurs qualifying internal expenditure of €40,000. It also incurs qualifying third-party expenditure of €80,000.

The third-party expenditure represents 200% of the qualifying internal expenditure, which is over the 15% limit. Furthermore, the third-party expenditure, although under the €100,000 limit, is not fully matched by qualifying internal expenditure. As such, the allowable external costs would be limited to €40,000. The total expenditure that could be included in an R&D Tax Credit claim in the above example would be €80,000 (i.e. €40,000 internal + €40,000 external).

EXAMPLE 3.15: OUTSOURCED R&D COSTS MATCHED AND LESS THAN €100,000

A company incurs qualifying internal expenditure of €120,000. It also incurs qualifying third-party expenditure of €90,000.

The third-party expenditure represents 75% of the qualifying internal expenditure, which is over the 15% limit. However, the third-party expenditure is under the €100,000 limit and is fully matched by qualifying internal expenditure. As such, the total external costs are allowable. The total expenditure that could be included in an R&D Tax Credit claim in this case would be €210,000 (i.e. €120,000 internal + €90,000 external).

Revenue Concession on Contractors   Because of the above third-party outsourcing restriction, many practical difficulties were faced by companies, particularly SMEs, which employed the services of contractors with specific skills to assist in their R&D activities for short periods of time, when the necessary resource/expertise did not exist in-house and the cost and long-term need for the expertise did not justify taking on a permanent employee.

A decision by the Appeal Commissioners in 2011 held that such use of a contractor did not constitute the company carrying on R&D activities itself and therefore the expenditure was not qualifying. Following this decision, a concession was introduced and included in subsequent issues of the Revenue guidelines[9] whereby it is possible to deem costs associated with such individual contractors as internal salary costs and thus not restrict these costs within the 15% or €100,000 third-party limits as

---

[9]   See Revenue Commissioners, *Research & Development Tax Credit Guidelines* (updated April 2015) p. 23.

discussed above. To qualify for this treatment the following criteria need to be met:

1. there is a specific R&D project being undertaken by an in-house team and the contractor can contribute specialised expertise that cannot be supplied by the in-house R&D team;
2. the contractor is an individual, not a company;
3. the individual contractor works on the company's premises;
4. the individual contractor works under the company's control; and
5. the engagement/contract period does not exceed six months.

3.5.2.6.2 University/Institute of Higher Education Costs

As discussed above at **Section 3.5.2.6**, section 766(1)(b)(vii) provides:
"where in any period a company–
  (I) incurs expenditure on research and development, and
  (II) pays a sum to a university or institute of higher education in order for that university or institute to carry on research and development activities in a relevant Member State,

so much of the sum so paid as does not exceed the greater of 5 per cent of that expenditure or €100,000, shall, to the extent that it does not exceed the expenditure referred to in clause (I), be treated as if it were expenditure incurred by the company in the carrying on by it of research and development activities".

Where a company incurs costs on the outsourcing of R&D activities to an EEA-based university or institute of higher education (hereafter collectively referred to as 'universities') and where these R&D activities are carried out within the EEA, it is possible to consider these costs for inclusion in an R&D Tax Credit claim. The amount of such costs that are allowable for inclusion in an R&D Tax Credit claim is limited to the greater of 5% of total qualifying internal spend, or €100,000. The €100,000 limit is subject to the claimant having matching internal spend. **Examples 3.16** and **3.17** below illustrate how these limits work in practice.

EXAMPLE 3.16: OUTSOURCED UNIVERSITY COSTS GREATER THAN 5%
BUT LOWER THAN INTERNAL COSTS AND €100,000

A company incurs qualifying internal expenditure of €400,000. It also incurs qualifying university expenditure of €80,000. The university expenditure represents 20% of the qualifying internal expenditure. Though this is over the allowable 5% threshold, it is possible to claim the full university expenditure of €80,000 on the basis that it is below the €100,000 limit and is matched by internal spend.

In this case, the total expenditure that could be included in an R&D Tax Credit claim would be €480,000 (i.e. €400,000 internal + €80,000 university).

EXAMPLE 3.17: OUTSOURCED UNIVERSITY COSTS
RESTRICTED TO INTERNAL COSTS

A company incurs qualifying internal expenditure of €40,000. It also incurs qualifying university expenditure of €80,000. The university expenditure represents 200% of the qualifying internal expenditure. Furthermore, the university expenditure, though under the €100,000 limit, is not matched by qualifying internal expenditure. As such, the allowable external costs would need to be limited to €40,000.

In this case, the total expenditure that could be included in an R&D Tax Credit claim would be €80,000 (i.e. €40,000 internal + €40,000 university).

3.5.2.7 Overheads

Where a company is carrying on R&D activities, it is likely that there will be overhead costs incurred in relation to these activities. As we have seen, section 766 TCA 1997 defines 'qualifying expenditure' as expenditure incurred by a company in carrying on R&D activities. Revenue's interpretation of this definition has shifted significantly over the past number of years, from a very broad view of allowable items within this expenditure category to an extremely narrow view of allowable items within this expenditure category. This has involved a change in Revenue's interpretation rather than a change in the legislation.

In calculating the amount of allowable costs for a given overhead line item, it is necessary that any apportionment to the R&D Tax Credit claim is 'just and reasonable'. Typically used, and Revenue-accepted methodologies, in this regard include apportionments to R&D activities based on:

1.

$$\frac{\text{R\&D allowable staff hours}}{\text{Total company staff hours}}$$

EXAMPLE 3.18: APPORTIONMENT METHODOLOGY BASED ON HOURS

Where a company has four full-time equivalents (FTEs) carrying on R&D activities and 12 FTEs in total in the company for the accounting period, then it should be reasonable to apportion 33% (i.e. 4/12) of relevant overheads to the R&D Tax Credit claim.

2.

$$\frac{\text{R\&D allowable staff costs}}{\text{Total company staff costs}}$$

EXAMPLE 3.19: APPORTIONMENT METHODOLOGY
BASED ON STAFF COSTS

Where a company has a qualifying R&D salary cost of €250,000 and a total salary cost of €1 million in the company for the accounting period, then it should be reasonable to allocate 25% (i.e. €250,000/€1,000,000) of relevant overheads to the R&D Tax Credit claim. This may be a more appropriate apportionment method than that used in 1. above in cases where different employment grades may be consuming more overheads, e.g. in a medical device company R&D engineers may have their own office space and computers, whereas manufacturing engineers may be based on a production line and have only shared access to computers. In such a scenario, the R&D engineers could be considered to be consuming a greater portion of certain overheads. If they have a higher average salary cost, this apportionment method may give a more reasonable estimate of the overheads consumed by the R&D engineers.

3.

$$\frac{\text{R\&D area footprint/floor space}}{\text{Total building footprint/floor space}}$$

EXAMPLE 3.20: APPORTIONMENT METHODOLOGY
BASED ON FLOOR SPACE

Where a company maintains 50% of its building for use purely for R&D activities, it should be reasonable to apportion 50% of relevant overheads to the R&D Tax Credit claim.

It may be appropriate to adopt different allocation methodologies for different cost items. What is important is that a detailed rationale for choosing an apportionment methodology and arriving at a given apportionment rate should be documented by claimants and consistently applied.

From a claimant's perspective, where there are costs that a claimant believes are related to its R&D activities, it is important that a strong link between the activities and the costs is made. Overhead items that may be difficult to have accepted as directly incurred in the carrying on of R&D activities would include support functions, such as marketing and sales. Revenue is also known to take issue with a number of specific overhead items, including:
- canteen costs;
- insurance;
- travel costs;
- recruitment fees;

- shipping;
- telephone costs;
- bank charges;
- business entertainment; and
- training.

Given the uncertainty in relation to Revenue interpretation in this area over the past number of years, each individual claim and associated over-head expenditure line item should be considered on a case-by-case basis. Where there is uncertainty with respect to any large items of expenditure, it may be beneficial for a claimant to seek advice from their tax advisor, or from Revenue, should the claimant wish to ensure that their claim is accepted without issue.

3.5.2.8 Non-allowable Expenditure

Section 766 TCA 1997 specifically provides that interest costs incurred by a company on R&D shall not be included in the calculation of the R&D Tax Credit, notwithstanding that such interest is brought into account by the company in determining the value of an asset that might be used in R&D activities.

Also, internal expenditure incurred by a company in the management or control of R&D activities where such activities are carried on by another person (i.e. someone outside the company) shall not be claimable. For example, where the R&D activities of a company are completely out-sourced to a third party, internal expenditure on the management of that arrangement, such as agreeing scope of work at the beginning and review-ing the completed work at the end, will not be claimable. In such a case, the company will not be considered to have any internal expenditure on qualifying R&D activities and therefore, the full cost of the outsourced R&D activities will be restricted (see **Section 3.5.2.6** above) and no claim for R&D Tax Credits will be possible.

3.5.2.9 Grant Aid

Under section 766(1)(b)(v) TCA 1997, any EEA Member State grant aid received or to be received in respect of R&D activities carried out in a given claim period must be netted off the related qualifying R&D expenditure that is included in an R&D Tax Credit claim to be made for that period.

When determining the grant aid amount to be netted off a claim, it is impor-tant to note that some cost items covered under certain grants are not deemed as allowable cost items for the purposes of the R&D Tax Credit regime. For example, where training or travel costs are being grant aided, it is likely that these costs will not be considered for inclusion in an R&D Tax Credit claim. On this basis, such costs should **not** be netted off the R&D Tax Credit claim. Given this mismatch between the allowable costs for grant purposes and for R&D Tax Credit purposes, there is a risk that a number of claimants may inad-vertently reduce their R&D Tax Credit amount by more than is necessary.

The high-level and detailed examples below show how this inadvertent R&D Tax Credit reduction can materialise.

EXAMPLE 3.21: R&D TAX CREDIT VS GRANT AID REVIEW
(HIGH-LEVEL)

Line Item	R&D Tax Credit Allowable Expenditure	Grant Amount Allowable Expenditure	Net R&D Tax Credit Qualifying Amount
Project 1	€1,000,000	€250,000	€750,000
Project 2	€500,000	€150,000	€350,000
Allowable R&D Tax Credit Expenditure			€1,100,000
R&D Tax Credit @ 25%			**€277,500**

EXAMPLE 3.22: R&D TAX CREDIT VS GRANT AID REVIEW (DETAILED)

Line Item	R&D Tax Credit Allowable Expenditure	Grant Amount Allowable Expenditure	Net R&D Tax Credit Qualifying Amount
Project 1 – Salary	€800,000	€100,000	€700,000
Project 1 – Materials	€200,000	€50,000	€150,000
Project 1 – Travel	€0	€70,000	€0
Project 1 – Training	€0	€30,000	€0
Project 1 – Total			€850,000
Project 2 – Salary	€420,000	€70,000	€350,000
Project 2 – Materials	€80,000	€40,000	€40,000
Project 2 – Travel	€0	€25,000	€0
Project 2 – Training	€0	€15,000	€0
Project 2 – Total			€390,000
Allowable R&D Tax Credit Expenditure			€1,240,000
R&D Tax Credit @ 25%			**€310,000**

3.5.3 The Scientific/Technological Criteria

The fundamental challenge to any R&D Tax Credit claim is ascertaining what qualifying R&D activities, if any, the company is carrying out. To establish this it is necessary to explore the technical definition of what qualifying R&D activities are for the purposes of section 766 TCA 1997, i.e. it is necessary to review the scientific/technological criteria that need to be met to qualify an activity as R&D for the purposes of the R&D Tax Credit. It is important to note that the R&D activities that will qualify for the R&D Tax Credit are a subset of what would be considered R&D more generally, given the definitions of R&D activities included in section 766 TCA 1997.

Section 766(1)(a) TCA 1997 provides:
"'research and development activities' means systematic, investigative or experimental activities in a field of science or technology, being one or more of the following–
  (i)   basic research, namely, experimental or theoretical work undertaken primarily to acquire new scientific or technical knowledge without a specific practical application in view,
 (ii)   applied research, namely, work undertaken in order to gain scientific or technical knowledge and directed towards a specific practical application, or
(iii)   experimental development, namely, work undertaken which draws on scientific or technical knowledge or practical experience for the purpose of achieving technological advancement and which is directed at producing new, or improving existing, materials, products, devices, processes, systems or services including incremental improvements thereto: but activities will not be research and development activities unless they—
   (I)   seek to achieve scientific or technological advancement, and
  (II)   involve the resolution of scientific or technological uncertainty".

R&D Tax Credit claims stand or fall on the scientific/technical merits of the activities and projects that underpin them. A company's understanding of what R&D involves can be different to that defined in the R&D Tax Credit legislation (see above). Typically, it is only a subset of the company's defined R&D activities that meet the stringent test of what qualifies as R&D activities. As claims are underpinned by the R&D activities carried out by companies, the first thing claimants need to be able to demonstrate to Revenue is that their R&D activities meet the relevant scientific/technical criteria set out in legislation.

The key legislative scientific/technological criteria are explained in detail in the following sections.

3.5.3.1 'Systematic, Investigative or Experimental Activities'

"'[R]esearch and development activities' means systematic, investigative or experimental activities ...".

Where a company is seeking to make a claim for the R&D Tax Credit, it is essential that there is documentation to support the R&D activities carried out. In the event of a review of a claim, Revenue would expect to see that the activities underpinning the claim have been carried out in a planned manner. Documentation that may be sought by Revenue would include:

1. documentation to clearly support the planned start and end date of each R&D project/activity;
2. examples of available project plans/charters/tracking documentation (such as MS Project Planners, evidence of agile development methodology, etc.);
3. results and data from tests, trials, studies and validations (including lab books or equivalent, where appropriate);
4. documentation relating to iterations of design, including reasons for failure/redesign of product;
5. relevant design drawings/specifications;
6. timesheet detail for all technical staff involved in the R&D projects/activities;
7. feasibility reports, summary reports, failure reports;
8. documentation of major milestones/key activities of R&D projects.

While the level and type of documentation generated as part of R&D activities will vary across sectors and company size, any company considering making a claim for R&D Tax Credits should implement project-tracking processes in order to ensure that this criterion is met. Typically, this will represent good business practice as well as meeting the requirements for claiming the R&D Tax Credit.

In relation to software development, in its guidelines updated in April 2015 Revenue confirmed that it considers agile development methodologies to be systematic in nature and thus qualifying to meet this requirement.[10] However, where agile approaches incorporating extremely light documentation processes are used, it may be necessary to overlay a high-level project-tracking process such that claimants can robustly defend the nature of the work carried on, personnel involved, goals and milestones of the project, etc., should Revenue choose to review a claim based on such a methodology.

3.5.3.2 *'Field of Science or Technology'*

"'[R]esearch and development activities' means … activities in a field of science or technology …".

The aim of the R&D Tax Credit regime is to incentivise companies to innovate in a number of key areas of science and technology. These areas are set out in the Taxes Consolidation Act 1997 (Prescribed Research and

---

[10] Revenue Commissioners, *Research & Development Tax Credit Guidelines* (updated April 2015) p. 18.

Development Activities) Regulations 2004[11] as well as in Appendix 1 of Revenue's *Research & Development Tax Credit Guidelines*. The list in the 2004 Regulations is included in **Appendix 3.2** to this chapter but is here summarised at a high level as follows:

1. Natural Sciences:
    (a) mathematics and computer science;
    (b) physical sciences;
    (c) chemical sciences;
    (d) earth and related environmental sciences;
    (e) biological sciences.

2. Engineering and Technology:
    (a) civil engineering;
    (b) electrical engineering;
    (c) various other engineering sciences, such as chemical, aeronautical and space, mechanical, metallurgical and materials engineering.

3. Medical Sciences:
    (a) basic medicine;
    (b) clinical medicine;
    (c) health sciences.

4. Agricultural Science:
    (a) agriculture, forestry, fisheries and allied sciences;
    (b) veterinary medicine.

As can be seen from even this truncated list, there are a wide range of fields within which activities are deemed to be qualifying for the purposes of the R&D Tax Credit regime.

Within the 2004 Regulations and also the Revenue guidelines (at Appendix 2), a full list of categories of activity that are not considered R&D activities is also set out. The list in the 2004 Regulations is included in **Appendix 3.3** to this chapter but is here summarised at a high level as follows:

1. research in the social sciences;
2. routine testing for quality control purposes;
3. cosmetic or stylistic alterations;
4. standalone management or efficiency studies;
5. standard corrective maintenance/action;
6. legal and administration work in connection with patents;
7. construction work associated with non-R&D areas or projects;
8. market research/testing;
9. prospecting, exploring or producing minerals, petroleum or natural gas;
10. commercialisation of products, processes, etc.;
11. administration and general support services not wholly and exclusively undertaken in connection with R&D activity.

---

[11] S.I. No. 434 of 2004.

Where there is uncertainty as to whether an activity will fit into a qualifying field, a brief discussion with Revenue or an R&D Tax Credit advisor should provide clarity.

3.5.3.3 *Type of Activity*

"'[R]esearch and development activities' means ... activities ... being one or more of the following—
   (i)   basic research, namely, experimental or theoretical work undertaken primarily to acquire new scientific or technical knowledge without a specific practical application in view,
  (ii)   applied research, namely, work undertaken in order to gain scientific or technical knowledge and directed towards a specific practical application, or
 (iii)   experimental development, namely, work undertaken which draws on scientific or technical knowledge or practical experience for the purpose of achieving technological advancement and which is directed at producing new, or improving existing, materials, products, devices, processes, systems or services including incremental improvements thereto".

The activities to be included in a claim for the R&D Tax Credit need to fall into at least one of the above three categories, namely:
1. basic research;
2. applied research;
3. experimental development.

'Basic research' can essentially be considered as 'blue sky' or fundamental research, a type of research typically confined to academia/universities. In practice, this type of research comprises a low percentage of R&D activities carried out by commercial organisations as, in many cases, basic research does not have a commercial application in mind at the time it is being carried out.

For example, basic research could take the form of research undertaken to understand the function of newly discovered molecules or research undertaken in an effort to understand unexplained phenomena in a particular field.

'Applied research' and 'experimental development' are the more common types of research that commercial companies undertake and, therefore, make up the majority of R&D Tax Credit claims. Furthermore, it is often the case that R&D projects contain both elements of applied research and of experimental development. This occurs in situations where claimants are seeking both to gain new, and draw on existing, knowledge within a given project.

For example, applied research could take the form of R&D efforts aimed at incorporating newly discovered molecules in a formulation that can be used for a particular clinical application.

Experimental development could take the form of R&D efforts aimed at improving the efficacy of an existing formulation over an extended shelf life. Knowledge regarding the existing formulation would be drawn upon in this instance in seeking to reduce the formulation efficacy degradation over time.

A key point to note from the definitions set out above is that the R&D Tax Credit is available to companies that are making incremental improvements to existing solutions. However, where a claim is being made in respect of incremental improvements, it is important that the claimant is able to demonstrate the scientific or technical merits of such improvements. This is discussed in more detail in the sections below.

3.5.3.4 Scientific/Technological Advancement

"activities will not be research and development activities unless they—
(I) seek to achieve scientific or technological advancement".

In considering the area of scientific/technological advancement, it is important to first be aware that there is a requirement that an advancement be **sought**, but that it is not a requirement that the sought advancement is actually achieved. This is an important point. As R&D projects are by their very nature uncertain, and the R&D Tax Credit is designed to encourage companies to take on this risk, it is essential that the R&D Tax Credit does not just reward successful R&D activities. It is also intended to reward R&D activities that would be considered as failures due to the fact that the scientific or technological advancement sought was not ultimately achievable.

An advancement in science/technology is considered as an advancement in the field as a whole, as opposed to an advancement solely for the company carrying out the R&D activity. However, to the extent that there is no information reasonably available to a company in relation to the advancement sought, e.g. no publically available information as to how a particular competitor solution was developed, then it is allowable for a company to consider making a claim for the R&D Tax Credit on the creation of a similar solution.

For example, Company A may be developing a piece of software for a particular challenging solution which would represent an advancement to the field of computer science. Company B may have already solved this problem with its software development efforts but has kept that information proprietary by way of a trade secret. As no information relating to the advancement achieved by Company B is reasonably available to Company A, Company A's efforts at achieving the same advancement should qualify for the R&D Tax Credit also.

The key questions to ask of a particular project in order to determine whether there may be potential for the project to be considered as making scientific or technological advances are:
1. Has the company confirmed that there is no comparable solution available on the market that it could utilise?
2. Has the company confirmed that there is no available information as to how to technically achieve the goal(s) set out as part of the project?
3. If successful and if shared, would the company be seen to be advancing the scientific/technological knowledge in the field as a whole, by reference to reasonably available information?

To the extent that a company would answer 'yes' to the above questions, then it is highly likely that the company's project(s) would be considered to be seeking to make scientific or technological advancements. If the company would answer 'no' to any of these questions, then it is unlikely that such a project would be considered as scientifically or technologically advancing.

In documenting R&D projects, it is important that the documentation addresses the three key questions listed above and that it can be clearly shown how/why there is no other solution or knowledge publically available. Furthermore, the company should document why, if successful, the project would act to increase the scientific/technological knowledge set in the relevant field as a whole.

3.5.3.5 State of the Art Review

The documentation referred to should include details of a review carried out prior to project commencement, typically referred to by Revenue as the 'state of the art review'. The purpose of documenting this review is to demonstrate that the advancement in science or technology sought has not already been achieved and made available elsewhere by other researchers.

This requirement can be difficult for claimants to comprehend as it effectively asks that a claimant proves a negative, i.e. that something does not exist.

Nevertheless, the type of documentation/evidence that Revenue typically requests include details of the following:
• a literature review;
• relevant journals reviewed/subscribed to;
• details of conferences/events attended on the subject matter;
• details of consortia/fora of which relevant staff are members and consult with on the subject matter.

As mentioned above, while it might seem counterintuitive to research and record what does not exist, this is currently an area of focus during Revenue audits and, as such, is an area that claimants should ensure they document carefully.

3.5.3.6 Scientific/Technological Uncertainty

In addition to the scientific/technological advancement required as discussed above in **Section 3.5.3.4**, it is also necessary that activities are seeking to resolve scientific/technological uncertainty. Specifically, section 766(1)(a) provides:

> "activities will not be research and development activities unless they—
> ...
> (II) involve the resolution of scientific or technological uncertainty".

Scientific or technological uncertainty can arise in two scenarios, as set out in the Revenue guidelines[12]:
1. uncertainty as to **if** a particular goal can be achieved; or
2. uncertainty as to **how** a particular goal can be achieved.

This means that while it is known that the goal could be achieved were there no constraints in place, it may not be known whether it is still achievable or how it is achievable once specific constraints or requirements are put in place. For example, the introduction of footprint limitations on a printed circuit board design may lead to uncertainty as to how temperature levels and heat dissipation can be controlled, something that may not be an issue were a larger footprint acceptable.

The distinction between the two types of uncertainty can be illustrated by the following example:

EXAMPLE 3.23: THE TWO TYPES OF UNCERTAINTY

1. Where an R&D effort is undertaken in order to realise a new drug product that can completely relieve an illness that is not currently relievable through the use of drug products, then this would present uncertainty as to **if** this goal can be achieved.
2. Where an R&D effort is undertaken in order to realise a drug product that can relieve an illness that is already relievable there is likely no uncertainty as to **if** this can be achieved, on the basis that a drug product already exists that can relieve this illness. However, the R&D effort may be seeking to realise a drug product that can relieve this illness within seven days, whereas drug products currently available take 14 days to relieve the same illness. In this scenario, such a requirement would present uncertainty as to **how** the drug could be developed.

For R&D carried out in a commercial context, there is often a large amount of uncertainty presented in terms of **how** something might be achieved and a lower level of uncertainty as to **if** something can be

---

[12] Revenue Commissioners, *Research & Development Tax Credit Guidelines* (updated April 2015) p. 17.

achieved. Potential claimants for the R&D Tax Credit quite often focus on the first scenario set out above, i.e. the 'if' uncertainty, and on this basis often incorrectly self-classify their activities as non-qualifying. However, if the claimants understood that the 'how' uncertainty is also a valid uncertainty for the purpose of making the claim, a more appropriate analysis of the activity might be made.

R&D staff are solution-focussed and when tasked by the company with a body of work, they will believe that they can complete it. However, what often does not get discussed in detail at company level is the complexity of the task and the number of alternative hypotheses within given constraints that have been trialled and tested by the R&D team prior to presentation of the solution to the company at the conclusion of the task. Where this type of scenario exists, i.e. uncertainty is driven by particular constraints or requirements, it is important that such R&D personnel are made aware of Scenario 2 above so that they do not incorrectly disqualify tasks or projects on behalf of the company.

In either of the scenarios above, the key questions to ask of a particular R&D project in order to understand whether there may be potential scientific or technological uncertainty associated with it are:

1. Has the company confirmed that it has not previously designed/developed something similar?
2. Has the company confirmed that there is no publically available solution/information that can be utilised to resolve the problem?
3. Has the company confirmed that the solution cannot be derived on the basis of discussions with technical peers?
4. Is the company an expert in the field of science/technology within which it is carrying out the R&D activity?

To the extent that a company answers 'yes' to all of the above questions, then it is highly likely that the company's R&D project would be considered as involving scientific or technological uncertainty. If a company answers 'no' to any of the above points, then it is likely that such a project would not be considered as involving scientific or technological uncertainty.

3.5.3.7 Interaction of the R&D Tax Credit with Other Government R&D Schemes

Government agencies other than the Revenue Commissioners, namely IDA Ireland, which promotes foreign direct investment into Ireland, and Enterprise Ireland, which supports the development and growth of Irish enterprises in world markets, are responsible for the administration of R&D grants on behalf of the Irish Government. Some of the qualifying scientific/technological criteria that need to be met in order to avail of these grants are similar to the scientific/technological criteria required for the R&D Tax Credit. In recognition of this, in February 2017 Revenue stated in its *eBrief* No. 17/17 that, as a rule, it will not seek to challenge the scientific/technological merits of any claim where:

1. an IDA Ireland or Enterprise Ireland R&D grant was received in respect of the project;

2. the R&D Tax Credit claimed for an accounting period of not less than 12 months is €50,000 or less[13];
3. the project is undertaken in a prescribed field of science or technology (as set out in **Section 3.5.3.2** above); and
4. the company is a micro or small-sized enterprise.[14]

This practice should provide SMEs meeting the above criteria with greater certainty in relation to their R&D Tax Credit claims.

This *eBrief* is a re-issue of a previous administration practice adopted by Revenue. However, the practice was dropped on the basis that cases arose where it was perceived that it was being abused by certain taxpayers. Should this arise again, it is understood that Revenue will not allow companies to rely on the concession where it is suspected that it is being abused.

It is important to note that while the scientific/technological criteria are similar under the R&D Tax Credit regime and the IDA/Enterprise Ireland R&D grant schemes, there are differences between them. While the IDA/Enterprise Ireland R&D grant scheme requires that companies seek to overcome scientific/technological challenges, from an advancement view-point the scheme is more focussed on the **business** advancement that will be attained if the project is successful. Where a strong business case cannot be made, then it is unlikely that a grant will be given by the IDA/Enterprise Ireland. This contrasts with the R&D Tax Credit regime in that the business advancement is irrelevant for R&D Tax Credit purposes, as the focus is solely on the scientific/technological merits of the project.

> Given this subtle but key difference in focus between the tax credit regime and the grant scheme, it is important that companies satisfy themselves that they meet the more stringent R&D Tax Credit criteria before they make a claim for the R&D Tax Credit.

3.5.3.8 R&D Start and End Dates

For the purposes of the R&D Tax Credit regime, qualifying activities are considered to commence at the point at which work on the resolution of the scientific/technological uncertainty commences. Qualifying activity is considered to end at the point at which work on the resolution of the scientific/technological uncertainty ends.

Where a company spends time in gathering market data and defining business requirements that will drive the R&D effort to be undertaken by the company, such time should not be considered for inclusion in an R&D Tax Credit claim. The expectation is that the scientific/technological

---

[13] This equates to a claim containing less than €200,000 of R&D expenditure.
[14] Revenue, *eBrief* No. 17/17, "R&D tax credit claims in respect of projects supported by Enterprise Ireland R&D grants".

requirements would have been defined based on the business requirements and that from that point the work on the resolution of scientific/techno-logical uncertainty would commence, i.e. the point at which it would be reasonable to consider the R&D Tax Credit qualifying activity to have commenced.

Once the scientific/technological uncertainty has been resolved, there may still be uncertainty as to whether the solution is commercially viable. Note, however, that work in establishing the commercial viability or gain-ing user acceptance of the solution would not be considered to be R&D Tax Credit qualifying activity.

The definition of, and documentation concerning, R&D project start and end dates is something that Revenue is likely to explore should an enquiry into a claim be carried out; companies should be comfortable that they have a clear process for establishing the start and end date of projects from an R&D Tax Credit perspective.

3.5.4 Documenting an R&D Tax Credit Claim

Prior to the submission of a claim, it is essential that claimants are com-fortable they can demonstrate that they meet the accounting and scientific/technological criteria as set out in the sections above. The fol-lowing sections outline the science and accounting tests that must be passed and the records that should be maintained by any claimants.

3.5.4.1 Documentation Supporting the Science Test

From a scientific/technological criteria perspective, a company must maintain detailed and contemporaneous documentation supporting the R&D activities carried out, the personnel involved in the activities and the advancements and uncertainties associated with the R&D activities. The documentation maintained by the claimant should evidence the following as set out in the Revenue guidelines:[15]

"**Records required to be maintained to satisfy the science test**
  (a) A description of the R&D activities, the methods to be used and what the company seeks to achieve by undertaking the activities concerned.
  (b) The field of science and technology concerned.
  (c) The scientific or technological advancement that is the goal of the R&D activities.
  (d) The scientific or technological uncertainty that the company is seeking to resolve in its R&D activities.
  (e) Evidence that the scientific or technological advance(s) sought had not already been achieved and that the scientific and/or

[15] Revenue Commissioners, *Research & Development Tax Credit Guidelines* (updated April 2015) pp. 40–41.

technological uncertainties that the company was seeking to over-come were not already resolved or that such resolution would not be available to a competent professional working in the field, for example, evidence that a comprehensive literature review to determine the current status of scientific or technological knowledge in the area had been conducted prior to commencing the project.

(f) Details of the systematic investigation, including
- the hypothesis advanced.
- the series of experiments or investigations undertaken to test the hypothesis.
- documentary evidence of the necessity for each major element and how it fits into the project as a whole.
- dated documents of the original scientific or technological goals, the progress of the work, how it was carried out and the conclusions.
- indicators or measures identified at the commencement of the project to determine if the scientific or technological objectives of the R&D activities are met.

(g) the qualifications, skill and experience of the project manager.
(h) the numbers, qualifications and skill levels of other personnel working on the project."

While documentation in support of the above points is typically maintained and available within large organisations and within organisations carrying out their R&D activities in highly regulated sectors, SMEs often struggle in this regard. As this is one of the key criteria to be met from an R&D Tax Credit perspective, it would be advisable that any potential claimant implement new, or augment existing, documentation processes in order to ensure that they can adequately evidence the R&D activities that were carried out, to ensure they satisfy the requirements of the science test.

3.5.4.2 Documentation Supporting the Accounting Test

From an accounting perspective, a claimant company must maintain detailed and contemporaneous documentation supporting all of the time/costs included in the claim as well as the methods used for the apportionment of these costs to the claim (see **Section 3.5.2**). The documentation maintained should evidence the following, as set out in the Revenue guidelines:[16]

"**Records containing the following information, if relevant, are required:**
(a) The dates of commencement and termination of the project. The date of resolution of the scientific or technological uncertainty is a determining factor when considering where an R&D activity ends, and activity associated with commercial exploitation begins. Costs incurred after the R&D phase is completed do not qualify for the relief;

---

[16] Revenue Commissioners, *Research & Development Tax Credit Guidelines* (updated April 2015) pp. 41–42.

(b) A project plan with appropriate milestones and deliverables for management of the project;

(c) Details of progress made against the project plan;

(d) Details of the personnel involved in the project, their qualifications and the amounts of their time allocated to the project;

(e) The location where the R&D activities took place, and a breakdown of costs associated with the location (e.g. apportionment of light, heat, etc.);

(f) Details of any amounts paid to universities or institutes of higher education and the qualifying R&D activity carried out by them on behalf of the company;

(g) Details of any amounts paid to non-academic subcontractors and the qualifying R&D activity carried out by them on behalf of the company;

(h) Details of the methods and bases of apportionment of all expenditure associated with the R&D."

3.6 How the Relief Is Claimed

Qualifying R&D Tax Credits are claimed through the company's corporation tax return and are used to offset corporation tax liabilities in the first instance. If the ability to offset the credit against corporation tax liabilities is not possible, then the credit may be claimed as a cash refund, subject to certain requirements being met.

3.6.1 Corporation Tax Return

Where a company is trading and has R&D Tax Credits available for a given accounting period, these credits must be applied for through the CT1 return within 12 months of the end of the given accounting period.

> **Note:** To the extent that the claim is not made within this 12-month window, the credit will be lost.

3.7 Revenue R&D Tax Credit Reviews

Given that the R&D Tax Credit costs the Irish exchequer over half a billion euros per annum (€553 million in 2014), there has been, and continues to be, a significant amount of Revenue action in the area.

Table 3.1 below shows the increase in the number of reviews and the associated increase in exchequer yield on Revenue R&D reviews from 2009 up to and including 2015. It is worth bearing in mind that the change in Revenue's interpretation of certain aspects of the scheme in the period from 2009 to 2014 may have contributed to these figures. In particular, interpretation changes in relation to the allowability of support costs and overheads may not have been understood widely, given the fact that there was no change in legislation in relation to these points.

TABLE 3.1: PUBLISHED RESULTS OF REVENUE REVIEWS OF
R&D TAX CREDIT CLAIMS[17]

Year	No. of Reviews	Yield €	Average Yield per Intervention €
2011	26	2,591,000	99,654
2012	49	5,413,000	110,469
2013	105	14,483,000	137,933
2014	162	10,106,000	62,383
2015	178	13,542,000	76,079

In reviewing an R&D Tax Credit claim, there are three main options that Revenue utilises:
1. an aspect query;
2. a Revenue audit; or
3. a Revenue audit including appointment of a technical expert.

Detailed analysis of the Revenue enquiry process, Revenue powers, the interest and penalties regime and the appeal process is beyond the scope of this book. However, outlined below are some aspects of these various processes that are specific to Revenue reviews of R&D Tax Credit claims. It is important to note that at the higher level Revenue reviews of R&D Tax Credit claims are bound by the same obligations, protections and rights of appeal afforded to taxpayers as with any other Revenue enquiry.

3.7.1 An Aspect Query

An aspect query from Revenue will commence with the provision of a letter from Revenue to the claimant seeking 22 points of information, the aim of which is to ascertain whether all of the relevant R&D Tax Credit criteria (as discussed in the sections above) have been met. The information points requested in this letter are set out in **Appendix 3.1** to this chapter.

If the information provided in response to an aspect query is sufficient to satisfy Revenue then it is likely that no further queries will be raised. Should the information be insufficient or should Revenue require further clarification on points, it may revert with additional queries in a further letter or, alternatively, it may request to carry out an on-site visit of the claimant company to discuss these queries.

---

[17] See http://oireachtasdebates.oireachtas.ie/Debates%20Authoring/
DebatesWebPack.nsf/takes/dail2017022800068#N16

The closure of an aspect query will occur once Revenue is happy with the information provided to it in support of a claim, or once Revenue and the claimant have come to a mutual agreement on any adjustments that might need to be made to a claim.

Where the options outlined above have been exhausted by Revenue and to the extent that there are still issues that have not been settled, Revenue can issue a letter notifying the company that its R&D Tax Credit claim will be subjected to a full Revenue audit. For completeness, it should also be noted that Revenue may move to carry out a full audit without going through the aspect query process. This can happen, for example, where there is significant cost or concern relating to a particular claim, e.g. the R&D Tax Credit claim might be the largest in scale in that particular tax district, or there could be a concern in relation to a specific industry sector that Revenue wishes to explore.

One key difference between the aspect query and audit processes is that claimants have an opportunity to self-correct under a reduced penalty (i.e. an unprompted disclosure) during an aspect query. Once a notification of audit has been made, more severe penalties can arise. Interest is chargeable to any liabilities in both cases. Furthermore, where a full audit is carried out, it is likely that Revenue will seek to incorporate other tax heads, thus increasing the time and effort required of the claimant to prepare for such an audit. For these reasons, claimants should ensure that they robustly and swiftly respond to Revenue when an aspect query letter is received.

3.7.2 Revenue Audits

3.7.2.1 General Audit Process

Where an R&D Tax Credit claim is to be subjected to a Revenue audit, notification of same will be sent from Revenue to the claimant company in advance of any such audit commencing. This letter may be specific to R&D Tax Credits or may seek to incorporate other tax heads.

The letter will usually ask that information be provided to Revenue in advance of any on-site visit. From an R&D Tax Credit perspective, the information that is requested is typically in line with that requested in an aspect query letter (see above and **Appendix 3.1**).

It will be necessary to agree on a suitable date and time for Revenue to come on-site to review the claim in detail. Revenue should be accommodated quickly: engaging as soon as proposed by Revenue will typically lead to a swifter review process as it is more likely that it has capacity around the time that the audit query is raised.

Prior to official commencement of the audit on-site, a claimant has the opportunity to make a 'prompted voluntary disclosure'. The benefit of making such a disclosure at this point is that the level of penalty is lower than that which would be applied if a disclosure was made after the audit commences. Also, details of any settlement made by the taxpayer under a qualifying disclosure should avoid publication by Revenue.

The duration of an audit can vary from two or three hours to a couple of days, depending on the claim size. During the audit, at a high level, Revenue will be seeking to understand:
1. What projects have been qualified for the R&D Tax Credit and why, i.e. has the company met the science test?
2. What associated costs have been qualified and why, i.e. has the company met the accounting test?

After an on-site meeting, Revenue typically requires follow-up actions to be addressed by the claimant in order to provide it with further clarification or additional information. Where the information provided during and after the on-site meeting is sufficient to satisfy Revenue, then it is likely that no further queries will be raised. Should the information be insufficient or should Revenue require further clarification on certain points, a series of correspondences may be required in order to address all queries.

The closure of an audit will occur once Revenue is satisfied with the information provided in support of a claim made, or once Revenue and the claimant have come to a mutual agreement on any potential adjustments that need to be made to a claim. At this point, Revenue will provide formal notification to the claimant of the closure of the audit.

Where it is not possible to satisfy Revenue that the claim is valid from a scientific/technological perspective, Revenue may seek to appoint a technical expert to review the claim. For completeness, it should also be noted that Revenue may move to appoint a technical expert without going through its own audit-review process, as outlined above. This can happen, for example, where there is significant cost or concern relating to a particular claim as discussed in **Section 3.7.1**. Revenue may also appoint a technical expert where it feels the area of science is going to be quite challenging for it to understand even at a basic level.

3.7.2.2 Revenue Audit: Appointment of Technical Expert

It is acknowledged that, in many cases, Revenue officials do not have the necessary technical expertise to competently evaluate the science test in detail as the science or technology in question should be at the leading edge of its field. Therefore, section 766 (7)(a) TCA 1997 allows Revenue to consult with a "person who in their opinion may be of assistance to them in ascertaining whether the expenditure incurred by the company was incurred in the carrying on by it of research and development activities" in accordance with section 766.

In this regard, each year Revenue issues an open invitation to join its technical expert panel. Applicants are screened by Revenue to ensure that they are suitably qualified in a relevant field of science or technology to be accepted for inclusion on the panel. This panel is typically made up of individuals from academia as this mitigates the potential for commercial conflicts of interest. Where Revenue requires the assistance of an expert in a given field, it refers to this panel of technical experts. On occasions where the specific skillset required is not available on the panel, Revenue may seek to engage an individual expert outside the panel.

Where Revenue intends to appoint a technical expert to review an R&D Tax Credit claim, written notification of this must be given to the claimant. The claimant then has an opportunity before such an appointment is made and before any commercial information is passed over from Revenue to the technical expert to consider whether they feel the proposed technical expert is suitable in terms of relevant experience in the area and whether they believe that any conflict of interest may arise.

When the technical expert appointment is agreed between Revenue and the claimant, a date(s) will be agreed for an on-site meeting between Revenue, its appointed technical expert and the claimant. During the on-site technical expert review, the duration of which can vary from two or three hours to a couple of days, depending on the number of projects to be reviewed, the technical expert will seek to understand:

1. how/why projects have been considered to qualify (see **Section 3.5.3**, The Science/Technology Criteria);
2. the methodologies used to track projects and associated activities (see **Section 3.5.3.1**);
3. the documentation available in support of all projects (see **Sections 3.5.3.5** and **3.5.4**).

Ultimately, the technical expert is tasked with providing Revenue with an opinion as to whether they believe that the projects meet all of the relevant criteria to be considered as qualifying R&D activities under the definitions set out in section 766 TCA 1997. This opinion is presented to Revenue in the form of a report and subsequently to the claimant.

It is important to note that the technical expert is commissioned by Revenue as an independent technical expert, and to form their opinion on the science test independently based on the information presented to them. This opinion is expected to be fully impartial and, as such, it should be made available to the claimant as soon as possible after it is provided to Revenue. Revenue has issued a revised practice note in relation to the manner in which independent experts interact with both Revenue and the claimant to help ensure an appropriate approach is consistently applied.[18]

Where the technical expert raises a concern regarding the eligibility of a project(s) in their formal report, it is generally possible for the claimant to provide additional detail for the technical expert to consider in an effort to mitigate any such concerns. Given the number of facets to a claim, and its associated projects, particular detail may be missed/misinterpreted, or a particular query may not have been raised by the technical expert, which would mitigate a concern that arises for them after the on-site meeting.

---

[18] https://www.revenue.ie/en/tax-professionals/tdm/income-tax-capital-gains-tax-corporation-tax/part-29/29-02-05.pdf

Where the information provided during and after the on-site meeting is sufficient to satisfy the technical expert and Revenue, then it is likely that no further queries will be raised. Should the information be insufficient or should the technical expert or Revenue require further clarification on points, a further series of correspondences may be required to address all queries.

3.8 Interactions with Other Reliefs

3.8.1 Start-up Companies Relief

As discussed in **Chapter 4** at **Section 4.5.4**, the Start-up Companies Relief and the R&D Tax Credit are compatible. The R&D Tax Credit is calculated before the Start-up Companies Relief and therefore can bring more companies within the limits of the Start-up Companies Relief. Also, the carry-forward provisions of the Start-up Companies Relief mean that should the R&D Tax Credit reduce all the company's corporation tax liabilities of the first three years of trading, the benefits of the Start-up Companies Relief are not lost but carry forward to future periods.

See **Chapter 4** for full details of the Start-up Companies Relief.

3.8.2 The Knowledge Development Box

The R&D Tax Credit and the Knowledge Development Box (KDB) (see **Chapter 5**) are fully compatible. As discussed in detail in **Section 5.7.5**, the KDB has been designed to build upon the R&D Tax Credit. However, in summary the two incentives are compatible and both can be availed of by a company.

3.8.3 Specified Intangible Asset Allowances

The interaction between the R&D Tax Credit and allowances for specified intangible assets (SIAs) is covered in detail in **Chapter 6** at **Section 6.9.3**. However, in summary, the R&D Tax Credit and SIA relief provided by section 291A TCA 1997 are not compatible. As discussed in **Chapter 6**, section 291A TCA 1997 provides an allowance for expenditure incurred on the provision of SIAs. The class of assets included in the definition of an SIA in section 291A include certain assets that may have been created as a result of R&D activities, e.g. patents. Section 291A provides that no allowance will be given in relation to any expenditure that has been previously relieved under the Tax Acts. If the R&D Tax Credit is claimed on any expenditure incurred on the creation of the SIA, then that expenditure will be considered to have been previously relieved under the Tax Acts and, therefore, not eligible for allowance under section 291A. **Section 6.9.3** includes a detailed analysis that companies should consider when deciding between claiming the R&D Tax Credit or allowances under section 291A.

3.9 Conclusion

The R&D Tax Credit regime is the most valuable corporation tax relief available to companies in Ireland. With potential benefits of up to 37.5% of the costs (25% tax credit plus 12.5% corporation tax deduction), the cost savings available to all companies carrying out R&D activities can be significant. The attractiveness of the regime is essential to the attractiveness of Ireland's FDI offering and helps the country to compete for some of the highest-level international research projects.

While this is an important relief that should be carefully considered by companies to ensure that they do not miss out, companies must fully understand the criteria to ensure that any claim they make will stand up to increasing Revenue scrutiny. Given the cost of the scheme to the Irish exchequer, it is incumbent on Revenue to ensure the scheme is not abused by unworthy claimants.

On Revenue's part, it is important that clear guidance is provided to taxpayers, which is consistently and fairly applied across the districts and various sectors to ensure that genuine taxpayers making genuine claims for the R&D Tax Credit based on a carefully considered interpretation of the legislation and guidelines do not find that they have inadvertently over-claimed.

The R&D Tax Credit is regarded as a key incentive to underpin and drive 'the smart economy' that successive governments see as the future of the Irish economy. With this in mind, it is important that the credit is reviewed regularly to ensure it is fit for purpose and is improved where necessary. In October 2016, a Department of Finance review of the R&D Tax Credit concluded that it is internationally competitive and encourages additional R&D activities in Ireland.[19] Given the increased focus internationally on attracting higher-end jobs and research projects, it is important that the R&D Tax Credit scheme and its administration are regarded as best in class.

---

[19] Department of Finance, "Economic Evaluation of the R&D Tax Credit" (October 2016). Available at http://igees.gov.ie/wp-content/uploads/2014/01/R-and-D-Credit-Evaluation-2016.pdf

For convenience, the main points relating to the R&D Tax Credit outlined in this chapter are included below in an 'At a Glance' summary.

AT A GLANCE: THE R&D TAX CREDIT

What is the relief?	It is a tax credit of 25% available on eligible expenditure on R&D activities.
This relief is potentially of value if:	• the business operates through a company; • the company is carrying on R&D activities; • these R&D activities are being carried out within the EEA.
This relief is likely to be of benefit to:	• Companies at any stage of their lifecycle that have incurred expenditure in the carrying on of R&D activities within the current or previous accounting period.
Interactions with other reliefs:	• It is complementary to the Knowledge Development Box, i.e. companies can avail of the benefits of both regimes. • It cannot be claimed in relation to expenditure upon which specified intangible asset allowances have been claimed. Therefore, a cost–benefit/opportunity analysis will be required to establish the optimum return.

Appendix 3.1: Detail Requested by the Revenue Commissioners in an Aspect Query

1. The number of R&D projects undertaken.
2. A summary of the R&D activities in relation to each project.
3. The date each R&D project commenced.
4. The date each R&D project ceased, if applicable.
5. The amount of the 2003 R&D expenditure threshold amount.[20]
6. Has all group expenditure been included in the threshold amount?
7. The field of science or technology involved.
8. Are the activities basic research or applied research or experimental development?
9. Outline the specific scientific or technological advancement that the company sought to achieve at the start of each R&D project.
10. Outline the specific scientific or technological uncertainty that the company sought to resolve at the start of each R&D project.
11. Once the uncertainty was resolved, confirmation that no further expenditure has been attributed to the R&D claim.
12. Was the solution already known and available to a competent professional in the field?
13. What was the location at which the R&D activities took place?
14. The number of staff employed in the R&D activities.
15 The project leaders and their qualifications.
16. How much (if any) R&D expenditure was paid to third-party contractors or service providers (excluding utilities)?
17. How much (if any) R&D expenditure was paid to a university or other third-level institution?
18. In respect of (17) and (18), briefly outline the work carried out by the other parties.
19. Where expenditure has been allocated to R&D by apportionment, state, in respect of each expenditure item, the method and basis used.
20. Where the claim includes expenditure on plant and machinery state:
    (a) the useful economic life of the asset;
    (b) the percentage use of the equipment on R&D over said lifetime.
21. Details of any grants received in respect of R&D.
22. A computation of the tax credit claimed, showing an itemised analysis of each expenditure item.

---

[20] As discussed in **Section 3.1**, the R&D Tax Credit was originally an incremental system with 2003 set as the base year for comparison R&D expenditure. While this has been changed to a volume system, for accounting periods commencing on or after 1 January 2015, the 2003 base year is still relevant in relation to accounting periods before this.

Appendix 3.2: Categories of Activity that May Qualify for the R&D Tax Credit[21]

Natural Sciences
1. Mathematics and computer sciences, including mathematics and other allied fields, computer sciences and other allied subjects, and software development.
2. Physical sciences including astronomy and space sciences, physics and other allied subjects.
3. Chemical sciences including chemistry and other allied subjects.
4. Earth and related environmental sciences including geology, geophysics, mineralogy, physical geography and other geosciences, meteorology and other atmospheric sciences including climatic research, oceanography, volcanology, paleoecology and other allied sciences.
5. Biological sciences including biology, botany, bacteriology, microbiology, zoology, entomology, genetics, biochemistry, biophysics and other allied sciences, excluding clinical and veterinary sciences.

Engineering and Technology
1. Civil engineering including architecture engineering, building science and engineering, construction engineering, municipal and structural engineering and other allied subjects.
2. Electrical engineering, electronics including communication engineering and systems, computer engineering (hardware) and other allied subjects.
3. Other engineering sciences such as chemical, aeronautical and space, mechanical, metallurgical and materials engineering, and their specialised subdivisions; forest products; applied sciences such as geodesy and industrial chemistry; the science and technology of food production; and specialised technologies of interdisciplinary fields, e.g. systems analysis, metallurgy, mining, textile technology and other allied subjects.

Medical Sciences
1. Basic medicine including anatomy, cytology, physiology, genetics, pharmacy, pharmacology, toxicology, immunology and immunohematology, clinical chemistry, clinical microbiology, and pathology.
2. Clinical medicine including anaesthesiology, paediatrics, obstetrics and gynaecology, internal medicine, surgery, dentistry, neurology, psychiatry, radiology, therapeutics, otorhinolaryngology and ophthalmology.
3. Health sciences including public health services, social medicine, hygiene, nursing, and epidemiology.

Agricultural Science
1. Agriculture, forestry, fisheries and allied sciences including agronomy, animal husbandry, fisheries, forestry, horticulture, and other allied subjects.
2. Veterinary medicine.

[21] These definitions are set out in the Taxes Consolidation Act 1997 (Prescribed Research and Development Activities) Regulations 2004 (S.I. No. 434 of 2004).

Appendix 3.3: Categories of Activity that Are Not Research and Development Activities[22]

(a) research in the social sciences (including economics, business management, and behavioural sciences), arts, or humanities;

(b) routine testing and analysis for purposes of quality or quantity control;

(c) alterations of a cosmetic or stylistic nature to existing products, services or processes whether or not these alterations represent some improvement;

(d) operational research such as management studies or efficiency surveys which are not wholly and exclusively undertaken for the purposes of a research and development activity;

(e) corrective action in connection with breakdowns during commercial production of a product;

(f) legal and administrative work in connection with patent applications, records and litigation and the sale or licensing of patents;

(g) activity, including design and construction engineering, relating to the construction, relocation, rearrangement or start up of facilities or equipment other than facilities or equipment which is to be used wholly and exclusively for the purposes of carrying on by the company of research and development activities;

(h) market research, market testing, market development, sales promotion or consumer surveys;

(i) prospecting, exploring or drilling for, or producing, minerals, petroleum or natural gas;

(j) the commercial and financial steps necessary for the marketing or the commercial production or distribution of a new or improved material, product, device, process, system or service;

(k) administration and general support services (such as transportation, storage, cleaning, repair, maintenance and security) which are not wholly and exclusively undertaken in connection with a research and development activity.

---

[22] These definitions are set out in the Taxes Consolidation Act 1997 (Prescribed Research and Development Activities) Regulations 2004 (S.I. No. 434 of 2004).

Appendix 3.4: Accounting for the Tax Credit

Introduction

Up to Finance (No. 2) Act 2008, the R&D Tax Credit was a non-refundable credit, i.e. it could only be used to reduce current and future corporation tax liabilities of a company; therefore, getting benefit for the R&D Tax Credit was dependent on the company having a corporation tax liability. The accounting treatment to be adopted for these types of credits was quite clear, i.e. the tax credit should be reflected as a reduction in the tax liability of the company in the tax line on the income statement.

Changes introduced by Finance (No. 2) Act 2008 allowed companies a refund of the R&D Tax Credits that are not used against corporation tax liabilities (see **Section 3.4.2**). This changed the nature of the R&D Tax Credit from an accounting perspective and, therefore, the approaches that could be adopted to account for the credit. The two available approaches were 'above the line' (i.e. accounting for the R&D Tax Credit in the profit-before-tax figure in the income statement) and 'below the line' (i.e. accounting for the R&D Tax Credit in the tax charge in the income statement).

Chartered Accountants Ireland issued Information Sheet 04/2009 entitled "Accounting Treatment of Research and Development Tax Credit" in May 2009, in which it set out the options for companies accounting for the R&D Tax Credit. It confirmed that, following the Finance (No. 2) Act 2008 changes, companies were allowed to account for the credit above the line. In fact, it recommended that the R&D Tax Credit be accounted for 'above the line' under IFRS. For old Irish GAAP, there was no explicit guidance on this matter and, therefore, either approach was acceptable.

With the below-the-line approach, the full credit a company was entitled to in a period was credited to the tax charge in the income statement and a corporation tax debtor of the same amount was recognised. As the credit was refunded or offset against the company's corporation tax liability over the years, the corporation tax debtor was reduced. Prior to the aforementioned changes implemented in 2008, this approach was required of all companies. However, with the transition from old Irish GAAP to new Irish GAAP (FRS 100 to FRS 105), which came into effect for accounting periods commencing on or after 1 January 2015, the below-the-line approach is no longer appropriate as the accounting treatment of the R&D Tax Credit under FRS 102 and FRS 105 is in line with the treatment under IFRS.

This appendix to **Chapter 3** sets out the approach that should now be taken in accounting for R&D Tax Credits as a result of Finance (No. 2) Act 2008, i.e. the above-the-line approach. Credits should be included as income or offset against R&D or payroll costs and included in other debtors. We will also consider the differences when accounting for the R&D Tax Credits under IFRS, FRS 102 and FRS 105.

International Financial Reporting Standards (IFRS)

Chartered Accountants Ireland Information Sheet 04/2009, referred to above, provided the following guidance on how the R&D Tax Credit should be accounted for under IFRS. Although Chartered Accountants Ireland has stated that this guidance is now out of date (presumably due to the fact that the guidance referred to the 'old' Irish GAAP), it is worth covering the main points in respect of the guidance relating to IFRS as there has been no intervening change to IFRS.

There is no specific guidance regarding how 'investment tax credits' should be accounted for as both IAS 12 *Income Taxes* and IAS 20 *Accounting for Government Grants and Disclosure of Government Assistance* exclude it from their scope.

IAS 8 *Accounting Policies, Changes in Accounting Estimates and Errors* requires that the substance of the R&D Tax Credit be considered so that it is accounted for correctly.

If the view is taken that the R&D Tax Credit is, in substance, a government grant towards the cost of R&D activities, it should be treated as a pre-tax government grant in the accounts, i.e. above the line.

FRS 102 and FRS 105

FRS 102 *The Financial Reporting Standard applicable in the UK and Republic of Ireland* (FRS 102) came into effect for accounting periods commencing on or after 1 January 2015, replacing existing old Irish GAAP. FRS 105 *The Financial Reporting Standard applicable to the Micro-entities Regime* came into effect for accounting periods commencing on or after 1 January 2016. As with Irish GAAP and IFRS, there is no specific guidance in FRS 102 or FRS 105 as to how the R&D Tax Credit should be accounted for. Section 29.21 (Income tax) of FRS 102 states that "an entity shall present changes in a current tax liability (asset) and changes in a deferred tax liability (asset) as tax expense (income)".[1] There is similar wording in FRS 105 (Section 24.12).[2] However, if the credit is treated as a government grant, it should not be presented as a current tax asset and, therefore, is not required to be accounted for through the tax charge in the income statement.

Section 24.5E (Government grants) of FRS 102 states that "[a] grant that becomes receivable as compensation for expenses or losses already incurred ... with no future related costs shall be recognised in income in the period in which it becomes receivable". There is similar wording in FRS 105 (Section 19.8).[2] It would appear to be clear that the R&D Tax Credit is a grant that is compensation for expenses already incurred with

---

[1] Revised version of FRS 102 issued in March 2018: FRS 102 *The Financial Reporting Standard applicable in the UK and Republic of Ireland* (March 2018).

[2] Revised version of FRS 105 issued in March 2018: FRS 105 *The Financial Reporting Standard applicable to the Micro-entities Regime* (March 2018).

no future-related costs and therefore, under Section 24.5E of FRS 102 (and Section 19.8 of FRS 105) should be recognised as income (or as an offset against expenses) rather than through the tax line of the accounts.

Appropriate Accounting Treatment

From 1 January 2009,[3] the R&D Tax Credit should be accounted for above the line as if it is treated as a quasi-government grant under FRS 102, FRS 105 or IFRS. The credit is generally booked as income.[4] The full R&D Tax Credit a company is entitled to in a period is credited to the income statement and the same amount is recognised as other debtors, such as government grants receivable.

As the R&D Tax Credit is refunded or offset against the company's corporation tax liability, this other debtor is reduced accordingly. The following example illustrates how this should work in practice.

EXAMPLE 1: STANDARD R&D TAX CREDIT

A company has the following profits, corporation tax liabilities and R&D Tax Credit claims:

	Year 1	Year 2	Year 3
Profit before tax (excl. R&D Tax Credit)	€400,000	€400,000	€2,400,000
CT liability (excl. R&D Tax Credit)	(€50,000)	(€50,000)	(€300,000)
R&D tax credit	€150,000	€150,000	€100,000
Profit after tax	€500,000	€500,000	€2,200,000
Amounts payable/ (refundable) in the following year, i.e. upon filing the tax return	(€33,000)	(€66,500)	€99,500

[3] It should be noted that any non-refundable R&D Tax Credits carried forward from accounting periods beginning before 1 January 2009 ('old' credits) should be recognised as a deferred tax asset, if appropriate, as they can only be offset against future corporation tax liabilities. It would be appropriate to recognise these credits as a deferred tax asset where it is likely that the company will have sufficient corporation tax liabilities to utilise the credits. For clarity, the accounting treatment outlined in this section does not apply to such credits.

[4] In practice, we have seen the R&D Tax Credit offset against R&D expenditure or against payroll costs, on the basis that the new R&D tax credit regime was initially envisaged as a refund of payroll liabilities and the refunds payable may be restricted to the company's payroll liabilities.

The R&D Tax Credit should be accounted for as follows (on the assumptions that no preliminary tax has been paid):

	Year 1	Year 2	Year 3
Income Statement			
Grant income	€150,000	€150,000	€100,000
Profit before tax	€550,000	€550,000	€2,500,000
Current year tax charge	(€50,000)	(€50,000)	(€300,000)
Profit after tax	€500,000	€500,000	€2,200,000
Balance Sheet – Corporation Tax			
Opening balance – Dr/(Cr)	€0	€0	€0
Current year (liability)/refund	(€50,000)	(€50,000)	(€300,000)
Government grant/other debtor	€50,000	€50,000	€200,500
Closing balance – Dr/(Cr)	€0	€0	(€99,500)
Balance Sheet – Government Grant / Other Debtor			
Opening balance – Dr/(Cr)	€0	€100,000	€167,000
Receivable re current year	€150,000	€150,000	€100,000
Refunded re Year 1	€0	(€33,000)	(€33,500)
Refunded re Year 2	€0	€0	(€33,000)
Offset against corporation tax	(€50,000)	(€50,000)	(€200,500)
Closing balance – Dr/(Cr)	€100,000	€167,000	€0
Tax Reconciliation Note			
Profit before tax	€550,000	€550,000	€2,500,000
Tax @ 12.5%	€68,750	€68,750	€312,500
Non-taxable income (being R&D credit)[5]	(€18,750)	(€18,750)	(€12,500)
Current year tax charge	€50,000	€50,000	€300,000

Plant and Machinery

Where plant and machinery is included in an R&D Tax Credit claim (see **Section 3.5.2.4.1**), the same analysis described above should apply.

---

[5] Calculated as €150,000 (Year 1 and 2) and €100,000 (Year 3) × 12.5%. The R&D Tax Credit is not a taxable receipt.

However, when using the above-the-line approach, as the plant and machinery portion of the 'government grant' relates to assets, the income should be recognised over the expected useful life of the asset. Therefore, where a company has sufficient tax payable against which the R&D Tax Credit may be offset, the credit will be received in full in Year 1 but it will be recognised in the income statement over a number of years.

EXAMPLE 2: PLANT AND MACHINERY

A company has the following profits, corporation tax liabilities and R&D Tax Credit claims (it is assumed all of the R&D Tax Credit relates to plant and machinery for the purpose of the example):

	Year 1	Year 2	Year 3
Profit before tax (excl. R&D Tax Credit)	€2,000,000	€2,000,000	€2,000,000
CT liability (excl. R&D Tax Credit)	(€250,000)	(€250,000)	(€250,000)
R&D Tax Credit	€150,000	€0	€0
Economic profit before the application of accounting standards	€1,900,000	€1,750,000	€1,750,000

The R&D tax credit should be accounted for as follows (on the assumption that no preliminary tax has been paid and that the plant and machinery has a useful life of five years):

	Year 1	Year 2	Year 3
Income Statement			
Grant income	€30,000	€30,000	€30,000
Profit before tax	€2,030,000	€2,030,000	€2,030,000
Current year tax charge	(€250,000)	(€250,000)	(€250,000)
Profit after tax	€1,780,000	€1,780,000	€1,780,000
Balance Sheet – Corporation Tax			
Opening balance – Dr/(Cr)	€0	(€100,000)	(€250,000)
Tax payments	€0	€100,000	€250,000
Current year (liability)/refund	(€250,000)	(€250,000)	(€250,000)
Government grant/other debtor	€150,000	€0	€0
Closing balance – Dr/(Cr)	(€100,000)	(€250,000)	(€250,000)

Balance Sheet –
Government Grant /
Other Debtor

Opening balance – Dr/(Cr)	€0	€0	€0
Receivable re current year	€150,000	€0	€0
Offset against corporation tax	(€150,000)	€0	€0
Closing balance – Dr/(Cr)	€0	€0	€0

Balance Sheet – Deferred
Income

Opening balance – Dr/(Cr)	€0	(€120,000)	(€90,000)
Receivable re current year	(€150,000)	€0	€0
Recognised as grant income	€30,000	€30,000	€30,000
Closing balance – Dr/(Cr)	(€120,000)	(€90,000)	(60,000)

Tax Reconciliation Note

Profit before tax	€2,030,000	€2,030,000	€2,030,000
Tax @ 12.5%	€253,750	€253,750	€253,750
Non-taxable income (being R&D credit)6	(€3,750)	(€3,750)	(€3,750)
Current year tax charge	€250,000	€250,000	€250,000

Conclusion

Historically, there was flexibility under Irish GAAP to account for the R&D Tax Credit above or below the line. However, IFRS is more restrictive and it is recommended under this standard that the credit be accounted for above the line. As FRS 100–105 were introduced to bring GAAP more in line with IFRS, accounting for the R&D Tax Credit above the line would also be the recommended method under those accounting policies (i.e. Section 24.5E of FRS 102 and Section 19.8 of FRS 105).

As with the accounting treatment and presentation of a number of other items, companies that transitioned from old Irish GAAP to FRS 100 to 102 (now FRS 100–105) would have needed to consider the transitional measure to be taken if they had previously been accounting for the R&D Tax Credit below the line.

---

[6] Calculated as €30,000 × 12.5% – the R&D tax credit is not a taxable receipt.

CHAPTER 4

START-UP
COMPANIES RELIEF

4.1 Introduction

In the midst of the global financial crisis of 2008 and the Irish banking and property crisis, the Start-up Companies Relief was introduced by Finance (No. 2) Act 2008 as an incentive to encourage entrepreneurship and job creation.

Chapter 3 dealt with the R&D Tax Credit, which is a relief that companies receive as a result of expenditure incurred. This chapter, together with **Chapters 5** and **6**, deals with reliefs that reduce the tax liability arising on income by either relieving the tax directly or giving a tax-deductible allowance against the income that will reduce the taxable profits of the company.

RELEVANT STAGE(S) IN THE INNOVATION LIFECYCLE

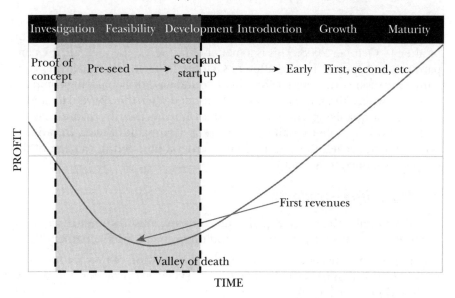

The Start-up Companies Relief provides newly incorporated companies carrying on new trades relief from tax in the first three years of trading. Therefore, it is relevant for companies at the early stages of the innovation lifecycle. As we shall see, the ability to carry forward the relief to later periods (see **Section 4.3.7**) means that while companies may claim in the early period, the financial benefit of the relief may not be achieved until later stages, i.e. after a company's first profitable period, which could be after the first three years of trading.

4.2 The Relief

Section 486C of the Taxes Consolidation Act 1997 (TCA 1997) (relief from tax for certain start-up companies) provides a corporation tax relief for new companies commencing to trade after 1 January 2009 and (by various Finance Act extensions) before 31 December 2018. The relief applies to the profits of qualifying trades of new companies and chargeable gains on the disposal of assets used by the company for the purposes of the new trade.

The relief works by reducing the corporation tax liabilities of new companies commencing a new trade in the first three years of trading where the corporation tax payable by the company for an accounting period does not exceed €40,000. Where such a company's corporation tax liability is less than €40,000, where qualifying criteria (see **Section 4.3** below) are met, this liability can be reduced to nil. Marginal relief is available for companies with corporation tax payable between €40,000 and €60,000.

Since Finance Act 2011, the relief is linked to the amount of employers' PRSI paid by the company in the relevant accounting period (see **Section 4.3.5** below).

4.3 Qualifying Criteria

4.3.1 Qualifying Start-up Company

In accordance with section 486C(1)(a) TCA 1997, a qualifying company is a company that has been incorporated within the European Economic Area on or after 14 October 2008. This is a matter-of-fact test to be met, i.e. the company was incorporated on or after 14 October 2008 and is a qualifying company, or it was incorporated before this date and it is not a qualifying company. However, where the company was incorporated after the above date and is, therefore, a qualifying company, this does not necessarily ensure that the company will be able to avail of the Start-up Companies Relief. In order to qualify for the relief, the various further criteria outlined in the rest of this chapter also need to be met.

4.3.2 Qualifying Trade

In order to claim the relief, a qualifying company must commence a qualifying trade on or after 1 January 2009 and on or before 31 December 2018.[1]

The purpose of the relief is to incentivise the creation of new trading businesses. In this regard, section 486C(2)(a) TCA 1997 provides that the following will not be a qualifying trade:
1. a trade that "was previously carried on by another person and to which the company has succeeded", e.g. where a sole trader incorporates their business as a new company;

---

[1] Originally, Finance (No. 2) Act 2008 fixed the end date at 31 December 2014. Subsequent Finance Acts have extended the relief such that it now applies to new trade commenced up to 31 December 2018. At the time of writing, it is anticipated that this relief would be further extended in the coming Finance Act.

2. a trade the activities of which were previously carried on as part of another person's trade or profession;
3. an 'excepted trade';[2]
4. a trade the activities of which would be regarded as that of a service company if the company was a close company within the provisions of section 441 TCA 1997;[3]
5. a trade the activities of which form part of an undertaking to which subparagraphs (a) to (h) of Article 1 of Commission Regulation (EC) No. 1998/2006[4] apply (an EU Regulation on state aid for specified activities); or
6. a trade the activities of which, if carried on by an associated company of the new company, would form part of a trade carried on by that associated company. This provision is an anti-avoidance provision which prevents a company that foresees itself breaching the relevant corporation tax limits from commencing a new element which would be part of a qualifying trade to a connected company in order to maintain the relief. In such a situation, neither company will be entitled to any relief under section 486C for current or subsequent years. Unfortunately, this can also prevent genuine business restructuring plans. For example, it is not uncommon for commercial reasons to operate a new business venture through a new company.

4.3.3 Relevant Corporation Tax

Companies can have corporation tax liabilities arising on a number of income sources, for example trading income, rental income and various investments, such as interest or dividend income. However, the Start-up Companies Relief only allows relief from 'relevant corporation tax'. For the purpose of the relief, relevant corporation tax relates to:
1. corporation tax payable by a company on trading profits of a qualifying trade for that accounting period; and
2. corporation tax payable on chargeable gains on the disposal of qualifying assets in relation to the trade.

Qualifying assets are relevant assets used by the qualifying trade for the purposes of the qualifying trade which are disposed of in the relevant period in relation to that trade. For example, if a company realised a gain on the disposal of a premises that was used for the purpose of the qualifying trade, the

---

[2] 'Excepted trade' is defined in section 21A TCA 1997 and includes activities such as dealing in or developing land, and working with minerials or petroleum-type activities that are subject to the higher rate of corporation tax, i.e. 25% rather than 12.5%.
[3] A detailed review of what a service company is within the meaning of section 441 is beyond the scope of this book. Briefly, however, a service company is a close company whose business consists of carrying on a profession or the provision of professional services or exercising an office or employment, e.g. a company carrying out accounting or legal services would be a service company.
[4] Commission Regulation (EC) No. 1998/2006 of 15 December 2006 on the application of Articles 87 and 88 of the Treaty to de minimis aid.

corporation tax liability arising on the gain would be regarded as a relevant corporation tax for the purpose of the relief. Relevant assets exclude shares, securities or other assets held as investments.

In addition, a relevant asset does not include any asset that has been acquired from an associated company which availed of any capital gains tax group relief schemes as outlined in sections 617 or 631 TCA 1997 in determining its base cost. This anti-avoidance provision aims to prevent assets with gains from being transferred to a company carrying on a qualifying trade and then sold on to a third party and availing of a reduction in capital gains tax.

It should be also noted that relevant corporation tax excludes:
• close company surcharges under sections 440 and 441 TCA 1997;
• profits attributable to dealing in residential development land (section 644B);
• non-qualifying trade-related chargeable gains for the period;
• income tax that is withheld by a company (e.g. tax relief at source on health insurance premiums that is witheld by the company when the health insurance premiums are paid by the company on behalf of employees); and
• the corporation tax chargeable on the part of the company's profits that is charged at the rate specified in section 21A TCA 1997, i.e. the 25% rate.

In identifying the profit attributable to income, a company must deduct any charges on income, management expenses or non-trade charges. The allocation of these deductions to income profits reduces the amount of income qualifying for the relief.

4.3.4 Relevant Maximum Amounts

The Start-up Companies Relief does not provide relief for qualifying companies from an unlimited amount of corporation tax. In this regard, the legislation has limited the amount of relevant corporation tax that can be relieved (i.e. 'the relevant maximum amount') by the qualifying companies. Section 486C(5) TCA 1997 defines the relevant maximum amounts as follows:
1. the lower relevant maximum amount is €40,000; and
2. the upper relevant maximum amount is €60,000.

The section also provides for a proportional reduction in these amounts where the accounting period of the company is less than 12 months.

This means that, subject to the restrictions outlined below at **Section 4.3.5**, if a company has a relevant corporation tax liability of €40,000 or less, the full amount of the relevant corporation tax can be relieved and the company will have a no relevant corporation tax liability. If the company has a relevant corporation tax liability of greater than €40,000 but less than €60,000, marginal relief will be available (see **Section 4.3.6**). If the relevant corporation tax liability of the company is greater than €60,000, no relief will be available under this section.

4.3.5 Pay-related Social Insurance (PRSI) Restriction

As mentioned above at **Section 4.2**, for accounting periods beginning after 1 January 2011, the value of the relief is directly linked to the amount of employers' PRSI paid by a company in an accounting period. The purpose of this change was to better target the relief to generate employment.

This restriction means that where the total amount of corporation tax payable does not exceed €40,000, the aggregate amount of corporation tax payable relating to income and chargeable gains of the qualifying trade will be reduced by the amount of the 'specified contribution'.

Section 486C(1)(a) TCA 1997 provides that the 'specified contribution' is the amount of employers' PRSI paid by the company in the accounting period, subject to a maximum of €5,000 per employee or director. Credit is also given for any employers' PRSI exempted under the Employer Job (PRSI) Incentive Scheme in respect of a company's employees in determining the amount of corporation tax relief available to the company.

Class S PRSI contributions, i.e. self-employed PRSI contributions, paid by a company for directors are not qualifying contributions for the purposes of the relief.

In summary, this means that to get the full benefit of the relief, the start-up company will have to employ at least eight employees or directors, each of whose related employers' PRSI contribution is €5,000 or more, i.e. on an income of €46,512 or greater (i.e. €5,000 ÷ employers' PRSI rate 10.75%).

4.3.6 Marginal Relief

As noted above in **Section 4.3.4**, where the relevant corporation tax liability of the company is €40,000 or less, then the full liability will be relieved. Marginal relief applies where the total corporation tax payable by the company for an accounting period exceeds €40,000 (i.e. the lower relevant maximum amount – see **Section 4.3.4**) but does not exceed €60,000 (i.e. the upper relevant maximum amount – see **Section 4.3.4**). Marginal relief allows some relief from the relevant corporation tax liability but on a marginal basis, i.e. the company does not get full relief from the corporation tax liability. Marginal relief is applied by applying the formula as set out in section 486C(4)(b)(ii):

$$3 \times (T - M) \times \frac{A+B}{T}$$

where:

T is the total corporation tax payable by the company for the accounting period;

M is the lower relevant maximum amount;

A is the corporation tax payable by the company for the accounting period so far as is referable to income from the qualifying trade for that accounting period; and

B is the corporation tax payable by the company for the accounting period so far as is referable to chargeable gains on the disposal of qualifying assets of the qualifying trade.

Example 4.1 below illustrates the effect of a marginal relief claim on the corporation tax liability of a manufacturing company.

EXAMPLE 4.1: MANUFACTURING COMPANY – MARGINAL RELIEF

Income

Case I	€380,000
Case V	€40,000

Tax

Case 1	€380,000 × 12.5% = €47,500
Case V	€40,000 × 25% = €10,000

T = €57,500
M = €40,000
A = €47,500
B = €Nil

$$3 \times (€57{,}500 - €40{,}000) \times \frac{(€47{,}500 + 0)}{€57{,}500} = €43{,}370$$

The total corporation tax payable for the period is €53,370 (i.e. €43,370 + €10,000 (Case V tax liability)).

4.3.7 Carry Forward of Unused Relief

Many start-up companies incur losses in their early years and therefore benefit very little from the Start-up Companies Relief. Finance Act 2013 amended section 486C TCA 1997 to allow any unused relief in excess of the tax liability to be carried forward to offset against tax in subsequent years.

4.3.7.1 Carry-forward Calculation

Where the total corporation tax payable by a qualifying company in the first three years of trading is less than the lower relevant maximum (i.e. €40,000 – see **Section 4.3.4**) and the total contribution (i.e. 'total contribution' is the lower of the specified contribution (see **Section 4.3.5**) and the lower relevant maximum amount, i.e. €40,000) is greater than the corporation tax referable to the qualifying trade for that accounting period, the amount of excess (the 'first relevant amount') can be carried forward and used to reduce the corporation tax referable to the qualifying trade for an accounting period after the relevant period (i.e. an accounting period after the first three years of trading).

This is restricted to the maximum amount of relief in any one year not exceeding the eligible amount of employers' PRSI paid in that year.

EXAMPLE 4.2: CALCULATION OF CARRY FORWARD OF START-UP COMPANIES RELIEF

	2018 Year 1 €	2019 Year 2 €	2020 Year 3 €	2021 Year 4 €
Case I income	10,000	25,000	60,000	90,000
Corporation tax (CT) @ 12.5%	1,250	3,125	7,500	11,250
Director PRSI	2,000	2,000	2,000	2,000
Employers' PRSI	0	4,000	4,000	10,000
Revised CT liability after applying section 486C	1250	Nil	3,500	
Unused relief carried forward	Nil	875	Nil	(875)
Excess PRSI to carry forward to 2018 (Note 1)	Nil			
Relief claimed in years after three-year period				875
Corporation tax payable in 2018 (Note 2)				10,375

Notes:
Note 1: Any unused relief arising in the three-year period may not be used until Year 4 and/or subsequent years.
Note 2: This is the revised corporation tax in Year 4 after claiming relief under the Finance Act 2013 measure (i.e €11,250 – €875 = €10,375).

4.3.7.2 Carry-forward Calculation for Marginal Relief

Where a company qualifies for marginal relief in an accounting period within the first three years of trading and does not fully utilise the relief, such relief can also be carried forward. The following formula is used to calculate the amount of relief (the 'second relevant amount') that can be carried forward and used against corporation tax payable referable to the qualifying trade after the relevant three-year period:

$$[C - (3 \times (T - M) \times C/T)] - R$$

where:

C is the total contribution for the accounting period;

T is the total corporation tax payable by the company for the accounting period;

M is the lower relevant maximum amount; and

R is the amount of relief to which the company is entitled under section 486C(4)(b) for the accounting period.

4.3.7.3 The 'Specified Aggregate'

The aggregate of all first relevant amounts (see **Section 4.3.7.1**) and second relevant amounts (see **Section 4.3.7.2**) are referred to as the 'specified aggregate'. Any excess as calculated above at **Sections 4.3.7.1** and **4.3.7.2** are combined together to form the specified aggregate.

Where a company has a specified aggregate amount and continues to carry on the qualifying trade after the relevant period, i.e. after Year 3, the specified aggregate is used to reduce the future corporation tax liabilities of these future periods.

However, the use of the specified aggregate is limited each year to the lesser of:
1. the corporation tax of the accounting period in question; and
2. the total contribution (see **Section 4.3.5**) of the accounting period in question.

In other words, the use of the carry forward is also limited to the same corporation tax and employers' PRSI ceilings that apply in the year the relief is generated.

Note: the specified aggregate can only be applied once by a company to reduce corporation tax.

4.3.8 Steps to Consider when Analysing whether a Company Is a Qualifying Company

Figure 4.1 opposite summarises the analysis steps that need to taken to determine whether a company will be able to avail of the Start-up Companies Relief.

FIGURE 4.1: SUMMARY OF STEPS TO ESTABLISH IF A COMPANY
QUALIFIES FOR START-UP COMPANIES RELIEF

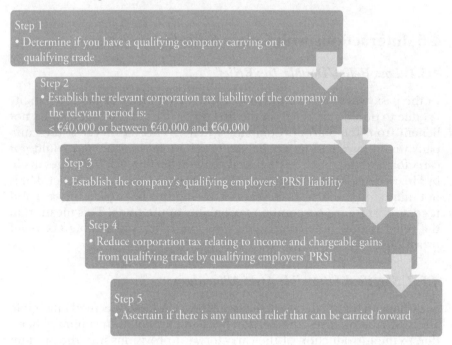

Step 1
• Determine if you have a qualifying company carrying on a qualifying trade

Step 2
• Establish the relevant corporation tax liability of the company in the relevant period is:
< €40,000 or between €40,000 and €60,000

Step 3
• Establish the company's qualifying employers' PRSI liability

Step 4
• Reduce corporation tax relating to income and chargeable gains from qualifying trade by qualifying employers' PRSI

Step 5
• Ascertain if there is any unused relief that can be carried forward

4.3.9 Making a Claim

Claims are made on the company's corporation tax return, form CT1. As there is no specific time limit for making a claim under section 486C TCA 1997, the general four-year provisions for making a claim for a refund of tax under section 865 TCA 1997 apply. While it would be expected that the relief would be claimed when a qualifying company files its corporation tax return, which is due to be filed in the ninth month after its accounting period end, if this for some reason did not happen, the company has up to four years to amend the return to include the claim and reduce the tax liability of the period.

4.4 State Aid Disclosures

EU Regulations provide a de minimis ceiling for state aid of €200,000 (€100,000 for the road transport sector) over a three-year period. Any relief received under section 486C TCA 1997 needs to be taken into account when assessing whether this ceiling has been breached. The Revenue Commissioners or any authorised officer will disclose this information to any board established by the State and also provide such information as may be requested by the European Commission in accordance with Article 3 of Commission Regulation (EC) No. 1998/2006.[5]

4.5 Interactions with Other Reliefs

4.5.1 Loss Relief/Double Tax Relief

In the past, where a start-up company incurred losses or had no liability tax due to double tax relief[6] in the first three years of trading, it could not benefit from the Start-up Companies Relief. This was because the company would have had no tax liablity to relieve and in the past could not carry forward the relief. As discussed above at **Section 4.3.7**, changes made by Finance Act 2013 now mean that any Start-up Companies Relief that is not utilised in the first three years of trading can be carried forward and used against future corporation tax liability of the trade. This means that the relief is now fully compatible with loss relief and double tax relief provisions.

4.5.2 Specified Intangible Asset Allowances

See **Chaper 6** for full details of section 291A TCA 1997, specified intangible asset (SIA) allowances and **Section 6.9.1** in particular. In summary here, due to the introduction of the carry-forward provisions into the Start-up Companies Relief, similar to the interaction with the loss relief above, the benefits of the SIA allowances and the Start-up Companies Relief are compatible.

4.5.3 The Knowledge Development Box

As discussed in **Chapter 5**, the Knowledge Development Box (KDB) reduces the effective tax rate on qualifying intellectual property trading profits from 12.5% to 6.25%, thereby reducing a qualifying company's tax liability. The KDB and the Start-up Companies Relief are compatible and, given its effect on companies' tax liabilities, the KDB is likely to give rise to more companies being able to claim Start-up Companies Relief.

---

[5] Commission Regulation (EC) No. 1998/2006 of 15 December 2006 on the application of Articles 87 and 88 of the Treaty to de minimis aid.

[6] Relief for foreign tax suffered on income earned, which could arise where the company earns income that is subject to tax in a foreign jurisdiction. Double taxation relief could result in no Irish corporation tax being payable on the income depending on the rate of tax of the foreign jurisdiction.

EXAMPLE 4.3: COMPANY AVAILING OF KDB AND THE START-UP COMPANIES RELIEF

Currently a company can have taxable profits of up to €320,000 (i.e. €320,000 × tax rate of 12.5% = €40,000 tax liability) fully exempt from corporation tax each year for the first three years of trading under the Start-up Companies Relief. If the company is also eligible for the KDB, the amount of taxable profits (assuming all qualifying profits of the company are eligible for KDB) that could be fully relievable is increased to €640,000 (i.e. taxable income €640,000 − KDB allowance €320,000 = taxable profit €320,000 at 12.5% = €40,000).

4.5.4 The R&D Tax Credit

As discussed in **Chapter 3**, the Start-up Companies Relief and the Research and Development (R&D) Tax Credit are compatible. The R&D Tax Credit will reduce the tax liability of the company before the calculation of the Start-up Companies Relief. This may result in the tax liability falling below the thresholds either for full relief, i.e. €40,000, or marginal relief between €40,000 and €60,000. This may allow companies to benefit from the start-up relief where they would not otherwise have done so due to higher profits. As the Start-up Companies Relief now carries forward, even if the R&D Tax Credit completely eliminates the corporation tax liability of the company in the first three years, the company may still get the benefit of the Start-up Companies Relief in future periods.

4.6 Conclusion

The Start-up Companies Relief can be a valuable relief for start-up companies, for which cash flow is very important. The potential to reduce tax liabilities at the early stages of becoming profitable can reduce the funding burden on nascent companies. While the Start-up Companies Relief is general corporation tax relief available to any trading company, i.e. innovative and non-innovating companies, in practice many innovative companies in the early stage of their lives avail of this relief; therefore, it is appropriate that this relief is explored by innovative companies. In the next two chapters, we will look at two further corporate tax reliefs (Knowledge Development Box and specified intangible asset allowances) that are more specifically targeted at helping innovative companies of any size or any stage in the innovation lifecycle reduce their corporate tax liability.

For convenience, the main points relating to the Start-up Companies Relief outlined in this chapter are included below in an 'At a Glance' summary of the relief.

AT A GLANCE: THE START-UP COMPANIES RELIEF

What is the relief?	This is a relief from corporation tax for start-up companies which in the first three years of trading have a corporation tax liability each year of less than €40,000 (with marginal relief available where liability is between €40,000 and €60,000).
This relief is potentially of value if:	The company is: • new, i.e. less than three years old; • has commenced a new trade; • is profit-making; and • has a tax liablity of less than €60,000.
This relief is likely to be of benefit to:	Start-up companies that generate modest or minimal taxable profits in the first three years of trading.
Interactions with other reliefs:	• Fully compatible with the R&D Tax Credit (see **Chapter 3**). • Fully compatible with the Knowledge Development Box (see **Chapter 5**). • Fully compatible with specified intangible asset allowances (see **Chapter 6**).

CHAPTER 5

THE KNOWLEDGE DEVELOPMENT BOX

5.1 Introduction

Then Minister for Finance, Michael Noonan, announced in his Budget 2015 speech that he was publishing a "road map to secure Ireland's place as the destination for the best and most successful companies in the world". In this regard, he announced his intention to introduce "a 'Knowledge Development Box' along the lines of patent and innovation boxes which have existed for many years in countries that compete with us for foreign direct investment." The Minister acknowledged that at the time, EU and OECD discussions in relation to an acceptable 'Box Regime' were ongoing and that once these discussions were concluded, an Irish regime, compliant with international standards, would be introduced that would be "best in class and at a low competitive and sustainable rate of tax".

Encouraging the commercial exploitation of intellectual property (IP) has been shown to be beneficial to economies from where such activities arise. In this regard, governments seek to encourage companies to locate and exploit IP in their countries to help grow their economies. One of the methods used by governments to encourage such activities in their local jurisdiction is the use of preferential tax treatment for income arising from such activities through the use of patent and innovation boxes or patent income exemptions. Historically, such tax measures were focussed on providing preferential treatment on the income generated from the exploitation of the IP without regard to where the activities that created that IP, i.e. the research and development (R&D) activities, took place. Companies could create the IP through R&D activities located in one country and then transfer the assets arising from the R&D activities to another country to avail of the preferential tax treatment offered by that country.

The EU and OECD discussions in relation to the patent and innovation boxes that were in existence in a number of countries at the time, e.g. the UK and The Netherlands, were seeking to address what were perceived as harmful international corporate tax practices arising from the use of these boxes. It was felt that regimes "that provide for a tax preference on income relating to intangible property raise the base-eroding concerns",[1] i.e. they were facilitating the inappropriate transferring of tax bases from one jurisdiction to another.

On 11 November 2014, the UK and Germany agreed on the 'modified nexus' approach to addressing this concern. This agreement was subsequently adopted as the international best practice by the EU and OECD.

The principle underlying the modified nexus approach is that, while preferential tax treatment relating to income from IP may be provided by countries to companies, to enjoy such preferential tax treatment the companies should undertake substantial economic activity in the jurisdiction granting it. 'Substantial ecomonic activity' involves R&D activities and, therefore, R&D expenditure connected with the creation of the IP asset that is to receive the preferential treatment.

This approach has meant that any new patent and innovation box regimes must adopt the modified nexus approach and existing boxes must be changed to comply with the principle of modified nexus, e.g. the UK and Dutch boxes (though existing boxes have been given a period of reprieve to allow current claimants to plan for the introduction of modified nexus-compliant regimes – in this regard they can retain their existing benefits until June 2021).

Upon conclusion of these international developments, the Department of Finance in January 2015 issued a public consultation paper on an Irish 'Knowledge Development Box'. Following this, a feedback statement was issued in July 2015 and legislation was drafted and introduced in section 32 of Finance Act 2015. The enacted legislation forms Chapter 5 of Part 29 of the Taxes Consolidation Act 1997 (TCA 1997) and includes sections 769G–769R TCA 1997. The legislation is effective for companies whose accounting period commences on or after 1 January 2016.

This chapter explores the details of the Knowledge Development Box (KDB), how companies can qualify for the allowance, and how they can reduce their corporation tax liabilities.

The KDB allowance helps a company reduce its taxable profits and, therefore, it will be relevant to companies who have started to make profits, i.e. companies that are in the growth or maturity stages in the innovation lifecycle as illustrated opposite.

---

[1] OECD, *Countering Harmful Tax Practices More Effectively, Taking into Account Transparency and Substance* (OECD, 16 September 2014). Available at http://www. oecd-ilibrary.org/taxation/countering-harmful-tax-practices-more-effectively-taking-into-account-transparency-and-substance_9789264218970-en

RELEVANT STAGE(S) IN THE INNOVATION LIFECYCLE:
THE KNOWLEDGE DEVELOPMENT BOX

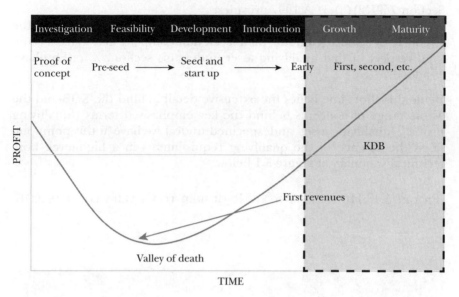

5.2 The Relief

The KDB provides an allowance that gives companies an effective rate of tax of 6.25% on qualifying income, i.e. half the normal 12.5% corporation tax rate. To achieve this effective rate of tax, Chapter 5 of Part 29 TCA 1997 (taxation of companies engaged in knowledge development) grants companies an allowance in the amount of 50% of the qualifying profits. This allowance then reduces the qualifying profits and the balance is taxed at 12.5%. The following is a high-level example of how the relief works.

EXAMPLE 5.1: SIMPLIFIED KDB CALCULATION

Qualifying KDB profits	€1,000,000
KDB allowances (€1,000,000 × 50%)	€500,000
Taxable Profits	€500,000
Tax at 12.5%	€62,500
Proof (above calculation results in expected effective rate of tax):	
Effective tax rate on profits after KDB Allowance (€62,500/€1,000,000)	6.25%

5.3 Qualifying Criteria

Section 769I(2)(a) TCA 1997 provides:

> "Where **qualifying profits** in respect of a **qualifying asset** arise in the course of a **specified trade**, then a relevant company may make a claim in respect of that qualifying asset under this section, …". (Emphasis added.)

While this short line belies the extensive detail behind the KDB and the whole range of concepts behind the key emphasised terms ('qualifying profits', 'qualifying asset' and 'specified trade') we have at this point outlined the essence of the qualifying requirements in a high-level, non-technical summary in **Figure 5.1** below.

FIGURE 5.1: HIGH-LEVEL STEPS REQUIRED TO QUALIFY FOR THE KDB

As can be seen from **Figure 5.1**, the company must carry on R&D activities, those R&D activities must result in a qualifying asset, and the company must generate trading income and profits from the qualifying asset. In such a scenario, the company can apply for a KDB allowance (i.e. a tax-deductible amount) that will result in the company having an effective corporate tax rate of 6.25% on the profits derived from the qualifying asset.

Having outlined the essence of the KDB and how it works, we need now to look at the detail and concepts behind its legislative definition to ensure that proper tax treatment is adopted.

5.3.1 'Qualifying Asset'

Section 769G(1) TCA 1997 provides that a 'qualifying asset' is an asset that is IP, other than marketing-related IP, which is the result of R&D activities.

'R&D activities' for this purpose has the same definition as that provided for by section 766, which is covered in detail in **Chapter 3**, **Section 3.5.3**.

'Intellectual property', for the purposes of Chapter 5 of Part 29 TCA 1997, is defined in section 769G(1) as:

"(a) a computer program, within the meaning of the Copyright and Related Rights Act 2000, but, where a computer program is a derivative work or adaptation, the portion of the computer program that represents the derivative work or the adaptation of the original work and the original work shall be treated as two separate computer programs, or
(b) an invention protected by–
  (i) a qualifying patent,
  (ii) any supplementary protection certificate issued under Council Regulation (EC) No. 469/2009 of 6 May 2009 concerning protection for medicinal products or any such certificate extended in accordance with Article 36 of Regulation (EC) 1901/2006,
  (iii) any supplementary protection certificate issued under Regulation (EC) No. 1610/96 of the European Parliament and of the Council of 23 July 1996 concerning protection for plant protection products, or
  (iv) any plant breeders' rights within the meaning of section 4 of the Plant Varieties (Proprietary Rights) Act 1980".

Therefore, there are three categories of potentially qualifying assets:
1. computer programs;
2. qualifying patents; or
3. miscellaneous certificates/rights relating to medicinal products, plant protection products or plant breeders' rights.

The first two categories of potentially qualifying assets are the most common and we will focus on these.

Marketing-related IP is specifically excluded from the definition of IP by section 769G(1) and includes:
1. trademarks;
2. brands;
3. image rights; and
4. other IP used to market goods or services.

Finally, aquistion costs (see **Section 5.3.2.3.1** below), are also excluded from the definition of IP.

5.3.1.1 Computer Programs

The original proposal on the modified nexus approach was that the only qualifying asset category would be patents, or other IP assets that are functionally equivalent to patents. This was seen as being disadvantageous towards certain sectors that do not rely on patents for various reasons. The IT sector, for example, tend not to get patents on software due to the difficulty, particularly in Europe, of securing same. The inclusion of computer programs as qualifying assets was a welcome accommodation on this point for the sector.

As we have seen, a 'computer program' is defined in section 769G(1) TCA 1997 as:

"(a) a computer program, within the meaning of the Copyright and Related Rights Act 2000, but, where a computer program is a derivative work or adaptation, the portion of the computer program that represents the derivative work or the adaptation of the original work and the original work shall be treated as two separate computer programs".

Section 2 of the Copyright and Related Rights Act 2000 provides:

"'computer program' means a program which is original in that it is the author's own intellectual creation and includes any design materials used for the preparation of the program."

As with all category classes of potentially qualifying assets, a computer program will not be a qualifying computer program for the purpose of the KDB unless the work that led to its creation involves activities meeting the definition of 'R&D activities' for the purposes of the R&D Tax Credit (section 766 TCA 1997). See **Chapter 3** for more details.

5.3.1.2 Qualifying Patents

Section 769G(1) TCA 1997 provides:

"'qualifying patent' means—

(a) a patent granted following substantive examination for novelty and inventive step, or

(b) a patent, other than a short term patent within the meaning of section 63 of the Patents Act 1992, or an equivalent provision in another jurisdiction, where—

  (i)   the Patents Office in the State, or equivalent Office elsewhere, has caused a search to be undertaken in relation to the invention and a search report (within the meaning of section 29 of the Patents Act 1992) prepared, and

  (ii) either—

    (I)   the patent was granted prior to 1 January 2016, or

    (II) the patent was granted on or after 1 January 2016 and before 1 January 2017 and a patent agent, within the meaning of section 106 of the Patents Act 1992, certifies that in his or her opinion such a patent meets the patentability criteria, in that the invention is susceptible of industrial application, new and involves an inventive step,

but this paragraph is subject to section 769I(6)(a)(i)(VII)".

In order to align with the provisions of the KDB, changes were required to the way in which the Irish Patents Office granted patents to ensure that Irish patents would be qualifying patents for the purpose of the KDB. By way of background, there are broadly two types of systems for granting a patent by national patents offices:

1. patents granted that are not subject to substantive examination for novelty and inventive steps; and

2. patents that are only granted following a substantive examination for novelty and inventive steps.

Section 769G TCA 1997 specifies that only patents that have been granted following a substantive examination for novelty and inventive steps are qualifying, i.e. patents that have been granted under the second type of system outlined above. However, historically, the Irish Patents Office granted some patents without a substantive examination and, therefore, such Irish patents under this provision would not qualify for the KDB.

To effect the required changes to the Irish Patent Office, the Knowledge Development Box (Certification of Inventions) Act 2017 was enacted and came into effect on 19 May 2017. This Act includes provisions amending the Patents Act 1992, which provides that the Irish Patents Office will grant patents following a substantive examination. This new patent regime applies to patent applications received on or after 19 May 2017.

The guidelines of the Revenue Commissioners on the KDB helpfully provide a list of jurisdictions that currently grant patents after carrying out a substantive examination for novelty and inventive steps and which are therefore potentially qualifying patents for the purpose of the KDB.[2] As well as the European Patent Office, these include:
• Austria
• Bulgaria
• Czech Republic
• Denmark
• Estonia
• Finland
• Germany
• Hungary
• Japan
• Poland
• Portugal
• Romania
• Slovakia
• Sweden
• United Kingdom
• United States.

5.3.1.2.1 Transitional Measures

While the KDB legislation was introduced before the Irish patents application system would require substantive examination for novelty and inventive steps and therefore result in qualifying patents (i.e. before the commencement of the Knowledge Development Box (Certification of

---

[2] Revenue Commissioners, *Guidance Notes on the Knowledge Development Box* (updated August 2016), Appendix 1. Available at http://www.revenue.ie/en/ tax-professionals/tdm/income-tax-capital-gains-tax-corporation-tax/part-29/29-03-01.pdf

Inventions) Act 2017), as can be seen in the quote above, section 769G(1)(b) TCA 1997 does provide some transitional arrangements whereby companies that have an Irish patent could potentially benefit from the KDB. The requirement that needs to be met to qualify for the transitional measure depends on whether the patent was granted prior to 1 January 2016, or after 1 January 2016 but before 1 January 2017.

If a company has an Irish patent that was granted before 1 January 2016, the patent will be a qualifying patent if it has caused a search to be undertaken in relation to the invention and a search report prepared, i.e. a substantive examination for novelty and inventive steps.

If the patent is granted after 1 January 2016 and before 1 January 2017, while a search and search report must also have been completed, it will still not be a qualifying patent unless a patent agent (i.e. a patent attorney not working in the Irish Patents Office) certifies that the patent "meets the patentability criteria, in that the invention is susceptible of industrial application, new and involves an inventive step".

These transitional measures also apply to non-Irish patents, once the jurisdication that has granted the patent has done so under provisions equivalent to those of the Irish Patents Act 1992.

Table 5.1 below summarises the position regarding the transitional measures for the patent-granting systems that have been in place:

TABLE 5.1: TRANSITIONAL MEASURES FOR PATENTS REGISTERED
UNDER EXISTING PATENT SYSTEMS

Date Patent Granted	Required Patent Registration Process
Pre 1 January 2016	Registration, if full search carried out by Irish Patents Office.
1 January 2016 – 31 December 2016	• Registration if full search carried out by Irish Patents Office; **and** • Patent agent certification confirming patentability.
Post 1 January 2017	Substantive examination for novelty and inventive steps.

5.3.1.2.2 Excluded Patents

The following types of patents are not qualifying patents for the purposes of the KDB:
1. short-term patents;
2. petty patents;
3. utility models; and
4. marketing-related IP (see **Section 5.3.1** above).

5.3.1.3 *Intellectual Property for SMEs (the 'Third Category')*

Section 769R TCA 1997 provides an additional category of assets that can be regarded as qualifying assets, specifically for small and medium-sized enterprises (SMEs). Section 769R(1) provides that "'intellectual property for small companies' means inventions that are certified by the Controller of Patents, Designs and Trade Marks as being novel, non-obvious and useful". Thus, clearly a lower test is required for such inventions/IP than for patents; furthermore, it is not required that such inventions be made public, as is required for inventions granted a patent.[3]

For the purpose of section 769R(2)(a), an 'SME' is defined as:
1. a company that has 'average overall income from intellectual property' of less than €7,500,000 (in a 12-month period);
2. if it is a member of a group, the group turnover must not exceed €50,000,000 (in a 12-month period); and
3. a company that is in one of the following size categories:[4]

Size category	Criteria
Micro	< 10 employees, and either: • turnover ≤ €2,000,000; or • balance sheet ≤ €2,000,000.
Small	< 50 employees, and either: • turnover ≤ €10,000,000; or • balance sheet ≤ €10,000,000.
Medium	< 250 employees, and either: • turnover ≤ €50,000,000; or • balance sheet ≤ €43,000,000.

The 'average overall income from intellectual property' in an accounting period is the lower of:

the overall income from intellectual property for the accounting period; or

$$\frac{\text{the average monthly overall income from intellectual property for the last 60 months}}{\text{the number of months in the accounting period}}$$

---

[3] At the time of the enactment of section 769R, the Irish Patents Office did not have the legislative authority to carry out the certification of such IP for small companies. New legislation to this effect was introduced on 19 May 2017 which grants the Irish Patents Office the power to make such certifications (Knowledge Development Box (Certificate of Inventions) Act 2017 – see **Section 5.3.1.2** above).
[4] Size criteria set by Annex to Commission Recommendation 2003/361/EC of 6 May 2003.

The following example outlines the steps an SME would need to consider to establish if it would be entitled to qualify for the KDB under the IP for SMEs provision.

EXAMPLE 5.2: SME INTELLECTUAL PROPERTY
QUALIFYING FOR THE KDB

Signal Ltd has created a new wireless antenna that uses new technology to provide optimum signal transmission. The company does not want to take out a patent on the new product for confidentiality reasons as it is felt that its inventive breakthrough, once known, could be replicated by a competitor without infringing on the patent, causing loss of competitive advantage. In this regard, the company wants to consider if it would qualify for the KDB under the IP for SMEs provision, which does not involve public disclosure of inventive steps. The company currently employs 60 employees and has an annual turnover of €5,500,000. The company has been selling the antenna for five years and has no other IP. Revenue from the antenna for the last five years is €8,000,000 with €2,000,000 of this amount earned in the last year. Signal Ltd is not part of a group.

In order to determine if the company will qualify as an SME for the purpose of the KDB, we check the size of the company. The company is a medium company as it has less than 250 employees and turnover of less than €50,000,000 (we do not need to analyse the balance sheet as it only has to meet one of the financial tests to qualify for the size classification in question).

Next, we need to establish the company's 'average overall income from intellectual property'. This is ascertained by taking the lower of the following two figures:
1. overall income for the accounting period: €2,000,000; or
2. the average monthly overall income from IP for the last 60 months/the number of months in the accounting period, i.e. (€8,000,000/60)/12 = €1,599,999.

Therefore, the average overall income from IP is €1,599,999. As this is lower than the threshold amount of €7,500,000, the company should be in a position to avail of the KDB relief in relation to income from the asset if the company successfully applies to the Irish Patents Office for certification that the product is novel, non-obvious and useful.

5.3.1.4 Supplementary Protection Certificates and Plant Breeders' Rights

As we have seen, the following miscellaneous IP types are included in the definition of qualifying assets for the purposes of the KDB in section 769G(1)(b) TCA 1997:

"(i) any supplementary protection certificate issued under Council Regulation (EC) No. 469/2009 of 6 May 2009 concerning protection for medicinal products or any such certificate extended in accordance with Article 36 of Regulation (EC) 1901/2006,

(ii) any supplementary protection certificate issued under Regulation (EC) No. 1610/96 of the European Parliament and of the Council of 23 July 1996 concerning protection for plant protection products, or

(iii) any plant breeders' rights within the meaning of section 4 of the Plant Varieties (Proprietary Rights) Act 1980".

To encourage innovation, supplementary protection certificates extend the rights associated with a patent in compensation for the long period it takes to achieve regulatory approval required for certain products, e.g. medicines. Supplementary protection certificates granted under the above legislation are specifically included as qualifying assets.

'Plant breeders' rights' under section 4 of the Plant Varieties (Proprietary Rights) Act 1980 are rights "in respect of any variety of a botanical genus or species, or any variety within such genus or species, being a variety which has a particular manner of reproduction or multiplication or a certain end use". Again, once the right in this regard meets this definition, the asset is a qualifying asset for the purpose of the KDB.

5.3.1.5 Family of Assets

In its work on preferential IP regimes,[5] the OECD has acknowledged that practical difficulties can arise in the tracing and tracking of income and expenditure to individual qualifying IP assets where they are interlinked in their development, use or exploitation to such an extent that any apportionment of income and/or expenditure would be arbitrary. Where such complexities arise, a product-based or 'family of assets' approach may be adopted by companies. This approach allows companies to group qualifying IP assets as a single unit, i.e. as a family of assets, for the purpose of the modified nexus calculation (the modified nexus calculation is discussed in **Section 5.3.2.3** below).

It is important, however, to remember that, where possible, the company must track income and expenditure on qualifying IP assets individually and, in this regard, any family of assets should comprise the smallest group of

---

[5] OECD, *Countering Harmful Tax Practices More Effectively, Taking into Account Transparency and Substance,* Action 5 – 2015 Final Report (OECD, 2015) Chapter 4, pp. 31–34.

assets beyond which an arbitrary decision would be required (i.e. a decision that does not have a technical or obvious logical basis). Therefore, just because a company has a valid family of assets does not necessarily mean that all of its qualifying assets can be included in this family. The following examples illustrate the application of the 'family of assets' concept in different scenarios in practice:

EXAMPLE 5.3: QUALIFYING ASSETS DEVELOPED SEPARATELY BUT THAT ARE INTERDEPENDENT

Pharma Co. develops a process to prevent a particular enzyme from becoming denatured during the manufacturing process. Separately, it develops a new drug formulation. Both of these assets are used in the realisation of a new drug. As it would not be possible to quantify the income from the asset otherwise than based on an arbitrary apportionment of the sales proceeds, the assets should be grouped into a family of assets.

Charateristics of scenario: a number of qualifying assets developed separately but dependent on each other in the final product.

Problem: while development expenditure may be traceable, any apportionment of income would be arbitrary.

Solution: group the assets as a family of assets.

EXAMPLE 5.4: QUALIFYING ASSETS DEVELOPED AS A SINGLE PROCESS BUT SOLD SEPARATELY

IT Co. develops a software platform that has various features, each of which represents a qualifying asset. While the company charges separately for each feature, any apportionment of the development expenditure across the various features would be arbitrary given that a single process developed all. Therefore, it is appropriate to group the assets as a family of assets for the purpose of calculating profits qualifying for the KDB.

Charateristics of scenario: a number of qualifying assets developed as a single process, but sold separately.

Problem: though the income is traceable, the expenditure incurred would require an arbitrary apportionment.

Solution: group the assets as a family of assets.

EXAMPLE 5.5: ONE QUALIFYING ASSET USED IN A NUMBER OF PRODUCTS

Manufacturing Co. develops a patented manufacturing process that represents a qualifying asset. This process is used in the manufacture of a number of products.

Pharma Co. patents the API formulation for an indigestion treatment. The company makes a number of iterations of the product based on the patented formulation, e.g. sugar-free, gluten-free, liquid and tablet varieties. As any apportionment of the development costs between the products would be arbitrary, the products should be grouped as a single family of assets.

Charateristics of scenario: one qualifying asset is used in a number of products.

Problem: though sales proceeds and expenditure are traceable, to split the expenditure over the various assets would require an arbitrary apportionment.

Solution: group products as a family of assets.

5.3.1.6 'Resulting from R&D Activities'

We have stated it a number of times, but it is important and worth repeating: having an IP asset that falls within one of the categories outlined in the previous sections (i.e. **Sections 5.3.1** to **5.3.1.4**) does not mean that a company has a qualifying asset for the purposes of the KDB unless that asset exists as a result of 'R&D activities' carried out by the company as defined by section 766 TCA 1997.

While the definition of a 'qualifying activity' is covered in detail in **Chapter 3**, **Section 3.5.3**, in summary, for activities to be considered R&D for the purposes of section 766, the following criteria must be met:
1. they must be in the area of basic research, applied research and/or experimental development;
2. the activities must have been carried out in a systematic, investigative and experimental manner;
3. they must be in an approved field of science/technology as set out in the TCA 1997 (Prescribed Research and Development Activities) Regulations 2004 (S.I. No. 434 of 2004);
4. the activities must seek to achieve a scientific or technological advancement; and
5. involve the resolution of scientific or technological uncertainty.

If the IP asset in question did not arise from activities that meet the above criteria, it will not be a qualifying IP asset for the purposes of the KDB.

While the above criteria are, *inter alia*, requirements that need to be met in order to claim the R&D Tax Credit (again, see **Chapter 3**), it is not a requirement that the company has claimed the R&D Tax Credit for the KDB. There could be a number of reasons why the company has not claimed the R&D Tax Credit, e.g. the R&D activities were completely outsourced to a third party and therefore the company was prohibited from making a claim for credit, the 12-month deadline for claiming the credit may have been missed, etc. The key point is that the company has records to be able to justify that the R&D activities meet the definition in accordance with section 766 TCA 1997.

5.3.1.7 Intellectual Property: Legal Ownership and Location

It is common in groups of companies that all IP protection matters are managed centrally within the group. This might include applying and holding patents, monitoring use and defending any infringement by third parties. Where this happens, it is typical that the legal ownership of the IP is also held centrally in one entity within the group, which would be located in a particular jurisdiction. However, having legal ownership of the asset held in Ireland or in the company that carried out the R&D leading to the IP asset is not a requirement of the KDB. The key requirement is that the company that carried out the R&D that led to the creation of the IP asset has the right to exploit the asset. **Example 5.6** illustrates a typical structure.

EXAMPLE 5.6: COMPANY EXPLOITING CENTRALLY HELD
INTELLECTUAL PROPERTY

Pharma Co. is an Irish pharmaceutical company that develops and manufactures 'orphan' drugs in Ireland for treating rare diseases. It is a member of a large multinational group of companies. The group has a centralised IP management function, 'IP Co.', which is located in the US and comprised of IP attorneys and patent experts. This group is responsible for the registration and protection of all the group's IP assets. Pharma Co. carries on R&D on a new drug in Ireland which qualifies for the R&D Tax Credit under section 766 TCA 1997. The drug has received all required approvals and IP Co. has been granted a patent in relation to the drug. The patent is legally held by IP Co.

Pharma Co. commences commercial manufacture of the drug and sells the completed product to third-party distributors. As it is exploiting the IP asset, and it carried out the R&D that led to the creation of the asset, Pharma Co. should be able to avail of KDB relief on the profits generated from the asset.

5.3.1.8 *Assessing whether a Company Has a Qualifying Asset*

In summary, when considering if an asset will qualify for the KDB relief, it is usually best to adopt the following assessment approach:

FIGURE 5.2: ASSESSING IF A COMPANY CAN AVAIL OF KDB RELIEF

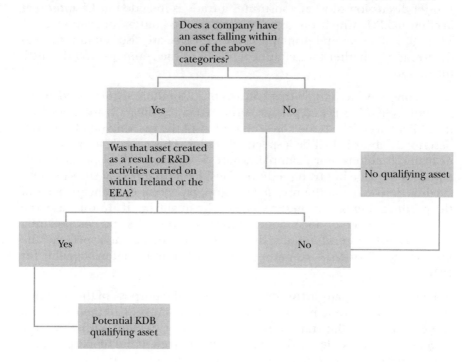

5.3.2 *'Qualifying Profits'*

"Where qualifying profits in respect of a qualifying asset arise in the course of a specified trade, then a relevant company may make a claim in respect of that qualifying asset under this section, ...".

5.3.2.1 Income of the 'Specified Trade'

For the purposes of the KDB, 'specified trade' is defined in section 769G(3)(a) TCA 1997 and is quite similar to the definition of 'specified trade' for the purposes of section 291A (specified intangible asset allowances, discussed in **Chapter 6**). For the KDB, a specified trade means a trade or part of a trade that includes one or more of the following:

"(i) the managing, developing, maintaining, protecting, enhancing or exploiting of intellectual property,

(ii) the researching, planning, processing, experimenting, testing, devising, developing or other similar activity leading to an invention or creation of intellectual property, or

(iii) the sale of goods or the supply of services that derive part of their value from activities described in subparagraphs (i) and (ii), where those activities were carried on by the relevant company".[6]

A brief discussion of what constitutes a trade is included in **Chapter 6** at **Section 6.3.2.1**, which discusses trading in the context of section 291A TCA 1997. The general principles covered there are also relevant here in determining whether the relevant activities of the company would constitute a trade.

If the company has a trade that consists partly of the activities listed above (section 769G(3)(a)) and partly of other activities, the legislation provides that "that part of the trade consisting solely of the carrying on of activities described [above] shall be a specified trade". This is likely to be the case in many situations. For example, where a company sells a product with embedded qualifying IP, it might be considered that part of the sales proceeds is derived from the product's brand, part from the other aspects of the product, and part from the value of the qualifying IP. In this case, the company will need to do an apportionment of the sales and costs relating to the asset between the qualifying IP and non-qualifying aspects of the product, the former representing the specified trade that may qualify for KDB relief.

Finally, if the company incurs expenditure for the purpose of the specified trade **before** the trade has commenced, for the purpose of the KDB, with the exception of the transitional measures (see **Section 5.5** below) the expenditure will be deemed to have been incurred in the first accounting period in which that company commences to trade.

5.3.2.2 Profits of the Specified Trade

As alluded to above, once it is determined that there is a specified trade, the next step is to ascertain the total profits of the specified trade. Obviously, there are two factors in determining profits: income and expenditure. It is necessary to ascertain the overall income of the

---

[6] Section 769G(3)(a) TCA 1997.

specified trade and from that deduct expenses incurred in earning that income as well as any relevant capital allowance in relation to assets used for the purpose of the trade.

Section 769G(1) TCA 1997 defines 'overall income from the qualifying asset' as follows:

"(a) any royalty or other sums in respect of the use of that qualifying asset,

(b) where the sales price of a product or service, excluding both duty due or payable and any amount of value-added tax charged in the sales price, includes an amount which is attributable to a qualifying asset, such portion of the income from those sales as, on a just and reasonable basis, is attributable to the value of the qualifying asset,

(c) any amount for the grant of a licence to exploit that qualifying asset, and

(d) any amount of insurance, damages or compensation in relation to the qualifying asset,

where that amount is taken into account in computing, for the purposes of assessment to corporation tax, the profits of a trade, and overall income from qualifying assets shall be construed accordingly".

The income of the specified trade is as one would expect, i.e. any income relating to the exploitation of the qualifying asset, be it royalty income, licence income or the sales value of a product or service that derives its value from the qualifying asset. In situations where there is a straight royalty or licence fee due in relation to the use of the qualifying asset, the calculation of the income is relatively straightforward. However, it is a little more complicated if a company is selling a product or service of which only part of the sales value derives from the qualifying asset. In such scenarios, the company will have to make an apportionment of the sales value to the qualifying asset on a 'just and reasonable basis'. While 'just and reasonable' is a familiar concept in tax, ultimately it is for the individual Inspector of Taxes to confirm if the apportionment made by a company is just and reasonable given the circumstances of the case.

In some cases, companies will have a clear understanding of how much the qualifying IP adds to the sales value of their products or services as it may respresent a unique selling point that allows the company to charge its customers a premium over its competitors. However, in many cases a clear comparison such as this may not be readily available and an economic analysis and report may be required to ascertain and support the apportionment position taken.

While the appropriate method of allocation may vary from sector to sector, product to product and company to company, key questions that always need to be answered are as follows:

(a) What would a third party pay for a licence to use the IP asset in their product or service?

(b) What portion of the sales price is made up of non-qualifying assets, e.g. how much of the sales value is driven by brand, other IP assets that were not developed in country, etc?

In the case of small and micro companies,[7] Revenue's guidance on the KDB notes that it is prepared to accept up to a 10% notional royalty rate for key embedded IP unless there is evidence to the contrary that such a rate is not appropriate.[8] This can be a beneficial safeharbour for small and micro companies and may allow them dispense with the need for a costly economic analysis to be undertaken.

On the cost-allocation side, Revenue has noted that the apportionment of expenses and capital allowances between the company's normal trade and its specified trade in addition to a 'just and reasonable' manner must be done "in such a way that the expenses of the specified trade are the expenses that an independent company would incur in earning the same income from the qualifying assets".[9] Revenue further notes that it will accept the apportionment where the allocation factor has been chosen in a manner that is "bona fide, based on facts and not unreasonable".[10]

Whatever allocation method is used both on the income and cost side, it would be expected that this method would be used consistently from one year to the next, except where there is a significant change in the circumstances requiring a change to ensure that the methodology remains just and reasonable.

It is worth noting that if a company has established that it has a family of assets (see **Section 5.3.1.5** above), a methodology can be established that can calculate apportionments to the family of assets as if it was one asset (i.e. a similar allocation methodology can be applied to a family of assets as to a single asset, if this can be shown to be reasonable). Furthermore, Revenue has indicated that where a company has a number of qualifying assets, the company may choose to calculate profits on an individual-qualifying-asset basis or simply calculate the profits of the specified trade (including all qualifying assets) and then apportion same to the qualifying assets on a just and reasonable basis.

---

[7] For the purposes of the Revenue guidance on accepting the notional royalty rate of 10% relating to small and micro companies, the company must have fewer than 50 employees and an annual turnover and/or annual balance sheet total of €10 million or less. If the company is a member of a group, the whole group must meet these thresholds. This is a different size criteria than that for SMEs set out in **Section 5.3.1.3**.

[8] Revenue Commissioners, *Guidance Notes on the Knowledge Development Box* (updated August 2016).

[9] *Ibid.*, p. 14.

[10] *Ibid.*, p. 22.

5.3.2.3 Establishing Qualifying Profits (the Modified Nexus Calculation)

Once we have established the profits of the specified trade, the next step is to determine what proportion of the IP asset value was created by the Irish company, i.e. 'the substantial activity requirement'. Expenditures act as a proxy for the substantial activities (i.e. it is assumed that the activities are located where the expenditure arises). This is the essence of the modified nexus approach: there must be a 'nexus', i.e. connection, between the country in which the costs (representing the substantial activity) of creating the IP asset by the company are located and the country where the income earned by the company is located in respect of that IP asset is recognised. The test is a proportionality test rather than a quantum test, i.e. the modified nexus method requires the company to establish what proportion of the asset arose out of the substantial activities carried out in Ireland. To achieve this, the following fraction was established by the OECD when it outlined the requirements of the modified nexus approach to help determine the proportion of profits from the specified trade that can qualify for the KDB.

FIGURE 5.3: THE MODIFIED NEXUS FRACTION

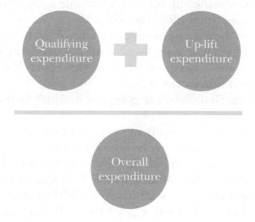

Each of the terms included in the formula are explored in the following sections:
- qualifying expenditure;
- up-lift expenditure;
- overall expenditure.

5.3.2.3.1 Qualifying Expenditure

Section 769G(2) TCA 1997 provides that 'qualifying expenditure' means expenditure incurred by the company wholly and exclusively in the carrying on by it of R&D activities (as defined by section 766 TCA 1997 – see **Chapter 3**) in a relevant Member State (i.e. EU or EEA Member State) where such activities lead to the development, improvement or creation of the qualifying asset. The expenditure must be tax deductible for the purpose of the trade of the company (or would be deductible if it had not been capitalised by the company). If the expenditure is incurred on the provision of plant and machinery, the item of plant and machinery must be eligible for capital allowances under Part 9 TCA 1997, with the exception of items that are eligible for capital allowances under section 291A (specified intangible assets – see **Chapter 6**).

Qualifying expenditure also includes amounts paid to third parties that undertake R&D activities on behalf of the company, even if that work was carried on outside the EEA. The amounts paid must represent an arm's length price.

Section 769G(2)(b) explicitly excludes the following items from the definition of qualifying expenditure:

1. Acquisition costs in relation to the qualifying assets. Acquisition costs are defined by section 769G(1) as expenditure incurred on the acquisition of IP, or rights over IP, where that IP is reflected in the value of the qualifying asset.
2. Any interest paid or payable.
3. Any amounts paid to a group member, directly or indirectly, to carry on R&D activities, whether under a cost-sharing agreement or otherwise, i.e. group outsourcing of R&D activities.
4. If the R&D activities are outsourced to a third party but that outsourcing arrangement is managed by a group member, any payment to the group member above what is paid to the third party is excluded for the qualifying expenditure calculation.
5. R&D activities carried on by the company in a jurisdiction that is not an EEA Member State.
6. Finally, the definition of qualifying expenditure excludes any expenditure incurred by the company for which the company gets a tax deduction, capital allowance or relief of any other description for the purposes of tax in a territory other than Ireland. This significantly restricts any expenditure incurred by the company on R&D activities carried on by the company outside Ireland, e.g. where an Irish company carries out R&D activities in a foreign jurisdiction through a branch of the company, the branch may get a tax deduction in the foreign jurisdiction in relation to the expenditure on the R&D activities and, therefore, the company cannot include this expenditure in its calculation of qualifying expenditure for the purpose of the KDB relief.

Acquisition Costs and Group Outsourcing Costs As discussed above at **Section 5.3.2.3**, the modified nexus approach attempts to identify by whom the substantial activities that led to the creation of the qualifying asset were carried on and where. In this regard, the approach looks to the location of where the expenditure is incurred as a proxy for where the substantial activities are carried out.

It is considered that acquisition cost (see point 1 in the list above) represents substantial activities leading to IP assets of some description being created by some other entity. Where these IP assets are reflected in the value of the qualifying asset of a company seeking to avail of the KDB, the modified nexus approach seeks to reduce the amount of the income from the qualifying asset that can avail of the preferential rate in proportion to the value of the qualifying asset versus the value of IP assets created by the other entity, i.e. the acquisition costs.

Similarly, R&D activities carried out by a group member on behalf of the company are seen to represent substantial activities not carried out by the company, and again the modified nexus approach seeks to limit the benefits offered by the KDB in the same proportion.

Buying services from group companies that do not constitute R&D activities are not regarded as group outsouring costs, e.g. the secondment of staff from a group member.

Revenue's guidelines classify items 3, 4, 5 and 6 in the above list as 'group outsourcing costs' but recognise the misnomer in using this term in that activities at point 4 and 5 may not involve any other group member, a branch not being a separate legal entity. What point 3 excludes is R&D activities not carried out by the company. Points 4 and 5, in most cases,[11] exclude R&D activities carried out by the company where those activities are not carried on in Ireland. Therefore, items classified as 'group outsourcing costs' include costs incurred on activities that do not have any involvement of a 'group' company.

However, despite the slight misnomer, this classification is helpful in the definition of up-lift expenditure and overall expenditure (see **Sections 5.3.2.3.2** and **5.3.2.3.3** below, respectively). The following example outlines how various cost items would be classified as qualifying or non-qualifying expenditure.

EXAMPLE 5.7(A): QUALIFYING AND NON-QUALIFYING EXPENDITURE

QE Ltd incurs the following expenditure in the creation of its qualifying IP asset:

Cost Item	Amount	Qualfying expenditure analysis	Reason
Salary costs of QE Ltd's R&D team based in Ireland	€500,000	Qualifying	The activities qualify under section 766 TCA 1997 as R&D activities, and the company would be entitled to a tax deduction for the expenditure in Ireland.

[11] There are conceivable situations, albeit rare, where a company could carry on R&D activities in a foreign jurisdiction without triggering a taxable presence in that jurisdiction and, therefore, not receive relief from tax in the foreign jurisdiction.

Salary costs of QE Ltd's R&D team based in its Polish branch	€100,000	Non-qualifying	While the R&D activities are carried out in the EEA, the company will get a tax deduction for the expenditure in another territory, i.e. Poland, through its branch return.
Salary costs of QE Ltd's R&D team based in its US branch	€100,000	Non-qualifying	The R&D activities are not carried on in a relevant Member State, i.e. the EEA.
Cost of R&D manager secondment to QE Ltd from another group company	€30,000	Qualifying	The company incurs the cost and will be entitled to a tax deduction. The service provided is not outsourced R&D activity.
Computer and lab equipment used by the R&D team	€30,000	Qualifying	The company will be entitled to plant and machinery capital allowances on expenditure.
Material used in the R&D process in Ireland	€50,000	Qualifying	The company would be entitled to a tax deduction for the expenditure in Ireland.
Outsourced R&D activities to its parent company, BCA Ltd	€20,000	Non-qualifying	Related-party outsoucing costs explicity excluded.
Outsourced R&D activities to 'Outsource Ltd', an unrelated third-party company located in the US	€75,000	Qualifying	Third-party outsourcing is allowable irrespective of the location of the activities.
Interest costs relating to the funding of R&D activities	€35,000	Non-qualifying	Interest costs explicitly excluded.

| Purchase of a patent that is used in the R&D process of the company | €25,000 | Non-qualifying | Patents are rights over IP and, therefore, if the costs of the patents are reflected in the value of the asset, they will be acquisition costs and excluded. |

Therefore, of the total expenditure of €965,000, the total qualifying expenditure in the above example is €685,000.

5.3.2.3.2 Up-lift Expenditure

'Up-lift expenditure' is effectively an allocation of a portion of the acquisition costs and group outsourcing costs to the qualifying pool of expenditure. This allows some elements of these costs to be included in the numerator of the modified nexus fraction (see **Figure 5.3** in **Section 5.3.2.3**).

The up-lift expenditure element of the modified nexus comprises the 'modified' element of the modified nexus approach. It was felt by the OECD when designing the new KDB systems that a full nexus approach was excessively difficult and punative for companies (particularly smaller companies) that acquire IP or outsource part of their R&D activities to related parties, even though they are still responsible for much of the value creation. A full nexus approach would exclude all elements of such costs from the numerator in the modified nexus fraction, thereby reducing the amount of qualifying profits that could avail of the preferential tax treatment provided by the KDB allowance.

Thus, the up-lift expenditure provisions allow a limited amount of acquisition costs and related-party outsourcing costs to be included above the line in the modified nexus fraction. The maximum level of up-lift expenditure allowed by the OECD in its approved approach is 30% of qualifying expenditure (see **Section 5.3.2.3.1**). In Ireland the full 30% is allowed, meaning that up-lift expenditure in the Irish KDB is defined as follows by section 769G(1) TCA 1997:

"'up-lift expenditure', in relation to a qualifying asset, is the lower of—
(a) 30 per cent of the amount of the qualifying expenditure on the qualifying asset, or
(b) the aggregate of acquisition costs and group outsourcing costs".

Example 5.7(B): Up-lift Expenditure

Following on from **Example 5.7(A)** above, the total qualifying expenditure was €685,000 and the following costs were excluded from the definition of 'qualifying expenditure':

Outsourced R&D activities to its parent company BCA Ltd	€20,000
Salary costs of QE Ltd's R&D team based in its Polish branch	€100,000
Salary costs of QE Ltd's R&D team based in its US branch	€100,000
Purchase of a patent that is used in the R&D process of the company	€25,000
Total	€245,000

Therefore, the up-lift expenditure is the lower of:
1. 30% of the qualifying expenditure, i.e. €205,500 (30% × €685,000);
   or
2. the aggregate of acquisition costs and group outsouring costs, i.e. €245,000 (acquisition cost of €25,000 plus group outsourcing costs €220,000).[12]

In this example, therefore the up-lift expenditure is €205,500.

5.3.2.3.3 Overall Expenditure

The 'overall expenditure' is all the qualifying expenditure plus the non-qualifying expenditure. The modified nexus method is designed such that the modified nexus fraction (see **Figure 5.3** in **Section 5.3.2.3**) would be 1/1 (i.e. the portion of qualifying income for the asset would be 100%) if the company incurred all the relevant expenditure in the creation of the qualifying asset itself; in other words, it had no acquisition costs or group outsourcing costs.

To ensure it is possible to have a 100% allocation of qualifying profits where appropriate, it is necessary that the overall expenditure does not include any item of expenditure that could never be considered as qualifying expenditure, i.e. expenditure items that do not form part of qualifying costs even if the activities relating to the costs are carried out by the company. This means that expenditure like interest costs, building costs and other capital costs not qualifying for plant and machinery allowances would not be included in the calculation of overall expenditure as they are not costs that could ever qualify as qualifying expenditure,

---

[12] The extended definition of 'group outsourcing' costs includes branch costs where a company receives a tax deduction in the foreign jurisdiction (see **Section 5.3.2.3.1**).

irrespective of where or by whom they are incurred. In other words, only the cost of activities that contribute to the value of the qualifying asset should be included in the overall expenditure calculation.

Therefore, we can express the overall expenditure as follows:

Qualifying expenditure + acquisition costs + group outsourcing costs

The following example demonstrates the overall expenditure calculation continuing the facts included at **Examples 5.7(A)** and **5.7(B)** above.

EXAMPLE 5.7(C): OVERALL EXPENDITURE

Again, to continue with **Example 5.7**, the following would be the overall costs:

Qualifying expenditure	€685,000
Acquisition costs	€25,000
Group outsourcing	€220,000
Overall expenditure	€930,000*

(* Proof: total cost (€965,000) minus 'non-substantial activities cost', in this case interest (€35,000).)

5.3.2.3.4 Bringing it all Together

In the last three sections we have dealt with how to determine the component parts of the modified nexus formula, i.e. the following fraction:

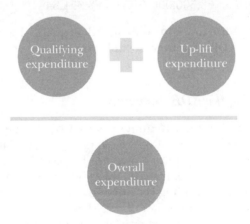

which is also expressed in section 769I TCA 1997 as

$$\frac{QE + UE}{OE}$$

In **Examples 5.7(A)**, **5.7(B)** and **5.7(C)**, QE Ltd's modified nexus ratio (MNR) is as follows:

€685,000 (QE) + €205,500 (UE)/€930,000 (OE) = 95.75%

We now apply this MNR to the profits of the specified trade (see **Section 5.3.2.2**) to arrive at the qualifying profits that can avail of the preferential treatment of the KDB. The following is the full modified nexus formula:

FIGURE 5.4: MODIFIED NEXUS FORMULA

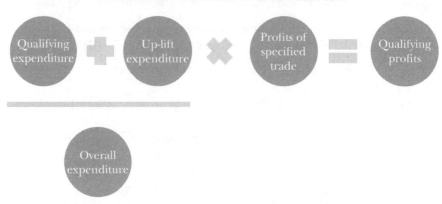

In QE Ltd's case we see that the profits of the specified trade (expressed as 'QA' in section 769I TCA 1997) are €3,500,000 and applying the MNR calculated above, 95.75%, we establish that the qualifying profits are €3,351,344. Alternatively, expressed as the full calculation of the qualifying profit as set out in **Figure 5.4**, we determine the following for QE Ltd:

$$((€685,000 \text{ (QE)} + €205,500 \text{ (UE)})/€930,000 \text{ (OE)}) \times$$
$$€3,500,000 \text{ (QA)} = €3,351,344.$$

Having calculated the amount of profits that qualify for the preferential treatment of the KDB, it is now possible to calculate the amount of that relief.

5.3.3 Calculating the KDB Allowance

The Irish KDB preferential treatment is that qualifying companies can avail of an 'effective' tax rate of 6.25% on qualifying profits as opposed to the 12.5% normal trading rate. However, the KDB has not introduced a new Irish corporate tax rate. Instead, the relief is given by way of an allowance that is treated as a trading receipt and can be used against qualifying profits. The qualifying profits, net of the KDB allowance, are then taxable at the 12.5% trading rate of corporation tax. The allowance is calculated as 50% of the company's qualifying profits, which gives an effective rate of 6.25% of tax on these profits.

The KDB allowance is calculated after capital allowances but before reliefs for any trading losses (see **Section 5.7.2** for further discussion on the use of such losses). The following figure provides a high-level illustration of how the KDB allowance reduces the qualifying profits to give the profit figure that will be subjected to corporation tax at 12.5% but, due to the allowance, results in an effective rate of tax at 6.25%.

FIGURE 5.5: CALCULATING TAXABLE PROFITS AFTER KDB ALLOWANCE

EXAMPLE 5.7(D): CALCULATING THE KDB ALLOWANCE
AND TAX PROFITS

Continuing **Example 5.7** involving QE Ltd, in **Sections 5.3.2.3.1** to **5.3.2.3.3** above we ascertained that the portion of the profits of the specified trade that qualifies for KDB relief, i.e. specified profits were €3.5 million and MNR is 95.75%. If the company had capital allowances of €150,000 relating to the specified trade, the KDB allowance calculation is as follows:

KDB Allowance Calculation

Profits of specified trade	€3,500,000
Capital allowances	€150,000
Specified profits after capital allowances	€3,350,000
Qualifying profits (i.e. €3,350,000 × 95.75%)	€3,207,715
KDB allowance 50%	€1,603,858
Taxable qualifying profits	€1,603,858
Tax at 12.5%	€200,482

Proof:

Qualifying profits after capital allowances	€3,207,715
Taxed at 6.25%	€200,482

It is important to remember that the non-qualifying profits from the specified trade of QE Ltd must also be taxed, at 12.5%. Thus, there is €3,500,000 of taxable profits, of which €3,207,715 is qualifying profits, leaving non-qualifying profits of the specified trade of €292,285. This will give the following total tax computation for the company:

Total Tax Computation for QE Ltd

Taxable qualifying profits after KDB	€1,603,858
Taxable non-quaifying profits	€292,285
Total taxable profits	€1,896,143
Tax at 12.5%	€237,017

5.4 Tracking of Expenditure and Income Relating to Qualifying Assets

5.4.1 Tracking and Documenting the Key Aspects of the KDB Allowance

As mentioned previously, the Irish KDB has been designed to conform with the work of the OECD in this area, which is part of a larger body of work being carried out by the OECD and the EU to mitigate harmful international tax practices. Because it is important that the new international corporate tax regime is considered appropriately designed, robust and defendable in the manner in which it is implemented and administered by tax authorities of individual countries, the OECD has provided details of the types of tracking required for a preferential IP regime to meet the international standard it has set. ('Tracking' in this context means the ability of companies to have a reasonable method to track the link between expenditures and income related to qualifying assets and provide evidence of this to the relevant tax authority.) In Ireland, these requirements have been set out legislatively in section 769L TCA 1997 and practically in Revenue's KDB guidelines.[13]

Section 769L provides that a qualifying company should maintain all records as may reasonably be required to determine that the qualifying profits relating to a qualifying asset are calculated in accordance with the provisions of the KDB legislation.[14] This includes evidencing that the criteria set out in this chapter are met.

This means that a company will have to be able to provide evidence of the following to substantiate a KDB claim:
1. documentation that demonstrates that the company has a qualifying asset;
2. documentation tracking the qualifying expenditure incurred on the development of the qualifying asset;
3. documentation in relation to any acquisition costs incurred which are included in the value of the asset;
4. evidence of any group outsourcing costs (see **Section 5.3.2.3.1**);
5. documentation linking the income and expenditure related to the qualifying asset, in particular the elements of the modified nexus calculation, i.e. the overall income, qualifying expenditure and overall expenditure in relation to the qualifying asset; and
6. confirmation that all relevant expenses are expenses a third party would have included if the trade was carried on by a separate company (see **Section 5.4.2.1**).

---

[13] Revenue Commissioners, *Guidance Notes on the Knowledge Development Box* (updated August 2016).

[14] The documentation requirements included in section 769L do not apply to expenditure incurred prior to 1 January 2016.

If the company has taken a position in relation to the asset, i.e. the existence of a family of assets (see **Section 5.3.1.5**) or derivative works or adaptations (see definition of 'computer program', **Section 5.3.1.1**), specific documentation must be maintained to evidence the assertion made by the company in this regard. If the company has made a claim for the KDB allowance under the family of asset provisions (see **Section 5.3.1.5**), section 769L(1)(c) TCA 1997 specifically requires records supporting the following aspects to be kept:
1. the commonality of scientific, technological or engineering challenges underlying the R&D activities that led to the creation of the qualifying asset;
2. the consistency of the chosen method of grouping of the R&D activities;
3. the creation of a nexus between expenditures and the family of assets; and
4. the choice of a family of assets with which to create that nexus.

If a company has claimed KDB allowance on the basis that a derivative work or an adaptation represents a qualifying asset, section 769L(1)(b) provides that the following should also be maintained:
1. documentation that identifies the original work and the derivation or adaptation;
2. records of the costs relating to the original work and the derivation or adaption; and
3. details of any income apportionment method used between the original work and the derivation or adaptation.

In practice, there should be a significant crossover on the technical and qualifying expenditure elements with the R&D Tax Credit compilation process, with much of the documentation that supports a claim for the R&D Tax Credit being sufficient for the KDB relief (see **Chapter 3**, **Section 3.5.4** for an overview of the R&D Tax Credit documentation requirements). This should include technological/scientific details and related costs of carrying out R&D. In some cases, the R&D documentation will provide some evidence of the existence of the qualifying asset, e.g. a computer program. However, in most cases it is likely that further documentation will be required in relation to the qualifying asset, e.g. patents or IP for SMEs (see **Section 5.3.1.3**). Also, there may be some aspects to the R&D Tax Credit documentation that satisfy the documentation requirements in relation to a position on a family of assets and derivations/adaptations, though again there may be further specific documentation required to fully support this aspect of any claim.

The items that are less likely to be covered by the R&D Tax Credit documentation are the components of the modified nexus calculation, including the overall expenditure, acquisition cost, overall income from qualifying assets, and profits of the qualifying assets.

The legislation requires that the KDB documentation needs to be prepared on a timely basis and that it is available for review. While this does not mean that the documentation needs to be prepared contemporaneously,

Revenue's view, as expressed in its KDB guidelines, is that the documentation should be prepared in advance of making the KDB claim. In practice, documentation in relation to R&D activities of the company is typically completed contemporaneously with the activities, e.g. project plans, experiment results, lab notebooks, etc., and therefore one would expect companies to be able to satisfy the 'timely' requirement. In relation to documenting the various elements required for the modified nexus calculation, this is important and will need significant consideration by the company before making the claim for the KDB relief; thus, it would seem logical that the basis for the calculation would be recorded at the time the claim is made. Therefore, while the documentation requirement may seem onerous, it would be difficult for a company to make a valid KDB claim if the required documentation is not in place before calculating and claiming the relief.

It is necessary that a company maintains its records in relation to a KDB allowance claim for six years after the end of the last accounting period in which a return has been delivered in respect of the last accounting period in which the asset was a qualifying asset, e.g. if a company makes a claim in September 2018 for the KDB in respect of its accounting period ended 31 December 2017, the company would have to maintain records in relation to the KDB claim for that period until 31 December 2024, i.e. six years after the year in which the return is filed. In practice, this means that original R&D and costing documentation supporting the KDB relief claim may need to be held indefinitely. For example, a patent can last 20 years and a company can still make KDB claims in relation to a qualifying patent even after that patent has expired. In this case, the original documentation of the R&D activities and costing of the patent will need to be maintained for six years after the last accounting period within which a claim for the KDB relating to that qualifying asset was made.[15] The following example illustrates the potential length of time a company could have to maintain records.

EXAMPLE 5.8: KDB ALLOWANCE ON LONG-LIFE QUALIFYING ASSET

Longterm Ltd has a qualifying patent which arose out of R&D activities it carried out in the accounting period ended 31 December 2018. Despite the patent lapsing in 2035, the company is still exploiting the asset and making claims for relief under the KDB legislation in accounting period ended 31 December 2041. Therefore, the company will be required to maintain documentation in relation to the R&D activities and costs incurred in 2018 until at least 2048, i.e. 30 years (the 2041 corporation tax return will be delivered in 2042 and therefore, records must be maintained six years after the end of the 2042 year end).

---

[15] Records may be maintained electronically.

Revenue may, by notice in writing, require that a company furnish such information necessary to support a claim for KDB relief. Failure to maintain or produce sufficient records in relation to any qualifying asset for which a claim for KDB relief has been made will result in a withdrawal of same by Revenue in relation to the qualifying asset.

Section 769L(6) TCA 1997 empowers Revenue to make regulations it deems necessary for the efficient and effective administration of the KDB. While Revenue's KDB guidelines (from August 2016) note that it does not anticipate "that regulations will be made in the short term",[16] at the time of writing the authors envisage that as the first claims for the KDB relief are made, this position will be reviewed and any necessary amendments or additions will be included.

5.4.2 Standard of Documentation Required

5.4.2.1 Large Companies

Under Part 35A TCA 1997, large companies[17] are subject to Irish transfer-pricing rules in relation to trading transactions. Where these provisions apply to a company, section 769N requires that documentation in relation to the following aspects of any claim for the KDB relief is drawn up and maintained in line with OECD requirements:

1. the market value of any IP for the purposes of determining 'acquisition costs';
2. income apportionment for the purposes of determining 'overall income from the qualifying asset';
3. R&D activities for the purposes of determining 'qualifying expenditure on the qualifying asset';
4. any apportionment included in section 769I TCA 1997, i.e. the modified nexus calculation (see above at **Section 5.3.2.3**);
5. any apportionment included in section 769O, i.e. the transitional measures (see **Section 5.5** below).

Part 35A TCA 1997 is designed to prevent erosion of the Irish tax base and achieves this by requiring that transfer-pricing adjustments are made only where Irish taxable income is understated or Irish tax-deductible expenditures are overstated. As these transfer-pricing requirements are based on OCED transfer-pricing principles, the documentation must also support the fact that income is not overstated and expenditure not understated. In this regard, the transfer-pricing requirements of Chapter 5, Part 29

---

[16] Revenue Commissioners, *Guidance Notes on the Knowledge Development Box* (updated August 2016), p. 52.
[17] For the purposes of Part 35A TCA 1997, a large company is defined as an enterprise that employs more than 250 persons and which has an annual turnover exceeding €50 million, and/or an annual balance sheet total exceeding €43 million: Commission Recommendation 2003/361/EC of 6 May 2003.

TCA 1997 are to a higher standard than those provided generally under Irish corporation tax legislation.

5.4.2.2 Small and Medium-sized Enterprises

The standard of proof for companies below the large company definition discussed above is, by degree, lower. However, while Revenue does not expect transfer-pricing standard documentation from SMEs, the Revenue guidelines on the KDB note that as SMEs get closer in size to large companies, it is expected that "the documentation available will be closer to the standard required by transfer pricing rules".[18]

This is not to suggest that SMEs do not require significant documentation to support a claim for KDB relief, but rather the burden of proof is less than that required from large companies. Revenue has indicated that it will accept a just and reasonable apportionment methodology, which represents a lower burden of proof for SMEs.

Expense apportionment methodologies should be developed by companies claiming the KDB allowance, having considered the key drivers of the expense, something that may be less complex to establish in smaller companies. Where such apportionment methodologies are just and reasonable they should be acceptable to Revenue, as outlined above.

For small companies, valuation of IP may be made on discounted cashflow expectations, with certain smaller companies entitled to rely on the notional royalty concession allowed by the Revenue guidelines, as discussed in **Section 5.3.2.2** above. In most instances, smaller companies will have less complex structures requiring less documentation. For example, smaller companies would not be expected to have significant marketing/brand-related IP to which profits would need to be allocated. The Revenue guidelines note that "reasonable apportionment by the Directors, identifying the various IPs which are involved (e.g. trade secrets, brand, patents, 3rd category of assets, etc.) based on stated and sound assumptions, will be acceptable in smaller companies",[19] whereas large companies would be expected to have experts' reports underlying such apportionments.

5.5 Transitional Measures

Section 769O TCA 1997 deals with a number of transitional matters that are quite unique to the introduction of the KDB allowance. The KDB is effective on qualifying profits arising on or after 1 January 2016. However, the creation of, and related expenditure incurred on, those assets may have taken place many years ago. The transitional measures

---

[18] Revenue Commissioners, *Guidance Notes on the Knowledge Development Box* (updated August 2016), pp 57–58.
[19] *Ibid.*, p. 58.

attempt to provide a set of rules for the calculation of the qualifying profits in the context of these historic costs. The rules can be set out in two timeframes: 1 January 2016 to 31 December 2019 and after 1 January 2020. The rules outlined in section 769O in relation to the various elements are outlined in **Table 5.2** below.

TABLE 5.2: TRANSITIONAL MEASURES

Cost Type	Periods arising 1 January 2016 to 31 December 2019	Periods after 1 January 2020
Acquisition costs in relation to a qualifying asset	Include expenditure incurred prior to 1 January 2016	Include expenditure incurred prior to 1 January 2016
Group outsourcing costs in relation to a qualifying asset	Include expenditure incurred prior to 1 January 2016. If such costs relate to more than one qualifying asset, apportion to each asset on a just and reasonable basis	Include expenditure incurred prior to 1 January 2016. If such costs relate to more than one qualifying asset, apportion to each asset on a just and reasonable basis
Qualifying expenditure on a qualifying asset	All such costs incurred in the 48-month period ending on the last day of the accounting period and calculated as a portion of the total qualifying expenditure on qualifying assets, where the expenditure is incurred prior to 1 January 2016; however, where the company is able to support actual costs incurred prior to 1 January 2016, it may use actual costs in the calculation rather than the above 48-month costs	Do not include any such expenditure incurred prior to 1 January 2016

The result of the above is potentially penal. All of the pre-1 January 2016 cost categories that reduce the modified nexus fraction, i.e. acquisition costs and potentially group outsourcing, remain constant, while the cost category that increases the modified nexus fraction, i.e. qualifying expenditure, can potentially fall away with time. This could result in a reducing MNR (see **Section 5.3.2.3.4** above) over time for companies, thereby reducing the percentage of qualifying profits that can avail of the KDB allowance.

However, the effect of this is mitigated by section 769O(4), which provides that where qualifying expenditure is incurred prior to 1 January 2016, it can be included in the calculation post-1 January 2020 if there is documentation in relation to the cost that satisfies section 769L(1) (see **Section 5.4.1** above). In such circumstances, the rolling 48-month average discussed above is replaced with these actual qualifying costs.

5.6 Making a Claim

5.6.1 Time Limits

A company has 24 months from the end of the accounting period to which the KDB claim relates to make the irrevocable election to have the KDB treatment apply to a qualifying asset. The time limit is not from the accounting period in which the asset is created but instead from when the company wants the KDB treatment to apply to the qualifying asset.

EXAMPLE 5.9: ELECTING FOR THE KDB TREATMENT TO APPLY
TO A QUALIFYING ASSET

Patent Co. Ltd carries out R&D leading to a qualifying patent in the accounting period 31 December 2017. The company fails to commericalise the product until 2019, at which stage the company starts earning significant profits. The company has until 31 December 2021 to decide whether it will make the irrevocable election to have KDB treatment apply to the qualifying asset. Once the election is made within the two-year period, the normal four-year rule for claiming a refund of tax under section 865(4) TCA 1997 applies to actually claiming the KDB allowance for the period. For example, in relation to the 31 December 2019 period end, once the company has made the election to have the KDB treatment applied to the asset by 31 December 2021, the company has until 31 December 2023 to claim the KDB allowance and obtain the refund of taxes paid in relation to the 31 December 2019 period.

5.6.1.1 Patents Pending

Given the length of time it can take to get a patent granted, section 769P TCA 1997 provides that a company can choose one of two options to ensure that the benefits of the KDB are not lost to the company in the patent-pending period because of the above time limits. Companies that have patent pending can:
1. Elect to have the patent pending treated as a qualifying patent and claim relief under the KDB. If the patent pending is subsequently

refused, a refund of the KDB benefits together with interest will be clawed back through an amended return for the period. No penalty will apply in this scenario.

or

2. The company can make a protective claim each year on its Form CT1 return in relation to the patent pending, which effectively notifies Revenue of the company's intention to claim if and when the full patent is granted. This mechanism protects the full claim from timing out, even if the patent is not granted within the above time limits.

5.6.2 Claiming KDB Allowances on Corporation Tax Return

5.6.2.1 Election to Have KDB Apply to Qualifying Assets

An election to have the KDB treatment applied to a qualifying asset should be made in the corporation tax return of the company, Form CT1, in the year in which the company decides to have the qualifying asset so treated.

The CT1 will request the following information from the company:

1. how many qualifying assets it has at the start of the accounting period;
2. how many new qualifying assets it is electing to have KDB treatment applied to;
3. the total number of qualifying assets that exist at the end of the accounting period.

This information should be provided for each class of asset, i.e. qualifying patents, computer programs, family of assets, IP for SMEs, and other assets.

Discontinued assets should not be included in this list.

5.6.2.2 Claiming the Allowance

Form CT1 has been amended to capture the KDB separate trade in a specific KDB section, which requires details in relation to the profits, losses, capital allowances, charges and group relief so that the trading results of the KDB separate trade are fully returned.

5.7 Interactions with Other Reliefs

5.7.1 Double Tax Relief

In some instances, residents of one jurisdiction can be taxable on profits generated in a second jurisdiction in addition to being taxable on those same profits in their country of residence. Double taxation relief provides relief from this double taxation in certain instances.

Double taxation relief calculations are complicated and beyond the scope of this book; however, for our present purposes, it can be noted that the effective tax rates imposed on the income from both jurisdictions are important in ascertaining the amount of double taxation relief available. This is important in the context of the KDB, as the Irish effective tax rate for the purpose of calculating double taxation relief is ascertained after the deduction of the KDB allowance.

5.7.2 Loss Relief

Section 769K(1) TCA 1997 provides that to ascertain the loss arising on a separate KDB trade, the same KDB fraction should be used (see **Section 5.3.2.3**), i.e.:

$$\frac{QE + UE}{OE}$$

When relieving KDB separate trade losses against future KDB profits, the losses need to be reduced by 50%, as the losses are offset against the future KDB profits after the calculation of the KDB allowance. Without this 50% reduction, too much relief would be given for the losses as they are calculated without the KDB allowances, whereas the profits would be calculated after the KDB allowance.

Generally, the Irish tax system gives relief for trading losses and charges against different sources of income. However, the value of those losses are reduced where the tax rates applying to the different sources are not equal, i.e. value-base loss relief. This concept has also been applied to the use of the KDB losses.

In this regard, section 769K(2) TCA 1997 provides that where a company makes a claim in respect of charges/losses from a KDB separate trade under either section 243A (restriction on relevant charges on income), section 396A (relief for relevant trading losses) or section 420A (group relief: relevant losses and charges), the amount of the relief must be reduced by 50%.

Where relief is claimed on the value basis under either section 243B (relief for certain charges on income on a value basis), section 396B (relief for certain trading losses on a value basis) and section 420B (group relief: relief for cetain losses on a value basis), the formula to calculate the value-based charges/losses available for surrender is adjusted to ensure that the KDB nature of the losses are reflected. This is achieved by reducing the 'R' (which represents the rate of corporation tax) in the formula included in those sections by 50%.

EXAMPLE 5.10: LOSS RELIEF

Drum Innovations Ltd had the following results for the year ended 31 December 2017.

General trading income	€1,000,000
Loss on specified trade (after KDB allowance)	(€100,000)

Corporation Tax Computation for Drum Innovations Limited 31 December 2017

Case I General trade	€1,000,000	
Current year loss relief section 396A(3)(b), as amended by section 769K(2)(b)	(€50,000)	Note 1
Taxable profits	€50,000	
Tax at 12.5%	€6,250	

Loss utilisation	
Specified trade loss incurred	€1,000,000
Relieved on a current-year basis	(€100,000)
Carry forward loss	€0

Note 1
Loss on specified trade fully used up being €100,000 on value base of 50%, i.e. €50,000.

5.7.3 Start-up Companies Relief

Discussed in more detail in **Chapter 4**, **Section 4.5.3**, in summary both reliefs are claimable: where the KDB allowance results in corporation tax of less than €40,000 (or €60,000 for marginal relief) the company will be able to avail of the Start-up Companies Relief where the other criteria set out in **Chapter 4** have been met. In this regard, the KDB may mean that more companies should be able to claim the Start-up Companies Relief as KDB – reducing the corporation tax liability of companies will mean more companies will meet the corporation tax threshold set out in the Start-up Companies Relief legislation.

See **Chapter 4** for full details of this relief.

5.7.4 Specified Intangible Asset Allowances

The KDB relief and the specified intangible asset (SIA) allowances are designed to be compatible; therefore, a company can avail of both (see **Chapter 6**, particularly **Section 6.9.2**).

The company will only receive an effective tax deduction of 6.25% for the SIA allowance given the order of calculation of the relief, i.e. take the capital allowances away from qualifying profits before working out the KDB allowance. Also, it must be remembered that it is quite likely that the capital cost of acquiring the SIA will represent an acquisition cost for the purpose of calculating the modified nexus ratio. This may have the effect of reducing the qualifying profits for the purpose of the KDB allowance.

5.7.5 The R&D Tax Credit

The KDB has been designed to build upon the R&D Tax Credit and is inherently linked to it. Thus, the two regimes are completely compatible and, in the main, the full benefit of both can be availed of.

There is only one interaction with the KDB that can result in the R&D Tax Credit benefit being deferred. This scenario arises in the context of a company that is claiming both the KDB and the R&D Tax Credit but has excess R&D Tax Credits above the taxable profits of the company. R&D Tax Credit refundable claims are discussed in detail in **Chapter 3**, **Section 3.4.2**; however, for the purposes of this discussion it is sufficient to know that if a company has more tax credits than tax liabilities, the credits are refundable to the company over a maximum of three years, subject to some limitations.

Section 769J TCA 1997 provides that the company must calculate any R&D Tax Credit excess for the purposes of the refund provisions as if the KDB did not exist. The effect of this provision is that the refundable element of the credit is limited, though the amount that is limited is available for carry forward to be used against future tax liabilities. In short, part of the refundable amount is converted into a non-refundable credit that is available against future corporation tax liabilities. In most instances, this will be a deferral rather than a reduction in the quantum of tax credits. However, if this applies to a company that never achieves taxable profits, the credit will be an unuseable tax credit that will carry forward indefinitely.

It should be noted that these provisions do not affect the calculation of the excess R&D Tax Credit for the purpose of setting the excess credit back against the prior year corporation tax liability of the company. This is best illustrated by way of a simple example.

EXAMPLE 5.11: INTERACTION OF R&D TAX CREDIT
CASH REFUND AND THE KDB

Marginal Co. Ltd has only specified trading income and carried out all the R&D activities that lead to the creation of the qualifying asset; therefore, its MNR is 1 : 1. For the year ended 31 December 2017, the company had qualifying KDB profits of €500,000 and R&D Tax Credits of €100,000. For the year ended 31 December 2016, the company had a corporation tax liablity of €5,000.

Step 1: Work out the R&D excess

	2016	2017
Qualifying KDB profits	€80,000	€500,000
KDB allowance	€40,000	€250,000
Taxable profits	€40,000	€250,000
Tax at 12.5%	€5,000	€31,250
R&D Tax Credits	€ –	€31,250
Excess R&D Tax Credits carry back from future period	€5,000	€ –
Tax liability	€ –	€ –
R&D Tax Credits excess	€ –	€68,750
R&D Tax Credits set off against prior-year liability	€ –	–€5,000
Excess R&D Tax Credits after prior-year set off	€ –	€ 63,750

Step 2: Work out the split of R&D Tax Credit excess between refundable credits and non-refundable credits

	2017
Taxable profits ignoring KDB allowances	€500,000
Tax at 12.5%	€62,500
R&D Tax Credits	€100,000
Less excess carried back to prior years	€5,000
Excess R&D Tax Credits after prior carryback	€32,500
Excess R&D Tax Credits for the purpose of the refund	€32,500
Excess R&D Tax Credits that are ringfenced to future corporation tax liabilities	€31,250
Total excess	€63,750

Proof credit usage:

R&D Tax Credit	€100,000
Against 2017 corporation tax	(€31,250)
Against 2016 corporation tax	(€5,000)
Payable as a cash refund	(€32,500)
Carry forward against future corporation tax	(€31,250)
Unused	€ –

5.8 Conclusion

The KDB allowance allows companies an opportunity to reduce corporation tax liabilities (by 50%) on profit attributable to qualifying assets that is the result of R&D activities carried out by the company. Where it applies, it provides an internationally competitive system of encouraging the commercial exploitation of IP-related assets from Ireland. However, having been designed, and the approach to such system mandated, by the OECD to reduce harmful tax practices, the system is quite cumbersome and, in this regard, it may be difficult for certain companies to qualify, or the cost of the administration of the system may outweigh the potential benefits. However, companies that are carrying on R&D activities which result in profit-generating assets should carefully consider the KDB allowance as a way of reducing corporation tax liabilities.

In the next chapter, on specified intangible asset allowances, we will explore allowances for capital expenditure incurred on the acquisition or development of IP assets.

As a reminder of its key features and requirements, we include below an 'At a Glance' summary of the Knowledge Development Box relief.

AT A GLANCE: THE KNOWLEDGE DEVELOPMENT BOX

What is the relief?	The relief is an allowance granted to companies that have qualifying trading profits from qualifying intellectual property (IP) assets that gives the company an effective corporation tax rate of 6.25% on such profits. This is a 50% reduction from the normal corporation tax rate of 12.5% on trading profits.
This relief is potentially of value if:	The company is: 1. Irish tax-resident; 2. has developed, through R&D activities, qualifying IP assets in Ireland or the EEA; and 3. profit-making.
This relief is likely to be of benefit to:	Profitable companies that generate income from qualifying IP.
Interactions with other reliefs:	• Fully compatible with the R&D Tax Credit (see **Chapter 3**). • Fully compatible with specified intangible asset allowances (see **Chapter 6**).

CHAPTER 6

SPECIFIED INTANGIBLE ASSET ALLOWANCES

6.1 Introduction

Specified intangible asset (SIA) allowances provide companies with a tax deductible allowance in respect of capital expenditure incurred on the provision of a SIA. These allowances are used by the company to reduce the company's taxable profits.

Similar to the Knowledge Development Box (KDB) (see **Chapter 5**), the SIA allowances are designed to encourage companies to locate and commercially exploit certain intangible assets from Ireland. However, while the KDB allowance is calculated by reference to the relevant profits generated by the company, the SIA allowances are calculated by reference to the capital cost incurred by the company on the provision of an SIA. This chapter explores in detail the rules relating to the SIA allowances as provided by section 291A of the Taxes Consolidation Act 1997 (TCA 1997).

At this stage in its innovation lifecycle, the company has incurred capital expenditure on the provision (development or acquisition) of a piece of valuable intellectual property (IP). It meets the various accounting criteria, its auditors are willing to recognise the cost of the asset on its balance sheet and the company is now about to generate income from the exploitation of this IP.

Historically, the main benefits to companies developing and exploiting IP was the patent exemption. However, this was considered to be too restrictive in terms of the IP that would qualify (i.e. only qualifying patents) and was not fit for purpose in a modern global economic environment. Also, there were other perceived issues with the patent exemption regime that would lead to its abolition. In acknowledging these shortcomings, however, the 'Innovation Taskforce' urged the introduction of a fit-for-purpose regime before the existing system was withdrawn.[1] This did not

---

[1] The 'Innovation Taskforce' was established to deliver a report on positioning Ireland as an international innovation hub in line with the economic framework, *Building Ireland's Smart Economy*, launched by the Government in 2008. The taskforce consisted of a number of experts from the public and private sectors, and published its findings in March 2010. In the report, it stated it would be "counter-productive to remove the (now more restricted) patent income exemption concurrently with stimulating the smart economy": *Innovation Ireland: Report of the the Innovation Taskforce* (March 2010) p. 118. Available at https://www.knowledgetransferireland.com/Reports-Publications/Report-of-the-Innovation-Taskforce.pdf.

happen; the patent exemption scheme was withdrawn in 2007 but its 'replacement'[2] was not introduced until 2009, in section 291A of the TCA 1997.

Section 291A intangible asset allowances, commonly known as specified intangible asset allowances, were introduced by Finance Act 2009. They involve tax allowances on the capital cost of acquiring or creating specified intangible assets. The relief granted under section 291A is given by way of a capital allowance on the qualifying expenditure.

The purpose of the allowances was to incentivise Irish companies to incur capital expenditure on the acquisition or creation of intangible assets with a view to the exploitation and generation of taxable profits from these assets in Ireland.

The intangible assets targeted by this relief are the various forms of IP such as patents, copyright and design rights, but also include marketing IP such as trademarks and brands. In this regard, this relief extends to a much larger range of assets than those covered by the Knowledge Development Box (see **Chapter 5, Section 5.3.1**).

If a company is to avail of the SIA relief, there are a number of key criteria it must meet, namely:
1. the company must have incurred expenditure on the provision of a specified intangible asset;
2. that asset must be recognised on the balance sheet of the company;
3. the company must be using the asset in the carrying on of the trade of exploiting, managing or developing the specified intangible asset or selling goods or services that derive their value from the specified intangible asset.

While the SIA relief is available at any stage in the innovation lifecycle where capital expenditure on the provision of a qualifying asset has been incurred, it is of most value when the company has taxable profits that need to be sheltered, typically in the growth and maturity stages. These are the stages in the innovation lifecycle of a company in which one would expect to see value accrue from SIA relief claims being made.[3]

---

[2] 'Interim replacement' may perhaps better describe the introduction of section 291A. The KDB is more akin to the old patent exemption, though significantly modified to address some of the perceived abuses of the patent exemption and to be more relevant to modern business.
[3] While the SIA relief will benefit companies in the post-profit phase, claims may have been made in a pre-profit period and carried forward to shelter future taxable profits.

RELEVANT STAGE(S) IN THE INNOVATION LIFECYCLE: SPECIFIED
INTANGIBLE ASSET ALLOWANCES

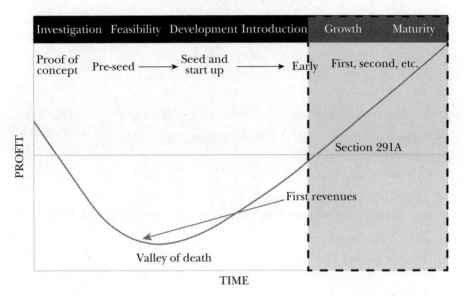

6.2 The Relief

The relief is a tax-deductible amount in the form of a capital allowance (tax
depreciation). Section 291A TCA 1997 deems 'qualifying assets' to be plant
and machinery for the purposes of section 284 (wear and tear allowances).
Therefore, a qualifying company is allowed a capital allowance for each year
that the asset is used in its trade as a tax-deductible amount in the calculation of the company's taxable liability from its specified trade for the period.
For SIA allowance claims made in accounting periods beginning before 1
Janurary 2015 and for claims made in relation to SIAs purchased on or after
11 October 2017,[4] the maximum amount of profits that can be sheltered by
this tax-deductible capital allowance plus any interest incurred on the provision of the SIA is restricted to 80% of the company's taxable profits from its
specified trade in a particular year. The rate of capital allowance is the rate
at which the company writes off the value of the asset each year to the
income statement in line with the appropriate accounting treatment.
Alternatively, the company may elect to write off the cost of the asset over
15 years at an allowance rate of 7% for the first 14 years and 2% in Year 15.
Example 6.1 below is a simple example of how the relief works in practice.

---

[4] Upon its introduction by Finance Act 2009, section 291A TCA 1997 had this
80% restriction. It was subsequently rescinded by Finance Act 2014 and so the
restriction did not apply to the accounting periods beginning on or after
1 January 2015. The restriction was reintroduced by Finance Act 2017 and
applies to SIAs purchased on or after 11 October 2017.

EXAMPLE 6.1: SPECIFIED INTANGIBLE ASSETS RELIEF

Taxable profits from specified trade before section 291A allowance/write off	€1,000,000
Cost of specified intangible asset on balance sheet	€500,000
Accounting treatment: write off to the income statement over 10 years	
Therefore, annual charge to the income statement	€50,000

Annual allowance under election option:
€35,000: Years 1–14
€10,000: Year 15

Therefore, it is better to take a tax deduction in line with the accounting treatment and the tax computation would be as follows:

Tax Computation

Taxable profits	€1,000,000
Section 291A allowance	€50,000
Taxable profits	€950,000
Tax at 12.5%	€118,750

In the above example, if the section 291A relief was not available, the tax would have been €125,000, meaning that there is a tax saving of €6,250 each year for 10 years, i.e. €500,000 at 12.5% per annum €62,500.

6.2.1 Reintroduction of Restriction on Usage of Allowances

When the SIA relief was originally introduced, the percentage of allowance that could be used against relevant trading activities was restricted. Until Finance Act 2014, a company could only shelter up to a maximum of 80% of its profits from relevant trading activities with allowances under section 291A and any interest relating to the capital expenditure. This potentially reduced further the value of a company making a claim under this section because in some industries the opposite of the above problem was the experience, i.e. rather than there being losses in the first number of years, significant profits were made which would only last for the first number of years, minimal profits generated thereafter. This was particularly prevalent in industries with high rates of innovation, such as Information Communication and Technology (ICT) and medical device manufacturing.

The 80% restriction was removed by Finance Act 2014, meaning that companies could shelter up to 100% of the taxable profits arising from companies' relevant trading activities (see **Section 6.3.2.3**) in a given year subject to having sufficient capital allowances in the period.

However, in Budget 2018 Minister for Finance Paschal Donohoe reintroduced the 80% restriction, with subsequent Financial Resolution No. 3 effecting the change in respect of any expenditure incurred by a company on the provision of an SIA on or after 11 October 2017.[5] This restriction was reintroduced on the recommendation of a report, *Review of Ireland's Corporation Tax Code,* undertaken by Mr Seamus Coffey in 2017, which argued that the measure was required "[i]n order to ensure some smoothing of corporation tax revenues over time".[6]

As shown below, the resolution amends the existing section 291A(6)(a) TCA 1997 to include the 80% restriction (highlighted in bold), with the amendment coming into affect for expenditure incurred on or after 11 October 2017:
> "(6)(a) Subject to paragraphs (b) and (c), the aggregate amount for an accounting period of—
>   (i) any allowances to be made to a company under section 284 as applied by this section, and
>   (ii) any interest incurred in connection with the provision of a specified intangible asset by reference to which allowances referred to in subparagraph (i) are made,

shall not exceed **80%** of the amount which would be the amount of the trading income from the relevant trade carried on by the company for that accounting period if no such allowances were to be made to the company and no such interest were to be deducted in computing that income for that accounting period and, for the purposes of this paragraph, the whole or part of any such allowances shall not be allowed for that accounting period and, only if it is then necessary for the purposes of this paragraph, the whole or part of any such interest shall not be deducted for that accounting period."

Therefore, a company can only shelter up to a maximum of 80% of its profits from relevant trading activities with allowances under section 291A and/or interest costs related to the purchase of SIAs for expenditure incurred on SIAs on or after 11 October 2017. Where the maximum amount to which the 80% restriction applies to both SIA capital allowances and interest costs on same, the company should restrict the use of capital allowances in the first instance and, if the maximum restrictions have not been met, then start restricting the interest costs.

As noted above, the removal of the restriction applied to accounting periods beginning on or after 1 January 2015. However, the reinsertion of the restriction applies to assets purchased on or after 11 October 2017. This means that for SIA claims purposes, a company may have two SIA asset types:

---

[5] Dáil Éireann, Financial Resolution No. 3: Intangible Assets (11 October 2017).
[6] Seamus Coffey, *Review of Ireland's Corporation Tax Code* (30 June 2017), p. 6. Available at http://www.finance.gov.ie/wp-content/uploads/2017/09/170912-Review-of-Irelands-Corporation-Tax-Code.pdf.

- SIAs purchased before 11 October 2017, allowances relating to which can be used to fully shelter specified trading profits; and
- SIAs purchased after 11 October 2017, allowances relating to which can only be used to shelter up to 80% of the trading profits of a particular year.

EXAMPLE 6.2: THE 80% RESTRICTION

Bad Timing Ltd purchased a patent for the manufacture of a new diabetes drug on 20 November 2017 for €10 million. The company borrowed 75% of the purchase price and incurred annual interest expenses of €950,000.

Apart from this diabetes drug, the company had no other trading activities. It commenced selling the product on 1 January 2018 and its annual results were as shown below.

The company recognises the patent as an intangible asset on the balance sheet and agrees to amortise the asset on a straight-line basis over its estimated useful economic life of 10 years.

	31 Dec 18	Notes	31 Dec 19	Notes
Income	€20,000,000		€80,000,000	
Cost of sales	€18,500,000		€30,000,000	
Profit before interest and amortisation	€1,500,000		€50,000,000	
Interest	€950,000		€950,000	
Intangible asset amortisation charge	€1,000,000		€1,000,000	
Profit before tax and interest	(€450,000)		€48,050,000	
Tax Computation				
Profits per accounts	(€450,000)		€48,050,000	
Add back				
Amortisation on SIA	€1,000,000		€1,000,000	
Disallowable interest	€0		€0	
Deduction				
Section 291A allowance	€250,000	1	€1,750,000	4
Taxable profits	€300,000		€47,300,000	
Tax at 12.5%	€37,500		€5,912,500	

Note 1
Section 291A allowance and interest calculation
Maximum relief

Profit before interest and amortisation	€1,500,000		€50,000,000	
80% restriction	**€1,200,000**		**€40,000,000**	

Maximum deductions available

Maximum capital allowance	€1,000,000		€1,000,000	
Maximum interest	€950,000		€950,000	
Maximum total	**€1,950,000**		**€1,950,000**	

Restriction calculation

Restriction required	€750,000	2	€0	
Disallowed capital allowances	€750,000	3	€0	
Allowable capital allowances	€250,000		€1,000,000	
Disallowable interest	€0	5	€0	5
Allowable interest	€950,000		€950,000	

Note 2
Restriction required = maximum total – 80% restriction
€1,950,000 – €1,200,000 = €750,000

Note 3
Reduce capital allowances before reducing allowable interest
€1,000,000 – €750,000 = €250,000

Note 4

Capital allowance brought forward	€0	€750,000
Capital allowances available	€1,000,000	€1,000,000
Utilised	€250,000	€1,750,000
Capital allowance carry forward	€750,000	€0

Note 5

Unrelieved interest brought forward	€0	€0
Interest expense available	€950,000	€950,000
Utilised	€950,000	€950,000
Capital allowance brought forward	€0	€0

6.3 Qualifying Criteria

In order for a company to claim allowances under section 291A, it must be carrying on a specified trade and it must have incurred capital expenditure in the provision of a qualifying asset which is used in that specified trade. The following sections cover each aspect of these requirements in more detail.

6.3.1 Qualifying Asset

6.3.1.1 Intangible

A qualifying asset must, in the first instance, be an 'intangible asset'. Section 291A(1) provides that an intangible asset "shall be construed in accordance with generally accepted accounting practice", i.e once the company satisfies the criteria necessary to have the intangible asset recognised on its balance sheet under the relevant accounting standard, the asset will be an intangible asset for the purpose of section 291A.

International Accounting Standard 38 *Intangible Assets* (IAS 38) provides that an intangible asset is an identifiable non-monetary asset without physical substance. An asset is a resource that is controlled by an entity as a result of past events (e.g. purchase or self-creation) and from which future economic benefits (inflows of cash or other assets) are expected.[7]

Thus, the three critical attributes of an intangible asset are:
- identifiability;
- control (power to obtain benefits from the asset);
- future economic benefits (such as revenues or reduced future costs).

Note: a similar definition is included in FRS 102 *The Financial Reporting Standard applicable in the UK and Republic of Ireland*, section 18.

6.3.1.2 Acquired vs Internally Generated

In practice, the capitalisation of intangible assets is more common in cases where the asset has been purchased from a third party. This is because in such circumstances it tends to be easy to:
1. identify an asset, i.e. the asset that has been purchased;
2. demonstrate control, as the purchase documentation will usually set out the legal rights of the purchaser; and
3. demonstrate future ecomonic benefit, as it is presumable there will have been a business case prepared to justify the purchase.

However, internally generated IP may prove more problematic, particularly if the project makes incremental progress over a period of time. It is worth noting that in relation to the capitalisation of internally generated IP resulting from the research and development (R&D) activities of the

---

[7] IAS 38, paragraph 8.

company, the process needs to be divided into both of the following phases:
- the research phase; and
- the development phase.

Under the accounting standards (both FRS 102 and IAS 38), no intangible asset arising from the research phase may be recognised, and cost relating to such should be expensed. However, it is possible to generate and recognise an intangible asset as a result of a development phase once the above criteria exist, i.e. the asset is identifiable, control can be demonstrated and there is future economic benefit.

Activities are considered to be 'research' when they involve original and planned investigation undertaken with the prospect of gaining new scientific or technical knowledge and understanding. 'Development', on the other hand, is the application of research findings or other knowledge to a plan or design for the production of new or substantially improved materials, devices, products, processes, systems or services before the commencement of commercial production or use.[8]

Some detail is provided below in **Table 6.2** in **Section 6.9.3**, in relation to the points to be considered when deciding whether to capitalise or expense development work.

6.3.1.3 Specified Intangible Assets

Not all intangible assets qualify for relief under section 291A. Therefore, once a company establishes that it has an intangible asset for accounting purposes, it then needs to consider whether that intangible asset meets the further qualifying criteria required under section 291A.

Section 291A includes a list of **specified intangible assets** (reproduced below), which are regarded as intangible assets qualifying for relief under this section. The list is quite broad; it is also worth noting that it includes certain goodwill deriving its value from the core SIAs (see below at **Section 6.3.1.4**).

"(a) any patent, registered design, design right or invention,

 (b) any trade mark, trade name, trade dress, brand, brand name, domain name, service mark or publishing title,

 (c) any copyright or related right within the meaning of the Copyright and Related Rights Act 2000,

(ca) computer software or a right to use or otherwise deal with computer software other than such software or such right construed in accordance with section 291(3),

 (d) any supplementary protection certificate provided for under Council Regulation (EEC) No. 1768/92 of 18 June 1992,

---

[8] IAS 38, paragraph 8.

(e) any supplementary protection certificate provided for under Regulation (EC) No. 1610/96 of the European Parliament and of the Council of 23 July 1996,

(f) any plant breeders' rights within the meaning of section 4 of the Plant Varieties (Proprietary Rights) Act 1980, as amended by the Plant Varieties (Proprietary Rights) (Amendment) Act 1998,

(fa) any application for the grant or registration of anything within paragraphs (a) to (f),

(g) secret processes or formulae or other secret information concerning industrial, commercial or scientific experience, whether protected or not by patent, copyright or a related right, including know-how within the meaning of section 768 and, except where such asset is provided directly or indirectly in connection with the transfer of a business as a going concern, customer lists,

(h) any authorisation without which it would not be permissible for—
(i) a medicine, or
(ii) a product of any design, formula, process or invention,
to be sold for any purpose for which it was intended, but this paragraph does not relate to a licence within the meaning of section 2 of the Intoxicating Liquor Act 2008,

(i) any rights derived from research, undertaken prior to any authorisation referred to in paragraph (h), into the effects of—
(i) a medicine, or
(ii) a product of any design, formula, process or invention,

(j) any licence in respect of an intangible asset referred to in any of paragraphs (a) to (i),

(k) any rights granted under the law of any country, territory, state or area, other than the State, or under any international treaty, convention or agreement to which the State is a party, that correspond to or are similar to those within any of paragraphs (a) to (j), or

(l) goodwill to the extent that it is directly attributable to anything within any of paragraphs (a) to (k)".

6.3.1.4 Goodwill

As noted above, goodwill directly attributable to any of the items listed can be regarded as an SIA and potentially qualify for allowance under section 291A. However, it is important to note that under the accounting standards[9] only acquired goodwill will be recognised on the balance sheet of a company as an intangible asset. Therefore, while internally generated goodwill is not specifically excluded from allowance by the legislation, in practice it will not qualify by virtue of the accounting rules and hence only acquired goodwill will qualify for relief.

Acquired goodwill is ascertained by comparing the cost of the acquired business to the fair value of the identifiable assets less the liabilities of

---

[9] IAS 38 and FRS 102.

the business. It is important that the goodwill is directly attributable to the listed assets outlined above. In practice, the goodwill of a business may be attributable to a number of factors and, therefore, it may be necessary to ascertain the portion of the goodwill applying to the specified asset.

6.3.1.5 Computer Software

Since its introduction by Finance Act 1994, section 291 TCA 1997 specifically grants companies a capital allowance on capital expenditure incurred on the acquisition of computer software for the purposes of the trade of the company. This provision envisaged a scenario in which computer software purchased by a company would be used as a tool in the carrying on of the company's trade, e.g. a Microsoft Office licence for a hotel.

When section 291A was subsequently introduced, it was envisaged that companies incurring capital expenditure on the provision of software that would then be a product which the company's trade managed, developed or exploited, or received a royalty, etc., from, would be entitled to allowance under this section, i.e. the value of the traded product or service was related to the purchased software. However, it became apparent that under the original wording of section 291, such capital expenditure could qualify for allowance under both sections 291 and 291A. Therefore, companies could choose to claim allowances under section 291 in relation to a purchase that should really have been claimed under section 291A. Choosing to claim under section 291 was advantageous because:

1. the eight-year write-off period is, in many cases, shorter than the write-off period required under the accounting standards;
2. none of the 80% restrictions apply to section 291 claims, meaning that 100% of the profits from the entire trading activities of the company could be sheltered.

Therefore, changes were introduced in 2010 which distinguished between computer software acquired for commercial exploitation, i.e. in part of an 'on-supply' to a customer, versus computer software purchased for use in the trade, i.e. in an 'end-user' scenario.

For example, if a software company purchases computer software and incorporates it into its own software offering, then this is regarded as purchased for commercial exploitation and allowances should be claimed under section 291A, whereas if a furniture manufacturing company purchases a software package with which to design its products it can claim allowances under section 291 as it is the end user of that software, i.e. it uses the software "in the operation of the trade carried on by the company".

6.3.2 Trading Status

In order to be entitled to relief under section 291A, it is necessary to be carrying on a trade. While what constitutes a 'trade' is a grey area in tax law generally, in certain cases, when it comes to the exploitation of IP, it can be particularly troublesome.

6.3.2.1 General Trade

What constitutes a 'trade' has been the subject of much debate over the years. There is a significant body of case law on the issue and a number of Royal Commissions[10] have also been established and have provided their opinion on the issue. While a complete review of this issue is beyond the scope of this book, set out below are a number of the key principles arising from the various sources of law and interpretation in this area that are of most significance for establishing the trading status when it comes to IP.

Furthermore, as the trading status of a company in Ireland determines whether it qualifies for the 12.5% trading rate of corporation tax or the 25% rate of corporation tax for passive income, this has been for many years a very important tax question and, given its significance, is one on which the Revenue Commissioners have regularly provided advance opinions to companies. Such opinions have tended to provide a level of comfort (but not a guarantee) to companies that their operations will be considered by Revenue to be 'trading' should a review arise. Usefully, these opinions are published (with redactions to avoid disclosure of the taxpayers' identities) on the Revenue website.[11] While many are not relevant to the current topic, **Appendix A** to this book provides a sample of some of Revenue's opinions relating to IP operations.

6.3.2.2 Intellectual Property Trades

Where a company is developing IP regularly and then exploiting that IP through its sale to numerous third parties on a regular basis or incorporating it into products for resale, it is reasonably clear that the company is trading. However, at the other end of the spectrum, if a company acquires an SIA and then simply licences that asset to another party on a once-off basis for a fee or royalty, without the need for active management, it is highly unlikely that this will constitute a trade; instead, it would appear to be more in the nature of a passive investment in a valuable asset from which a passive (non-trading) return is made. In this situation, the company would not be considered to be trading and, therefore, is unlikely to qualify for allowances under section 291A.

As with general trading enquiries (see **Section 6.3.2.1** above), there is an option available to get an advance opinion from Revenue on whether the activities of a company in relation to its IP would constitute a trade.

6.3.2.3 Relevant Activities and Separate Trade

Where it is established that a company is carrying out sufficient activity to be considered as trading, it is necessary to decide whether the activities relating

---

[10] For example, the Royal Commission on Taxation of Profits and Income (June 1955).

[11] See https://www.revenue.ie/en/tax-professionals/tdm/income-tax-capital-gains-tax-corporation-tax/part-02/02-02-06.pdf (accessed May 2018).

to the SIA are part of a subset of the wider trading activities of the company. This subset of trading activities will be considered to be the relevant activities of the company. For the purposes of the corporation tax computation of the company, the income and expenditure relating to the relevant activities will be considered to be a separate trade of the company.

The definition of 'relevant activities' in section 291A(5)(a) is in two parts, as follows:

"(i) the whole of such activities, if any, that
    (I) comprise the sale of goods or services which are goods or services that derive the greater part of their value from, or
    (II) consist of managing, developing or exploiting,
        a specified intangible asset or specified intangible assets in respect of which allowances under this Chapter have been made to the company, and
(ii) such parts of other such activities, if any, being parts that—
    (I) consist of managing, developing or exploiting such assets, or
    (II) contribute to the value of goods or services by using such assets".

There are two main scenarios in which a company will meet the above criteria:

1. The first scenario is where a company is deriving value from embedded IP, i.e. it is selling goods and/or services that have the relevant SIA as part of the core. For example, if a company sells a smart phone which includes a piece of unique technology, part of the value received from the sale of the phone is derived from the underlying IP of that technology.
2. The second scenario involves the active trade of the relevant SIA. For example, a company may develop software for licence to third parties. It may license this software to a large number of clients and be continually developing and enhancing that software with updates, etc., i.e. it is developing and exploiting the asset.

Each of these two scenarios, in turn, need to be analysed into two further scenarios:

1. sales of goods and services; and
2. activities that consist of managing, developing or exploiting SIAs.

6.3.2.4 Sale of Goods and Services

Where the company is selling goods and services, the value of which is derived from an SIA, it is necessary to ascertain if the greater part of the value is derived from the SIA or not. The 'greater part' is taken to be more than 50%, i.e. if more than 50% of the value of a product is derived from the SIA it meets the 'greater part test'.

If the greater part of the value is derived from the SIA, the whole of the sales proceeds is taken into the relevant trading activities calculation. Where less than the greater part of the value is derived from the SIA, an apportionment of the sales price needs to be made to ascertain the amount to be included in the relevant trading activities calculation.

6.3.2.5 Activities that Consist of Managing, Developing or Exploiting SIAs

Where all of the activities relate to the managing, developing or exploiting of an SIA or SIAs, then the whole of the income from those activities will logically fall to be considered part of the relevant trade. The legislation also envisages where part of an activity consists of such activities, though this is unlikely to arise in practice. Where it does, an apportionment would also have to be made to determine the appropriate income from the relevant trade.

6.3.2.6 Ascertaining Profits of the Separate Trade

Once the relevant activities have been determined and the income deriving from same ascertained, it is then necessary to establish the taxable profit of the separate trade. Where there are other trading activities being carried on by the company, the company's costs will need to be allocated between separate trade activites and general trade activities. Direct costs of each trade, such as material, labour, etc., should be allocated directly. Where there are costs that are not specific to either trade, an appropriate method of apportionment will need to be established. In many cases, a turnover basis of allocation may be appropriate. For individual line items, there may be more relevant methods of apportionment, e.g. power may be allocated on a machine-hour basis. Whatever allocation methodologies are adopted, they should be just and reasonable, and they should be consistently applied from one financial period to the next. The rationale behind the methodologies adopted should be documented for consistency of application and also to demonstrate the process to Revenue.

6.3.2.7 Relevence of the Separate Trade Calculation

Relief under section 291A is only available against profits from a company's separate trade, i.e. the exploitation, management, etc., of SIAs, and is not allowed against any of the company's other profits. Obviously, this can reduce or delay the benefit of the allowance because the separate trades may not be profitable in the first number of years after the creation of the SIA and, therefore, the allowances will only carry forward against profits from future relevant trading activities. If sufficient profits are never made from relevant trading activities against which the allowance can be used, they will effectively be a useless, indefinite carry-forward number on the tax computation for the company, i.e. no tax relief will ever accrue to the company in relation to these assets.

In most cases, companies will be required to make an apportionment of their profits between their separate trade and their general trading activities. While this apportionment should be done on a just and reasonable basis, it should not exceed the profits that would have been attributable to the activities if they were carried out by an independent person dealing on an arm's length basis, i.e. if carried on by a third-party company.

The following example illustrates the calculation of separate trade profits and the potential deferral/loss of tax capacity as a result of having a separate trade rather than just one general trade.

EXAMPLE 6.3: APPORTIONMENT BETWEEN
GENERAL AND SEPARATE TRADE ACTIVITIES

SIA Ltd sells an 'internet of things'-enabled kettle. In 2016, it purchased a piece of software for €1,000,000 from a third party that manufactures a smart kettle. The software is leading edge and makes SIA Ltd's kettle more efficient and reliable than any other smart kettle on the market. The company has had an independent economic study carried out and it is estimated that the value of sales of the kettle have increased by 70% due to the inclusion of the new software. The company has the following income statement for the year ended 31 December 2017. It is established that 60% of the company's turnover relates to sales of this new kettle. The company has no interest costs.

Income	€3,000,000
Cost of sales	€1,500,000
Accounting amortisation of SIA to P&L	€100,000
Administration costs	€300,000
SIA cost	€1,000,000

The results of the company need to be apportioned between the value arising from the exploitation of the SIA and the value arising from the general sales of the company. As the smart kettle derives the greater part of its value from the SIA (more than 50%), the full value of the sales of the kettle can be taken into the specified trade calculation:

SIA cost: €1,000,000

Amortisation rate: 10%

	Company Income Statement	Specified Trade	General Trade
		60%	40%
Income	€3,000,000	€1,800,000	€1,200,000
Cost of sales	€1,500,000	€900,000	€600,000
Administration costs	€300,000	€180,000	€120,000
Profits before SIA amortisation	€1,200,000	€720,000	€480,000
Accounting amortisation of SIA to income statement	€100,000	€100,000	
Accounting profits	€1,100,000		
Taxable profits		€620,000	€480,000

As can be seen from the above, the apportionment does not change the overall total taxable profits of the company, i.e. the total taxable profits are €1,100,000. However, if the figures are changed slightly, we see the potential loss of tax capacity as a result of the separate trade. For comparison, if the company paid €15,000,000 for the asset, the result would be as follows.

SIA cost: €15,000,000

Amortisation rate: 10%

	Company Income Statement	Specified Trade	General Trade
		60%	40%
Income	€3,000,000	€1,800,000	€1,200,000
Cost of sales	€1,500,000	€900,000	€600,000
Administration costs	€300,000	€180,000	€120,000
Profits before SIA amortisation	€1,200,000	€720,000	€480,000
Accounting amortisation of SIA to income statement	€1,500,000	€576,000*	
Accounting profits	(€300,000)		
Taxable profits		€144,000	€480,000
SIA allowances carried forward		€924,000**	

* Restriction applied to SIA allowance (€720,000 × 80%).
** SIA carried forward: €1,500,000 less €576,000 utilised.

In this case, the taxable profit of the company is €624,000, even though the profit and loss account shows a loss of €300,000. This is because the SIA allowance available is ringfenced and limited to 80% of the specified trade profits. This means that the excess SIA allowances cannot be used against the non-specified trade income; it is allowed as a carry forward against future profits from the specified trade.

6.3.3 Capital Expenditure

6.3.3.1 Incurred Capital Expenditure

Generally, in order for capital allowances to be claimable, it is necessary that the company making the claim actually incurred the capital expenditure. In this regard, a capital expenditure is incurred when the expenditure in relation to the asset is due and payable by the company.

Revenue has confirmed that the acquisition of an intangible asset where the acquirer issues shares will only qualify for allowances where the company incurs capital expenditure in the course of that acquisition.[12]

6.3.3.2 Enhancement Expenditure

Where further capital expenditure on a SIA is incurred by the company following its original provision, allowances will also be available in relation to this enhancement expenditure. The rate of write-off applying will be the same rate, i.e. the account-based rate or the fixed rate (see **Section 6.4** below), as applies to the original asset. If the company has elected for the fixed write-off rate, the 15-year period in relation to the enhancement expenditure will commence in the accounting period within which the expenditure is incurred.

6.3.3.3 Pre-trading Expenses

Revenue has confirmed that expenditure incurred on the provision of an SIA prior to the commencement of trade of the company can qualify for section 291A allowances once the trade commences and the asset is brought into use in the trade.[13] In such circumstances, the allowances become claimable in the accounting period in which the asset is first brought into use in the trade.

6.3.3.4 Interaction of SIA Allowances with Annual Royalty Payments

Where a SIA is acquired, and the acquisition consists of a capital payment plus annual royalty, it is necessary to understand the nature of the payment more closely. Generally, royalty payments are revenue deductible in

---

[12] See https://www.revenue.ie/en/tax-professionals/tdm/income-tax-capital-gains-tax-corporation-tax/part-09/09-02-05.pdf (accessed May 2018).
[13] Revenue Commissioners, *Tax Briefing* Issue 09 – July 2010.

that, despite their accounting treatment as capital, they may be tax deductible as a charge on income in accordance with sections 243, 243A and 243B TCA 1997. Therefore, even where an annual royalty charge is capitalised in a company's accounts, section 291A allowances will not be available, which is in line with the requirement under section 291A(7) that the expenditure on the provision of the SIA must not have received relief under any other provision of TCA 1997 (see **Section 6.7** below).

6.4 Rate of Capital Allowance

Under section 284 TCA 1997, the rate of wear and tear allowance on plant and machinery generally is 12.5%, i.e. a tax deduction is given for the cost of plant and machinery over an eight-year period. Section 291A amends this rate in relation to SIAs. In short, a wear and tear allowance is granted on an SIA at one of two rates:
1. the accounting rate of write-off; or
2. the election rate of write-off.

While the accounting rate of write-off is the default rate for companies, they also have the option, as the name suggests, to 'elect' into a fixed rate.

6.4.1 The Accounting Rate of Write-off

The 'accounting rate of write-off' gives companies the option of taking a tax deduction for the cost of the provision of an SIA in line with the manner the asset is written off to the income statement under generally accepted accounting principles (GAAP). The rate is determined by the following formula:

$$A/B \times 100$$

where:

A is:
(a) the amount, computed in accordance with GAAP, charged to the income statement of the company, for the period of account which is the same as the accounting period, in respect of the amortisation and any impairment of the SIA; or
(b) where the period of account beginning in the accounting period is not the same as that accounting period, so much of the amount, so computed and charged in that respect to the profit and loss account of the company for any such period of account, as may be apportioned to the accounting period on a just and reasonable basis taking account of the respective lengths of the periods concerned and the duration of use and ownership of the asset in each of those periods;

and

B is the actual cost, within the meaning of paragraph (ad) of section 284(2), of the SIA or, if greater than the actual cost, the value of that asset by reference to which amortisation and any impairment have been computed for the period of account referred to in paragraphs (a) or (b) above.

6.4.2 *The Election Rate of Write-off*

Companies can opt for a fixed rate of write-off that may not align with the accounting rate. To avail of this, a company must make an irrevocable election to have the cost of the SIA written off for tax purposes at the rate of 7% for the first 14 years and 2% for Year 15. The election is made in the return of the company for the accounting period within which the expenditure on the provision of the asset is first incurred, but also applies to all further capital expenditure incurred on the asset, i.e. enhancement expenditure.

6.4.3 *Which Rate to Choose*

The specific circumstances of a company will determine the most appropriate rate for it to adopt. Generally, the principle of taking a tax deduction as early as possible has a cash flow advantage for companies. In this regard, it is usual that the accounting principle adopted is likely, to be prudent, to seek to write the asset off over a shorter period than 15 years. Therefore, most companies would adopt this approach. This also allows for an acceleration in capital allowances if the asset is impaired over its life.

Patents tend to be the general exceptions to the above in that the accounting depreciation period may track the life of the patent, which could be up to 17 years. Also, in some instances, certain assets may not be depreciable from an accounting perspective, e.g. certain brands such as Coca-Cola, etc. In this case, without the election rate, no capital allowances would be available.

6.5 Clawbacks – Balancing Allowance/Charge

Section 288 TCA 1997 provides that a balancing allowance (effectively a catch-up for the unrelieved lost economic value of an asset) or a balancing charge (effectively a recoup of capital allowance given for economic value that has not been used up) will arise if any of the following events occur:
1. where the plant and machinery ceases to belong to the company;
2. where the plant and machinery ceases to be used in the trade of the company;
3. where there is a permanent cessation of the trade of the company;
4. in the case of rights to use or otherwise deal with computer software, where one entity grants to another entity the right to use in consideration for a capital sum.

The most common situations in which a balance allowance or charge arises is where the asset in question is sold by the company that has claimed SIA allowances.

Upon the introduction of section 291A TCA 1997, if any of the above events arose in the 15 years following the year that allowances were first claimed on the SIA in question, a balance allowance or balance charge arose. However, Finance Act 2014 reduced this clawback period to five years. Therefore, if any of the above events arise after five years, there is no balance allowance/charge calculation required.

If there is a disposal of an SIA after a five-year period to a connected party for an amount that exceeds the amount of unused capital allowances, the transaction is deemed to have been at an amount equal to the amount of unused capital allowance resulting in a situation where no balance charge arises, though, importantly, the purchasing connected party can claim capital allowances on the unrelieved expenditure of the selling company (see **Example 6.4** below.)

EXAMPLE 6.4: BALANCE ALLOWANCES/CHARGE CALCULATION

Tech Co Ltd purchases two SIAs in 2015 for €1,000,000 each. The company accounting policy is to write the SIAs off over 10 years and it claims full section 291A capital allowances on both assets from 2015 based on the accounting rate of write-off and does not reach the 80% restriction. In 2017, the company sells one of the SIAs for €900,000. In 2021, the company sells the second SIA for €1,500,000.

Balance Allowance/Charge Calculation 2017	
Proceeds	€900,000
Tax written-down value	€800,000 (€1,000,000 – €100,000 for 2015 and 2016)
Balancing (allowance)/charge	€100,000

Therefore, Tech Co Ltd will have an additional taxable amount of €100,000 in its corporation tax computation for 2017.

As the second asset is sold after five years from the date of purchase, Tech Co Ltd does not need to carry out a balancing allowance/charge calculation.

If there is a disposal of an SIA within five years to a connected party, a balancing charge in the first instance will arise; however, under section 312 TCA 1997, where both companies make a joint election to the Revenue Commissioners to have section 312 applied, the sales proceeds are deemed to be an amount equal to the unrelieved tax written-down value of the asset. Therefore, no balance allowance/charge arises on the seller and, for tax purposes, the purchaser can claim capital allowances on the remaining tax written-down value of the asset.

6.6 Connected-party Acquisitions

Separate to the capital allowance implications outlined above in relation to related-party transactions, section 291A deals specifically with the acquisition of assets from connected parties and the interaction of the relief granted under section 291A and other capital gains tax (CGT) reliefs that are potentially available.

By way of brief background, a number of CGT sections, i.e. sections 615 and 617 TCA 1997, provide relief from CGT in situations where an asset is transferred from one member of a group of companies to another by deeming the transaction to take place at an amount that would secure neither a gain nor a loss for the transferor. If section 291A did not specifically deal with this situation, the interaction of the SIA allowances with the group relief allowances could give allowances on untaxed gains. The following example demonstrates how transfer of assets between members of a group of companies works in practice.

EXAMPLE 6.5: TRANSFERS OF SIAS BETWEEN
MEMBERS OF A GROUP OF COMPANIES

Company A incurs capital expenditure of €1.2 million on an SIA. Upon completion, the market value of the asset is €2.5 million, at which point it disposes of the asset to Company B, a group company of Company A. Company A avails of relief from CGT under section 617 TCA 1997 such that no CGT arises on the €1.3 million gain. Without the provisions of section 291A(9), Company B would be entitled to claim capital allowances on the full €2.5 million of purchase costs. This would mean that the group would be getting allowances on €2.5 million of expenditure when it had in fact only incurred on a group basis €1.2 million on the provision of the asset.

To prevent this mismatch between tax allowances and group expenditure incurred, section 291A(9)(a) provides that capital allowances will not be available under section 291A where the asset was purchased from a connected party who availed of relief under either section 615 or 617 such that the transaction gives rise to a no gain/no loss situation.

However, section 291A(9)(b) allows purchaser allowances on connected-party transfers where the transferor and transferee make a joint election under section 615(4) or 617(4). These elections disapply the respective relieving section and mean that where a gain arises, that gain will be subject to CGT for the transferor. Therefore, in connected-party transfers it is necessary to do an analysis of the likely CGT cost for the transferor on the transfer without the benefit of the relieving provisions of section 615 or 617 versus the potential tax saving for the transferee on receipt of capital allowances under section 291A.

6.7 Expenditure to which SIA Allowances Do Not Apply

Allowances under section 291A will not be available in relation to any other expenditure which is not laid out wholly and exclusively for bona fide commercial reasons and that was incurred as part of a tax-avoidance arrangement. Also, the relief does not apply to the extent that the expenditure on the provision of the SIA is in excess of an arm's length amount payable between independent parties.

These provisions allow Revenue to reject or amend any claims for capital allowances under section 291A where there is a perceived abusive or artificial arrangement that is not within the spirit of the legislation.

Finally, under the provisions of section 291A(7) the relief will not be available where a company has received a relief or deduction for that expenditure under the Tax Acts, i.e. if you have received a tax deduction for the expenditure previously, this section will not allow you a double deduction. Outside a claim for the R&D Tax Credit, the instances of this happening are rare, but one could envisage a scenario where relief was given under section 765 TCA 1997 (allowance for capital expenditure on scientific research) which may also qualify for section 291A and, therefore, the company would have to consider which relief to be of the greater benefit.

6.8 Administration

6.8.1 Appointment of an Expert

Similar to other innovation-related reliefs, the legislation recognises that it is not practical for Revenue to have specific experts in relation to IP for all industries that may come under its review. In this regard, the legislation empowers Revenue to consult and disclose confidential information to any person, an 'expert', who in its opinion may be of assistance in ascertaining:
1. the extent to which such expenditure is incurred on the SIA; and
2. where the SIA is acquired from a connected party, the amount that would have been paid in an arm's length situation, i.e. if the acquisition was from an unrelated third party.

To protect a company's confidentiality and potentially valuable IP, in advance of disclosing information to such an expert Revenue is obliged to notify the company of the appointment of the expert, detailing the following:
1. the identity of the expert with whom it is intended to consult; and
2. the information it intends to disclose.

The company has the opportunity to veto the intended expert if it can satisfy Revenue (or the Appeal Commissioners) that the disclosure of the intended information to the intended individual could prejudice the company's trade. In practice, Revenue will usually seek to appoint such an expert from the academic community to reduce the potential risk of commercial conflicts of interest arising.

6.8.2 Claim to Be Made within 12 Months

Generally under Irish tax law, with a few notable exceptions, most claims for a refund of tax must be made within four years of the end of the accounting period for which the right to claim arises. Any claim made under section 291A TCA 1997 must be made within 12 months of the end of the accounting period within which the capital expenditure was incurred.

On the face of it, this may seem like a sufficient time period for a claim to be made; however, in practice, it may prove quite difficult. It may take the company quite some time to collate and agree all the costs attributable to the SIA, particularly where the asset was internally created as opposed to being a capital acquisition. It is then necessary to justify and agree the recognition and write-off period of the capital expenditure as a capital asset on the balance sheet in a manner that is acceptable to the company's statutory auditors. Then, it will be necessary for the company to do a cost–benefit analysis of claiming the R&D Tax Credit versus section 291A relief. Finally, the 12-month window gives the company very little time to determine how profitable the product might be in the market. It is important to remember that election into the section 291A allowances treatment is irrevocable (see **Section 6.4.2**), making it, therefore, an important decision requiring careful consideration and judgement.

6.9 Interactions with Other Reliefs

6.9.1 Start-up Companies Relief

Allowances under section 291A TCA 1997 are deductible in calculating a company's corporation tax liability before ascertaining whether Start-up Companies Relief is applicable (see **Chapter 4**). If, following the inclusion of allowances under section 291A in the first three years of trading, the tax liability of the company is less than €40,000 (or between €40,000 and €60,000), full exemption (or marginal relief) under the Start-up Companies Relief should apply, assuming the other criteria of the start-up relief are met. In this regard, the two reliefs are not mutually exclusive.

Historically, section 291A may have displaced the Start-up Companies Relief because the start-up relief did not carry forward. For example, if a company could shelter its entire taxable profits with section 291A allowances in the first three years of trading, the Start-up Companies Relief did not apply. However, as the Start-up Companies Relief can, since 2013, be carried forward (see **Chapter 4, Section 4.3.7**), the benefit of the start-up relief should still accrue to the company against future taxable profits of the trade.

See **Chaper 4** for full details of the Start-up Companies Relief.

6.9.2 The Knowledge Development Box

The provisions of section 291A TCA 1997 and the Knowledge Development Box (KDB) (see **Chapter 5**) are not mutually exclusive and, therefore, it is possible to avail of the benefits of both tax reliefs. The KDB gives a company an allowance to reduce its corporate tax rate from 12.5% to 6.25% in relation to qualifying activities. This relief is calculated after relief from capital allowances under section 291A, which means that while the company does benefit from both, its relief under section 291A has an effective tax saving of 6.25% as opposed to 12.5% if it were not also claiming relief under the KDB.

6.9.3 The R&D Tax Credit

As discussed above at **Section 6.7**, no allowance will be given under section 291A in relation to any expenditure that has been previously relieved under the Tax Acts.

As discussed in **Chapter 3**, the R&D Tax Credit is a relief for expenditure incurred by companies in the carrying on of qualifying R&D activities. The credit is available on all revenue expenditure incurred in the carrying on of qualifying R&D activities irrespective of the accounting treatment of such items in the financial statements of the company, i.e. the R&D Tax Credit is available on all revenue expenditure incurred in the carrying on of R&D activities, even if this is capitalised in the accounts of the company.

It is in this area that there is potential for an overlap between the R&D Tax Credit and allowances under section 291A. While it can arise, it is unusual for the cost of the purchase of a capital intangible asset to qualify for the R&D Tax Credit and, therefore, the typical situation in which the overlap between the two reliefs arises is in the case of internally generated IP. Where there is an overlap, it is necessary to analyse the potential benefits and costs under both reliefs to ensure that the company makes the most financially beneficial decisions. Outlined in **Table 6.1** below are factors that need to be considered to ensure the correct decision is made.

TABLE 6.1: R&D TAX CREDIT VS SECTION 291A ALLOWANCES

R&D Tax Credit	Allowance under section 291A
Credit is 25% of costs incurred.	Allowances are an effective tax reduction of 12.5% of the costs incurred.
The benefit of the credit is received by the company over a maximum of three years, or a shorter period if the company has sufficient tax capacity to utilise the credit.	The benefit is received by the company over the period of write-off in accordance with accounting treatment (which could be 5 to 17 years) or over 15 years in accordance with the fixed-rate election option.

The credit can be utilised against all taxable profits of the company. If it does not have taxable profits, a refund up to the maximum of two years' payroll costs can be received by the company or the corporation tax paid in the last 10 years.	The allowances can only be utilised against taxable profits of a specified trade. If the specified trade does not generate sufficient taxable profits over the lifecycle of the SIA, the allowances are effectively lost.
No clawback.	If the SIA is sold within five years, some or all of the allowances granted could be reclaimed through a balancing charge.

Generally, the R&D Tax Credit will be more beneficial to companies where there is a conflict between claiming it and allowances under section 291A, because of the following:
1. The R&D Tax Credit is a 25% tax credit on the costs, whereas the section 291A allowance only gives a tax deduction, meaning that net tax benefit is 12.5% of the costs.
2. The full benefit of the R&D Tax Credit will be given against all taxable profits of the company over a maximum of three years.

In addition to the tax considerations outlined above, there are a number of other tax and non-tax commercial considerations that need to be considered when deciding to capitalise development work. Some of these issues are outlined below in **Table 6.2**.

TABLE 6.2: DECISION ON WHETHER TO
CAPITALISE DEVELOPMENT WORK

Not to capitalise	Capitalise
No base cost on future disposal	Base cost on future disposal
Tax deduction up front at 12.5%	No upfront tax deduction
Income statement cost affects the financial state of the balance sheet	Balance sheet is in the stronger condition as an asset is recognised and cost-to-income statement reduced
If R&D Tax Credit is claimed, potential tax saving in Year 1 is up to 37.5% (i.e. tax credit of 25% plus tax deduction of 12.5%)	If R&D Tax Credit is claimed, potential tax saving is 25% (i.e. you do not get a 12.5% tax deduction for the revenue expenditure and if you claim the R&D Tax Credit, you cannot claim the section 291A allowances)
No clawback of the R&D Tax Credit on the sale of any asset that arises out of the R&D activities, albeit no base cost	Potential clawback of any allowances claimed on the sale of an SIA, albeit base cost on disposal

6.10 Conclusion

Specified intangible asset allowances can provide a valuable tax deduction to companies for capital expenditure incurred in the creation of some intangible assets. This has been an important corporate tax relief for multinational companies that have transferred substantial operations to Ireland, including valuable intellectual property assets. By giving companies a corporate tax deduction on capital expenditure incurred on the provision of SIAs, the SIA allowances have encouraged companies to generate income from such assets from Ireland, thereby helping to grow the Irish economy.

This chapter ends Part I, Phase B of this book, 'Development and Growth', in which details of the main corporate tax relief available to companies have been discussed. Part I, Phase C – 'Realisation/Exit', provides details of reliefs available to the shareholders of companies when they divest their interest in the company through a disposal or gift to family.

As a reminder of its key features and requirements, we include below an 'At a Glance' summary of the specified intangible asset allowances as outlined in this chapter.

AT A GLANCE: SPECIFIED INTANGIBLE ASSET ALLOWANCES

What is the relief?	They are deductible capital allowances (tax depreciation) on capital expenditure incurred on the provision of certain intangible capital assets.
This relief is potentially of value if:	1. the business operates through a company; 2. the company has taxable profits, or will in the future, which it wants to shelter; 3. the company has incurred capital expenditure on the provision of intangible assets that are recognised on its balance sheet.
This relief is likely to be of benefit to:	Companies that have taxable profits at any stage of their lifecycle, which have incurred capital expenditure on the provision of an intangible asset.

Interactions with other reliefs:	1. Complementary to the KDB, i.e. companies can avail of the benefits of both regimes. 2. It cannot be claimed in relation to expenditure upon which R&D Tax Credits have been claimed. Therefore, a cost–benefit/opportunity cost analysis will be required to establish the optimum return. 3. Section 101 stamp duty relief on the purchase of the IP in conjunction with the allowances.[14] 4. Can be used in conjunction with the Start-up Companies Relief (see **Section 6.9.1**).

---

[14] Section 101 of the Stamp Duty Consolidation Act 1999 provides an exemption from stamp duty on the sale, transfer or disposition of intellectual property as defined by section 101. While stamp duty is beyond the scope of this book, it is referenced here for completeness.

CHAPTER 7

THE HOLDING COMPANY REGIME

7.1 Introduction

As outlined in the Introduction, Phase C of Part I discusses the various strategies and reliefs that should be considered when investors have developed value in a business and are now seeking to personally realise some/all of that value in a tax-efficient manner.

In this chapter we will examine in detail the 'holding company regime', which allows trading companies that are held corporately to be disposed of in a tax-efficient manner. **Chapter 8** then explores Revised Entrepreneur Relief, which provides tax relief to entrepreneurs selling their company. Finally, **Chapter 9** discusses Retirement Relief, which allows business owners over 55 years of age to tax efficiently sell/gift their business to third parties/family.

Also, as noted in the introduction to Part I, the topics covered in these three chapters are general tax reliefs available to most trading companies, i.e. not just innovating companies. In this regard, the chapters are intended to give readers an introduction to the issues for consideration rather than be an in-depth technical examination.

The holding company regime is a relief for companies from any capital gains tax (CGT) liability that would otherwise arise on the disposal of trading subsidiaries. The holding company regime is typically availed of by a company when it is divesting a trading subsidiary (or one of its trading subsidiaries) by way of a third-party sale.

From an investor perspective, the holding company regime allows an investor to realise gains (indirectly through a holding company) on the disposal of a trading company without having to incur personal CGT. The full proceeds (i.e. proceeds without any charge to tax) are then available to the investor's holding company to reinvest in other business interests that the investor might like to pursue corporately.

RELEVANT STAGE(S) IN THE INNOVATION LIFECYCLE:
THE HOLDING COMPANY REGIME

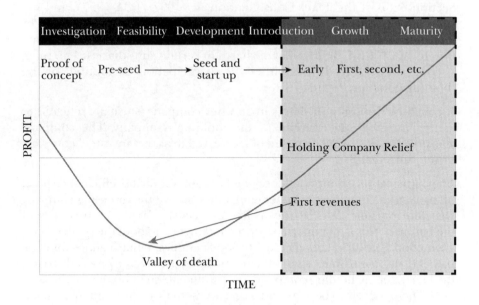

The holding company regime would generally be used by companies that have subsidiary operations which have moved into a profitable phase and are therefore at the growth or maturity stages of the innovation lifecycle as shown above. However, increasingly larger companies are buying earlier stage companies that may have made progress on the development of intellectual property (IP) that is of interest to the acquiring company, even though the assets have not yet been commercially exploited by the developing company. In this regard, the market is seeing start-up companies that are anticipating a sale in the short to medium term setting up a holding company structure from inception to avail of this relief should a potential purchaser come to the table, sometimes within as short a period as 12 months.

It is important for investors to consider the likelihood of a potential sale of a trading company in the medium to short term and then decide how they hold that trading company (i.e. directly/personally or indirectly through personal holding companies) as early as possible in the process, as there is a 12-month holding period (see **Section 7.3.1** below) that needs to be satisfied in order to avail of the holding company regime. On many occasions, successful investors who are considering a disposal of a trading company discover too late that its holding structure is not set up in a manner that can avail of the holding company regime.

7.2 The Relief

Generally, when an Irish-resident company disposes of shares in another company, the company is subject to CGT on the difference between the cost of acquiring those shares and the proceeds received upon disposal, at the rate of 33%.

Section 626B of the Taxes Consolidation Act 1997 (TCA 1997), and the supplementary provisions of Schedule 25A TCA 1997, were introduced by Finance Act 2004 and provide Irish-resident companies with an exemption from CGT on the disposal of shares in certain subsidiaries. The relief is commonly referred to as either the 'participation exemption' or the 'holding company regime'.

A company disposing of shares in another company is usually referred to as the 'investor', the 'parent' or the 'holding' company. The company whose shares are being disposed of is referred to as the 'investee' company or the 'subsidiary'.

The participation exemption is designed to allow for the tax-efficient disposal of interests in companies by other companies, so that the disposing company has more available cash (i.e. the tax-free proceeds) to invest in other parts of the business. This is an important aspect to remember about the participation exemption, that it is a tax relief for corporate entities. While it allows for companies to dispose of interests in other companies, the tax-free proceeds are for the benefit of the holding company, for the ultimate shareholders of the business. There is likely to be a tax cost to get access to those proceeds personally.

EXAMPLE 7.1: REALISATION OF TRADING COMPANY HELD CORPORATELY VS PERSONALLY – IMPACT ON INVESTOR

Conor and Eoin incorporate Innovation Exits Ltd in 2015. The company researches, develops and manufactures medical devices. They each own 50% of the company. Eoin holds his 50% through his own holding company.

Innovations Exit Ltd is sold in 2017 for €2 million. While Conor has a tax liability upon disposal of €330,000, Eoin's holding company has no tax liability on the disposal and therefore has 100% of the sales proceeds available for reinvestment through the holding company in other business interests. Should Eoin wish to personally access the funds in his holding company, there will be tax costs. While Conor has suffered a tax cost on the actual disposal of the shares, the net-of-tax proceeds are now held by him personally.

7.3 Qualifying Criteria

7.3.1 'Parent Company'

Generally, two companies would be regarded as having a parent–subsidiary relationship if the parent company owns at least 51% of the shares of the subsidiary. However, for the purposes of section 626B TCA 1997, a company shall be a parent of another company if it directly or indirectly holds not less than 5% of the shares in the company for an uninterrupted period of not less than 12 months.

7.3.2 *Investee Company's Residence*

The investee company must be resident in a relevant territory. Section 626B(1) TCA 1997 provides that a relevant territory is either:
1. a Member State of the European Communities; or
2. a country with which Ireland has entered into double taxation treaty arrangements.

The following example illustrates some of the foreign-resident companies that would and would not meet the residence test for the purpose of section 626B(1).

EXAMPLE 7.2: ANALYSIS OF HOLDING COMPANY WITH FOREIGN
SUBSIDIARY IN VARIOUS JURISDICTIONS

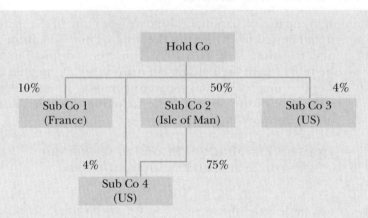

In the above structure, assume that Hold Co has owned all the shares for at least 12 months. Set out below is the analysis of the relationship for the purposes of section 626B.

Entity	Analysis	Outcome
Sub Co 1	Hold Co owns > 5% of its shares. Sub Co 1 is tax resident in a relevant territory as France is an EU Member State.	Hold Co is Sub Co 1's parent for the purpose of section 626B.
Sub Co 2	Hold Co owns > 5% of its shares. Sub Co 2 is not tax resident in a relevant territory.	Hold Co is not Sub Co 2's parent for the purpose of section 626B, as it fails the tax residency test.

Sub Co 3	Hold Co owns < 5% of its shares Sub Co 3 is tax resident in a relevant territory as Ireland has a double taxation treaty with the US.	Hold Co is not Sub Co 3's parent for the purpose of section 626B as it does not meet the 5% shareholding requirement.
Sub Co 4	Hold Co owns > 5% of its shares (indirectly). Sub Co 4 is tax resident in a relevant territory as Ireland has a double taxation treaty with the US.	Hold Co is Sub Co 4's parent for the purpose of section 626B as it meets the holding requirement, albeit indirectly.

7.3.3 Extended Period for Disposal

If the holding company is a parent, i.e. holds 5% or more of the shares for an uninterrupted period of 12 months, the disposal may qualify for relief from CGT under section 626B TCA 1997. However, a disposal may also qualify for the relief where the holding company is not at the time of the disposal a parent company, but was a parent company within a two-year period from the date of the disposal. The following example illustrates how these rules might work in practice.

EXAMPLE 7.3: MINIMUM PERIOD OF OWNERSHIP
AND THE EXTENDED PERIOD FOR DISPOSAL

HoldCo Ltd owns 25% of InvestCo Ltd for five years. It then sells 22.5% of the company to a third party. Eighteen months later, it sells its final 2.5% interest in the company.

At the time of the first disposal, HoldCo Ltd is a parent, as it has a greater than 5% interest in InvestCo Ltd, which it has held for more than 12 months. At the time of the second disposal, HoldCo Ltd does not have at least 5% of the shares of InvestCo Ltd. However, it may still be able to avail of relief from CGT under section 626B as it was a parent company within the two-year period prior to the disposal.

7.3.4 Wholly or Mainly Trading

Section 626B relief from CGT is designed for the efficient disposal of trading entities/groups. In this regard, section 626B(2)(c) provides that at the time of the disposal the investee company must be:

(a) a company whose business consists wholly or mainly of the carrying on of a trade or trades; or

(b) the investor company, any company the investor company is a parent of and any company of which the investee company is a parent company taken together consists wholly or mainly of the carrying on of a trade or trades, i.e. the activities of the investor company, the investee company and any 5% subsidiaries of the investee company when taken together wholly or mainly trading. For example, an investor company may have a 100% subsidiary that holds 100% of a trading subsidiary. When you look at the first subsidiary it is not trading and, therefore, does not qualify as an investee company under (a) above. However, when you take its activities and that of its subsidiary together, the activities would be considered wholly or mainly trading, therefore, the first subsidiary would qualify as an investee company under (b) and, therefore, the investor company could sell the first subsidiary and avail of the holding company regime assuming the other criteria were met.

This means that the company being disposed of must be trading or be a holding company of another company(ies) that are wholly or mainly trading entities. 'Wholly or mainly' means greater than 50% looking at, *inter alia*, net trading profits to other non-trading profits and net trading assets to other non-trading assets.

7.3.5 Exclusions

The provisions of section 626B TCA 1997 do not apply to shares deriving their value, or the greater part of their value, from specified assets which are land and buildings in the State or assets related to mineral, mining or exploration rights in the State.

The relief will also not apply where the disposal is for consideration that would give a no gain/no loss situation by virtue of the deeming provisions of other legislation, i.e. where certain sections of the Tax Acts provide that certain disposals should not give rise to a charge to CGT or generate a CGT loss, e.g. section 617 TCA 1997 (group relief).

7.3.6 Losses

Where a loss arises on the disposal of shares to which section 626B TCA 1997 applies, that loss is not available for offset against other chargeable gains.

7.4 Interactions with Other Reliefs

7.4.1 Corporate Reliefs

The realisation/exit reliefs (covered in Phase C of Part I, i.e. **Chapters 7**, The Holding Company Relief, **8**, Revised Entrepreneur Relief, and **9**, Retirement Relief) are reliefs for the shareholders rather than the company. In this regard, there is no interaction between the knowledge development box (KDB), the R&D Tax Credit, Start-up Companies Relief or section 291A (specified intangible asset) relief. However, there could be an impact on other shareholder reliefs and these are discussed briefly below.

7.4.2 Retirement Relief

As mentioned above, at **Section 7.2**, if you have a holding company structure and you dispose of a trading subsidiary tax free, the proceeds are in the hands of the holding company as opposed to the ultimate shareholder. For example, take the case of a simple structure involving one shareholder owning 100% of the shares in a holding company with one trading subsidiary. If the holding company disposes of the trading subsidiary it can take the proceeds tax free. However, the proceeds are now in the holding company and need to be extracted from the company to get the proceeds into the personal ownership of the shareholders. The shareholder may have missed the opportunity to avail of retirement relief as the holding company now no longer meets the trade test. However, if instead of availing of the holding company regime the shareholder had sold their interest in the holding company, they could have availed of retirement relief.

7.4.3 Revised Entrepreneur Relief

As discussed in **Chapter 8,** Revised Entrepreneur Relief ('Entrepreneur Relief') applies to the disposal of shares in certain companies by individuals, whereas Holding Company Relief applies to the disposal of certain shares in trading companies by corporate entities. Therefore, the transactions do not generally overlap.

Entrepreneur Relief can apply to the disposal of a qualifying holding company. Therefore, with the sale of a trading company that is held by a holding company, the vendor will need to decide if it is preferable to:
1. sell the holding company, thereby taking the proceed personally and receive the benefits of the Entrepreneur Relief; or
2. have the holding company sell the trading company, thereby receiving the gross proceeds tax free in the holding company.

While, in all scenarios, the second option will result in lower tax on the disposal, the shareholders still need to extract the proceeds from the holding company and this is likely to have a tax cost. Furthermore, the decision is likely to be driven by the following considerations:
(a) the amount of the proceeds;
(b) whether Entrepreneur Relief lifetime limit has already been used up; and
(c) if the plan is to reinvest the proceeds into other business opportunities through the holding company or if the proceeds are needed personally by the shareholders.

7.5 Conclusion

The holding company regime provides investors with a way to manage realisations/exits of trading companies in a tax-efficient manner. It facilitates the receipt of proceeds from the disposal of a trading business tax free at a corporate level; this then allows the corporate to reinvest the full proceeds into other business ventures. In this regard, the relief should be considered by investors at the structuring stage to ensure that the relief may be available to them when a realisation event, such as a disposal, occurs.

The next chapter, **Chapter 8**, provides high-level details of a CGT relief (Entrepreneur Relief) that provides benefits to individuals rather than corporate entities.

As a reminder of its key features and requirements, we include below an 'At a Glance' summary of the holding company regime as outlined in this chapter.

AT A GLANCE: THE HOLDING COMPANY REGIME

What is the relief?	This relief provides an exemption from CGT on the disposal by a company of certain interests in subsidiary companies.
This relief is potentially of value if:	1. the company has held a minimum of 5% of the shares of another company for at least 12 months in the last two years; 2. the holding company sells its interest in that company.

CHAPTER 8

REVISED ENTREPRENEUR RELIEF

8.1 Introduction

The Revised Entrepreneur Relief is a relief for investors from any capital gains tax (CGT) liability that would otherwise arise on the disposal of a trading company by a eligible entrepreneur. It allows the entrepreneur to realise value/exit their company by way of a disposal of shares in a tax-efficient manner. In this regard, it is presented in Part 1, Phase C (Realisation/Exit) of this book. Revised Entrepreneur Relief was introduced to encourage individuals to become entrepreneurs, which is accepted as being beneficial for the economy.

The holding company regime, as covered in **Chapter 7**, allows a CGT exemption by the disposal of a company by a trading company (the relief is not available to individuals who are not corporates). Revised Entrepreneur Relief allows a reduced rate of CGT for individuals rather than corporate shareholders on the disposal of a trading company.

The Startup Refunds for Entrepreneurs (SURE) covered in **Chapter 1** gives entrepreneurs an opportunity to reclaim PAYE already claimed by allowing a deductible amount equal to the investment they have made in shares and is, therefore, an income tax relief. Revised Entrepreneur Relief is a CGT relief as it provides the entrepreneur relief from CGT on a gain on the disposal of shares in their company.

The relief was introduced by Finance Act 2015 by the inclusion of section 597AA in the Taxes Consolidation Act 1997 (TCA 1997) and is referred to as 'Revised Entrepreneur Relief'. Prior to this, section 597A, Entrepreneur Relief, provided limited relief to investors from CGT. However, this was considered to be too limited and, therefore, was abolished for disposals made on or after 1 January 2016, at which point the Revised Entrepreneur Relief under section 597AA came into effect. As the original Entrepreneur Relief has been abolished, it is not covered in this book; the term 'Entrepreneur Relief' is used in this chapter and elsewhere in the text to refer to the Revised Entrepreneur Relief, as this is the term that is commonly used in practice when referring to the current relief provided under section 597AA.

As Entrepreneur Relief is usually related to a realisation of value/disposal, it can be seen from the figure opposite that it is generally in the later stages of the innovation lifecycle.

RELEVANT STAGE(S) IN THE INNOVATION LIFECYCLE:
ENTREPRENEUR RELIEF

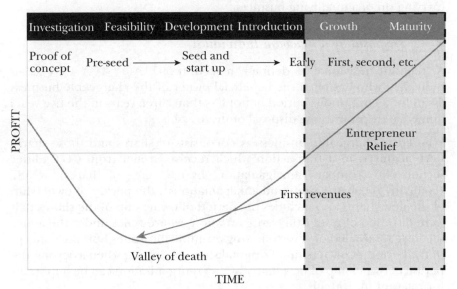

TIME

Entrepreneur Relief is typically used by businesses that have moved into profit and are therefore at the growth or maturity phases of the innovation lifecycle. Increasingly, however, larger companies are buying earlier-stage companies that may have made progress in the development of intellectual property (IP) that is of interest to the acquiring company, even though the IP has not yet been commercially exploited by the developing company. In this regard, after the company has been incorporated for at least three years, Entrepreneur Relief may be relevant.

8.2 The Relief

Section 597AA TCA 1997 reduces the rate of CGT from 33% to 10% on the disposal of certain business assets ('chargeable business assets') made by certain individuals ('relevant individuals') on the first €1 million of chargeable gains in the relevant individual's lifetime. Any chargeable gains made by the relevant individual in excess of €1 million is chargeable to CGT at the full 33% rate of tax.

8.3 Qualifying Criteria

8.3.1 Qualifying Business and Qualifying Group

The relief is designed to reward the entrepreneurs of trading business generally. Therefore, a 'qualifying business' is defined as a business other than the following:
(a) the holding of securities or other assets as investments;
(b) the holding of development land; or
(c) the development or letting of land.

Also, a qualifying group is a group in which the business of each 51% subsidiary (other than a holding company) consists wholly or mainly of the carrying on of a qualifying business.

8.3.2 Disposal by a Relevant Individual

A 'relevant individual' is defined in section 597AA(1) TCA 1997 as an individual who has been the beneficial owner of the chargeable business assets for a continuous period of not less than three years in the five years immediately prior to the disposal of those assets.

Where the chargeable business asset consists of shares and those shares were acquired in a transaction which received relief from CGT under section 586 (company amalgamations by exchange of shares) or 587 (company reconstructions and amalgamations), the period of ownership of the new shares also includes the period of ownership of the shares that were disposed of under the reorganisation, where relief under the above sections was availed of. The following example illustrates how the concept of the period of ownership of original shares counting when assessing the period of ownership of new shares after a reorganisation can be important for relevant individuals.

EXAMPLE 8.1: ENTREPRENEUR RELIEF AFTER A REORGANISATION

John owns 100% of the share capital of Entre Holdings Ltd, which is the 100% parent of the trading company Entre Trading Ltd. John incorporated Entre Trading Ltd 10 years ago and held 100% of the shares directly in the company. Two years ago he incorporated Entre Holding Ltd and transferred his shares in Entre Trading Ltd into Entre Holding Ltd in a share-for-share swap. Relief under section 586 TCA 1997 was received such that no CGT was payable on the disposal of John's shares in Entre Trading Ltd to Entre Holding Ltd.

John has now received an offer from a third party of €800,000 for the shares in Entre Holding Ltd.

For the purpose of the 'relevant individual' test, it would appear that John only holds the shares in Entre Holding Ltd for two years and, therefore, would fail the not-less-than-three-of-the-last-five-years test.

However, because the transfer of the shares in Entre Trading Ltd by John to Entre Holding Ltd qualified for relief under the provisions of section 586 TCA 1997, John's period of ownership of Entre Trading Ltd is included in the calculation of the period of ownership of Entre Holding Ltd. Therefore, for the purposes of section 597AA, John is deemed to have held the shares in Entre Holding Ltd for 10 years and so satisfies the ownership test and is a relevant individual.

8.3.3 Chargeable Business Asset

Generally, section 597AA TCA 1997 envisages two asset types that may qualify for the lower rate of CGT:
- assets used for a qualifying business; and
- shares in companies carrying on qualifying business.

Specifically section 597AA(2)(a) provides that 'chargeable business asset' "means an asset, including goodwill which–
    (i) is, or is an interest in, an asset used for the purposes of a qualifying business carried on by an individual, or
   (ii) is a holding of ordinary shares in–
       (I) a company whose business consists wholly or mainly of carrying on a qualifying business, or
     (II) a holding company of a qualifying group, in respect of which an individual–
          (A) owns not less than 5 per cent of the ordinary share capital, and
          (B) is a qualifying person in respect of the company or, if the company is a member of a qualifying group, of one or more companies which are members of the qualifying group."

The definition of 'chargeable business asset' excludes non-trading assets such that the following are not regarded as chargeable business assets for the purposes of section 597AA:
(a) shares (other than shares as mentioned in paragraph (a)(ii)), securities or other assets held as investments;
(b) development land; or
(c) assets on the disposal of which no gains accruing would be chargeable gains.

8.3.4 Share Disposal: Minimum Holding and Qualifying Person

Where the chargeable business asset being disposed of consists of shares in a company or group carrying a qualifying business, there are two additional criteria that need to be met.

First, the relevant individual must hold not less than 5% of the ordinary share capital of the company. Secondly, the individual must be a qualifying person. A qualifying person, for the purposes of this section, is defined in section 597AA(1)(a) as–:
"an individual who is or has been a director or employee of the company (or company in a qualifying group) who–
(a) is or was required to spend not less than 50 per cent of that individual's working time in the service of that company (or those companies) in a managerial or technical capacity, and
(b) has served in that capacity for a continuous period of 3 years in the period of 5 years immediately prior to the disposal of the chargeable business assets of which the disposal of shares in the company (or one of those companies) forms the whole or part".

While what constitutes a 'managerial capacity' might intuitively seem more obvious than in a 'technical capacity', both terms are not without ambiguity but would seem to go beyond a normal employee.

8.4 Relevant Person's Lifetime Limit

As noted above, the lower rate of CGT only applies on the first €1 million of chargeable gains in the relevant person's lifetime. Therefore, the relevant individual needs to consider any disposal made in relation to any qualifying assets where the disposal took place on or after 1 January 2016 to ensure that this lifetime limit is not exceeded by the cumulative proceeds of any transactions that took place on or after 1 January 2016.

Where the relevant individual had no previous disposal of chargeable assets since 1 January 2016, the first €1 million of chargeable gain will be at the 10% rate of CGT, saving the relevant individual €230,000, i.e. (€1,000,000 × 33% = €330,000) – (€1,000,000 × 10% = €100,000). Any amount of consideration in excess of the €1 million will be subject to CGT at the normal rate of 33%.

EXAMPLE 8.2: DISPOSAL OF SHARES AND LIFETIME LIMIT

Niamh owns 100% of the shares in Innovation Systems Ltd for the past 10 years, during which time Innovation Systems Ltd has been trading and Niamh has been a full-time working director.

In September 2016, Niamh disposes of 50% of her shares in the company resulting in a chargeable gain for her of €800,000.

Niamh's CGT liability for 2016 will be as follows:

2016

Chargeable gain	€800,000
Small gains exemption	€1,270
	€798,730
CGT at 10%	€79,873
Lifetime threshold	€1,000,000
Threshold remaining	€201,270

In September 2017, Niamh decides that she wishes to completely exit the business and sells her remaining shares for €800,000. Niamh's CGT liability for 2017 will be as follows:

2017

Chargeable gain	€800,000	
Small gains exemption	€1,270	
	€798,730	
CGT at 10%	€20,127	(€1,000,000 – €798,730) = €201,270 × 10%
CGT at 33%	€197,162	(€798,730 – €201,270) = €597,460 × 33%
Total CGT	€217,289	
Tax saved 2016	€183,707.90	
Tax saved 2017	€46,292	
Total tax saved	€230,000	

Any subsequent disposal by Niamh of a qualifying company will be liable to CGT at the full rate of 33% unless other reliefs apply.

8.5 Interactions with Other Reliefs

8.5.1 Corporate Reliefs

The realisation/exit reliefs (examined in Part 1, Phase C of this book, i.e. **Chapter 7**, The Holding Company Regime, **8**, Revised Entrepreneur Relief, and **9**, Retirement Relief) are reliefs for the shareholders rather than the company. In this regard, there is no interaction between the Knowledge Development Box (KDB – see **Chapter 5**), the R&D Tax Credit (see **Chapter 3**), Start-up Companies Relief (see **Chapter 4**) for or section 291A specified intangible asset allowances (see **Chapter 6**). However, there could be an impact on other shareholder reliefs and these are discussed briefly below.

8.5.2 Retirement Relief

The interaction with Retirement Relief is discussed in detail in **Chapter 9** at **Section 9.4.2**; however, in summary Retirement Relief and Entrepreneur Relief can apply to the same transaction. This can mean that the Entrepreneur Relief lifetime limit discussed above at **Section 8.4** can be used up on a transaction that is already sheltered from CGT under the Retirement Relief provisions.

8.5.3 The Holding Company Regime

The interaction with the holding company regime is discussed in detail in **Chapter 7** at **Section 7.4.3**. However, in summary, the two reliefs generally do not overlap, as the holding company regime provides CGT relief to companies, whereas the Entrepreneur Relief provides CGT relief to individuals. The interaction of the two reliefs can impact decisions on whether to sell a holding company (availing of the Entrepreneur Relief) or to have the holding company sell the trading company (availing of the holding company regime).

8.6 Conclusion

Entrepreneurship is very important to any economy. The Revised Entrepreneur Relief is an important CGT relief that seeks to reward individuals for taking the risk of entrepreneurship and its introduction by Finance Act 2015 was welcomed by the business community. Reducing the rate of CGT from 33% to 10% for relevant individuals is a generous relief. However, the lifetime limit of €1 million is considered to be restrictive. In terms of international comparisons, the UK version of the relief allows the lower rate of CGT to apply to the first €10 million of relief and, therefore, is considered more encouraging of entrepreneurship.

There are no age criteria to avail of the Entrepreneur Relief, which means that the relief is available to all age groups. The next chapter, **Chapter 9**, examines Retirement Relief, which provides CGT relief for owners of businesses that have reached a certain age (55 years) and are divesting their interest in the business.

As a reminder of its key features and requirements, we include below an 'At a Glance' summary of Revised Entrepreneur Relief as outlined in this chapter.

AT A GLANCE: REVISED ENTREPRENEUR RELIEF

What is the relief?	This relief reduces the rate of CGT on qualifying disposals from 33% to 10% on the first €1 million of chargeable gains.
This relief is potentially of value:	Where the assets have been held for at least three years, if the assets being disposed of are qualifying shares where: 1. the entrepreneur has owned at least 5% of a business for at least three years; and 2. the entrepreneur has been working in the business for three of the last five years.

CHAPTER 9

RETIREMENT RELIEF

9.1 Introduction

Retirement Relief is a relief from capital gains tax (CGT) for owners of businesses (corporately or directly held businesses) that would otherwise arise on the disposal or transfer of their interest in those businesses.

Retirement Relief allows for the disposal of a business to third parties or the transfer of a business to certain members of business owners' families in a more tax-efficient manner. While there are similarities between Entrepreneur Relief (see **Chapter 8**), unlike Entrepreneur Relief there is a qualifying age criteria (i.e. the business owner must be over 55 years of age) that must be met to avail of Retirement Relief. In this regard, Retirement Relief is typically used by more established companies and this is reflected in the innovation lifecycle figure below.

One of the reasons Retirement Relief was introduced was to encourage business owners to pass on their businesses to the next generation (in a family scenario), thereby encouraging the next generation to keep the business as a going concern, as well as driving further entrepreneurship.

Interestingly, under the provisions of Retirement Relief, there is no requirement that the business owner actually retires from the business. This is to encourage a period of transition whereby the original owner can still work in the business and share their experience with the next generation to help ensure future success.

RELEVANT STAGE(S) IN THE INNOVATION LIFECYCLE:
RETIREMENT RELIEF

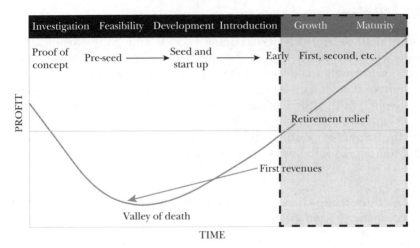

Retirement Relief is usually considered during the process of a business owner exiting a business. The business must have been owned by the individual for a period of at least 10 years and it must have a market value. Thus, Retirement Relief is primarily used by owners when their business is in the maturity stage. However, there have been some instances of the owners of a business in the growth stage availing of this valuable CGT relief.

9.2 The Relief

Section 598 of the Taxes Consolidation Act 1997 (TCA 1997) provides relief from the charge to CGT on the disposal made by individuals, who have reached 55 years or older, of certain business assets (qualifying assets) which have been owned by that individual for the qualifying period. Section 599 TCA 1997 provides a similar but more generous relief where the disposal is made to a child of the individual. Thus, the extent of the relief varies depending on the age of the individual and the consideration/value of the assets being disposed of.

Retirement Relief can be relevant in the case of a disposal of an asset or the gift of an asset. In the case of a gift to a connected party, the disponer is deemed to have made a disposal at the market value of the asset, i.e. even though the individual has gifted rather than sold their business, from a CGT perspective they are deemed to have sold their business at market value for the purpose of calculating their CGT liability.

The legislation relating to Retirement Relief is relatively complex, with many qualifying conditions and exclusions. Thus, the relief requires careful consideration when applying it to the facts of a particular case to ensure that it is appropriately applied. It is discussed here at a relatively high level as an introduction to the main issues; for more detailed analysis, the reader is referred to Chapter 3 of *Capital Gains Tax: A Practitioner's Guide* by Mark Doyle, which covers the topic in a more exhaustive manner.[1]

9.2.1 Retirement

Retirement Relief from CGT is designed to facilitate the efficient passing on of a business as a going concern through a gift/sale to the next generation, or through a sale to a third party when the business owner is in the twilight of their career. However, the term 'Retirement Relief' is somewhat misleading in that the legislation does not require the individual to actually retire from the business. For example, it is common for parents who are the owners of a business to pass the business on to their children while maintaining a sometimes significant role in the business.

---

[1] Mark Doyle, *Capital Gains Tax: A Practitioner's Guide*, 2nd Edition (Chartered Accountants Ireland, 2016).

9.2.2 Age Criteria

Until changes introduced by Finance Act 2012, as long as an individual was 55 years or older and various criteria (see **Section 9.2.5**) were met, the full provisions of Retirement Relief outlined below were applicable. The two key considerations were:

1. if the disposal was to a third party or to a child; and
2. if the disposal was to a third party, did the proceeds from the sale (on its own or together with other qualifying disposals by the seller) exceed the seller's lifetime limit?

In an attempt to encourage business owners to pass on their businesses at an earlier age, an upper age limit for availing of Retirement Relief was introduced; for anyone above this age limit, the benefits of Retirement Relief for the seller/disponer of qualifying assets were reduced. The new upper age limit was 66 years. Thus, in addition to considerations outlined in points 1 and 2 above, it is now also important to ascertain whether the seller/disponer is in the age category 55 to 66 years, in which case the full benefits of Retirement Relief are available. Conversely, if they are aged over 66 years, they can avail of reduced benefits only.

9.2.3 Disposal to Third Parties

Where there is a disposal of qualifying business assets to a third party, there are two lifetime limits available to the individual seller, depending on the age category into which they fall, as outlined below:

Age of individual making the disposal	Lifetime limit
55–66 years	€750,000
Over 66 years	€500,000

Therefore, where an individual is aged between 55 and 66 years, they can sell their qualifying business assets for up to €750,000 without the charge to CGT arising. If the proceeds exceed €750,000, marginal relief may be available. (Marginal relief allows some relief from CGT liability, but on a marginal basis, i.e. the individual does not get full relief from all of the CGT liability.) If the individual is aged over 66 years, the maximum amount they can receive without incurring a CGT liability is €500,000, with marginal relief available on proceeds above €500,000.

The above limits of €500,000 and €750,000 are cumulative lifetime limits, meaning that all disposals by an individual that qualify for Retirement Relief must be aggregated together when considering if the limit has been breached (see **Example 9.1** below).

EXAMPLE 9.1: RETIREMENT RELIEF LIFETIME LIMITS

Martin is aged 55 years and owns a business designing and manufacturing bespoke machinery for the medical devices sector. He founded the business 15 years ago. In the past three years he has also started a software development business. A third party wishes to buy the bespoke machinery business for €500,000. Martin sees this as an excellent opportunity to realise value from his established business and allow him to focus on developing his new software business.

As Martin is aged 55 years, but less than 66 years, and as the proceeds from the disposal of the qualifying business assets are less than €750,000, he can avail of Retirement Relief such that no CGT should be payable on the disposal of the assets.

...

Some 10 years later, Martin (now aged 65 years) has been successful in building his software business. He now wishes to retire, and he has received an offer of €600,000 for the software business. He is eligible for Retirement Relief and, as he is still in the 55–66 years age group, the €750,000 limit applies. However, as this is a lifetime limit, we need to aggregate the value of the two transactions. Specifically, due to the constraints of cumulative lifetime limits, Martin must calculate the current disposal on a cumulative basis with the prior transaction, i.e. consideration is deemed to be €1,100,000 (€500,000 + €600,000). Normal CGT rules, including the application of Retirement Relief, apply to the recalculated gain. Given the amounts in this example, marginal relief may apply to the recalculated gain (see below).

As discussed above, where the relevant limits of €500,000 and €750,000 respectively are exceeded, marginal relief may apply. As a result, this may limit the CGT payable to 50% of the excess of the sale proceeds over the relevant applicable limits. The following example illustrates how marginal Retirement Relief applies.

EXAMPLE 9.2: MARGINAL RETIREMENT RELIEF ON
DISPOSAL TO A THIRD PARTY

Mary has been running a successful software development company for the last 20 years. She purchased the company for €100,000 in 1998. Mary has recently turned 68 and has decided to sell the company in order to spend more time with her grandchildren. She has received an offer of €720,000 for her company. As Mary is over 66 and meets the qualifying criteria for Retirement Relief, and as the sale is to a third party, and the proceeds are over €500,000, she may qualify for marginal relief on the sale.

The marginal relief caps any CGT liability at 50% of the difference between proceeds and the relevant limit.

	€
Proceeds from sale	720,000
Original cost	100,000
Capital gain	620,000
Taxable at 33%	204,600

Difference between proceeds and relevant limit

(€720,000 – €500,000 = €220,000)

CGT cap for retirement relief

(€220,000 × 50%= €110,000)

Therefore, as Mary qualifies for marginal retirement relief, her CGT bill is reduced from €204,600 to €110,000 as a result of the marginal relief.

9.2.4 Disposal within a Family

More generous Retirement Relief provisions are included in section 599 TCA 1997, where an individual disposes of the assets by way of sale or gift to a 'child'. These provisions were introduced to encourage entrepreneurs to bring the next generation into their businesses. Like section 599 TCA 1997, the same age bands, i.e. 55–66 years and 66+ years, were introduced in Finance Act 2012 to encourage business owners to pass on the business at an earlier age to the next generation.

9.2.4.1 Child

For the purposes of section 599 TCA 1997, the definition of 'child'[2] includes a son or daughter of the individual making the disposal, but is also extended to cover the following individuals:

1. a child of a deceased child, i.e. a grandchild of the individual where the grandchild's parent is deceased;
2. a nephew or niece who has worked substantially on a full-time basis in the business for a period of five years ending with the disposal;
3. a minor who lived with and was under the care of the individual for at least five years;
4. children and potential grandchildren of civil partners.

9.2.4.2 Limits

Before the age categories were introduced in Finance Act 2012, where qualifying assets were transferred to a child, the full proceeds (or market

---

[2] The definition of 'child' for the purposes of the Taxes Act includes adopted children.

value, where the disposal was by way of gift or transaction that was not an arm's length transaction) were without limit exempt from CGT. However, following the changes introduced by Finance Act 2012, the position may be summarised as follows:

Age of individual making the disposal	Lifetime Limit
55–66 years	Unlimited
Aged over 66 years	€3 million

The following example illustrates how the age of the individual can affect the lifetime limits available.

EXAMPLE 9.3: LIFETIME LIMITS ON GIFTING A BUSINESS
TO CHILDREN

Bernard is aged 59 years and has a generic pharmaceuticals business, which he has owned and managed for the past 25 years. He now wishes to gift this business equally to his two sons, Dermot and Barry. The business is worth €20 million and Bernard has no base cost in the business because he developed it without any acquisitions. As the transfer of the business is to related parties (i.e. Bernard's children), the actual consideration is ignored for CGT purposes and instead the market value of the assets transferring is deemed to be the consideration received by Bernard. Thus, in the first instance Bernard has a chargeable gain of circa €12 million. However, assuming all Retirement Relief criteria are met, Bernard can entirely avoid any CGT liability on the chargeable gain.

Contrast this with the situation that would arise if Bernard was already aged over 66 years. In this instance, he would only be able to avoid CGT on the first €3 million of the chargeable gain, with the balance of €9 million liable to CGT at a rate of 33%.

9.2.4.3 Clawback

The Retirement Relief legislation provides a number of conditions that must be continued to be met for a number of years after the transfer. If these conditions are not met, the relief claimed is withdrawn or 'clawed back'. Where relief is granted to the individual under section 599 TCA 1997, and the child sells the assets that were subject to the relief within a period of six years from receipt by them of the assets, the CGT that would have applied to the individual who disposed of the asset to the child will be assessed and charged to the child in addition to any CGT accruing to the child on the child's disposal of those assets.

9.2.5 Qualifying Criteria

In order to avail of Retirement Relief as outlined above, a number of qualifying criteria must be met. First, the assets being disposed of must be 'chargeable business assets', i.e. assets used in a trade or shares in a trading company (see **Section 9.2.5.1** below). Secondly, under the criteria for qualifying assets, they must have been owned by the individual for at least 10 years (see **Section 9.2.5.2** below).

9.2.5.1 'Chargeable Business Asset'

As discussed above, the assets being disposed of must be what are regarded as 'chargeable business assets' for Retirement Relief to apply to the disposal. Section 598(1)(a) TCA 1997 provides the following important definition of a chargeable business asset:

"'chargeable business asset' means an asset (including goodwill but not including shares or securities or other assets held as investments) which is, or is an interest in, an asset used for the purposes of farming, or a trade, profession, office or employment, carried on by–
(i)   the individual,
(ii) the individual's family company, or
(iii) a company which is a member of a trading group of which the holding company is the individual's family company,

other than an asset on the disposal of which no gain accruing would be a chargeable gain."

In summary, chargeable business assets are assets used for the purpose of a trade by the individual or the individual's family company. They do not include assets held for investment purposes, e.g. premises held for rental purposes or shares as a portfolio investment.

For the purpose of the above definition, a company is deemed a family company of the individual if that individual has the power to exercise 25% of the voting rights, or at least 10% of the voting rights where not less than 75% of the voting rights are held by close family members.

9.2.5.2 Qualifying Assets

Once a chargeable business asset is identified, it is necessary to assess whether the chargeable business asset is regarded as a qualifying asset for the purposes of Retirement Relief. A qualifying asset includes the following:
1. chargeable business assets (apart from tangible moveable property) which have been owned for at least 10 years by the individual, and which have been chargeable business assets throughout the 10-year period ending on the date of disposal;

2. shares in a trading company or a company that is a member of a trading group which has been owned by the individual for not less than 10 years and where the individual has been a full-time working director of the relevant company for a period of not less than five years in that 10-year period;

3. land, machinery or plant which the individual has owned for not less than 10 years, but which was used by the individual's relevant company in its trade and which is disposed of by the individual to the same person at the same time as the disposal of the shares in the relevant company.

9.3 Tax Avoidance

Both sections 598 and 599 TCA 1997 provide standard provisions that deny Retirement Relief where it is not shown that the disposal of the qualifying assets was made for a bona fide commercial reason and did not form part of an arrangement or scheme, the main purpose of which was the avoidance of a liability to tax.

9.4 Interactions with Other Reliefs

9.4.1 Corporate Tax Reliefs

Retirement Relief is a CGT relief for the shareholder of a company, as opposed to a relief for the company itself. Therefore, various corporate tax reliefs such as the R&D Tax Credit (see **Chapter 3**), the Knowledge Development Box (see **Chapter 5**) and the specified intangible asset allowances (see **Chapter 6**), etc., are not affected by Retirement Relief.

9.4.2 Revised Entrepreneur Relief

As discussed in **Chapter 8**, Revised Entrepreneur Relief ('Entrepreneur Relief') is a lower rate of tax on any qualifying chargeable gain up to a lifetime limit of €1 million. Retirement Relief is a relief from CGT on any chargeable gain. Therefore, if a disposal qualifies for both reliefs, the Entrepreneur Relief lifetime limit could be used up on a transaction that would not have attracted a CGT tax liability in any event. In the following example we see how these two reliefs can overlap.[3]

---

[3] At the time of writing, this is a matter upon which clarity has been sought from Revenue by tax practitioners as it does not seem appropriate that the Entrepreneur Relief lifetime limit would be consumed by a chargeable gain that is not subject to tax.

EXAMPLE 9.4: ENTREPRENEUR RELIEF AND RETIREMENT RELIEF
APPLYING TO THE SAME TRANSACTION

John is aged 56 years and gifts his business, which is worth €2 million,
to his two sons, Daniel and Oran. John qualifies for both Entrepreneur
Relief and Retirement Relief on the transaction. His CGT calculation would be as follows:

Deemed proceeds	€2,000,000
Base cost	€–
Chargeable gain	€2,000,000
Annual exemption	€1,270
	€1,998,730
Tax	
Entrepreneur Relief	
€1,000,000 at 10%	€100,000
Balance at 33%	€329,581
CGT	€429,581
Retirement Relief	€429,581
CGT liability	€–

If John had not qualified for Entrepreneur Relief on the above
transaction, he would still have had a nil CGT liability by virtue of
Retirement Relief. If he starts a new business and holds it for the
required three years, he may qualify for Entrepreneur Relief, but
will not qualify for Retirement Relief, as he has not held the
assets for 10 years. However, because he has used his full lifetime
limit on the first transaction, he will not benefit from the
Entrepreneur Relief on this second transaction.

9.4.3 Capital Acquisition Tax Planning

Where the chargeable business assets are being disposed of by way of gift,
there are a number of capital acquisition tax (CAT) reliefs that should be
considered in order to help the recipient of the gift reduce their CAT liability. In particular, Business Asset Relief and Same Event Relief should be
considered.

9.5 Conclusion

Retirement Relief is usually used by business owners towards the end
of their business career when they exit a successful business that has

been operating for at least 10 years. The relief can provide significant benefit to a business owner who is aged over 55 years and is selling their business or passing it on to the next generation. It provides significant CGT reliefs on chargeable gains on the disposal or transfer. It is important for business owners to be aware of the various lifetime limits and age categories that apply to ensure that they get maximum possible benefit.

This chapter brings Part I of this book to a close, and our discussion of the tax incentives and reliefs that are available to innovative companies and their owners/investors. The focus of the book in Part II now turns to the funding of innovation and we will explore the various funding options available to companies (particular SMEs) in Ireland.

As a reminder of its key features and requirements, we include below an 'At a Glance' summary of Retirement Relief as outlined in this chapter.

AT A GLANCE: RETIREMENT RELIEF

What is the relief?	Retirement Relief is a CGT relief available to the owners of a business following the disposal or gift of certain business assets and shares in a case where the seller is aged over 55 years and where the business has been owned for a period of 10 years.
Interactions with other reliefs:	• Retirement Relief is an owner, as opposed to a corporate, tax relief and therefore does not change the corporate tax relief as discussed in **Section 9.4.1.** • Entrepreneur Relief is a lower rate of tax on chargeable gains. Retirement Relief is a relief from any CGT liability arising on any chargeable gains. Therefore, the benefits of both will not accrue to the same transaction.

PART II

SOURCES OF FUNDING FOR INNOVATION AND GROWTH

Business innovation is the main driver of both long-term business and economic growth. The accumulation of idle capital cannot continuously sustain growth unless new and improved products and services are developed and launched. The innovation of Ireland's small and medium-sized enterprises (SMEs) in new product/service development, and their expansion into new markets, are crucial catalysts of both existing and projected national growth.

As businesses grow from small to medium to large enterprises, their need for funding increases. Funding will be required to achieve the business's objectives, be it to innovate and improve products/services, enter new markets, hire or contract additional staff, expand facilities, or purchase new equipment and machinery. Raising funding for growth depends on a number of factors including, for example:
- the track record of the business and its owners;
- the objectives of the business;
- the current financial health of the business;
- the business ownership structure;
- the ability and track record of the owner/management team to plan; and
- the owner/management team's ability to convince investors/lenders to believe in them and their vision for the business.

The financing of a business, whatever its size or stage of development, is one of the most fundamental aspects of its management. Getting the financing right, in terms of both its quantum and type, will help achieve a healthy business, positive cash flows and, ultimately, a profitable and growing enterprise. Financing is required at all stages of a business's development. On commencement, start-up funding is required and as the business grows it will require finance to expand. The quantum and type of funding will vary, depending on the industry sector, growth opportunities, and the owner's appetite for and view of the various funding sources.

As all businesses, and more importantly their owners, are different, there is no 'one-size-fits-all' funding solution. Many businesses may be in the same sector, but their funding journey and sources will be very different. The objective of Part II is to provide SME owners, management and their advisors with an extensive outline of the possible sources of funding, including:
- equity finance;
- debt finance;
- government funding supports; and
- alternative lending sources.

Each source of funding is discussed in detail to assist the reader in considering and assessing if it is suitable for their business and, importantly, its growth. Finally, Chapter 15 explores the ideal funding mix between debt and equity funding and includes feedback and practical advice from an SME founder, a banker and a later-stage funder.

CHAPTER 10

THE CHANGING LANDSCAPE OF SME FUNDING IN IRELAND

10.1 Background

The European Union and the United States may not always see eye to eye on matters of trade and commerce, but there is one matter on which they are in complete agreement: both the European Commission and the Office of the United States Trade Representative see small and medium-sized enterprises (SMEs) as the backbone of their respective economies. In the US, a vibrant 30 million-strong SME sector has, according to the US trade office, accounted for almost two-thirds of new private-sector jobs in recent decades. The European Commission paints an even more vibrant picture: SMEs account for 99% of all businesses active in the EU, two-thirds of total private-sector employment and, since 2012, up to 85% of new jobs. Move to a more global or a more local level and the story is repeated. According to the International Trade Centre, SMEs represent 95% of global business and 60% of private-sector jobs, while in Ireland, the dominance of SMEs could hardly be more striking: according to the Central Statistics Office (CSO) SMEs represent no less than 99.8% of businesses active in the Republic. Figures from 2014 show a total of 238,000 businesses employing more than 1.3 million workers, or almost half of the entire (public and private) workforce. Of these, over 90% work in companies with less than 10 employees.

Also strikingly consistent at home and abroad is the high value assigned to SMEs as pathfinders of growth and development. SMEs are seen not just as enmeshed in the economic fabric of their communities but as in the driving seat of their economic futures. Words and phrases such as 'innovative', 'dynamic' and 'engines of growth' are routinely used to laud the SME sector. The European Commission shares the language of many national and international organisations when it describes "SMEs and entrepreneurship as key to ensuring economic growth, innovation, job creation and social integration".[1] Of national interest in this regard was a 2016 survey by the Commission, which found that Irish SMEs ranked as the best in innovation across the EU and beyond.[2] The Commission found Ireland's success in this regard was linked to its ability to "introduce more innovative products and generate more new jobs in fast-growing young companies".

---

[1] Refer to the website of the European Commission, "Growth" section: "Entrepreneurship and Small and medium-sized enterprises (SMEs)". See https://ec.europa.eu/growth/smes_en

[2] European Commission, The European Innovation Scoreboard 2016. Available at https://publications.europa.eu/en/publication-detail/-/publication/6e1bc53d-de12-11e6-ad7c-01aa75ed71a1/language-en#

The prominence of innovation and entrepreneurship as attributes of the SME sector can, in part at least, be linked to the emergence of high-potential technology startups in recent years. Typically driven by developments in ICT or software, or more recently, social media opportunities, these enterprises often contrast with SMEs in other sectors in a number of important respects. Whereas more 'traditional', often family-owned businesses, tend towards stable and steady models of growth, employment and revenue, these innovation-oriented SMEs more often involve a coming-together of like-minded professionals with a view to *disrupt* or *transform* existing customer behaviours, in many cases with the intent of rapidly scaling up the business on the strength of this.

In general, SMEs, particularly those in the ICT and software sectors, tend to differ from businesses in other sectors in their approach to funding. An inherent focus on fast growth and scaling up can also mean that, in many cases, these enterprises see their SME status as transitory, with business models geared towards international and even global expansion, whether as stand-alone entities or through merger and acquisition.

With this in mind, it may be useful to define what an SME is. The European Commission provides the following widely accepted definition, in which enterprises are classified according to their size (revenues and net assets) as well as the number of employees employed by the enterprise:[3]

- a '**micro enterprise**' is an enterprise that has fewer than 10 employees and has either an annual turnover and/or an annual balance sheet not exceeding €2 million;
- a '**small enterprise**' is an enterprise that has fewer than 50 employees and has either an annual turnover and/or an annual balance sheet total not exceeding €10 million;
- a '**medium enterprise**' has fewer than 250 employees and an annual turnover below €50 million or a balance sheet below €43 million;
- a '**large enterprise**' has greater than 250 employees and an annual turnover above €50 million or a balance sheet total above €43 million.

Having noted a conceptual difference between dynamic startups and more traditional SMEs, it would also be useful to gain a sense of what kinds of companies currently constitute the SME sector in Ireland. According to CSO data from 2014:[4]

- service providers, representing everything from law and accountancy firms to hospitality, food service, publishing, transport and telecoms companies, represent more than half (51.8%) of active businesses in Ireland;
- distribution, a sector that includes retail, wholesale and vehicle sales, represents 19.1% of active businesses;
- construction accounts for 19.9% of active enterprises;

---

[3] See http://ec.europa.eu/growth/smes/business-friendly-environment/sme-definition_en

[4] Available at https://www.cso.ie/en/releasesandpublications/ep/p-bii/bii2014/sme/

- general industry, including manufacturing, accounts for 6.9% of businesses; and
- financial services represent 2.8% of active businesses.

10.2 A Decade of Challenge

For all that they predominate in and contribute to our economy, and for all the plaudits they receive for innovation and dynamism, the SME sector has been through a difficult time over the last decade. The most explicit evidence of this comes from the CSO, whose data shows that, between 2008 and 2012 – arguably the depth of the recession – 15% of Irish enterprises went out of business, as the number of active businesses dropped from 216,265 in 2008 to 185,530 in 2012. While there has certainly been recovery since then – **Table 10.1** contrasts the improved situation that prevailed just two years later, in 2014 – there is a real sense that the SME sector continues to function in the shadow of the 2008 financial crisis and the recession that followed.

TABLE 10.1: SMEs ACTIVE IN IRELAND IN 2008 AND 2014[5]

	2008	2014	Increase/(Decrease)
Micro enterprises	222,030	219,888	(2,142)
Employees	425,018	373,342	(51,676)
Small enterprises	18,620	15,213	(3,407)
Employees	357,880	291,714	(66,166)
Medium enterprises	3,020	2,634	(386)
Employees	292,297	254,928	(37,369)
Large enterprises	525	514	(11)
Employees	436,725	414,307	(22,418)

While turmoil in the European and world banking systems set the framework for the crisis, over-reliance on the property sector in the Irish economy provided a particularly acute set of local circumstances, leading ultimately to the bailout and 'Troika' (the International Monetary Fund, European Central Bank (ECB) and European Commission) intervention in Irish public finances. The immediate post-2008 period will long be remembered as a time when consumer and business confidence plummeted, and financial projections that were once considered worst-case scenarios suddenly appeared wildly optimistic. In meeting a sudden and challenging change in circumstances, the natural response for many companies, large or small, was a

---

[5] Central Statistics Office, Business Demography NACE Rev 2 by Employment Size, County, Year and Statistic. Available at http://www.cso.ie/px/pxeirestat/Statire/SelectVarVal/Define.asp?maintable=BRA08&PLanguage=0

curtailment of costs and cash outflows. Wages and salaries – the biggest and most easily flexed overhead – were trimmed, and this, combined with heavy job losses in some sectors, only served to exacerbate the sense of a widespread loss of economic confidence.

Ireland's economic downturn affected, to some extent, virtually all sectors and organisations within the State, both public and private, so it is worth noting a particular set of structural issues that served to make SMEs more vulnerable. These also provide the context for the changed funding landscape that, as we shall see, has gradually evolved in Ireland over the last decade.

- For companies that were already small, downsizing options were limited.
- Being generally less diversified meant less opportunities to strategically recast economic activities.
- Lower capitalisation meant an inherently weaker financial structure.
- Cultural issues hampered the search for alternative finance when traditional routes closed off.
- Overleveraging on property assets created an unsustainable debt overhang for many.
- Startups in particular were likely to have had lower or indeed no credit rating, and so fewer financing options.
- Enterprises at early stages were likely to be heavily dependent on credit.

These were some of the structural challenges that confronted SMEs as they faced into a difficult trading environment. However, it requires no great research into the sector or deep knowledge of the experiences of its owner–managers to know that, for many, this challenge of survival could be crystalized into one single issue: **access to credit**. A sample of reports and findings from different organisations highlights the extent of the difficulties encountered in this regard:

- a 2012 survey by the Irish Small and Medium Enterprises Association (ISME) found that 50% of SMEs that had applied for funding had their loans refused by their banks[6];
- a 2012 report from the Central Bank found Irish SMEs faced a tougher challenge in accessing credit than any other eurozone country aside from Greece[7]; and
- a 2014 European Commission/ECB survey found that 23% of Irish SMEs saw access to finance as their biggest concern, compared to the eurozone average of 14%.[8]

Of course, access to funding was not an issue unique to Ireland. The European Commission has noted that "access to finance is the most

---

[6] See https://www.rte.ie/news/business/2011/1212/309762-isme/ (accessed April 2018).
[7] See https://centralbank.ie/docs/default-source/publications/economic-letters/economic-letter–vol-2012-no-8.pdf (accessed April 2018).
[8] See https://www.ecb.europa.eu/pub/pdf/other/accesstofinancesmallmedi-umsizedenterprises201404en.pdf (accessed May 2018).

pressing issue for many small enterprises",[9] while the World Bank has stated "access to finance is a key constraint to SME growth".[10] Addressing the annual conference of ISME in 2016, the Governor of the Central Bank of Ireland, Philip Lane, pointed out that:

"Even in good times, SMEs face a tougher financing environment compared to larger corporates, due to higher investment risks and limited firm-level information available to providers of debt and equity finance."[11]

10.3 Over-reliance on Bank Credit

There can be little doubt that the challenge for Irish SMEs was particularly severe and compounded by a major over-reliance on one source of funding: bank credit. A 2014 Oireachtas report found that the level of finance for SMEs in the Irish market coming from banks was well over 90%, a situation it described as "significantly higher than the European norm".[12] As recently as early 2017, ISME noted that banks remain the core lending source for Irish SMEs, with up to 70% of Irish businesses relying on banks for finance, a situation it contrasts with 30% for the rest of Europe.[13]

For Irish SMEs then, the downturn brought both a painful realisation and a double-pronged challenge: bank-sourced funding, the mainstay of its credit needs, was most needed just at the juncture when the banking sector entered its greatest period of dysfunction. This was an environment in which there were not only few alternatives in the market but, in many cases, little understanding of what those alternatives would look like.

To understand why Irish SMEs view their funding requirements as beginning and ending with a trip to the bank requires a deeper analysis of Irish culture and history than is possible here. Suffice it to say that, between the establishment of a country-wide banking system in the late 19th Century

9   See https://ec.europa.eu/growth/smes_en (accessed April 2018).

10 See https://openknowledge.worldbank.org/handle/10986/12515?show=full (accessed April 2018).

11 "Address by Philip R. Lane, Governor of the Central Bank of Ireland, at the Irish Small and Medium Enterprises Association Annual Conference 2016, Royal Dublin Society", press release 11 November 2016. Available at https://www.centralbank.ie/news/article/address-by-philip-r.-lane-governor-of-the-central-bank-of-ireland-at-the-irish-small-and-medium-enterprises-association-annual-conference-2016-royal-dublin-society (accessed April 2018).

12 Joint Committee on Jobs, Enterprise and Innovation, Houses of the Oireachtas, *Report on Access to Finance for Small and Medium Enterprises (SMEs)*, 16 July 2014. Available at https://webarchive.oireachtas.ie/parliament/media/committees/jobsenterpriseandinnovation/access-to-finance-for-smes-with-links-15-july.pdf (accessed August 2018).

13 ISME Quarterly Bank Watch Survey (Q1) 2017, statement by ISME CEO Neil McDonnell in accompanying press release: https://www.isme.ie/assets/170308-bank-watch-pr-3.pdf (accessed April 2018).

and the emergence of the 'Celtic Tiger' in the 1990s, hard-won bank finance was, by and large, deemed the only credible source of formal funding to businesses. The Celtic Tiger period brought with it a transformation in the availability of credit, but this only served to reinforce the predominance of banks as the natural 'go to' option, whatever the scale and nature of the credit requirement. Post-2008, the impact of the banking and liquidity crisis was deeply and widely felt, as much by banks themselves as their debtors. Banks found their balance sheets compromised by large-scale, non-performing toxic debts and their efforts to correct course saw both personal and corporate borrowers brought under unprecedented scrutiny. Banks were typically more focused on scrutinising existing loans to identify and manage possible impairments. This was the context in which SMEs, dealing with their own cash-flow issues, found increases in their bank credit facilities often impossible to secure.

In a time of much stress for all parties, SMEs often found that their fortunes were tied not just to the debts on their balance sheets but to the particular funding provider to whom those debts were tethered. There is a good deal of anecdotal evidence to suggest that the level of lending, forbearance, support or otherwise received by SMEs very much depended on which bank they were associated with. Added to this was the fact that, in the process of addressing their own balance sheet turmoil, a number of international banks made the decision to exit Ireland, a situation further complicating the experience of borrowers here.

The economic recovery and the restructuring of the banking sector seen in the last few years have certainly created a sense in which we have 'turned the corner'. With this has come, in theory at least, a steady improvement in overall credit availability to Irish businesses. Surprisingly, however, and despite any obvious transformation in thinking by SME owner–managers with regard to funding, there appears to be a distinct cooling off in the relationship between business owner–managers and their corporate financing service providers. Illustrative of this is a 2016 Central Bank survey that points to commercial banks experiencing significant declines in company applications for traditional banking credit.[14] The Central Bank's *SME Market Report* for H1 2016 notes that, in spite of sustained economic recovery, standard commercial loans applications by SMEs of all sizes have declined steadily since 2013, with a drop of 4% recorded between March 2015 and October 2016. Meanwhile, across SMEs of all sizes, the median debt-to-turnover ratio declined from 5.5% in September 2015 to 4.5% in March 2016 (having reached a peak of 10% in March 2014). On an annual basis, total business debt was a significant 12.2% lower compared to the same period in 2015.

Considering the clamour for credit among SMEs since the beginning of the financial crisis, these are, on the face of it, unexpected figures and

---

[14] Central Bank of Ireland, SME Market Report, 2016 HI. Available at https://www.centralbank.ie/docs/default-source/publications/sme-market-reports/gns-5-10sme-market-report-2016h1.pdf?sfvrsn=8

have prompted much commentary and analysis. One interpretation is that, despite strong headline figures pointing to a marked improvement in Ireland's economy, confidence amongst Irish SMEs remains far removed from pre-recessions levels. Business owner–managers who have survived the last number of years continue to look cautiously on highly leveraged balance sheets. Coupled with a sense of caution engendered by the political uncertainty in our closest and largest trading partners, this may explain why loan applications by Irish SMEs are considerably lower than our European neighbours.[15]

Plausible as it is, this explanation is not accepted by everyone. In late 2016, ISME wrote to Ireland's then Minister for Finance, Michael Noonan, and the Central Bank to raise concerns over a bank allegedly seeking signed, undated letters of resignation as collateral for business loans. ISME has long argued that aggressive and intimidatory practices are commonplace in the Irish banking system (arguments which the banks, it should be noted, consistently refute). However, perception is, in many cases, reality, and it would certainly be understandable if risk-averse SME owners/managers were reluctant to engage with banks in what they feel is an unfriendly environment.

The most likely explanation for the decline is a simple cost–benefit analysis of the value of Irish commercial loans. Despite the ECB's massive ongoing stimulus programme, the Irish retail banking environment has seen largely unchanged interest rates since the recession. The average interest rate for SMEs based on latest Central Bank data is 5.9%, which according to a 2015 H1 SME Central Bank Credit Demand Survey[16] is nearly 2% higher than the eurozone average and three times higher than the lowest rate available in Austria.[17]

Whether it is one or a combination of the reasons above, Irish SMEs have undoubtedly actively set out to reduce their dependence on bank borrowings even as Irish banks claim, with some credibility, to be opening the 'credit taps'. In 2014, for example, Bank of Ireland pledged it would make €12 billion available to SMEs over the following five years and the rejection rates for SME loan applications in Ireland almost halved between September 2015 and March 2016. In this context, it can only seem remarkable that 70% of SMEs that, when asked in a Red C Credit Demand Survey conducted in November 2014 to state their main reason for not applying for bank finance in the past six months, gave the response that they simply did not require it![18]

---

[15] Central Bank of Ireland, SME Market Report, 2017 H1. Available at www. centralbank.ie

[16] See http://www.centralbank.ie/docs/default-source/publications/sme-market-reports/sme-market-report-2015h1.pdf?sfvrsn=4

[17] It could be pointed out that this average rate applies to loans of up to €250,000 with rates falling to 2.4% for loans between €250,000 and €1 million. This, however, remains above the EU average.

[18] See http://merrionstreet.ie/en/allaboutjobs/Features-Articles/7_trends_from_today_s_Credit_Demand_Survey.html

Before moving on from the fraught issue of the relationship between banks and SMEs, it is also worth taking note of some recent observations on the matter by the Credit Review Office. The Credit Review Office was established by the Government in 2010 to provide a simple and effective review process for SMEs refused credit from Irish banks. The 17th report from the Credit Review Office, covering the period 1 January to 30 June 2016, describes a generally favourable outlook and improving performance in the SME sector, with the caveat that many still have a way to go to return to full financial strength.[19] The Credit Review Office, however, takes the opportunity to highlight its concern with what it sees as the growing remoteness of the relationship with borrowers (by financial institutions) and increasing reliance on credit decision-making software. On the former, the Credit Review Office notes:

> "Current service models however do not fully recognise that SMEs do not behave in the same way as larger businesses and corporates. SMEs, particularly Micro and Small Businesses and some Farms which are not as financially sophisticated, and many have difficulty in presenting credit proposals which recognise all the boxes which need to be ticked in current banks' credit decisioning systems."[20]

On the issue of increased reliance on credit decision-making software, the Credit Review Office advises as follows:

> "Banks must avoid over use of algorithms and credit scores to commoditise all SME lending, and ensure that their Relationship Managers have a good knowledge of all the credit tools which are available to assist SMEs."[21]

10.4 Addressing the Funding Gap

Notwithstanding the relationship challenges that have impacted on the behaviours of SME business owners, it remains an indisputable fact that access to credit is a cornerstone of business growth and development. As the underlying trend of bank deleveraging and the strategic exits by international credit institutions continues, it also becomes increasingly undeniable that a funding gap is emerging, one which may be seen as both a challenge and an opportunity for SMEs.

One of the few upsides to the 2008 financial crisis for Irish SMEs was the strong light it shone on their historic over-reliance on banks, whether through overdrafts, term loans, lease finance or invoice discounting. An important consequence of this was the serious pressure it put on the Government to investigate the opportunity for, and ultimately support,

---

[19] John Trethowan, *Credit Review Office Seventeenth Report*. Available at www. creditreview.ie/publications/
[20] *Ibid.* p. 2.
[21] *Ibid.* p. 3.

alternative sources of finance. Recognising that SMEs are the heartbeat of the economy and that their recovery would play a vital role in badly needed employment growth, a number of important initiatives were undertaken to help improve the supply of credit to SMEs. Notable among these were the creation of:

- the Strategic Banking Corporation of Ireland (SBCI);
- the Ireland Strategic Investment Fund;
- the Seed and Venture Capital Scheme; and
- Microfinance Ireland.

The intention behind these initiatives was to increase competition in capital markets for Irish businesses and deliver lower-interest-rate alternatives, through both traditional and non-traditional channels.

Designed specifically to promote competition in the SME lending market and to reduce the cost of credit for SMEs, the SBCI began lending in March 2015. Funded by the European Investment Bank, KfW (the German government-owned development bank) and the Ireland Strategic Investment Fund, by the end of 2015 the SBCI had committed €751 million to the three main bank lenders and two non-bank lenders, Merrion Fleet Management and Finance Ireland.

The Ireland Strategic Investment Fund is the successor to the National Pensions Reserve Fund, an €8 billion sovereign development fund mandated to support economic activity and employment in Ireland.

Through Enterprise Ireland, the Government has made €175 million available via the Seed and Venture Capital Scheme, which, running from 2013 to 2018, is intended to stimulate job creation and support the funding requirements of young, innovative Irish companies.

Microfinance Ireland is a further government initiative that offers unsecured three-to-five-year term loans of up to €25,000 to micro enterprises.

Additional funding options in the form of equity financing were also introduced during 2013 and 2014, including initiatives such as the MML Capital (worth €125 million), the BDO Development Capital Fund (€75 million) and the Cardinal Carlyle Ireland Fund (€290 million). These typically provide equity funding of between €2 million and €50 million to mid-sized, export-oriented businesses.

Existing alternative funding opportunities, such as the Employment and Investment Incentive Scheme (EII Scheme – see **Chapter 2**) also came to renewed prominence. For two decades, the EII Scheme (originally the Business Expansion Scheme (BES)), has provided an important source of alternative funding for businesses in Ireland.

In this evolved environment, a list of the potential sources of finance for Irish SMEs could now reasonably be said to include:
1. equity funding;
2. bank funding;

3. non-bank funding;
4. government funding and supports; and
5. alternative funding options, including, for example, crowdfunding.

10.5 The Irish Equity Conundrum

As noted earlier, and more recent frustrations notwithstanding, the view that funding a company's growth should come through bank (and, in some instances, family and friends) funding rounds remains deeply entrenched in the traditional SME mindset, as is the view that equity should only be conceded as a last resort.

For SMEs that view themselves as family businesses, funding that relinquishes equity is often seen as hugely problematic. Many Irish business owners see giving up equity in return for investment as akin to selling their family's birthright. When probed about the issue, some will link it to a feeling that it represents a failure of sorts: "You're taking in an investor – why can't you do it yourself?" In many cases, only the absolute refusal of the bank to fund what are perceived as traditionally solid proposals will succeed in changing business owners' mindsets.

There are consequences to such entrenched views. Where traditional bank finance options such as loans and overdrafts are the preferred choice for Irish entrepreneurs, the end result can often be ownership of 100% of a struggling business rather than 50% of a growing one. A simple analogy can help clarify the equity conundrum to many Irish business owners: would you prefer to own 100% of a local business or 50% of a large business with international locations?

As noted at the start of this chapter, this negative view of equity is prevalent throughout the Irish SME community across almost all industry sectors, with one notable exception: the ICT, software and social media sectors. These, in sharp contrast, have a tradition not only of openness but in fact an expectation with regard to giving equity in return for funding. This approach may reflect the distinctive ownership and growth journey of ICT companies, as well as the global nature of this sector. Whatever the reason, within these companies there is a strong cultural expectation that raising equity funding in the early days of a company's lifecycle is part of its natural development process. Whereas the traditional SME view is that an equity-for-funding swap is a last-gasp 'nuclear' option, the prevailing view here is that holding on to 100% of equity may hold a company back. Limiting options to traditional bank funding is often seen as evidence of lack of vision rather than an expression of business acumen. Effectively, what technology entrepreneurs are saying by their actions is that they see it as far preferable to own a smaller piece of a large and lucrative pie than all of a small and unremarkable one.

For SME owners/managers looking seriously at what is best for their company, it is important to recognise that perceptions of an equity conundrum are culturally based and not held to the same extent in other sectors and, indeed, other business cultures. In the first instance, the very phrase 'giving up equity' should be recognised for the misnomer it is. Nothing is actually being given away in this process; instead, investment is being made into the company at a valuation that is agreed between the investor and the entrepreneur. In choosing an equity partner, an SME owner/manager is also not just looking for an injection of finance but the opportunity to move the company significantly along a growth journey.

It is also important to recognise that fundamental change has taken place in the Irish funding landscape, posing questions and presenting opportunities that can no longer be ignored. While many funding requirements will undoubtedly remain best suited to bank debt, the role of equity must now be viewed as far more potent.

It is important to be realistic when making such assertions, of course. There is little doubt that banks will remain predominant as the lenders of choice for Irish SMEs. However, it should also be clear that business owners who dismiss what they see as a relinquishing of equity before considering its value may be doing their business a disservice: for every business and concept there is a set window of opportunity, one that does not stay open indefinitely. Take the following example, which is based on a discussion one of the authors had in 2016 regarding a potential €10 million equity investment.

EXAMPLE 10.1: SEIZING MARKET OPPORTUNITIES
WITH EQUITY FUNDING

A CEO/CFO team in an Irish software company was, in mid-2016, actively seeking equity funding with a view to entering a new market through the acquisition of a complementary company. The expectation was that this would add significant customers and revenues to the Irish SME. After long and protracted negotiations, the team was eventually brought around to seeing the benefits of an equity investment. The process of due diligence commenced, only to terminate with the discovery that the acquisition opportunity was lost, having been acquired by a competitor in the meantime.

The lesson is that when an entrepreneur sees a growth opportunity, they must be ready to seize it. It will not be there indefinitely. The market, competitors and technologies are always moving forward and do not stand on niceties.

10.6 The New Context of Growth

The rebound of the Irish economy from the depths of a grinding recession is, in some respects, as remarkable as the economic collapse that preceded it. Ireland's economy continues to grow strongly, with GDP expansion of 7.2% recorded in 2017.[22] This, coupled with the fact that Ireland's economy continues to grow strongly, with expected nominal GDP growth of 5.7% in 2018,[23] and expected increases in consumption and investment by Irish consumers and businesses, has made for a positive outlook for the Irish economy. A further barometer of an improved trading environment for SMEs is the downward trend in insolvencies as reported by Vision-net.[24]

As a small, open economy, Ireland's recovery always runs the risk of being impacted by external factors and uncertainties such as Brexit and the continuing implications of the outcome of the 2016 US presidential election. However, the Q3 2016 quarterly bulletin from the Central Bank still takes a broadly favourable outlook for the Irish economy:

> "[R]relative to a no-Brexit baseline, projected Irish GDP growth has been revised down by 0.2 and 0.6 per cent in 2016 and 2017, respectively. On this basis … GDP is projected to grow by 4.9 per cent this year and by 3.6 per cent in 2017."[25]

Irish SMEs can look forward to participating in this period of renewed growth. Given, however, the evidence that suggests they remain averse to bank debt as potentially higher risk with high interest rates, the question of how open they are to the diversity of other options for credit and liquidity becomes an increasingly urgent one.

Now that Ireland's funding market is no longer cornered by the mainstream commercial banks, awareness must be generated among business owners and managers about the benefits of alternative sources of finance, like venture capital, as a viable means for expansion in a 21st-century funding landscape. **Figure 10.1** opposite shows the four main pillars of SME funding in Ireland, which are grouped according to whether they are equity, debt, government, or other sources of funding.

---

[22] See https://www.rte.ie/news/business/2018/0719/979760-cso-quarterly-national-accounts/

[23] See https://www.rte.ie/news/business/2018/0503/959996-ireland-gpd-growth-forecast/

[24] Vision-net, *Business Barometer - Annual Review 2017.* Available at https://www.vision-net.ie/news/2017-annual-review-report/ (accessed April 2018).

[25] Central Bank of Ireland, *Quarterly Bulletin* 03 (July 2016), p. 8.

FIGURE 10.1: SOURCES OF FINANCIAL AND NON-FINANCIAL SUPPORTS IN IRELAND

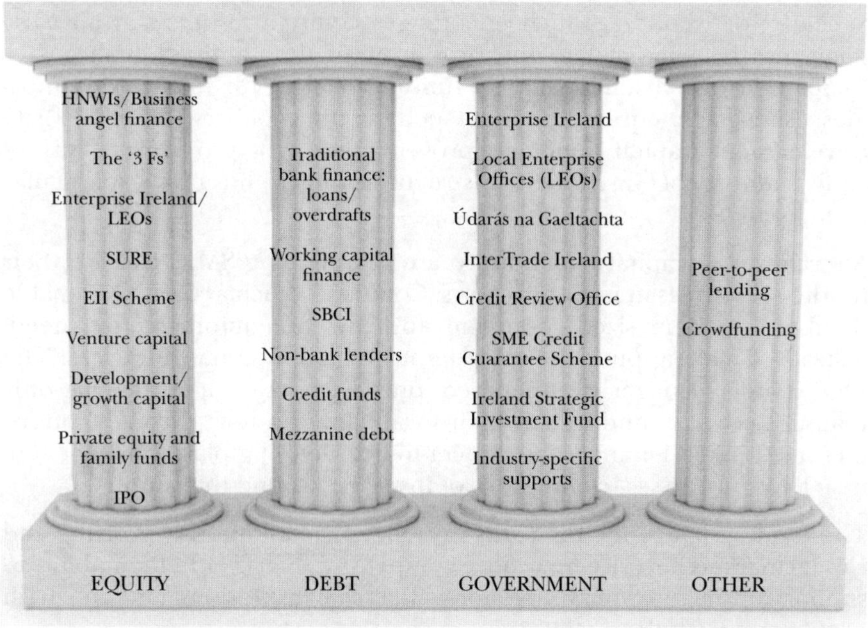

EQUITY	DEBT	GOVERNMENT	OTHER
HNWIs/Business angel finance	Traditional bank finance: loans/ overdrafts	Enterprise Ireland	Peer-to-peer lending
The '3 Fs'	Working capital finance	Local Enterprise Offices (LEOs)	Crowdfunding
Enterprise Ireland/ LEOs	SBCI	Údarás na Gaeltachta	
SURE	Non-bank lenders	InterTrade Ireland	
EII Scheme	Credit funds	Credit Review Office	
Venture capital	Mezzanine debt	SME Credit Guarantee Scheme	
Development/ growth capital		Ireland Strategic Investment Fund	
Private equity and family funds		Industry-specific supports	
IPO			

The chapters that follow will discuss in detail each of these 'funding pillars' available to an SME, what an investor looks for when considering an investment opportunity, how to get investor-ready, and the dos and don'ts of fundraising, as well as the views of an SME founder, banker and later-stage funder.

10.7 Conclusion

Traditionally, Irish business entrepreneurs, owners and managers operated in a business culture where taking on new lending took precedence over relinquishing business control in return for investment. The rise and success of the Irish ICT and software sector has convincingly challenged this norm. The question now must be whether SMEs in other sectors will look at the funding experiences of some of Ireland's most successful new businesses and recognise that these alternatives to bank funding not only work but can actively contribute to such success.

In making their assessment, SME owners/managers should recognise that the funding desert they have confronted over the last decade has given way to what might be seen as a flood of new opportunities: equity financing schemes and funds are now available to companies from the seed investment stage right through to later-stage growth/development capital.

These are not just emerging opportunities; they have an established track record of success. As detailed in **Chapter 1** and further covered in **Chapter 11**, the use of government tax policy in initiatives such as the EII Scheme, for example, which encourages equity investment at an early stage, has been crucial to the prosperity of thousands of Irish SMEs. **Chapter 11** also examines equity funding choices for mid-sized companies; later-stage equity funding such as that offered by the BDO Development Capital Fund has proven capable of providing a mix of equity and debt instruments, structured to a business's particular circumstances.

Alternatives to capital expenditure are also helping SMEs free up their funding resources in innovative ways. Companies such as GRENKE enable small and medium-sized companies to lease the equipment they need, instead of making purchases that tie up valuable capital resources. The SME owner/manager who believed, only a few years ago, that the only realistic access to funding was their local bank can now, through companies like Linked Finance, access peer-to-peer lending platforms that connect local businesses to a network of investors around the country.

The funding landscape for SMEs in Ireland is continuously evolving and capital markets here are now more competitive than ever in their ability to support business owners, investors, financial institutions and the Irish economy as a whole.

Irish SMEs can now plan for the future with a robust and diversified balance sheet funding base, an approach that will make them better able to withstand any future shocks and, equally important, avoid the risk that comes with being dependent on a single funder. This is an important consideration not just for individual SMEs but for Ireland's economy as a whole. A more diversified funding base means that the impact of any future recession on SMEs would be less pronounced, leading to potentially less economic damage and job losses as compared to the experience of the last decade.

Will this new array of innovative and flexible funding options persuade the mass of Irish SMEs to make a significant and historic shift? To be fair to the sector, we should acknowledge that changing mindsets is not simply a matter of changing habits. Results from the CSO's 2014 Access to Finance survey showed that 45% of SMEs decided to borrow from a bank with which they had an existing relationship, while 22% did so because the bank had a local branch presence.[26] Such relationships are hugely important in business and there are understandable reasons why entrepreneurs would prefer to build on existing options when the alternative seems a step into the unknown. That said, the business case for looking beyond the immediate should also be increasingly clear.

---

[26] See http://www.cso.ie/en/releasesandpublications/er/atf/accesstofinance2014/

CHAPTER 11

EQUITY CAPITAL (FUNDING PILLAR 1)

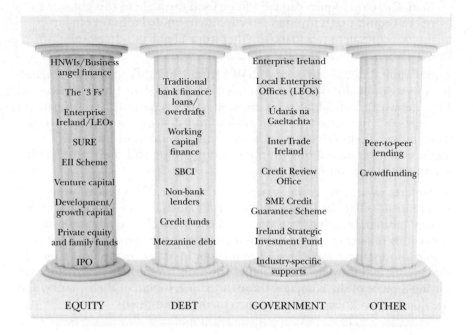

EQUITY	DEBT	GOVERNMENT	OTHER
HNWIs/Business angle finance	Traditional bank finance: loans/ overdrafts	Enterprise Ireland	
The '3 Fs'		Local Enterprise Offices (LEOs)	
Enterprise Ireland/LEOs		Údarás na Gaeltachta	
SURE	Working capital finance	InterTrade Ireland	Peer-to-peer lending
EII Scheme	SBCI	Credit Review Office	Crowdfunding
Venture capital			
Development/ growth capital	Non-bank lenders	SME Credit Guarantee Scheme	
Private equity and family funds	Credit funds	Ireland Strategic Investment Fund	
IPO	Mezzanine debt	Industry-specific supports	

11.1 Introduction

As shown in **Figure 10.1** towards the end of **Chapter 10** and above, equity capital is the first pillar of the SME funding landscape in Ireland. In fact, equity capital is the lifeblood of every business and company of whatever size and in whatever sector. Each business, from the smallest start-up enterprise to the largest Plc, requires equity capital in order to commence business, trade, acquire resources and grow. As the business grows and evolves, the equity capital requirement also evolves and changes, matching and reflecting the stage the company is at in its lifecycle.

Equity capital, at its simplest, is the funding invested in a business in return for an ownership stake. It is also known as the share capital or share ownership, a concept that is, of course, more important where the business has multiple owners and/or investors.

Equity capital typically enables a business to commence trading, obtain credit from suppliers, pay rent for its business premises and employ staff.

Equity capital is secured when its owners and/or a third-party investor buys a certain number of shares in a company in exchange for investing monetary capital in the company. This equity capital is unsecured and is the permanent capital in the company. In effect, by securing some of the share capital/share ownership in return for their cash, an investor gains the opportunity to share with the company's owners/founders the risks and rewards of the business's development.

> *Note:* The term 'equity capital' will be used throughout this chapter to refer to equity that is invested directly into unquoted private companies. It is not equivalent to a loan (whether from a bank or otherwise).

Equity capital can be invested in SMEs from a number of sources, including private individuals (be they friends or relatives of the business owners), high net-worth individuals who invest in SMEs as part of their investment strategy, and dedicated venture capital and development capital funds. The equity investment outlined below is in general terms; there would be slight variations depending on the investor profile and these are detailed separately in **Section 11.2.1** below.

Therefore, as 'equity' is the ownership that both the business owner and other investors have in a company, 'equity financing' is the process of raising money through bringing investors into the business. When a business owner uses equity financing, they are, from their perspective, giving part of the ownership interest in their business to an investor in return for cash to be used in developing and growing the business. Investors, from their perspective, are buying a piece of the company through the investment of their money, and are doing so in expectation of a return on their investment.

A company mainly grows and expands by selling more of its goods and services. In anticipation of future sales and expanding markets, it must purchase more materials, hire more staff, expand into new markets/territories, etc. Whatever its current selling success, a growing company is unlikely to be able to finance these resources through funds it already has. It will almost certainly require more funding (either in the form of equity capital or debt finance) to expand operations and ultimately generate more profits and cash. These profits will, in turn, support the business as well as reward the owners, the equity investors and/or the lenders through funding repayments.

We noted in **Chapter 10** that it is often neither possible nor desirable for business owners to get the capital required to trade and grow from borrowings or debt finance only. We also noted that, while there is cultural resistance in some sectors, there is a strong track record in the ICT and software sectors, in particular, of equity capital being utilised to not only accelerate growth, but to add credibility and inspire confidence among customers, suppliers, staff and other funders. In this chapter, we will look in greater detail at the different types of equity capital available and gain an understanding of how SMEs can engage in the process of securing equity finance. (For a definition of 'SME', see **Chapter 10**.)

At its simplest, there are two sources from which SMEs can obtain equity finance:

(a) **owners themselves**, providing their own capital in exchange for a share ownership in the business; and/or

(b) **external investors**, who can provide the business with start-up or expansion capital in return for a share ownership of the business.

In the evolution of many successful businesses, the equity funding will typically move from the first to the second of these, i.e. the business will commence through owner funding and expand through investor equity funding. An important consideration in this regard is timing. As a rule of thumb, it is better to delay raising equity capital from external investors (i.e. all investors excluding the original business founders) for as long as possible, allowing maximum time for the business concept to be proved and grow revenues, profitability and increase the value of the company. Before investing their own money, investors will naturally prefer that progress has been made in respect of implementing the business plan; they also generally seek evidence that the entrepreneurs/management team in which they are investing have aligned interests and have what is called 'skin in the game', i.e. the entrepreneurs have also invested and are backing their plan and idea from their own personal resources.

11.2 Unique Characteristics of Equity

Equity capital has a range of unique characteristics that distinguish it from other forms of SME funding and that are important to understand for those unfamiliar with the process of securing it. While equity capital brings with it the right of the investor to share in the success of the business in terms of its profits, as well as ownership, it is also important to be aware that it also brings with it the risk that, should the business fail, the equity invested will be lost and not repaid.

All businesses carry with them some level of risk and there is no guarantee that an enterprise will be successful. Arguably, the only thing close to certainty in business is that, without a sound business plan, adequate equity capital, management and planning, an enterprise will fail.

Understanding this risk, the owners/investors provide equity on the expectation that it will generate a significant return on the investment; for example, they will invest €100,000 on the expectation that, after a number of years, this will be worth, say, €300,000.

It is not surprising then that the majority of equity investors, whether the owners or external investors, exert considerable effort to manage this risk/return potential by having a say or influence in how the business is run and managed in order to mitigate the very real possibility of losing all of their investment through poor decisions. The expectations and requirements of the owners/equity investors can include:

• **A share in the profits** Equity investors expect businesses to generate a return on their investment in terms of profits, value and, ultimately, cash.

The expectation is that they will receive cash distributions or dividends in return for their investment and that, as the business grows and expands, its value increases resulting in an increase in the value of the share ownership.

- **Management participation** Equity investors may expect to participate in and/or contribute to the management of the business, or they may hire a management team with a proven track record to do it on their behalf. In smaller businesses, an owner may be the only manager, while in large businesses there may be several owners who may elect representatives to the board of directors to oversee the management of the business and protect their interests.
- **Share in sale proceeds** If the business is sold, the equity owners will share in the sale proceeds pro rata to the invested capital (or they may lose their investment if the business fails).

There are two important points, related to these expectations, which may not be immediately obvious:

1. The actual equity (as distinct from a percentage of equity) of a business owner increases when a business generates profits (or decreases in the case of losses). This is because, *ceteris paribus*, by generating profits a company increases the amount of its net assets (i.e. its assets less its liabilities). The corresponding increase (or decrease) is recorded in the owners' equity.
2. Once committed to a company, an equity investment is not easily liquidated into cash unless the company has a line-up of equity investors willing to buy the shares on offer. Depending on the performance of the company, it may be difficult to realise the investment in a short period of time. An equity investor, in other words, cannot 'cut and run' on a whim.

11.2.1 Types of Equity Shares

Equity in a company is recorded in its balance sheet and is represented by share capital plus, if applicable, share premium if the shares were issued at an amount above their par value (see **Section 11.2.2** below). It is typically referred to as the 'ordinary share capital' or 'owners' equity'. There may be different classes of shares reflecting different rights or entitlements attaching to each class of share. The rights and entitlements of each class of share in terms of voting, dividends and repayment of capital are set out in a company's constitution.

Having different classes of shares may seem to add an unnecessary layer of complexity to an emerging and growing business, but they can serve many useful purposes, including confining control of the company to certain individuals, offering shares with preferential dividend rights to encourage investment, or having different entitlements to the payment of surplus funds on the winding up of the company. The main categories of equity shares are as follows:

- **Ordinary shares/direct equity** This is a class of shares the founders of the business will hold and that will issue to new investors in the business in return of a percentage ownership, should the company fundraise with external investors in return for direct equity in the business.

- **Restricted/capped ordinary shares** These are, in most cases, a different class of ordinary share and their issue and existence can be differentiated from the ordinary shares by a letter, as in 'A' or 'B' ordinary shares. Typically, these shares can rank equally, i.e. *pari passu*, with the ordinary shares except for some key differentiators, which may be in terms of voting rights or return on capital. These can be the class of share that are issued when a company raises funds under the Employment and Investment Incentive Scheme (EII Scheme) (as discussed in detail in **Chapter 2**): such investments typically have a capped return and therefore do not share in the sale proceeds of a trade sale over and above the amount of the capped return.
- **Preference shares** These shares carry a preferential right to a fixed dividend and usually rank higher (i.e. have preference) than other share classes in the event of a winding up. The fixed rate of dividend is normally expressed as a percentage of the preference share nominal value and the dividend is normally cumulative, unless stated otherwise. This means that should a company fail to pay a dividend, it will accrue to the shareholder(s) and become payable on the next payment date. Preference shares typically do not carry voting rights, nor do they carry further rights to participate in profits beyond the applicable dividend rate. These dividend and other preference share rights are generally set out in the company's constitution. (Preference shares are typically used by Enterprise Ireland in its investment agreements.)
- **Redeemable shares** If a company's constitution permits it, a company may issue shares that can be redeemed by the company at their nominal value (or such other price as may be agreed with the investor) at an agreed date in the future or at the directors' discretion, provided that there are sufficient distributable reserves available. Redeemable shares offer a certain level of protection to the investor and allow control of the company to revert to those who controlled it before the investor invested by redeeming the shares.
- **Convertible redeemable preference shares** These are similar to preference shares except that they carry a right to convert into ordinary shares should they not be repaid on their due date. The conversion factor (i.e. how many ordinary shares each convertible redeemable preference share will convert into), will be decided at the time of issue and will usually be based on a company valuation metric. If such a conversion takes place, in most cases it means that the company has not achieved its business plan and, as a result, the investor converts in order to try to realise their investment and influence the decision-making in the business by utilising ordinary shares with voting rights.

11.2.2 Components of a Company's Equity

Share capital may not be the sole component of a company's equity, as detailed in the following illustrative balance sheet extract:

EXAMPLE 11.1: ILLUSTRATIVE BALANCE SHEET (EXTRACT)

Issued share capital	€150,000
Share premium	€50,000
Revenue reserves	€20,000
Other reserves	€0
Total	**€220,000**

Issued Share Capital As discussed above, this represents the amount invested by the owners from the day the business was incorporated. Additional capital may have been invested since the company commenced trading, which will increase the share capital on the balance sheet. Also, as detailed above, it is possible that the share capital account will include other forms of shares, whether a separate and distinct class of ordinary shares with restricted rights (in terms of voting, return, etc.) or preference shares that may rank ahead of the ordinary shares in terms of dividends and repayment.

Share Premium This is the amount over and above the par value (typically €1) of a share. For example, ABC Ltd has issued 100 shares, which have a par value of €1 each. However, the company has been paid €150, or €1.50 per share. The excess over the par value, i.e. €50, appears on the company balance sheet in the share premium account.

Revenue Reserves This represents the profits that the business has generated since incorporation and that have not been distributed or returned to the owners. If all profits are distributed every year then the revenue reserves will be zero, while if losses are continuously incurred, its revenue reserves will be negative.

Other Reserves A company may have other reserves that make up its equity, which can include a revaluation reserve, which represents any surplus recognised through an upward valuation of its fixed assets.

As a company issues more shares, the issued share capital increases with a corresponding increase in the company's cash balance. The ability to issue shares in a performing company with growth opportunities provides such a company with alternatives to debt finance (see **Chapter 12**).

11.3 Key Terms to Understand before Raising Equity Capital

We have noted already the attitude prevalent in many Irish SMEs that equity capital is in effect 'giving away' something valuable. Understanding the language of equity capital is an important part in educating owner/managers as to the actual role equity investment can play in meeting their growth opportunities.

'Pre-money valuation' vs 'post-money valuation' 'Pre-money valuation' refers to a company's value before it receives a new equity capital.

EXAMPLE 11.2: PRE- AND POST-MONEY VALUATION CALCULATION

An external investor (Investor A) agrees to a pre-money valuation of €2 million for a company. If she decides to invest €500,000, this makes the company's post-money valuation €2.5 million.

The percentage ownership of the company is set out as follows:

Post-money valuation	**€2,500,000**	A	
Made up of:			
Investor A	€500,000	B	20% (B/A)
Founder	€2,000,000	C	80% (C/A)

Thus, post-money valuation = pre-money valuation + new funding.

These terms and the above formula are very important because they determine the equity stake a business owner provides during the funding round. In **Example 11.2**, the investor's €500,000 investment means acquiring 20% of the company, with the existing owners now owning 80%. These are the percentages that will determine the share in profits, dividends and, ultimately, the proceeds on exit if the company is sold.

Similarly, if the existing owners wanted to 'buy back' the investor's equity stake, then the price to be paid (in very broad terms) would be 20% of the then agreed valuation of the equity at that time; and if the equity valuation increased to, say, €4.5 million, the investor would be entitled to 20% or €900,000 (€4.5 million × 20%). Similarly, if the valuation reduced to €1.5 million, the investor's 20% equity stake would be valued at only €300,000.

'Anti-dilution' This is a very important term to be aware of when raising equity capital and agreeing investment terms. If an anti-dilution clause is included in investment terms/agreement, it means that in the event the company sells shares (raises further equity) in the future at a valuation lower than that at which the investor invested, an adjustment will be made to the number of shares held by the existing investor to ensure that their percentage shareholding is not impacted by the lower valuation.

EXAMPLE 11.3: ANTI-DILUTION

Continuing on from **Example 11.2** above, assume that one year later the company raises further equity finance from a new investor, Investor B, and the pre-money valuation of the equity at this time is €1.5 million (compared to €2 million at the time Investor A invested).

If we assume a further equity raise of €500,000 from Investor B and that the original investor (Investor A) has an anti-dilution protection clause in her investment agreement, this will result in the shareholdings set out below:

Investor A's shareholding in the business has not been impacted by the fall in valuation due to anti-dilution protection. The founder's shareholding in the business has been diluted and impacted by, first, having to take on a further investor (Investor B) at a lower valuation and, secondly, Investor A's anti-dilution protection.

Revised post-money valuation	**€2,000,000**	A	
Made up of:			
Investor A	€400,000	B	20% (B/A)
Investor B	€500,000	C	25% (C/A)
Founder	€1,100,000	D	55% (D/A)

'Enterprise Value' and 'Equity Value' These are metrics used to value a company – see **Section 11.4**.

'Multiple' A 'multiple' is a number that is used in the calculation of the value of a business, being multiplied by its earnings number. In most cases, EBITDA (earnings before interest, tax, depreciation and amortisation) is the measure used for the earnings number. For example, assuming a multiple of 2 and earnings of €500,000, the multiple of earnings calculation means that the business may be valued for sale at €1 million.

'Burn Rate' The rate at which the company is consuming cash, usually expressed on a monthly basis.

'Pre-emption right' A pre-emption right provides that, when new shares in a company are issued, existing shareholders have a right of first refusal to purchase the shares in proportion to their existing shareholdings. Where pre-emption rights exist, external parties other than existing shareholders are only entitled to purchase newly issued shares in the company if the existing shareholders do not exercise their pre-emption rights.

'Drag right' A drag right enables the majority shareholder to force a minority shareholder to join in the sale of a company. The majority shareholder doing the dragging must give the minority shareholder the same price, terms and conditions as any other seller. Drag rights are designed to protect the majority shareholder.

'Tag right' The opposite of a drag right, a tag right is used to protect a minority shareholder. If a majority shareholder sells their stake, it gives the minority shareholder the right to join the transaction and sell their minority stake in the company on the same terms and conditions of the majority shareholder.

'**Exit strategy**' An investor's intended method for allowing their investment to achieve the maximum possible return. Strategies depend on the exit climate, including factors such as market conditions, industry trends and company performance.

'**Non-disclosure agreement (NDA)**' Essentially, this is a confidentiality agreement that is executed by the potential investor and the company seeking investment prior to the release of any information that is confidential and commercially sensitive to the company.

'**Cash conversion percentage ratio**' A cash-flow measure of how much of a company's profits turns into cash.

'**Free cash flow**' A measure of a company's financial performance, calculated as operating cash flow minus capital expenditures. It calculates the rate at which EBITDA converts into available cash.

'**Restricted transactions**' An investor may list certain transactions that require their consent prior to them being undertaken by the company. Examples include capital expenditure, bank borrowings or acquiring complementary businesses.

'**Warranties and covenants**' Warranties are statements made by the owners/seller to the effect that certain facts in relation to the business or the company are true. Should the investor/buyer later discover that a warranty was not true, which causes the investor/buyer to suffer a loss, this could give rise to a claim for breach of warranty, entitling the buyer to damages. Covenants protect the purchaser's interests post completion and compel the existing owners to conduct the business in a certain manner and, if applicable, to obtain the purchaser's approval for important or extraordinary matters.

'**Investment term sheet**' (also known as a '**letter of intent**' (LOI)) A nonbinding agreement setting out the basic terms and conditions under which an investment will be made. A term sheet serves as a template to develop more detailed legal documents. Once the parties involved reach an agreement on the details laid out in the term sheet, a binding agreement or contract that conforms to the term sheet details is then drawn up.

'**Exclusivity**' An exclusivity agreement stipulates that the seller cannot pursue an offer from another potential investor for a period of time subsequent to the signing of the LOI.

11.4 Valuing an Equity Stake

When completing equity investments, investors become co-owners of the business with the owners/founders. However, the amount of ownership held by each is dependent on a negotiation, which in turn is based on the funds invested and the agreed-on value of the business (as it is at present and as it may be in the future).

It is important to remember that business valuation is an art, not a science, and that the valuation is always to some degree subjective and dependent on the perspective of the valuer. Furthermore, business founders will typically seek as much investment as possible for as little equity as is acceptable, while investors will want as much equity as possible.

The final equity proportions and amount of investment raised generally involve a compromise based not just on the numbers but also the eagerness of the investor to invest and the level of urgency with which the founder/business owner is seeking that investment.

At the same time, however, the valuation of a company does have a hugely important objective purpose for both parties, as it is the basis for determining the 'cost' in terms of the equity being acquired by the investors. The valuation needs to be low enough to ensure that investors will achieve an attractive return but high enough to keep existing shareholders incentivised to successfully achieve the business plan (i.e. they need to still feel they are working for their own success, not someone else's).

Valuing a company is how an equity capital investment is 'priced', and valuation is not the only issue in this process; the terms of an investment are also important.

Various multiples or metrics can be applied to establish a valuation. Examples include an agreed multiple of recurring revenues and/or of maintainable EBITDA. The choice of multiple is determined by what is commonly applied in the sector in which the company trades. For example, companies providing goods to the retail sector may be valued by applying a multiple to the company's annual revenues. The multiple can vary and is typically based on historic transactions. For other sectors, the multiple is applied to annual EBITDA to determine a company's valuation. Any multiples and metrics arising from companies being sold in the sector relevant to the company seeking equity funding offer important guidance. Therefore, researching the sale of companies in the industry sector may also reveal what multiples are relevant. Public companies must disclose transaction details but private companies do not. As a result, finding pertinent examples for a private company may be a challenge. A common way to overcome this challenge is to apply a discount factor to the public company's multiple, the rationale for the discount being that the private company's shares are not as marketable or readily sold as the public company's. The amount of the discount can vary and in such circumstances it is appropriate to seek professional advice.

There are a number of ways to value a company and all depend on the specifics of each case. While we do not detail each of the possible valuation methods, **Example 11.4** below sets out how the valuation of a business can be arrived at using the maintainable EBITDA/earnings method.

EXAMPLE 11.4: MAINTAINABLE EBITDA/EARNINGS VALUATION

Maintainable EBITDA	**€3,000,000**
Multiple	4 ×
Enterprise value	€12,000,000
Debt	(€2,000,000)
Equity value/Pre-money valuation	€10,000,000
Investment (Investor A)	€2,000,000
Post-money Valuation	**€12,000,000**

In this example, Investor A will hold 16.67% (€2m/€12m) of the equity for their €2 million investment in the company.

11.5 What Equity Investors Look for in an Investment Opportunity

While what a company does (in terms of its products or services) is clearly important when selecting an investment opportunity and assessing and reviewing its suitability, experience shows that there are three more important factors or criteria for consideration and assessment:
1. the business founders and its management team;
2. the track record of the business; and
3. its potential for growth, and how the equity investment will unlock and secure the growth.

11.5.1 Business Founders and Management Team

Unsurprisingly perhaps, this is the number one, most important factor that will be assessed by investors. Investors invest in people and they will assess not just their CV, business track record and experience, but also some 'softer' elements, such as personality, outlook and values.

Experienced investors will spend a great deal of time getting to know and becoming comfortable with the owners and the management team to gain an understanding of their passion and ambition for the business. Can the investor trust and work with them? What are their values and beliefs? It is not just about the company and its products/services but understanding if the right people are there to drive the business forward.

An understanding of the owners' plans for the business during the investment lifecycle is key. Are they planning a trade sale when the time is right or do they sincerely believe in passing the business on to their children? The answer to this question will play a big part in how the equity investment may be structured and repaid.

Other points investors will assess of the owners and management team include:
- How do they react when things go wrong?
- How do they behave under pressure?
- Are they open to advice and indeed 'tough talking' when serious problems arise?

Experienced investors will continually assess these softer elements by getting to know the founders and the people around them in advance of and as investment terms are being negotiated. In seeking the clearest possible insight into owners' personalities when discussing terms, assessing and reviewing how they communicate and react to difficult investment negotiation points, an investor is addressing what are likely to be their overriding questions:
- Have the owners/management team a successful track record?
- Will this person or team drive the business growth and success required to repay the investment, and within the next few years?
- How in-depth is their knowledge of the market and the opportunity?
- Can I have confidence in their ability to execute the business plan?

A commonly used phrase in investing is 'people invest in people'. Although there may be no matters arising from the financial, legal and commercial due diligence, an investment may not happen (and many have not happened) because the potential investors are not comfortable with the entrepreneurs behind the business, or the values and personalities of the investors do not align with those of the entrepreneurs.

EXAMPLE 11.5: PEOPLE INVEST IN PEOPLE

A potential investor was completing a tour of the factory floor of a well-established food company with its CEO when one of the production lines stalled. The CEO immediately began to 'lose it' with the operatives and production manager. This gave the investor a valuable, if unflattering, insight into the temperament of the CEO. Although personality can appear a subjective matter, any astute and experienced equity investor will rate it as hugely important when choosing who to invest in.

11.5.2 Track Record of the Business

An investor will want to understand what the business has achieved, and how, over, say, the last three years. What have its growth rates been and how do they compare to the market average? Has this growth been in line with the market and sector growth rates and those of the business's competitors? How has it financed that growth to date?

Investors will also want to know if they are 'first in'. Has the company had previous external investors and have they been repaid? How has it reacted to any challenges over previous years in terms of price pressure from customers or competitors? Has it a track record of losing key customers or staff? Are there any fundamental changes in the market, either current or impending? If so, how has the company and its management team reacted historically and is it proactive in respect of current market and competitor threats?

11.5.3 Growth Potential of the Business

An understanding of the business's revenue and EBITDA growth potential is essential. What is driving the growth and how certain is it? Is it 'push' or 'pull' (i.e. is the market demanding the company's products/services ('pull') or is the company pushing them on to the market ('push'))?

A common statement from business owners seeking investment is: "If I have €X investment then €Y revenue and EBITDA projections will definitely happen." Unfortunately, unless the company is the new Stripe, it is unlikely to happen that way. Investors will want far more detail in order to understand when the funds invested will be spent and on what, and how this will serve to unlock the growth opportunity. The more certain and concrete you can make the growth trajectory through market data (while at the same time taking account of threats and weaknesses in the business model), the more likely an investor is going to believe that it is achievable.

11.6 Outline of a Typical Equity Investment Process

Once a business has decided to progress with an equity investment proposition, there are a number of actions and steps it will need to take in order to properly prepare for making that investment a reality. **Figure 11.1** below provides an overview of eight key steps of the equity investment process. For an equity investment to complete, it will, in the majority of cases, proceed through each of these eight steps. An equity investment may be declined at any stage when either an investor or the company decides to withdraw from the process, for whatever reason.

FIGURE 11.1: THE EQUITY INVESTMENT PROCESS

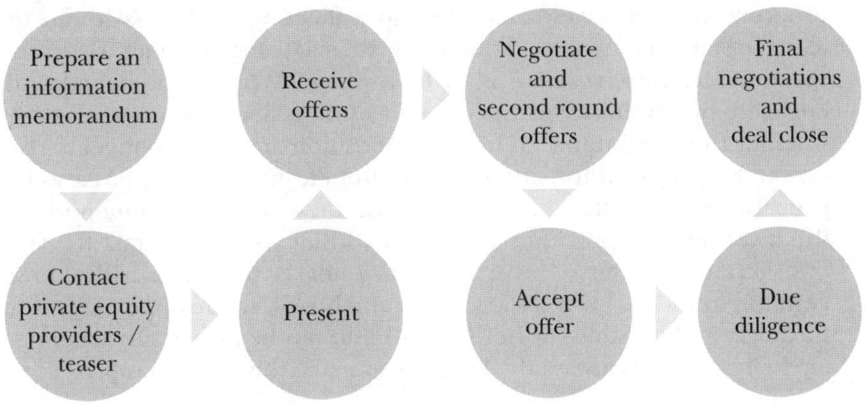

1. **Prepare an information memorandum** It cannot be overstated how important it is for any business seeking equity investment to map out clearly the information investors will require for making their decision. This will typically be done by way of an information memorandum (IM) or business plan and will include:
   (a) the background to the business, its history and ownership structure;
   (b) information about the company's products/services and its key financial metrics, e.g. gross margin per product/service, yield per manufactured product, etc.;
   (c) information about customers and markets, and projected market share and growth rates;
   (d) analysis of the company's competitors, its unique selling proposition (USP) and any protected intellectual property it may have (e.g. a patent on a manufacturing process);
   (e) a detailed financial model for the business, including profit and loss account, balance sheet and a cash-flow projection for the next five years, with details of assumptions supporting the model, including the sources and uses of the funding;
   (f) an organisation chart highlighting key employees; and
   (g) details of how the investment will be repaid or refinanced, be it with a bank or other investor or a trade sale.
2. **Produce a 'teaser' document for approaching potential investors** Prior to releasing the IM, a 'teaser' document or executive summary of the IM should be prepared. The rationale for this is to avoid circulating the company's important and confidential information to a wide pool of potential investors. The circulation of a teaser document will enable investor appetite to be assessed and the IM released to only those interested parties who have expressed an interest and have signed a confidentiality/non-disclosure agreement. The teaser document should summarise the information outlined above into a two-page (maximum) document about the business, the investment opportunity, and summary financial details. This document is used to gauge the interest of any prospective investor.

   How investors are approached is very important. It is strongly advised to engage corporate financiers to assist with this process. If the company is doing it themselves then it is probably most appropriate to pick up the phone and call prospective investors directly, outlining the investment proposition, with a view to setting up a meeting to discuss it and its teaser document further. Attempting to make first contact with prospective investors by email is to be avoided. When approached and engaged by phone, a prospective investor is likely to state directly whether they are interested in the proposition and want to meet to discuss it. Be prepared for, and be respectful of, 'no' answers, but also be prepared to ask if there is someone else they would recommend who the investment opportunity may suit and that you should talk to. The one certainty about a prospective investor is that they will almost certainly know the business world extremely well, so the opportunity for feedback and possible further leads should not be missed. To reiterate: a telephone call is always the best way to make this kind of approach to potential investors, introducing them to your business, and for gaining their respect.

If, on the other hand, the call is successful and the investor is willing to proceed to the next stage, to meet and discuss the proposition in more detail, the crucial next step is for the business owner to get a confidentiality or non-disclosure agreement (NDA) in place. This is standard practice for equity investors and you will gain their confidence requesting same; it demonstrates the level of professionalism and governance with which you run your business. It is important to ensure NDAs are prepared and that only approaches to carefully selected investors are made. The proposal and company documentation should then be honed as investor meetings and pitches are prepared for.

3. **Meeting and pitching to investors** The key to successful meetings with potential investors, particularly those at which there is an opportunity to pitch, is to be prepared. Always find out how much time the investor has and ensure that the meeting and any presentation sticks rigidly to this (unless, of course, the investor requests that it be extended). Focus on communicating the core proposition throughout and avoid using jargon or sound bites when more straightforward language is possible. Structure the presentation around the three key factors detailed in **Section 11.5** above:
   • the business founders and its management team;
   • the track record of the business; and
   • its potential for growth and how the equity investment will unlock and secure the growth.

4. **Receiving and negotiating offers** On receipt of an offer from an investor, which will be presented by way of an investment term sheet, it is strongly recommended that, unless you have raised equity finance previously, you get independent legal or business advice on the investment term sheet to ensure that you fully understand its clauses. Time spent in clarifying ambiguous points on the term sheet will help to ensure that the process for putting a formal legal agreement in place is as smooth as possible. This will also reduce the chances of the deal aborting (not succeeding) should something become problematic at the legal agreement stage.

The main items contained in an equity investment term sheet provide details about:
(a) the investment amount, its timing and proposed use in the business;
(b) the number of shares and percentage ownership;
(c) the equity and debt structure;
(d) dividend and interest (if applicable) rights, and voting rights;
(e) any management incentive schemes;
(f) exit clauses;
(g) investor board representation and investor veto rights;
(h) information and reporting requirements;
(i) costs of completing the investment;
(j) confidentiality;

(k) steps to closing; and
(l) exclusivity.

An exclusivity clause in an equity investment term sheet should be carefully considered. An exclusivity clause effectively stipulates that the company cannot pursue/engage in funding discussions from other potential investors for a specified period of time subsequent to the signing of the term sheet with a prospective investor. The reason investors seek exclusivity is to allow them a period of time to complete their diligence and avoid the possibility of another investor completing the same investment.

Though such an exclusivity clause will give a company a commitment from an investor for a period of time, it is important that the timeframe is reasonable (say six to eight weeks) so that, if the company or investor decides not to proceed, the company is not precluded from approaching other investors.

In addition to the above, negotiations between investors and companies should involve, at a minimum, the following factors:

- **amount of capital invested** – this may be a single amount or a combination of investments over a defined period;
- **timing of the investment** – investments may be timed or phased, with a specific amount invested initially and future amounts due on future dates or when certain milestones have been met;
- **return on investment** – the proportionate share of future earnings attributable to the investor over an agreed period of time;
- **timing of the return to the investor** – prospective payments in the future will be discounted to reflect the investor's opportunity costs and the risk-free return which they would have otherwise earned by forgoing the amount invested.

5. **Due diligence** Investors will undertake due diligence on a company prior to deciding to invest. Due diligence is a process that verifies and confirms statements and views about a business and its prospects and can include financial, legal, technical, market, tax and commercial diligence. Diligence can include, for example: a competitive analysis; validation of products/services IP; assessment of the company's structure; historic and projected financials and contracts; a check of company law compliance; and reference checks with customers.

> **Note:** Customer reference checks should only be carried out when the investor has completed all other due diligence, when legal agreements are materially agreed and the investor has all the required approvals to invest. It will undermine a business owner's credibility to have to explain to a customer that an expected investment did not proceed due to a last-minute hitch.

6. **Final negotiations and closing the deal** Depending on how smoothly the due diligence process has gone, the investor may wish to alter certain investment terms or add certain clauses to the equity investment

agreement to address the diligence findings. These can include post-completion covenants that the company will undertake to address any weaknesses found during due diligence; for example, employ a commercial director to assist accelerate growth or update certain customer/supplier contracts that may have expired.

11.7 Equity Investment Agreements

Once the investor's due diligence has been completed, the investment moves to legal completion, when the necessary legal documents to reflect the investment are drafted and reviewed by both the investor and the company, following which there is final negotiation and execution. Typically, the legal agreements to reflect an equity investment comprise the following:

- **Investment Agreements** Also known as a shareholders agreement, an investment agreement is essentially a contract between all of the shareholders in a company and the company itself. The purpose of such an agreement is to provide how the company is to be managed and, as far as possible, to address issues that might otherwise become divisive in the future if not agreed in advance. The agreement will, in a large part, mirror the equity investment term sheet and contain information and details on some or all of the following:
  - o the business of the company;
  - o the composition of the board of directors including the chairperson;
  - o the frequency of board meetings and the required quorum;
  - o information rights of the investor and the board;
  - o share matters, including pre-emption, drag and tag rights, anti-dilution and conversion of shares (see **Section 11.3**);
  - o investor realisation matters, setting out how and when an investor proposes to exit the business; and
  - o non-compete and confidentiality matters.

  Additional items included in the investment agreement can include restrictive covenants, restriction on share transfers, warranties and covenants, and good and bad leaver provisions.

- **Share-purchase Agreements** In situations where shares are purchased directly from the company owners, a share-purchase agreement will set out the terms of the purchase and the warranties the seller is giving in respect of the shares. Warranties are legal statements given by the company and existing shareholders to the investor that confirm certain facts are true at the date of the investment, as far as the warrantors are aware. (For example, a warranty that the selling shareholder(s) owns the shares being sold and they have not been pledged (i.e. used as security for a loan), the company's filings in the Companies Registration Office (CRO) are up to date, its management accounts are prepared on the same basis as the audited accounts, and that the company has no legal claims outstanding against it.) The warrantors can make the investor aware of any exceptions to the warranties by way of a disclosure letter.

- **Company Constitution** A company's constitution is its governing document and is registered with the CRO upon its incorporation. Accordingly, the constitution of a company is a public document and is open to inspection by the public. Any changes to the constitution of a company must also be filed with the CRO within a prescribed period of time, usually 21 days after.

  Depending on the terms of the equity investment and the type of equity instrument being issued (see **Section 11.2.1** on types of equity investment), the company's constitution will be required to be updated to reflect the share instrument issued and the rights and entitlements of the share. The constitution of a company can only be amended by a special resolution, which is a resolution passed by 75% or more of the shareholders present and voting at a general meeting of the company (as required by the Companies Act 2014). Among the standard provisions contained in most company constitutions are the following:

  (a) description of share capital (where there is more than one class of shares, a description of the rights attaching to the different classes of shares);
  (b) directors' powers to allot shares;
  (c) pre-emption rights regarding the issue of new shares;
  (d) purchase by the company of its own shares;
  (e) provisions concerning the convening and conduct of meetings of shareholders;
  (f) provisions concerning the convening and conduct of directors' meetings; and
  (g) the power of directors to appoint additional directors.

- **Service Contracts** As discussed above, people invest in people and investors will want to ensure that the executive management team and other key employees have up-to-date service contracts with the company setting out the terms of employment, termination and restrictive covenants, which are effectively non-compete clauses.

- **Warranty Deeds** As detailed above, these set out the matters that the owners warrant as being true and correct, with any exception to these being disclosed in the disclosure letter and disclosure bundle document.

> *Note:* Detailed legal advice and assistance should be sought with respect to all of the above documents.

11.8 How Investors Measure Return on Equity

Investors measure their return on how much their investment has increased over the investment term and what it has delivered in terms of dividends and exit value. All investors want to maximise investment returns and, as a result, they are aligned with the founders' objective.

The overall return is determined by comparing the equity value on the exit date to the equity value when the investment was made. The investor's return will be based on the investor's equity ownership percentage on the exit date equity value, which will be compared to the entry equity value and the uplift expressed as an 'x times return'. **Example 11.6** below details the calculation of an investor's return over a five-year period.

EXAMPLE 11.6: FIVE-YEAR INVESTOR RETURN CALCULATION

Entry equity value	€70 million
Investor equity investment	€7 million
Investor stake	10%
Five years later	
Company equity sold for	€210 million
Investor stake	10%
Investor return	**€21 million**

In this example, the investor made a **3 times return on their investment.**

A trade sale (i.e. a sale of 51% or more of the ownership of the company) or similar exit event presents an obvious point at which an investor exits a business, though, of course, such a sale is not inevitable. What is inevitable, however, is that point in time when the investor wishes to exit and it may be one that does not suit the business owner/management team. It is therefore critically important to understand from the beginning not just what the investor's objectives are but the timescale in which they expect to achieve them.

Broader economic events can occasionally help to dictate the timing of an investor's desired exit or 'cash out'. Certainly, the economic downturn of recent years saw instances where, due to personal circumstances, private investors sought funding back earlier than anticipated by the company invested in. This is, however, something that is much less likely to occur with venture capital or development capital funds, as such funds have a minimum time horizon and it is not typically inherent in their structures to seek funds back earlier than originally negotiated.

11.9 Matters to Consider when Raising Equity Capital

We noted in **Chapter 10** that equity investment can provide significant benefits to companies and business owners embarking on their growth journey. Business owners must, however, enter any equity agreement with their 'eyes wide open'. Drawn from direct experience, **Chapter 18** provides advice on the dos and don'ts of fundraising, including equity finance. The following matters should also be considered by any company in advance of undertaking the equity-raising process:

1. **It is a time-consuming process** A business owner must be prepared to put in considerable time and effort into the process both before, during and

after the actual investment transaction is completed, while at the same time investing all the required time and energy into ensuring the business continues to trade in line with its financial projections.

2. **Research into and align with the best-fit potential equity investors** It is essential to research the potential investors for the business, know about other investments they have completed, and understand their investment criteria. Do these align with your requirements for an investor in your business? Other than funding, what other 'value add' can they bring (see point 4 below)?

3. **Getting the investment amount right** The most indefensible mistake an entrepreneur can make when seeking equity capital is not asking for enough to make the business a success. Lacking sufficient capital to execute the business plan is like starting a long car journey with only half a tank of fuel: the odds that you will complete your journey are slim. When seeking funding, it is advisable for all companies to overfund, adding an amount for a contingency or buffer. This will also show the investor that you are realistic and aware that not everything will happen as planned. Evidence of such realism will increase the investor's confidence. If you are unsure as to the right funding amount to seek, consult with your business advisor before progressing.

4. **Considering an investor's 'value add'** This is an important consideration. Aside from money, what other 'value add' can the investor bring, such as introductions for new business opportunities or assistance in unlocking the growth potential of the business? If it is feasible to target multiple investors, what makes one investor more attractive than another in this regard?

5. **Exit** What is the investor's planned exit point? Is it aligned with the objectives of the company and its owner(s)? Any such misalignment needs to be addressed before proceeding with an investment, as well as discussing scenarios in case it becomes a reality during the investment period. If a company requires an equity investment for a three-year term, there is no point in taking on an equity investor who will want their investment back after one year: the objectives of the company and investor are not aligned.

11.10 Advantages of Equity Capital

Having discussed the issues, problems and stresses that may come with seeking equity finance, it is important to restate the many overriding advantages it offers in comparison with the traditional banking finance options usually favoured by Irish SMEs. These include:

1. **Cash-flow benefits** With equity capital, there is no loan to repay. This provides the business with a major cash-flow advantage since it does not have to factor in monthly loan repayments, which can be particularly important if the business does not generate profits initially. This also frees the management team to channel more money into growing the business.

2. **Credit issues eliminated** If you or your business lack creditworthiness – through a poor credit history or lack of an established financial track record – equity capital is not only preferable or more suitable than debt, it can offer a lifeline that delivers future growth and transformation for the business that would otherwise not be possible.
3. **Learn and gain insights from equity investors** With equity capital, as well as the financing, you can also gain from an external investor's experience, knowledge and business connections – benefits that rarely come with a bank loan and which can provide vital assistance to the growth of a business, giving it the best chance of succeeding.

11.11 Types and Sources of Equity Capital

Set out below is an overview of the possible sources of equity capital available according to the company's stage in the innovation lifecycle. (*Note:* it is possible for the funding sources to overlap as, ultimately, an equity investor can decide if they wish to invest in the management team and its growth opportunity.)

TABLE 11.1: SOURCES OF EQUITY ACCORDING TO A COMPANY'S STAGE IN THE INNOVATION LIFECYCLE

Company's Stage in the Innovation Lifecycle	Possible Innovation Lifecycle Sources of Equity
Investigation, Feasibility and Development	• High net-worth individuals (HNWI) and business angel finance • The '3 Fs' (friends, family and 'fools') • Startup Refunds for Entrepreneurs (SURE) • Local Enterprise Offices
Introduction	• HNWI and business angel finance • The '3 Fs' • Employment and Investment Incentive (EII) Scheme • Venture capital • Enterprise Ireland • Local Enterprise Offices
Growth/expansion and development	• HNWI and business angel finance • EII Scheme • Venture capital funds • Enterprise Ireland • Development/growth capital funds • Private equity and family funds • Trade sale/merger • IPO

Maturity/transfer/succession/turnaround/buy-out stage	• HNWI and business angel finance • Development/growth capital • IPO

11.11.1 High Net-worth Individuals (HNWI)/Business Angel Finance

> **HNWI/business angel finance is suitable for start-up companies, particularly companies at the development and introduction stages of the innovation lifecycle**

Generally, new companies will have owner/founder investment before approaching outside investors and lenders, including, for example, the '3 Fs' or availing of SURE. This is essential to demonstrate that the owners have 'skin in the game' and are willing to back themselves and their business plan. At this early stage, external investors may include HNWIs and business angels, i.e. private individuals unconnected with the founder who invest in the business in return for a share of ownership.

Business angels are private individuals who invest capital in early-stage and developing companies, as well as contributing their know-how and experience in company management. They can offer valuable expertise and guidance. Angels may seek active participation in the company in which they invest, which may include taking a seat on the board.

Business angels can be a very important substitute for bank financing or venture capital, which can be difficult to attract at the early stage of a company's lifecycle. They are primarily motivated by return on investment and business angel involvement can often help secure access to venture capital or bank loans.

The average initial investment by business angels ranges from between €50,000 and €250,000 individually, or they can form syndicates (partnerships with other business angels) for investments in excess of €250,000.

Unlike the '3 Fs', as detailed in **Section 11.11.2** below, HNWIs and business angels invest to maximise a return on their investment. The fact that a business angel/HNWI has invested in a company will be seen as a positive signal by future potential stakeholders, i.e. it can assist in securing venture capital or bank funding.

Key attributes to assess when considering the investment of a business angel include:
• commercial track record;
• business credentials and experience;
• funds readily available to invest; and
• relevant industry contacts.

11.11.1.1 Business Angel Exit

Business angels do not want to be invested in a business indefinitely – they tend to want to maximise the return on their investment over a period of five to seven years. Typical exit alternatives are by way of a trade sale of all the shares or of the business angel's shares only, whereby the company redeems the business angel shares only, which is financed by way of new equity finance.

11.11.1.2 Sourcing Business Angel Investment

There are a number of business angel networks that have been created and built by Enterprise Ireland, InterTradeIreland and business innovation centres (BICs) in Dublin, the South east, Cork and the west of Ireland, with the latter offering a matching service for companies and investors.

Additionally, Enterprise Ireland's Growth Capital Department can assist with access to business angels who have an ongoing relationship with the agency. As a joint initiative with InterTradeIreland, Enterprise Ireland also supports the Halo Business Angel Network (HBAN), which facilitates access to a network of registered business angels. This partnership is managed on a local level by the BICs.

Further information and sources of potential business angels can be found at www.hban.org

11.11.2 The '3 Fs' (Friends, Family and 'Fools')

> **The '3 Fs' are suitable for investigation, feasibility and development lifecycle stages**

When a business is in its start-up phase, or is about to experience rapid growth, obtaining equity finance is the key to getting things moving. As most loan finance options may not be available in the early stages of a business's lifecycle, it is common for business owners to seek finance from individuals or a group of individuals to provide the funding necessary to meet the company's initial trading needs.

Such individuals can usually be categorised as coming from one or more of the following three groups: friends, family members or 'fools' (the '3 Fs'). It is known as the '3 Fs' because, in many instances, it is friends and family that help fund early-stage and start-up companies. The term 'fools' derives from the phrase "fools and their money are easily parted" and is used because such investors have invested in a business at such an early stage, with all the related risks involved, including that such early-stage businesses have a high risk of failure, but also the potential for significant growth. In exchange for funding, and based on the amount they contribute, the owner offers a stake to each individual in the business. At this early stage of development, such individual investors may not have a say in the operation of the business as they are investing based on trust and their previous experience of, and often a personal relationship with, the business owner.

As the business is at an early stage of its development, it can be very difficult to put a value on it, particularly when the investment sought is intended for the development of a concept, prototype, etc. As a result, therefore, in such circumstances, the percentage ownership that an investor receives will be negotiated. Individual investment amounts and the number of investors will vary depending on the overall amount being raised.

It is worth noting that, subject to approval and qualification by the Revenue Commissioners, it may be possible for the investor to receive tax relief on their investment if they invest under the EII Scheme, which is covered in **Chapter 2** and summarised below.

11.11.3 Enterprise Ireland and Local Enterprise Offices

> **Enterprise Ireland funding and supports are suitable for companies that have greater than 10 employees, while Local Enterprise Offices provide funding and support for companies with less than 10 employees and suit companies at the feasibility, development, introduction and growth stages**

Enterprise Ireland is the state agency responsible for supporting the development of manufacturing and internationally traded services companies. It provides funding and supports for companies, from entrepreneurs with high-potential startup propositions to large companies expanding their activities, improving efficiency and developing international sales.

There are over 30 Local Enterprise Offices (LEOs) in Ireland, providing a range of financial supports designed to assist with the establishment and/or growth of local micro businesses, i.e. a business with fewer than 10 employees.

Both Enterprise Ireland and the LEOs can, subject to meeting the required criteria of the relevant support, complete an equity investment in an SME. For more on this, see **Chapter 13**, Government Funding and Supports.

11.11.4 Startup Refunds for Entrepreneurs

> **SURE is particularly suitable for entrepreneurs starting up their own company**

As discussed in detail in **Chapter 1**, at the time of writing the Startup Refunds for Entrepreneurs (SURE) is a tax-relief incentive scheme for entrepreneurs starting up their own company that, subject to Revenue qualification and rules, may entitle the entrepreneur to an income tax refund of up to 41% of the capital that is invested by the entrepreneur under the scheme.

As discussed in detail in **Chapter 1**, depending on the size of the investment, a refund of income tax paid over the six years prior to the year in which you invest may be available to be claimed. The SURE scheme provides an important source of equity finance for early-stage and start-up companies. For more details, see www.revenue.ie

11.11.5 The Employment and Investment Incentive Scheme

> **The EII Scheme is suitable for companies at all stages of development, subject to Revenue approval**

As discussed in detail in **Chapter 2**, at the time of writing the EII Scheme (previously known as the Business Expansion Scheme (BES)), is a tax-relief incentive scheme providing all-income tax relief to qualifying investors for equity investments in certain qualifying SMEs.

The EII Scheme offers one of the few remaining income tax reliefs and is one of the few sources of total income relief for private individuals. (The income tax aspects of the scheme are discussed in **Chapter 2**.)

The EII Scheme is available as a source of finance for companies and tax relief for private investors until 2020 (unless extended by the EU) and it facilitates qualifying companies (as approved by Revenue) to secure equity funding at a competitive cost of finance with no capital repayment until the end of the four-year investment period, which is the investment term set out under the scheme following which the investment can be repaid to the investors. Any repayments to investors prior to the expiry of the four-year investment term would likely lead to a claw back of investor tax relief.

The total amount of EII Scheme investment that a qualifying company can raise is €15 million with an annual maximum of €5 million.

The Revenue Commissioners' and EU qualification criteria for companies to avail of the EII Scheme, as well as the requirements for investors to claim income tax relief on investments made under the EII Scheme, are detailed in **Chapter 2**.

For more information on the EII Scheme, see Revenue's Tax and Duty Manual, Part 16-00-10 at www.revenue.ie

11.11.5.1 Use of EII Scheme Funding

Upon receipt of EII Scheme funding, the company must use the money raised from the share issue for the purpose of carrying on a qualifying trade, or if the company has not yet commenced to trade, in incurring expenditure on research and development.

In addition, the use of the funds must contribute directly to the maintenance or creation of employment in the company. Examples of what EII Scheme funding can be used for by the company include:
1. hiring of new staff to expand the company's workforce to enable it to increase its production capacity and output;
2. purchase of stock or new fixtures and fittings/plant and machinery, again to increase the company's production output;
3. purchase of a premises from which the trade will be carried on; and/or
4. extension to the company's premises.

An important restriction is that the money raised under the EII Scheme cannot be used to repay debt or equity of the company, or to fund the repayment/exit of existing shareholders.

It is important to note that if the company is part of a group of companies or under the control of a holding company, there are restrictions on the structure of the group, including that the money raised by a share issue can be used by a qualifying subsidiary for any of the above purposes. However, in order to avail of relief under the EII Scheme, the qualifying company must invest the money into the qualifying subsidiary by way of share issue.

From the perspective of an applicant company on receiving Revenue approval and completing an EII Scheme investment, there are significant benefits to raising EII Scheme funding. These include:

1. **Fixed cost of finance for four years** EII Scheme funding (unlike most bank and other forms of borrowing that can be subject to variable and changing interest rates) has a fixed cost of finance, with the majority of the cost of the finance being typically a cap/premium on the investment amount. This cap/premium is the maximum amount the EII Scheme shares can receive at the end of the four-year investment period and is the reason why most EII Scheme investments are structured by way of a different class of share, as detailed above in **Section 11.2.1**. It is payable to the investor, along with the original amount invested, at the end of the investment term. This fixed cost of finance provides the company with certainty over its cost of finance over the four-year investment term. (*Note:* Where funds are raised from a professional **EII Scheme designated investment fund manager** (as further detailed in **Section 11.11.5.2** below) there may be an additional cost in terms of an annual management/monitoring fee, which is typically a nominal 1%–2% of the funds raised.)

2. **No capital repayment until the end of the investment term** In addition to the fixed cost of finance, there is no capital repayments due on EII Scheme funding until the day after the fourth anniversary of the EII Scheme investment. Consequently, the company has full use of the EII Scheme funding to finance growth and expansion, which entails a significant cash-flow benefit.

3. **The existing shareholders retain control of the business** In order to qualify for the EII Scheme, the EII Scheme investor must subscribe for shares that represent new ordinary share capital in the qualifying company and, importantly, carry no preferential rights. Most EII Scheme investments are structured so that the investment is for a different class of ordinary share than the ordinary shares held by the founders of the company. These are shares that are distinguished from the existing ordinary shares in that they have restricted rights in terms of either voting or dividends as well as a return on capital, i.e. the cap/premium on the EIIS Scheme share investment. As a result of the restrictions on the EII Scheme shares and the fact that the existing ordinary shares have full voting control, the founders retain full control and do not, in most cases, suffer a dilution of their percentage ownership and control of the company. It is worth

noting, however, that some EII Scheme investments can be structured as ordinary shares, with no restrictions on voting rights, dividends or return on capital, i.e. are *pari passu* with the existing ordinary shares.

4. **An EII Scheme investment is equity, not debt** As detailed above, in return for their EII Scheme funding, the investor must receive new ordinary shares in the business. As a result, the investment is deemed equity and not debt which, importantly, has a positive impact on the company's balance-sheet gearing (i.e. its borrowing capacity).

5. **An EII Scheme investment may trigger further investment or bank funding** A significant effect and advantage of point 4 above is that, due to the new EII Scheme equity improving the company's gearing, other investors or bank lenders will look positively on a funding application. This improvement is due to the increase in share capital arising from the EII Scheme investment in the company; banks will see it as lower risk compared to a company with little or no share capital.

11.11.5.2 *Two Methods of Raising EII Scheme Funding*

A company has a choice of raising EII Scheme funding from either:
• a group of private investors, commonly referred to as an 'EII private placing'; or
• a designated investment fund.

EII private placings are typically undertaken by companies raising funds from the '3 Fs' (see **Section 11.11.2** above) and the investors are likely to be known to the business owners. As a company evolves through its funding lifecycle and it requires larger investment amounts, it can seek EII funding from designated investment funds. Such funds raise EII Scheme funding from private investors typically at the end of the calendar year for investment in companies during the following year.

The advantages of raising funding from an EII Scheme designated investment fund are as follows:
1. a designated fund will have the EII Scheme funds available for immediate investment, whereas individual investors may not have the required funds when approached by the company;
2. a designated fund represents and invests on behalf of a number of private individuals, dealing with them and any requests they may have directly, whereas under a private placing, a company can have a wide and diverse shareholder base to manage; and
3. a designated fund can take an active part in assisting an investee company execute its business plan, e.g. by providing introductions to new routes to market or assisting to strengthen its management team.

There are currently three recognised EII Scheme designated investment fund managers in Ireland:
1. the Davy EII Tax Relief Fund (www.bes.ie);
2. the Goodbody EIIS Fund (www.eiismanagement.ie); and
3. Business Venture Partners EII investment funds (www.bvp.ie).

The first two funds have a broad investment mandate and target established and profitable companies operating in all industry sectors. The key focus is on the experience and strength of the management team and the growth opportunity. Business Venture Partners' focus is on companies in the renewable energy, energy efficiency, industrial and agritech sectors. Additionally, Cantor Fitzgerald can complete EII Scheme fundraising for companies by raising EII Scheme investments from its private clients.

11.11.6 Venture Capital

> **Venture capital is suitable for early-stage and growing companies, particularly those at the introduction and growth stages**

Venture capital (VC) is defined as "the provision of capital for growth and expansion to companies with underdeveloped or developing products and revenues at an early stage in their corporate lifecycle".[1] VC is capital provided by venture capital firms (venture capitalists) who invest in ambitious, fast-growing companies with the potential to develop into significant businesses. Dedicated VC firms manage VC funds that have a mandate to invest in specific sectors and/or in companies at a specific stage of development. The investment monies are provided to the VC firm for investment by the specific fund's limited partners who can comprise institutional-type investors, e.g. the Ireland Strategic Investment Fund (ISIF), banks and pension funds.

In addition to providing capital to the company, the venture capitalist will also support the company by taking a seat on its board and providing access to their contacts to help drive the business plan and growth.

VC is a very important source of funding for early-stage companies that do not have access to capital markets. Though it often entails high risk for the investor, it also has the potential for significant returns. The downside for business owners is that venture capitalists usually get a say in company decisions, in addition to a portion of the equity.

Most VC comes from wealthy investors, investment banks and other financial institutions that pool such investments. This form of raising equity capital is popular among new companies or SMEs with limited operating history that cannot raise funds by issuing debt.

Venture capitalists will typically look to realise their investment at the end of the investment term, which is typically five years, through floatation on a public market, a trade sale of the entire company or for their stake to be bought out by either the company or another investor.

---

[1] Irish Venture Capital Association, *A Guide to Venture Capital*, 9th Edition (IVCA, October 2017) p. 5. Available at http://www.ivca.ie/wp-content/uploads/2017/10/Guide-to-Venture-Capital-9th-Edition.pdf

However, it is not unusual for venture capitalists to provide further invest-ment to SMEs (commonly referred to as 'following their money') when the company is executing on its business with further funding rounds being undertaken. In such circumstances, it is typical for venture capital-ists to partake in the subsequent funding rounds, thus avoiding their initial shareholding being diluted by a funding round in which they do not participate.

Venture capitalists usually invest in companies that are seeking equity funding typically from €500,000 upwards. The company can be in its start-up and/or growth/expansion stage; however, in the majority of cases it must be in a fast-growing, attractive sector, with a strong management team that offer high-growth potential for the business.

11.11.6.1 Venture Capital as a Funding Option

Not all companies are suitable for VC funding and not all owners of SMEs will suit working with a venture capitalist. To determine whether VC funding is suitable for your company, consider the following questions:
- Does your company have high-growth potential and is your team ambi-tious to grow the company rapidly?
- Does your product/service have a USP (unique selling proposition)?
- Can the USP be protected as an intellectual property right (e.g. patent)?
- Do you have a full, capable management team in place to execute the business plan or are there any gaps?
- Are you willing to give up some equity to a VC investor?
- What are the realistic exit opportunities for all shareholders in order to realise their investment?

If the answer is 'yes' to most of these questions, VC funding is worth con-sidering. If 'no', it may be that your proposal is not suitable for venture capitalists and it may take additional work to make the proposal investor-ready (see **Chapters 16** and **17**).

When considering VC, it is important to ensure you are talking to the right venture capitalist as well as making sure they have capital available for invest-ment. There are a number of VC firms that focus on specific sectors and markets, and it is important to research the venture capitalist's track record of investing in companies and exiting those investments. Do you know any of the business founders of the venture capitalist's investee companies? Can they share their experience of the venture capitalist? Experience of this kind is always worth searching out and considering.

The Irish Venture Capitalist Association (www.ivca.ie) contains the details of VC firms in the Republic of Ireland and Northern Ireland.

(**Note:** as discussed above in **Section 11.6**, prior to sharing any information with a potential investor, a company must always ensure that a confidenti-ality/non-disclosure agreement (NDA) is in place.)

11.11.7 Development Capital/Growth Funding

> **Development/growth capital is suitable for established, later-stage and scaling companies with export growth potential, i.e. those at the growth and maturity stage of the innovation lifecycle**

The concept of development/growth capital is only a recent development in Ireland. Prior to 2013, SMEs in Ireland did not have access to development capital funding, though it has played a key part in the growth of companies in the UK and in continental Europe, particularly Germany.

The role of development capital is to provide established, mid-sized and export-focused SMEs access to significant funding (from €2 million to €50 million) to assist them achieve their business objectives, which could include, for example:

- a merger/acquisition;
- a management buyout by the existing management team;
- funding to enter/expand in new/existing export markets;
- a partial liquidity event for existing shareholders, which provides an alternative to a premature sell-out; and
- new capital expenditure to fund increased production capacity.

Development capital funds will typically invest €2 million to €40 million in equity and quasi-equity, and focus on backing companies with experienced management teams with significant growth opportunities. 'Quasi-equity' is a category of debt that has traits of equity, including being convertible into equity should it not be repaid or certain key metrics like revenue or EBITDA targets are not met.

Developing capital can also be accessed by companies that are scaling, i.e. companies that have achieved revenues of between €3 and €5 million in a short period of time (usually between three and five years) and require significant funding to scale further.

There are four active development capital funds in Ireland:

1. **The BDO Development Capital Fund** (www.developmentcapital.ie) This is a €75 million fund that invests development and growth capital in established, mid-sized and profitable companies to support and accelerate their export growth plans. As of September 2018, the fund has completed nine investments with Version 1, Lifes2Good, Perigord, Obelisk, Netwatch, Broderick's, Blueface, Multihog and another confidential investment.

   The fund's investors include Enterprise Ireland, Bank of Ireland and some of Ireland's largest corporations, such as CRH plc, Glanbia plc and Glen Dimplex. Additionally, the fund makes available proven industry experts to investee companies to assist them in executing their business plans, including John Moloney, Helen Ryan, Jim Mountjoy, Noel Kelly and Alan Crosbie.

The BDO Development Capital Fund is sector-agnostic (i.e. it is not focused on investing in SMEs in a specific sector(s)) and can also provide alternatives to premature early-stage sell-out, by allowing the owners to 'take some money off the table'. A key aspect of this fund is that it employs flexible transaction instruments: its investments can involve both equity and quasi-equity instruments. This recognises that certain SME owners are averse to all-equity investment as they do not wish to dilute their shareholding. Quasi-equity instruments include convertible loans or convertible share instruments, which can convert into equity in certain circumstances, including, for example, a trade sale.

2. **The Carlyle Cardinal Ireland Fund** (www.cardinalcapitalgroup.com) This is a €292 million fund and is the largest private equity fund in Ireland (with an ISIF commitment of €125 million – see below). A 50:50 joint venture between Cardinal and the Carlyle Group, the US global asset manager, the fund has completed eight transactions as at September 2018, with investments completed in Lily O'Brien's, GSLS, Carroll Cuisine, Payzone, Abtran, Learning Pool, Sam McCauley Chemists and AA Ireland.

3. **MML Capital Ireland** (www.mmlcapital.ie) This is a €125 million fund focused on SMEs located on the island of Ireland with ambitious management teams to reach the next stage of their evolution, maximising growth opportunities at home and abroad. As at September 2018, MML had completed 11 investments with Lowe Refrigeration, Identigen, H&MV Engineering, Prim-Ed, Agenda Communications Conference Services, Fastway Couriers (Ireland), Sonas Bathrooms, Schivo Medical, Ashdale and the Travel Department.

4. **The Business Growth Fund** (www.bgf.co.uk) This is a new development capital and growth fund launched in November 2017. The €250 million fund is targeting SMEs with revenues between €5 and €100 million. At the time of writing, the fund had yet to announce an investment.

All of the above funds have Enterprise Ireland/Irish Strategic Investment Fund (ISIF) as investors with the balance of funding coming from the European Investment Fund, Irish plcs and institutional investors. The funds invest for both minority and majority equity stakes in the business.

Similar to VC, development capital investors will take a seat on the board and will look to add value by assisting the company accelerate its growth plan. The investment term is typically five years, following which the development capital investors will seek to realise their investment by way of refinancing to another development capital investor or a trade sale.

Similar to VC funding, it is imperative that the investee company's management team gets to know their potential development capital funder and know about their existing investee companies, what value-add they can bring and their track record as investors. (As an investor is carrying out due diligence in you and your company, it is important that you also learn what they are like as an investor.)

11.11.8 Private Equity and Family Funds

Private equity/family funds are typically suitable for established companies, i.e. the growth and mature stages in the innovation lifecycle

---

There are certain private equity and family funds that seek to invest equity capital in SMEs. Like development capital funds, they typically invest by way of equity instruments in established companies with significant growth prospects.

Private equity funds active in Ireland include:
* Broadlake Capital (www.broadlake.ie);
* Renatus Capital Partners (www.renatus.ie); and
* Causeway Capital Partners (www.causewaycapital.eu).

11.11.9 Initial Public Offering (IPO)

An initial public offering (IPO) involves making available for sale the shares of a private company to the public. IPOs (also known as a stock market listing or, simply, a 'listing') are often completed by companies seeking capital to expand, but they can also be undertaken by large, privately owned companies looking to become publicly traded.

There are several benefits in obtaining a listing, including:
* access to capital for growth;
* shareholder liquidity;
* broadening the shareholder base;
* enhancing the profile of the business;
* placing a market value on the business;
* encouraging employee commitment by, for example, providing share options as part of their annual remuneration; and
* increasing the company's ability to undertake acquisitions by using its now listed shares as consideration.

However, once listed, the business will face increased external scrutiny with related greater demands on the time of its management team.

Before embarking on an IPO, it is important to consider if the business is suitable for a listing, or if alternative financing or actions (such as a full or partial sale) would be more appropriate. Additionally, there are a number of factors to consider, including:
1. the most appropriate stock market on which to list;
2. getting IPO-ready – ensuring the correct business plan, business structure, equity growth story (detailing how the value of the company's equity will increase following the listing), corporate governance, investor relations, financial and IT systems are all prepared and in place;
3. the demands that come with being listed, including more detailed and higher frequency of reporting.

The Irish Stock Exchange (Euronext Dublin) notes that a company is suitable for a listing if it meets the following criteria:
- a compelling business proposition with strong growth prospects;
- visible and predictable earnings;
- strong board and management team;
- track record of delivery;
- strong intellectual property and developed customer relationships;
- competitive advantage in chosen market; and,
- a clear statement of how funds raised will be used.

(*Note*: as undertaking an IPO is a significant step, it is important to get independent legal and business advice.)

Following a listing, there are a number of compliance and reporting matters to be fulfilled by listed companies, as well as increased transparency and publically available information on the company's trading performance.

Also of note in this regard are the views of Orla O'Gorman, Head of Equity Listing Ireland at Euronext, which are set out in **Chapter 15**.

11.12 Conclusion

Equity capital is a key and necessary funding element for all companies irrespective of their size and scale of growth. As a business grows, it will require further equity capital to finance and maintain this growth. At some stage in a company's lifecycle, the founders of a business may have to raise equity capital externally and, as outlined in this chapter, there are several possible sources for that equity. However, prior to raising equity capital, it is important to consider whether the potential equity partner is the 'right fit' for the business in terms of their experience and the value-add they will bring ('more than just money'), for example introductions to possible customers, new suppliers, etc., as well as the timeframe for which they are willing to commit their funding. The use of different classes of shares can in some cases overcome any misalignment of interests. Most importantly, in advance of releasing any sensitive company information, a confidentiality/ non-disclosure agreement should be signed by potential investors receiving such information. Professional advice should be sought if the business owner is not comfortable with the proposed valuation of the company indicated by the equity investor. While it is not unusual for there to be differences between valuations proposed by seller and the buyer, it is important that both have a clear basis and logic for their respective valuations so that both can understand each other's basis of valuation.

As a company grows it is unlikely to continue to raise equity capital only; otherwise the founders would end up owning nothing. Other sources of finance are available and the continued growth of the company will depend upon getting the mix between equity capital and other sources, principally debt finance, correct. Debt finance will be examined in the next chapter.

AT A GLANCE: EQUITY CAPITAL

What is equity capital?	Equity capital is funding invested in a business in return for an ownership stake. It is also known as the share capital/share ownership, a concept that is, of course, more important where the business has multiple owners and/or investors.
What are the benefits of equity capital?	Benefits include: • improved cash flow; • credit risk is reduced; and • insights gained from experienced equity investors.
Are there any disadvantages?	• loss of control, in that the business owner is sharing the control and direction with the equity investor; • equity investors will share in profits generated.
How long does equity capital take to raise?	The length of time it takes to complete an equity investment can vary, from a number of weeks to months, depending on how quickly the equity investor wants to complete the investment and the required information for the equity investor to complete due diligence is furnished. For this reason, it is important that if an exclusivity period is requested by the equity investor it is kept to a minimum. Professional corporate finance advice will assist in keeping this period to a minimum.
Who provides equity capital to SMEs?	There are several equity investors seeking equity capital investments in SMEs at all stages of the innovation lifecycle (see **Section 11.11**).

CHAPTER 12

DEBT FINANCE
(FUNDING PILLAR 2)

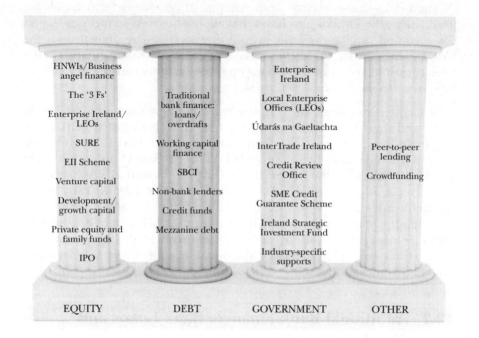

EQUITY	DEBT	GOVERNMENT	OTHER
HNWIs/Business angel finance		Enterprise Ireland	
The '3 Fs'	Traditional bank finance: loans/overdrafts	Local Enterprise Offices (LEOs)	
Enterprise Ireland/LEOs		Údarás na Gaeltachta	
SURE	Working capital finance	InterTrade Ireland	Peer-to-peer lending
EII Scheme	SBCI	Credit Review Office	
Venture capital	Non-bank lenders		Crowdfunding
Development/growth capital	Credit funds	SME Credit Guarantee Scheme	
Private equity and family funds	Mezzanine debt	Ireland Strategic Investment Fund	
IPO		Industry-specific supports	

12.1 Introduction: What Is Debt Finance?

Since the 2007/2008 global financial crisis, the Irish banking system has experienced a period of unprecedented change, with significant measures taken to try to prevent similar events occurring in the future. While many of the events from this time have been well documented and will remain topical for years to come, a real effect of this period of change is a smaller banking sector containing fewer active players with a reduced capacity to lend as well as a reduced (and arguably more appropriate) appetite for risk.

As detailed in **Chapter 10**, Irish small and medium-sized enterprises (SMEs), however, have always been highly dependent on banks for debt finance and the reduction in the number of active lenders in the market, and their reduced appetite for risk, has resulted in the emergence of an SME credit gap that the smaller banking system is unable to service. We have also seen the introduction of a number of government initiatives to encourage the remaining banks to provide funding solutions to fill this credit gap.

Additionally, the Government has encouraged alternative lenders to innovate and provide new ways of addressing the credit gap problem.

The principle of debt finance needs little or no introduction and as a result of the changes and emergence of alternative debt lenders, there are many different options available to SMEs to raise debt finance. These share the overall goal of providing sufficient funding to meet a business's needs while, at the same time, generating sufficient funds to manage the loan's scheduled repayments. Business needs that can comfortably be met through debt finance range from equipment purchases to materials for production, the kind of purchases that allow a business to meet its day-to-day costs and facilitate organic growth in its sector. The objective for the SME business owner, understandably, is to get access to this finance at the lowest feasible cost, ensuring repayment obligations can be met with as little stress to the business as possible.

This chapter examines the various types of debt finance available to SMEs and their sources. Debt finance comprises traditional bank funding, including loans and overdrafts, working capital facilities and commercial finance, which are provided by both banks and other debt providers. Following the financial crisis, which resulted in a reduction in bank credit, the Strategic Banking Corporation of Ireland (SBCI) was set up to provide access to flexible credit facilities for SMEs, while non-bank lenders have also entered the market to provide debt products to SMEs. Set out below is an overview of the various types and sources of debt facilities available to SMEs, which can be considered as a company evolves through its lifecycle.

12.2 Traditional Bank Finance: Bank Loans and Overdrafts

> **Bank loans and overdrafts are suitable for all companies throughout their lifecycles, subject to meeting the bank's lending criteria**

Bank loans and overdrafts are one of the most common forms of debt finance for SMEs. Bank approval depends on a number of factors including the business's credit history and rating, its industry sector, the number of years it is in operation, its repayment capacity and whether it has any assets that can be offered as security. Most banks may require businesses to provide an asset or personal guarantee as security for a bank loan. However, this can vary depending on the amount of funding being borrowed. If the business defaults on repayment, the bank/lender can seize the asset and sell it to cover the cost of the loan.

Repayment of bank loans (which can also be referred to as 'amortisation') can be structured (with agreement of the bank) to be capital/principal repayment with an interest-only period, and can be short-, medium- or long-term, depending on the purpose of the loan and the needs of the business.

Most bank loans will be structured with a clause that allows the bank to call for the immediate repayment of the loan despite the loan repayment being restructured over a number of months or years. This is called 'on demand' and allows the bank to take action in respect of its loan facilities if the company is not performing within the bank-agreed metrics, as set out in the loan facility letter.

EXAMPLE 12.1: MATCHING THE LOAN TO THE BUSINESS'S NEEDS

A company is involved in the manufacture of children's toys and a large portion of its revenue is generated in November and December each year. As a result of the company's seasonality and uneven cash flow, it funds its operation by way of a short-term bank loan drawn (for a six-month term) at a cost of 4% per annum in July of each year.

The loan is repayable the following February in one lump sum and the company uses the cash generated from the November/December sales to repay the loan facility.

In this scenario, the company borrowed funds and matched the loan to the cash flow of the business to enable it to meet market demand.

Like bank loans, bank overdrafts are repayable on demand and are closely monitored by banks to ensure that the overdraft stays within the sanctioned limit set by the bank. Overdrafts are generally more expensive than a bank loan and are usually used to fund short-term cash flow.

12.2.1 Key Terms to Understand before Raising Bank Debt Finance

'**Loan facility/agreement**' The loan/credit arrangement through which a company can borrow funds up to an agreed sum.

'**Fixed interest rates**' Interest that remains at the same rate for the entire life of a loan.

'**Variable interest rates**' Interest that changes rate on the basis of changes in an agreed-upon index (usually the European Central Bank (ECB) rate of interest).

'**Loan term**' Loan terms vary from short to long term, as determined by the bank in consultation with the company, and is the length of time the loan is available to the company. The loan term will include any period of time that the company is required to make interest-only payments, plus the period of time of both capital and interest payments.

'**Amortisation period**' This is the period of time over which a debt is paid off. If a company is making equal payments each month to pay off a loan, an amortisation period of 20 years will result in higher monthly payments than a period of, say, 30 years. With agreement from the bank, the amortisation period may be extended beyond the length of the original loan term with agreement from the bank.

'**Collateral**' Also known as security, collateral is the asset(s) used to provide security for a debt; the strength of the collateral can affect the rate, amortisation period and term of a loan.

'**Loan covenants**' These are conditions, both financial and non-financial, to a loan that require the borrower to fulfil, or which restrict the borrower from undertaking, certain actions.

'**Interest cover**' A measure of a company's ability to meet its loan interest payments. Capital I cover is calculated by dividing earnings before interest and taxes (EBIT) by the annual loan interest cost.

'**Gearing**' Gearing represents a company's leverage, meaning how much of the business's funding comes from creditors (debt holders) compared to the company's owners (shareholders).

'**Headroom**' In the context of a loan facility/arrangement, 'headroom' is the amount of the facility as yet undrawn.

'**Loan pre-conditions/conditions precedent**' The conditions precedent detail the necessary consents and approvals required to be satisfied prior to a loan being available for drawdown by a company, e.g. provision of an independent valuation for an asset being provided as security (collateral), audited financial statements or independent confirmation that the company is tax compliant.

'**Gross leverage**' Usually used as a financial covenant metric, gross leverage sets the level at which a company's borrowings can be in excess of its EBITDA (earnings before interest, tax, depreciation and amortisation). For example, a gross leverage ratio of 3.5 to 1 means that borrowings are 3.5 times EBITDA. If this number increased, it would reveal that EBITDA is falling and, if set as a financial covenant metric, the company would be in breach of this performance ratio.

'**Debt service ratio (DSR)**' DSR is calculated by dividing a company's EBITDA by the amount of debt service required to be made, i.e. annual interest and capital repayments. A bank will set a level of DSR to be maintained by the company during the term of a loan.

'**Events of default**' A list of events as a result of which, if they occur, the bank may demand immediate repayment of the loan along with all accrued interest. Examples of events of default include breach of a covenant, significant decrease in the value of a secured asset or any other matters where the bank may deem their loan repayment is compromised, i.e. a winding-up petition.

'**Letter of offer/credit**' A letter from a bank/lender detailing the terms and conditions of the offer of a loan, specifying the amount of the loan, its term, interest rate, fees and costs, any pre-conditions of drawdown, security required, information rights and covenants to be complied with.

'**Fixed charge security/debenture**' A charge/lien on a specific fixed asset (such as land/buildings) to secure the repayment of a loan. Under this arrangement, the asset is signed over to the lender and the borrower cannot sell it without the lender's permission. The lender also registers a charge against the asset, which remains in force until the loan is repaid.

'**Floating charge security**' A charge/lien on more than one asset (which floats from asset to asset) that changes in quantity and/or value from time to time (such as debtors or stock), to provide security for the repayment of a loan. Under this arrangement, no charge is registered against the asset and the owner of the asset can deal in it as usual. If a default occurs, or the borrower goes into liquidation, the floating asset 'freezes' into its then current state, 'crystallizing' the floating charge into a fixed charge and making the lender a priority creditor. The proceeds from the disposal of these charged assets will be used to discharge the lender as a priority creditor.

12.2.2 Costs of Bank Loans and Overdrafts

Bank loans and overdrafts are provided at a cost, which is generally interest charged on the owed amount. Other fees and charges may be applicable, depending on the type of loan and on the lender. There are generally seven elements of bank loan/overdraft costs that need to be explained:
1. arrangement fees;
2. interest;
3. insurance;
4. interest break cost;
5. early repayment fees;
6. covenant compliance costs; and
7. legal and professional advice.

1. **Arrangement fees** These are payable to the lender to reserve the funds and to cover account/loan opening costs. Arrangement fees will vary, depending on the complexity of the business, the loan, its quantum and risk.

2. **Interest** The most common types of interest rate are fixed or variable, which include the bank's margin (or profit). Bank loans are generally priced based on the European Central Bank rate (Euribor plus bank margin). Interest charged will also vary depending on risk of default.

3. **Insurance** Key person insurance may be a pre-condition of loan drawdown and in the majority of cases is assigned (meaning it is for the benefit of the bank/lender) to the lender to cover some or all of the principal owed in case the borrower becomes incapacitated or dies. The amount and cost of this insurance varies and is dependent on the health history of the insured person and the quantum and term of the borrowings.

4. **Interest break cost** This is the cost of breaking and changing a fixed interest rate loan to a variable rate loan. The bank may charge a fee to compensate for the loss of the fixed interest rate if this is higher than the variable rate.

5. **Early repayment fees** These are fees that may be charged if a company repays a loan over a shorter period of time than the approved term of the loan.

6. **Covenant compliance costs** These include costs that may be required to be incurred in order to satisfy the bank's pre-condition of the draw down of funds, including, for example, the cost of an independent valuation of an asset being provided as security, or a third-party review of fit-out costs of a new building.

7. **Legal and professional advice** Legal fees may be applicable and payable if bank professional and legal advice is required on the loan, while such fees are also likely to apply when providing an assets(s) as security for a loan for which the bank will want to confirm both the value of the security and that the asset has no prior charges on it (i.e. provided to other lenders, or if there were, that they are now discharged).

12.2.3 Bank Loan Covenants

For business loans, there are generally requirements to maintain certain financial ratios within set parameters. These are called 'bank loan covenants' and establish benchmark metrics that are intended to ensure that the borrowing company stays financially healthy and, more importantly, that the bank's loan is protected.

Bank loan covenants are generally classified in two broad categories, restrictive or financial, and within these categories can either be positive or negative.

A positive covenant requires a company to meet certain standards defined by the bank, such as maintaining a minimum level of liquidity, revenues or EBITDA, for example a minimum level of annual sales and/or EBITDA, minimum gross leverage and debt servicing levels. Restrictive (negative) covenants are intended to restrain a business from taking certain actions, such as adding more debt, making capital expenditure above a certain amount or replacing top management, without the bank's consent.

Covenants are measured by the bank on either an annual, semi-annual or quarterly basis, and the bank generally requires the company to furnish a covenant certificate certifying that the covenants have been complied with.

12.2.4 Information Rights

As a condition of granting the loan, as well as a condition of its continued availability, the bank will almost certainly request certain information, such as the latest audited company financial statements, generally within 90/120 days of the company's year end; management accounts, which could be on a monthly or quarterly basis, 20 or 45 days after the month or quarter end; and the annual financial and cash-flow projections, generally 45 days in advance of the preceding year end. This information will be agreed prior to sanctioning the loan facility and will be set out in the bank's letter of offer.

12.2.5 Timeframe for Arranging Bank Loans

The timeframe for arranging a bank loan will vary, depending on the stage of readiness of the business and the type of loan applied for. Unsecured loans can take between one and four weeks, whereas secured loans can take between two and three months. However, this varies depending on the bank and the amount and purpose of the loan, and is subject to the established track record the company may have with the bank, as well as whether the bank currently holds the security for the loan.

Similar to raising equity capital, independent professional advice should be sought.

12.2.6 Advantages and Disadvantages of Bank Loans

There are a number of advantages to funding SMEs by way of bank loans, including:
- the business is guaranteed the money for a certain period, generally three to 10 years (unless it breaches the loan conditions/covenants);
- while interest must be paid on the loan, it is not necessary to provide the bank with a share in the business;
- the loan amount, length of term, repayment schedules and type of interest rate can be tailored to suit the business, including both cash-flow and income generation;
- due to the current climate of low interest rates, the borrowings usually are at a low annual cost;
- interest and bank arrangement fees are normally tax-deductible in the company's annual corporation tax return; and
- loans can be matched to the lifetime of the equipment or other assets for which the loan was made.

Possible disadvantages or drawbacks of bank loans include:
- as with other types of debt, if the loan is secured and the business fails to repay, the lender may take action to seize the security provided for the loan;
- a loan is not flexible and may not provide the best use of capital for businesses with fluctuating finance requirements (for example, a growing business might take a loan out for €500,000 but due to various factors finds it only needs €250,000, meaning that interest is being paid on €250,000 of excess finance); and
- defaults on loan repayments can lead to a fall in a company's credit rating, increased interest rates for existing and future loans, collateral being seized and legal proceedings against the company. Company directors may also be personally affected, depending on how the loan is structured. There could also be an impact on the directors personally arising from any possible breaches under the Companies Act 2014.

12.3 Working Capital Finance

12.3.1 Introduction

As companies evolve and grow through their innovation lifecycle, an increasing amount of cash/funding is consumed within the business. This is known as its 'working capital', which effectively signifies how much of a company's cash is 'tied up' in its day-to-day operations.

Working capital is determined or calculated from a company's balance sheet by deducting a company's current liabilities (i.e. short-term debts that are payable within 12 months) from its current assets (i.e. stocks, trade debtors, etc.). (*Note*: in representing the cash required to manage a business on a day-to-day basis, a company's working capital requirement has no direct correlation with its profits or losses.)

An example of a working capital calculation is set out below in **Example 12.2**.

EXAMPLE 12.2: WORKING CAPITAL CALCULATION

ABC Ltd
BALANCE SHEET (extract)
For year ending 31 December

Current Assets		Current Liabilities (short-term)	
Stock	€300,000	Trade creditors	€350,000
Trade debtors	€450,000	Payroll taxes	€65,000
Bank/Cash	€250,000	Bank loan	€65,000
Total current assets	€1,000,000	Total current liabilities	€480,000
	A		B

ABC Ltd's Working Capital = €520,000 (A – B)

This means that ABC Ltd has €520,000 of cash tied up in its day-to-day operations, sufficient assets to pay off its short-term debts.

Positive working capital means that a business is able to pay off its short-term liabilities as they fall due for payment. Also, a high working capital can be a signal that a company may be able to expand its operations or has too much investment in stocks, debtors or other assets.

Negative working capital means that a business is unable to meet its short-term liabilities with its current assets. Therefore, an immediate increase in sales, profitability or additional capital into the company may be necessary in order to continue its operations.

Working capital also provides an indication of a company's operational efficiency. Money tied up in inventory or accounts receivable cannot pay off any of the company's short-term financial obligations. Therefore, working capital analysis is very important, though also very complex.

For example, an increase in working capital could be explained by an increase in debtors (through an increase in sales), but it could also be due to slow debtor cash collection or too much of an increase in inventory. The precise circumstances would need to be carefully reviewed on a case-by-case basis.

12.3.2 Evaluating Working Capital

As detailed above, working capital is a measure of a company's liquidity and overall financial health. Due to the fact that its calculation (as set out above) comprises cash, stocks, trade debtors, creditors and other liabilities due within one year, a company's working capital reflects a number of day-to-day operational activities, including stock management, debtors control, cash collection and payments to suppliers.

Positive working capital generally indicates that a company is able to pay off its short-term liabilities almost immediately. Negative working capital generally indicates a company is unable to do so. This is why investors tend to be sensitive to a company's working capital requirement. If its requirement is deteriorating, this needs to be reviewed and interpreted very carefully and may suggest that the company is struggling to maintain or grow sales, is paying bills too quickly, has too much stock or is collecting receivables too slowly. Increases in working capital, on the other hand, suggest the opposite and suggests a well-managed company with opportunity and balance sheet funding available for growth. There are several ways to evaluate a company's working capital further, including calculating days and comparing the ratios both to prior periods and with other companies within the same sector/industry: the stock–turnover ratio (i.e. how many times stock is turned over or sold and replaced during a period), trade debtors days (which measures on average how many days it takes a company's customers to pay for its products/services),[1] and creditor days (which measures on average, how many days it takes the company to pay its suppliers).[2]

One of the most significant uses of working capital is stock. The longer stock sits on the shelf or in the warehouse, the longer the company's working capital is tied up. Hence, the importance of continuously reviewing the stock-holding policy. If a company's stock–turnover ratio is decreasing, it could suggest that the company is holding too much stock or that sales are falling and the reasons/drivers behind this should be reviewed and investigated.

---

[1] The longer it takes for its customers to pay it, the less liquidity a company will have and could indicate that certain debtors/customers are problematic/not recoverable.

[2] An increasing number of creditor days would indicate that the company may be financing its day-to-day operations by delaying payment to its suppliers. Such a ratio should be further investigated.

EXAMPLE 12.3: EVALUATING WORKING CAPITAL

Using the scenario of ABC Ltd in **Example 12.2** above, if ABC's stock–turnover ratio was 10 times and in the subsequent financial year it decreases to five times, all other things being equal, this could (subject to investigation) suggest that the company currently has too much stock, declining sales or obsolete stock and the reasons for same should be investigated. For certain companies, stock is a material component of its working capital; examining the details above, €300,000 of ABC's working capital of €520,000 is comprised of stock.

Therefore, although ABC Ltd has a positive working capital, the liquidity of each of the elements comprising it should be closely examined to ensure ABC Ltd has sufficient cash to fund its day-to-day operations. For example, in addition to the €300,000 tied up in stocks, €450,000 is due from the company's debtors. Depending on how quickly ABC's stock turns (i.e. is sold) and how frequently its debtors pay will determine how liquid/realisable these elements of its working capital are. These are part of ABC's working capital cycle, i.e. how quickly stocks, debtors, etc. are realised and its creditors are paid. An advantage of ABC's working capital component is that it has €250,000 of cash, which can be used to fund its operations. However, not all companies have readily realisable current assets or sufficient cash to fund their working capital cycle. For these companies, working capital finance is often required.

12.3.3 Financing Working Capital

In the majority of cases, a company's customers, i.e. its trade debtors, do not pay immediately for the goods/services provided and can take 30 days (or longer) credit. Therefore, a company must fund this investment by either having sufficient cash to pay for its suppliers, employees, etc., or seek a dedicated working capital facility to provide it with interim funding.

Subject to the type of company and its working capital composition, there are a number of options to finance a company's working capital requirement, including equity capital (see **Chapter 11**) which can be used to fund a company's initial and ongoing working capital requirement. Working capital facilities for SMEs include the following:
1. invoice discounting/debtor finance;
2. invoice factoring;
3. supplier finance; and
4. asset finance.

12.3.4 Invoice Discounting/Debtor Finance

Invoice discounting (also known as debtor finance) is where a company's trade debtors (customers that are sold goods/services on credit) are used as collateral for a loan issued by a bank/finance company.

Essentially, invoice discounting accelerates cash flow for a company from its trade debtors: instead of waiting for these customers to pay within the agreed credit terms, the company receives cash almost as soon as the invoice is issued. The bank/finance company earns revenue both from the interest rate it charges on the loan (which is well above the ECB rate), and from a monthly fee it charges to maintain the arrangement.

The invoice discounting finance provider will generally take a floating charge over the company's trade debtors/receivables (which, as set out in **Section 12.2.1**, is a secured charge by the lender over assets which change in quantity or value from time to time, allowing the invoice discounting provider to recover any unpaid amounts by the company from all amounts owing from the company's trade debtors). Invoice discounting is not possible, however, if another lender already has title to all of the company assets (i.e. fixed and floating charges) as collateral on a different loan. In such situations, the other lender would need to waive its right to the company's trade debtors collateral and, instead, take a second-ranking charge on the trade debtors behind the invoice discounting finance company's debt.

The amount of the invoice discounting facility provided by the finance provider is always less than the total amount outstanding from trade debtors, typically 75%–80% of all invoices less than 90 days old, which provides the finance provider with an element of 'headroom' should some trade debtors not pay (i.e. the finance provider is only providing funding on debts at a rate of 80% and for those debts that are less than 90 days old).

For debtors that are funded by the invoice discounting provider and, in turn, take a credit term greater than 90 days, this will reduce the amount available to the company to draw in the future. The invoice discounting provider will deduct the amount from the remaining available facility as part of its month-end reconciliation.

From an operational perspective, the company sends an accounts receivable report to the finance provider at least once a month, aggregating receivables into the categories required by the invoice discounting provider. The finance company uses this information to adjust the amount of funding that it can lend the company under the terms of the agreed invoice-discounting lending agreement. The company retains control over the accounts receivable, which means that it is responsible for extending credit to customers, invoicing them and collecting from them. Customers do not need to be notified about the discounting arrangement.

Invoice discounting provides a short-term, once-off cash-flow benefit and should be considered carefully because of the ongoing associated fees. As noted above, to be in a position to avail of invoice discounting as a financing alternative, companies should exclude accounts receivable from the security for any other financing arrangements.

Benefits of invoice discounting can include:
- the immediate release of cash that has been, or is due to be, locked into customer invoices for a period of time (which can be very useful in funding a company's working capital cycle);
- an immediate reduction in a company's working capital cycle as it receives up to 75%–80% of the invoiced amount in cash, allowing it to fund its payments to suppliers/employees, etc.;
- confidentially between the company and finance provider. The company may not want its customers to know that it is borrowing money on their promise to pay an invoice. The customer will not notice any difference.

Potential drawbacks of invoice discounting include:
- as a source of finance it can cost more than the charges associated with a bank loan and so may impact on profit margins;
- some businesses can become overly dependent on invoice discounting as a funding source and find it difficult to leave without impacting their operations and funding of future sales; and
- in order to be accepted by an invoice-discounting provider, the company must have established credit-collection processes and procedures in place. Additionally, the provider will conduct quarterly audits of the borrower's debtors, sales and credit-collection procedures.

12.3.5 Invoice Factoring

Another type of working capital finance, invoice factoring works in a similar way to invoice discounting, with a key difference being credit control. With invoice factoring, rather than simply advancing cash to the borrowing company and then leaving the collection of its trade debtors to the company, the lender takes control of the sales ledger and deals directly with customers so as to ensure invoices are paid on time.

The main reason that a company may choose to factor its trade debtors is to receive cash immediately rather than waiting for the credit period to complete, i.e. the 30 to 60 days it often takes customers to pay. Like invoice discounting, factoring allows companies to quickly increase their cash flow, which makes it easier to discharge creditors, pay employees, and increase production/service throughput to fulfill increasing customer orders.

There are two types of invoice factoring (or 'factoring'):
- recourse; and
- non-recourse.

Recourse factoring is where a company sells its invoices to a factoring company (a 'factor') with the stipulated agreement/condition that the company will buy back the invoices if the monies owed on them cannot be collected. This type of factoring plan is generally affordable since the company is agreeing to absorb some of the risk involved in the transaction.

With **non-recourse factoring** a company sells its invoices to a factoring company without the obligation of buying the invoices back if the monies owed on them cannot be collected. Instead, if the customers renege on their payments or pay their invoices late, any losses are absorbed by the factor, leaving the business unscathed. For this reason, this type of facility is generally more costly.

While improving cash flow is the main reason a company may choose to factor its invoices, factoring has other advantages, including:

- factors provide free back-office support, including managing collections from customers, which can allow business owners more time and resources to focus on growing the company;
- factoring is based on the quality of the credit history of a company's customers, not the company's credit or business history;
- it can be customised and managed to provide capital as and when an individual company needs it; and
- it is scalable, meaning that the amount of funding available can increase as its trade debtors grow.

12.3.5.1 Disadvantages of Factoring

Some of a company's customers may prefer to deal directly with it. How the factor deals with customers may affect what those customers think of the company. For this reason, it is important that a reputable factor is used that will not damage a company's reputation.

12.3.6 Supplier Finance

Supplier finance provides a company with a line of credit to pay suppliers, without impacting on its existing funding arrangements. The finance provider assesses the company's creditworthiness and obtains credit insurance on the company. The finance provider sanctions a line of finance to the client, matching the credit insurance limit. Once the facility is in place, the funder simply pays supplier invoices on behalf of the client. The funder usually gets repaid from proceeds from debtor receipts.

Supplier finance is ideal for financially strong companies and frees up cash that would be required to pay suppliers, allowing the company to invest cash elsewhere in the business.

12.3.7 Debt Finance Sources for SMEs: Bank Loans, Overdrafts and Working Capital Facilities

12.3.7.1 The Domestic Banks

All of the domestic banks (AIB, Bank of Ireland, Ulster Bank, Permanent TSB and KBC) provide term loan, overdraft and working capital finance options (i.e. invoice discounting, factoring, supplier and asset finance) for SMEs at all stages of their development. Typically, each bank has dedicated relationship managers to assist SMEs in securing loans and/or working capital finance. The quantum, use of the funds, repayment capacity, security and cash-flow forecasts will all be assessed to determine the SME's suitability for the debt finance being sought.

At the time of writing, all of the above banks are actively seeking lending opportunities in the market, creating a competitive environment that allows SME owners to shop around for the best terms for their business.

12.3.7.2 The Strategic Banking Corporation of Ireland

In addition to the domestic banks, the Strategic Banking Corporation of Ireland (SBCI, see http://sbci.gov.ie) was established by the Irish Government in 2014 for the purpose of making low-cost credit aimed specifically at Irish SMEs and startups. The SBCI's funding partners include:
• the European Investment Bank (EIB);
• KfW (the German Development Bank); and
• the Ireland Strategic Investment Fund (ISIF).

Lending commenced in March 2015 through the SBCI's specialist on-lenders, which include both bank and non-bank partners. As of December 2017, nearly 18,725 SMEs had borrowed €783 million of loans, with an average loan of €41,798.

The SBCI's goal is to ensure access to flexible funding for Irish SMEs by facilitating the provision of:
1. financial products with longer maturity and capital repayment flexibility, subject to credit approval;
2. lower cost funding to financial institutions, the benefit of which is passed on to SMEs; and
3. access for new entrants to the SME lending market, creating competition.

All of the above are intended to create a more competitive and dynamic environment for SME debt funding with the funding being available to SMEs through both bank and non-bank specialist on-lenders.

The SBCI aims to deliver lending products for SMEs, including the following:

TABLE 12.1: SBCI LENDING PRODUCTS

Product	Key Features
SBCI Investment & Working Capital Loans	• Lower interest rates • Loan amounts up to €5 million • Used for investment and working capital purposes • Term: 2–10 years • Repayment flexibility
Refinance of Facilities with Exiting Banks	• Lower interest rates • Loan amounts up to €5 million • Used for refinancing facilities with banks that are exiting the Irish market

Agricultural Investment Loans	• Lower interest rates • Loan amounts up to €5 million • Used for SMEs involved in primary agricultural production, the processing or marketing of agricultural products • Term: 2–10 years • Repayment flexibility
Leasing and Hire-purchase Solutions	• Leasing scheme that offers flexible asset finance funding solutions, including leasing and hire-purchase that will allow SMEs finance assets including cars, commercial vehicles, plant and machinery • Lease terms are usually between 2 and 5 years and provide SMEs with fixed monthly rental payments for the term
Invoice Financing Solutions	The SBCI invoice financing facility provides SMEs with finance of up to 90% of a company's trade debtors

For more information, see https://sbci.gov.ie

12.3.7.2.1 Where and How to Apply for SBCI Lending Products

SBCI's products are available through both bank and non-bank financial institutions (called SBCI's 'on-lending partners'). The SBCI provides access to the same, lower-cost funds to all its on-lending partners. While the on-lending partners may use different pricing approaches, the SBCI ensures (through detailed monitoring) that the financial advantage of the lower-cost funding obtained by the on-lenders is fully passed on in the SBCI loans provided to eligible SMEs. It is also important to note that all of the SBCI's products are subject to the financial institutions' own credit policies and procedures.

In 2016, the SBCI announced new on-lending agreements with four non-bank lenders: Finance Ireland, Merrion Fleet, First Citizen and Bibby Financial Services Ireland. This was a vital step in creating greater competition for SME lending in the Irish market, by supporting smaller indigenous players and providing funding for a broader range of products, including investment and working capital loans, lease and hire-purchase, invoice discounting and refinancing.

In April 2018, a €300 million SME Brexit Loan Scheme was launched by the Irish Government and will be operated by the SBCI. The scheme provides low-cost funding (at 4% or less), which is supported by the European Investment Fund, to SMEs that are innovating in response to the challenges posed by Brexit. The scheme covers loans ranging from €25,000 to €1.5 million, with loans of up to €500,000 being unsecured.

The SBCI will engage directly with Brexit-impacted businesses to assist them with the eligibility process and in applying for loans. SMEs can start the process by visiting the SBCI website (www.sbci.gov.ie) and completing an application form to establish their eligibility for the scheme. Once an SME is confirmed as qualifying for the scheme, it is provided with a unique code from the SBCI confirming that it is eligible, which it can then bring to any of the three lenders in the scheme. These are (at the date of writing) Bank of Ireland, Ulster Bank and AIB.

As Ireland's national strategic bank, the SBCI is committed to leveraging these existing on-lender relationships and encouraging the entry of new on-lending partners to improve access to low-cost, flexible, longer-term finance for the SME sector, increasing competition in the SME financing market and thereby supporting SME growth and investment. The introduction of new lending arrangements with non-bank lenders as well as the new Brexit SME Loan Scheme are testament to a continuing flexibility and speed of response to changing economic conditions and the potential impact on SMEs. The positive impact of adding over half a billion euro to the Irish economy, supporting SMEs and job creation cannot be understated.

12.3.8 Asset Debt Finance

Asset debt finance is used by companies to obtain assets, typically vehicles, plant and equipment, which are needed to grow and scale the business. It involves making regular payments for the use of such assets over an agreed period of time, thus avoiding the full cost of buying the assets outright. The company gets immediate use of the asset to assist in generating additional sales while the amount owing to the finance provider for the leased asset is recorded as a liability on the company's balance sheet. The most common types of asset debt finance products are:
- leasing;
- hire-purchase; and
- asset refinance.

12.3.8.1 Leasing

Leasing gives a company the full use and benefits of the asset for a monthly fee; however, the company does not have ownership of the asset. At the end of the primary rental term, the company has the option to return the equipment or use it through a secondary rental agreement for a lower reduced fee.

12.3.8.2 Hire-purchase

Hire purchase enables a company to buy an asset(s) by spreading the cost of the asset over an agreed time frame. At the end of the term, the company has the option to purchase the asset for a small fee. The finance provider owns the asset until the final instalment is paid; however, the company has full use of the asset throughout the repayment period, which is usually between two and five years.

12.3.8.3 Asset Refinance

Asset refinance (also known as sale and leaseback) allows a company to release cash tied up in unencumbered assets. The company sells the asset to the finance provider and then leases it back, paying a monthly fee. At the end of the term, there is a nominal 'purchase fee'.

12.3.8.4 Advantages of Using Asset Finance

Asset finance can be used to fund most assets, including, for example, IT and telecoms systems, CCTV equipment, shop fit-out, office furniture, catering equipment, vehicles, plant and machinery, etc. It offers an optimal solution if the business needs new equipment that might otherwise be unaffordable. The various forms of asset finance provide the following advantages for businesses:

- access to required equipment without incurring the cash-flow disadvantage of an outright purchase;
- finance agreements can often be tailored to the business's needs, with flexibility on both the term and repayment schedule;
- leasing and hire-purchase support accurate budgeting, as payments are usually fixed, allowing improved cash-flow management; and
- asset finance providers often specialise in a particular type of asset about which they have expert knowledge.

All of the domestic banks offer asset debt finance products and, as set out in **Section 12.4** below, there are a number of non-bank lenders that also provide asset finance products.

12.4 Non-bank SME Lenders

There are several specialist working capital funders that can provide specific financial products to SMEs. Set out below in **Table 12.2** is a summary overview of some of the potential funders.

TABLE 12.2: SUMMARY OF NON-BANK SME LENDERS

BIBBY FINANCIAL SERVICES IRELAND   Bibby Financial Services Ireland (www.bibbyfinancialservices.ie) provides SMEs with invoice discounting and factoring facilities for both startups and established companies, irrespective of business sector. It also offers invoice export and recruitment finance, which is focused on export and recruitment companies.   **Required company stage of development**:   SMEs at all stages of development, subject to lending criteria.   **Types of funding and support**:   Invoice discounting and factoring.

CAPITALFLOW

Capitalflow (www.capitalflow.ie) provides SMEs with a choice of invoice discounting, asset finance (hire-purchase, lease and asset re-finance) and property finance products.

Required company stage of development:

SMEs at all stages of development, subject to lending criteria.

Types of funding and support:

Working capital finance including:

- invoice discounting;
- hire-purchase;
- lease finance;
- asset refinance; and
- property finance.

CLOSE BROTHERS COMMERCIAL FINANCE

Close Brothers Commercial Finance (www.closecommercialfinance.ie) provides invoice and asset finance products tailored to companies' specific requirements. Close Brothers also offers SMEs asset-based lending products, which provide larger SMEs with invoice finance as well as finance from other assets of the SME, e.g. stock, property or plant and machinery, etc.

Required company stage of development:

SMEs at all stages of development, subject to lending criteria.

Types of funding and support:

Invoice and asset finance.

CONVERTIBILL

Convertibill (www.convertibill.com) provides SMEs with the following finance products including:

- order finance – to fulfil orders/contracts;
- supplier finance – to pay suppliers;
- invoice finance (discounting and factoring) – to release cash tied up in trade debtors;
- sales finance – to provide business's customers with credit;
- distribution finance – to finance the supply and distribution cycle;
- lease finance – to finance equipment and other assets required by the company; and
- project finance – to fund both large, medium and small projects.

The different forms of finance offered by Convertibill are designed to meet the varying needs of business.

Required company stage of development:

SMEs at all stages of development, subject to lending criteria.

Types of funding and support:

See above.

FINANCE IRELAND

Finance Ireland (www.financeireland.ie) specialises in providing SMEs motor finance, finance and leasing (incorporating hire-purchase, contract hire, short-term car rental), commercial mortgages, asset management (primarily debt purchase and recovery) and agri-finance.

In 2016, the Irish Strategic Investment Fund (ISIF) invested €30 million in Finance Ireland for a 32% equity stake in the company, with the funding being used to expand its financial offerings. Finance Ireland also manages a €100 million 'Milkflex' fund, which offers dairy farmers access to flexible, low-interest loans, and which is aimed at assisting dairy farmers (specifically members of the Glanbia Co-op) to increase dairy production. The funding can be used for a wide variety of purposes, with an element allocated for new entrants to dairy farming. The fund stakeholders are the ISIF, Glanbia Co-op, Rabobank and Finance Ireland.

Required company stage of development:

SMEs at all stages of development and farmers, subject to lending criteria.

Types of funding and support:

- motor finance;
- SME and agri-asset backed loans;
- commercial property loans, from €1 million to €10 million; and
- Milkflex loans for dairy farmers.

GRENKE

Grenke's core product offering is leasing (www.grenke.ie). Very small asset purchases can be financed with a Grenke leasing arrangement, starting with assets costing €500.

Grenke operates independently of vendors and banks, meaning SMEs are not tied to a particular brand or manufacturer. Its leasing offering focuses on office and communications equipment, medical devices, security systems and production equipment. However, on request, it may be possible to lease other items.

Required company stage of development:

SMEs at all stages of development, subject to lending criteria.

Types of funding and support:

See above.

GROWCAP FINANCE

Growcap Finance was established in 2015 and provides trade and supply-chain funding to SMEs in Ireland (www.growcapfinance.com).

Required company stage of development:

Established SMEs, subject to lending criteria.

Types of funding and support:

Trade and supply-chain funding to finance a company's purchases from abroad. Growcap provides the overseas supplier with a letter of credit (which is a form of payment commitment) to allow the supplier to release the goods knowing that it will be paid, which is the pre-agreed facility with Growcap.

For an SME it means that the goods acquired will be delivered at the agreed date and place, while the supplier will be equally confident that it will receive payment from Growcap's bank.

MICROFINANCE IRELAND LTD

MicroFinance Ireland (MFI) (www.microfinanceireland.ie) is a not-for-profit lender, established to deliver the Government's Microenterprise Loan Fund, which was put in place to support 'micro enterprises' with less than 10 employees and with an annual turnover of less than €2 million that are having difficulties in accessing funding from banks and other commercial lenders.

Helping to create or sustain jobs is a key tenet of MFI business. Startups, newly established and growing micro enterprises may have difficulty in accessing funding from banks due to trading difficulties or for other reasons such as lack of security, current level of bank debt, difficulty with existing borrowings or lack of a track record. Irish-based businesses can apply to MFI Ireland for unsecured business loans from €2,000 to €25,000.

Required company stage of development:

Early-stage development loan finance for Irish-based businesses with less than 10 employees. Sole traders and partnerships, as well as companies, can apply, subject to lending criteria.

Types of funding and support:

Unsecured business loans from €2,000 up to €25,000 for start-up, cash-flow or expansion purposes. The repayment terms of MFI loans vary from three to five years. In addition, MFI can provide mentoring from an experienced business mentor on the local enterprise office (LEO) mentoring panel.

SME FINANCE & LEASING SOLUTIONS

SME Finance & Leasing Solutions (www.smeleasing.ie) provides leasing for lower-priced assets (€1,000–€15,000) and so facilitates the capital expenditure requirements of SMEs, irrespective of size.

SME Finance & Leasing Solutions does not offer leasing services directly to SMEs; it provides finance through a nationwide network of independent equipment vendors, sales organisations and other dealer-based origination networks, focussing on a number of key market segments. SME Finance & Leasing Solutions also offers a financial product called 'Sales Aid Leasing', which allows an SME offer its customers a finance option for purchasing the SME's products/services.

Required company stage of development:

SMEs at all stages of development, subject to lending criteria.

Types of funding and support:

Leasing for all types of business equipment as well as Sales Aid Leasing (as described above).

THE WESTERN DEVELOPMENT COMMISSION (WDC)

The Western Development Commission (WDC) (www.wdc.ie) manages the WDC Investment Fund (WIF) which provides investment funding for SMEs, community and micro enterprises, based in or relocating to the Western Region.

Required company stage of development:

Funding is available to micro, small and medium-sized enterprises as well as social enterprises in counties Clare, Donegal, Galway, Leitrim, Mayo, Sligo and Roscommon, subject to lending criteria.

Types of funding and support:

Equity investments from €100,000 to €1 million, and both loan and micro loan finance facilities ranging from €5,000 to €300,000 are available, subject to the company's needs and business plan.

12.5 Credit Funds

In addition to the non-bank lenders described above in **Section 12.4**, the Irish Government further responded to the financial crisis by creating alternative equity funds (discussed in **Chapter 11**) and a dedicated SME credit fund, BlueBay Credit Fund, which provided a funding alternative to the SME market. This was a €450 million fund supported by the ISIF and other institutional investors, managed by BlueBay and advised and managed by DunPort Capital Management.

BlueBay provided alternative debt capital solutions to mid-sized Irish companies for refinancing, growth, acquisition and shareholder re-organisation purposes.

DunPort is targeting the provision of similar flexible, alternative debt capital solutions to SMEs and mid-corporates through a €283 million successor fund announced in April 2018.

Further details can be found at www.dunportcapital.ie

An alternative debt funder is BMS Finance, which provides a range of SME lending products. Further details are set out in **Chapter 13**, **Section 13.8.4**.

12.6 Mezzanine Debt

Another source of debt finance is mezzanine debt (commonly referred to as 'mezz debt'), which sits between secured senior debt and equity. This type of capital is usually secured by assets and is lent strictly based on a company's ability to repay the debt from free cash flow. Albeit more costly, it assists a growing business to bridge any gap between what conventional banks will lend against assets and the total value of a new project or acquisition.

A company owner should only consider mezzanine debt instead of equity, when the business is producing stable, free cash flow, since this allows the company to obtain financing without issuing equity and diluting the ownership of the business.

The interest cost varies between 10% and 14%, and there are a number of providers of mezz debt, including BMS Finance, AIB and DunPort.

12.7 Conclusion

As a result of government-led initiatives since the financial crisis, the Irish banking system has reduced in size, and contains fewer active players with a reduced capacity to lend and a reduced (and arguably more appropriate) appetite for risk. However, a new debt funding market with a significant number of alternative non-bank lenders has emerged to fill the resultant void, specifically the SME credit gap.

Today, the non-bank funding market is playing a greater and ongoing role in funding SMEs. This will result in companies having to adopt more diverse capital structures as they use a number of sources to fund themselves, which will lead to SMEs having a lower dependence on a single funding source, as well as lower refinancing risks as corporate and commercial Ireland will be less exposed to any future changes in the banking sector. This new funding landscape, combined with other SME government supports (discussed in **Chapter 13**) will assist fund the growth of SMEs both existing and starting up.

AT A GLANCE: DEBT FINANCE

What is debt finance?	Debt finance involves a company borrowing money from a third-party lender but not giving up shares/ownership. The amount of debt borrowed is repaid to the lender plus interest at agreed dates, and there are usually strict conditions or covenants.
What are the benefits of debt finance?	Benefits include: • low cost due to the current low interest rate market; • no loss of control/shares; and • the company/SME has use of the funding for the period of the loan.
Are there any disadvantages?	• Security, in terms of an asset, is usually required to secure bank debt finance; therefore, if the business defaults in terms of repayments, the asset could be seized by the lender. • Additionally, there could be costs if the company/SME pays the loan back early.
How long does debt finance take to raise?	Securing debt finance can vary from a number of weeks to months depending on how quickly the information required by the debt funder is provided and security for the loan is reviewed. (Set out in **Chapter 15** are further insights from a corporate banker on timeframes to complete a banking proposal.)
Who provides debt finance to SMEs?	All of the domestic banks are actively seeking SME lending opportunities, and there are a number of alternative debt providers that have emerged since 2014 (see **Section 12.4**).

CHAPTER 13

GOVERNMENT FUNDING AND SUPPORTS (FUNDING PILLAR 3)

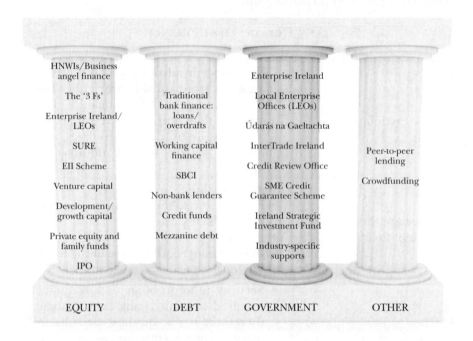

EQUITY	DEBT	GOVERNMENT	OTHER
HNWIs/Business angel finance		Enterprise Ireland	
The '3 Fs'	Traditional bank finance: loans/ overdrafts	Local Enterprise Offices (LEOs)	
Enterprise Ireland/ LEOs		Údarás na Gaeltachta	
SURE	Working capital finance	InterTrade Ireland	Peer-to-peer lending
EII Scheme	SBCI	Credit Review Office	
Venture capital	Non-bank lenders	SME Credit Guarantee Scheme	Crowdfunding
Development/ growth capital	Credit funds	Ireland Strategic Investment Fund	
Private equity and family funds	Mezzanine debt	Industry-specific supports	
IPO			

13.1 Introduction

Business startups and SMEs at all stages of development can apply for government funding supports to assist them to grow and expand. The range of supports is considerable and, as a first step, business owners can access details through the online tool at www.supportingsmes.ie. This cross-government initiative provides information on over 170 state business supports that are available to SMEs from circa 30 different government departments, agencies and initiatives. By answering eight straightforward questions, SMEs are directed to the government supports most relevant to their business sector and location. In addition, members of the SME State Bodies Group (see https://www.finance.gov.ie/wp-content/uploads/2017/05/SME-State-Bodies-Group-SME-SBG.pdf) and specially trained 'jobs ambassadors' regularly attend SME sector-specific events nationwide to promote the use of www.supportingsmes.ie and engage with SMEs as part of the Government's Supporting SMEs campaign, which was launched in May 2014. Over 100,000 businesses and entrepreneurs have availed of the online resource tool since the campaign was launched.

Government financial supports are delivered through a variety of government departments, state agencies and partnerships with third parties. In May 2015, the Government announced that there is circa €2 billion of government aid, grants and loans available to SMEs. Irrespective of their stage of development, companies can apply for various funding supports. As noted above, a full listing of such funding and supports can be found at www.supportingsmes.ie. In this chapter, we will provide an overview of the main funding and support options available through:

1. Enterprise Ireland;
2. Local Enterprise Offices;
3. Údarás na Gaeltachta;
4. InterTrade Ireland;
5. the Credit Review Office;
6. the SME Credit Guarantee Scheme; and
7. the Ireland Strategic Investment Fund

Other government-led supports such as the Strategic Banking Corporation of Ireland (SBCI) and MicroFinance Ireland are discussed in **Chapter 12**.

Note: This is a high-level summary of the government agencies and schemes that manage and provide financial and non-financial supports for SMEs. Because such supports are continuously updated and refined, further detail on the criteria, eligibility and deadline dates (if applicable) should be researched through the relevant websites.

13.2 Enterprise Ireland

Enterprise Ireland (EI) (www.enterprise-ireland.com) is the government agency responsible for the development and growth of Irish enterprises in global markets (including manufacturing and internationally traded services companies). EI works in partnership with Irish SMEs to help them start, grow, innovate and win export sales, thereby assisting and sustaining economic growth and regional development, and securing and growing employment.

13.2.1 SME Relevant Stage of Development for Enterprise Ireland Supports

Funding supports from EI are closely aligned to a business's stage of development. The agency can provide funding and supports for companies with greater than 10 employees targeting export markets, including business propositions for high-potential startups (HPSUs) (defined as startup businesses with potential to develop an innovative product or service for sale in international markets that would create at least 10 jobs and €1 million in export revenues within three to four years) through to large companies expanding their activities, improving production efficiencies and growing international sales.

EI also provides funding and supports for third-level researchers to assist in the development, protection and transfer of technologies into industry through licensing or spin-out companies.

EI's New Frontiers Entrepreneur Development Programme is Ireland's national entrepreneur development programme for early startups and is run in partnership with the Institutes of Technology. The programme is designed to support entrepreneurs with innovative business ideas who are planning to establish and run their own company. A range of supports including mentoring, incubation spaces and €15,000 scholarship payments are provided to help accelerate the development of the business and to equip the promoter(s) with the skills and contacts needed to successfully start and grow their company.

13.2.2 Types of Enterprise Ireland Funding and Support

The types of support available from EI are broadly dependent on the business's stage of development, its requirement for funding and the jobs and export-growth potential. **Table 13.1** below outlines a selection of the funding and supports available from EI for SMEs.

TABLE 13.1: ENTERPRISE IRELAND FINANCIAL AND
NON-FINANCIAL SUPPORTS

Equity investments	These are investments made by EI in SMEs typically for preference share instruments. Funding decisions are determined by: • the SME's need for financial support to fund a project; • potential employment and sales growth; • previous EI funding provided to the company; and • regional location of the company.
Financial grants	EI financial grants vary from time to time and depend on the objective that EI is seeking to assist the SME to achieve. Examples include: grants for capital (i.e. assets), key employees (i.e. experienced hires), business process improvement (including lean manufacturing), research and development and new market entry to name but a few.
Innovation vouchers	An Enterprise Ireland innovation voucher provides an SME with funding worth €5,000 to assist it explore a business opportunity or solve a business problem with a registered knowledge provider, which are higher education institutes/public research bodies.

EI equity investment, financial grants and innovation vouchers for startups, established SMEs and large companies can be significant, depending on the company's job and export growth potential, and have played an important part in the growth and development of numerous successful Irish companies.

EXAMPLE 13.1: AN ENTERPRISE IRELAND SUPPORT
AVAILABLE TO SMEs: THE MARKET DISCOVERY FUND

A recent example of an EI support for companies, including SMEs, potentially impacted by Brexit is the Market Discovery Fund, which aims to support such companies to diversify by targeting and launching in new markets.

Companies can access funding of up to €150,000 to help them take the first step into new markets, with the funding being applied towards internal and external costs incurred in researching new markets for products and services.

Companies can apply for support from the Market Discovery Fund more than once, provided each application considers a new market for an existing product or an existing market for a new product.

The Market Discovery Fund is available across three levels:
• Level 1: Grants up to €35,000
• Level 2: Grants greater than €35,000 but less than €75,000
• Level 3: Grants greater than €75,000 but less than €150,000

The Market Discovery Fund is open to applications from:
• HPSUs (Levels 1 and 2 only)
• SMEs (Levels 1–3)
• Large companies (Levels 2 and 3)

Support may be approved for eligible expenditure across a range of categories, including: salaries, overheads, travel and subsistence (overseas), consultancy, trade fairs, market reports and rent of office space.

For more information, see www.enterprise-ireland.com

As important as such financial supports are, equally important are the non-financial supports EI can provide to SMEs, such as involvement in trade missions to potential export markets, introductions to key contacts when entering new markets and the use of office space in foreign markets. There are numerous examples of Irish companies competing on the world stage that have successfully entered new markets on foot of assistance from EI, including, for example, Netwatch and Blueface.

EI is constantly monitoring foreign market trends that may negatively impact exporting SMEs, and, where possible, EI helps SMEs to take corrective action and change policies to counter them. For example, as detailed in **Section 13.1**, EI is actively formulating and implementing a strategy to assist SMEs address the uncertainty of Brexit, as demonstrated by the funding support 'The Market Discovery Fund'.

EI also runs and manages a number of focused events to assist SME management teams develop, such as Finance4Growth workshops and Leadership4Growth programmes. These workshops and programmes are delivered in collaboration with leading international providers (e.g. Stanford University in California) and seek to provide SME management teams with the tools and techniques to operate more effectively and achieve strategy objectives in international markets.

To avail of EI funding and supports, a company must become an EI client and be allocated a development advisor who will assist the startup/SME avail of the correct supports. Further details on how to become an EI client and the current supports available can be found at www.enterprise-ireland.com

13.3 Local Enterprise Offices

There are 31 Local Enterprise Offices (LEOs) across the country (www.localenterprise.ie) providing a range of financial supports designed to assist with the establishment and/or growth of local micro enterprises. A micro enterprise, for these purposes, is any business that employs up to 10 people, has an annual turnover of less than €2 million, can be a new or established business, and has the potential to generate export sales.

13.3.1 SME Relevant Stage of Development for Local Enterprise Office Supports

As detailed above, to avail of LEO supports, a business must be a micro enterprise, as defined above. LEOs do not provide financial support to businesses in the following sectors: retail, professional services (i.e. accountants, solicitors, etc.), personal services (i.e. hairdressers, crèches, etc.), construction, and distribution. Nor do LEOs provide the financial support of 'displacement', i.e. where a new business could only prosper by diverting sales or employment away from an existing local business already providing essentially the same offering, thus placing existing jobs and the viability of the existing business at risk.

13.3.2 Types of LEO Funding and Support

LEOs provide both financial and non-financial (soft) supports to micro enterprises. Financial supports include those set out opposite in **Table 13.2**:

TABLE 13.2: LOCAL ENTERPRISE OFFICE FINANCIAL SUPPORTS

Feasibility Study Grants	Grants to research market demand for a product or service, and for examining its commercial sustainability.
Priming Grants	A business startup grant, available to micro enterprises within the first 18 months of business commencement. The maximum priming grant payable to a micro enterprise is 50% of the expenditure eligible to be covered by the grant or €150,000, whichever is the lower.
Business Expansion Grants	Business expansion grants assist businesses in their growth phase after the initial 18-month start-up period. The maximum business expansion grant payable is 50% of the expenditure eligible to be covered by the grant or €150,000, whichever is the lower.
Technical Assistance for Micro Exporters	This is a grant to assist micro enterprises investigate, research and develop new market opportunities. The maximum grant payable is subject to a maximum of €2,500 or 50% of eligible expenditure.

LEOs also offer micro enterprises the following non-financial supports:
1. training courses, including, e.g. start your own business, marketing and social media, selling, time management, tax, presentation skills;
2. training, mentoring and business advice from a panel of business experts; and
3. networking supports for specific industry sectors, e.g. Dublin Food Chain (see www.dublinfoodchain.ie).

Further details can be found at www.localenterprise.ie

13.4 Údarás na Gaeltachta

Údarás na Gaeltachta's website (www.udaras.ie) carries a clear and concise description of its objective and role:
"Established in 1980, Údarás na Gaeltachta is the regional authority responsible for the economic, social and cultural development of the Gaeltacht. The overall objective of Údarás na Gaeltachta is to ensure that Irish remains the main communal language of the Gaeltacht and is passed on to future generations.

The authority endeavours to achieve that objective by funding and fostering a wide range of enterprise development and job creation initiatives and by supporting strategic language, cultural and community based activities."[1]

---

[1] http://www.udaras.ie/en/faoin-udaras/ar-rol (accessed August 2018).

13.4.1 SME Relevant Stage of Development for Údarás na Gaeltachta Supports

Údarás na Gaeltachta offers qualifying businesses and companies from various sectors a range of incentives and supports at the start-up, development and expansion stages of the innovation lifecycle, and/or to locate in a Gaeltacht region, which is a requirement to avail of its supports. Eligible sectors are very broad and include, for example, pharmaceutical and medical devices, manufacturing, food processing, audio-visual and digital media, information technology, financial and customer services, aquaculture and fish processing, language-based enterprises and tourism.

13.4.2 Types of Údarás na Gaeltachta Funding and Support

Údarás na Gaeltachta offers enterprises a choice of incentives and supports to start up, develop, expand or locate businesses in a Gaeltacht area. In addition to direct equity investments, the authority provides grants for feasibility studies, research and development, capital, employment and training and consultancy services as well as trade fair participation schemes and innovation vouchers for exploring a business opportunity or problem with a registered knowledge provider, i.e. higher education institutes. It also has a wide range of business premises available for lease, purchase or development. According to Údarás na Gaeltachta, properties are available at competitive rental rates and leasing arrangements can be flexible; additionally, buildings can be adapted to suit the particular business requirements.

According to Údarás na Gaeltachta, funding eligibility and amounts will depend on the type of business proposed, geographical location, employment skills level required (high-end or manual) and the potential employment level of the project. All Údarás na Gaeltachta-supported businesses must agree to promote and develop the use of the Irish language in their activities.

Further details can be found at www.udaras.ie

13.5 InterTradeIreland

InterTradeIreland (www.intertradeireland.com) is a cross-border trade and business development body funded by the Department of Business, Enterprise and Innovation in the Republic of Ireland and the Department for the Economy in Northern Ireland. The objective of IntertradeIreland is to support businesses, through innovation and trade initiatives to take advantage of North/South co-operative opportunities to improve capability, drive competitiveness, growth and jobs.

13.5.1 SME Relevant Stage of Development for InterTradeIreland Funding and Supports

According to InterTradeIreland's website, it helps SMEs across the island by "offering practical cross-border business funding, intelligence and contacts".

Ambitious and established SMEs with a satisfactory trading record in the manufacturing and services sectors are eligible for InterTradeIreland funding and supports.

13.5.2 Types of InterTradeIreland Funding and Support

InterTradeIreland provides SMEs with support under the three categories listed in **Table 13.3** below:

TABLE 13.3: INTERTRADEIRELAND FINANCIAL
AND NON-FINANCIAL SUPPORTS

1. Market Intelligence	• 'Trade accelerator vouchers' provides financial support up to £1,000 to assess a cross-border business plan. • Tender workshops provide SMEs with knowledge and practical skills to assist them to tender successfully for public sector contracts across the island of Ireland. • Market assistance to improve the cross-border trading of SMEs.
2. Funding	• Funding support of up to 50% of the cost of a sales person's salary in the first year, subject to a maximum cost of €37,500/£30,000, with the 'Acumen Programme'. • Product/service innovation through the 'Fusion Programme', which provides financial support to assist SMEs focus on technology innovation by providing funding for a graduate hire to be based in the SME for 12 or 18 months, with mentoring provided from the academic partner of the programme (i.e. a third-level institute) along with the InterTradeIreland Fusion Programme consultant. The support can be for 12 months (£31,000/€41,000) or 18 months (£44,250/€58,700). • €6,000/£5,000 of specialist consultancy support for small businesses under the 'Elevate Programme', assisting identification of cross-border markets and customers. Eligible businesses are those with fewer than 10 employees and annual revenues below €1.8 million/£1.5 million.
3. Contacts	InterTradeIreland runs a series of events including conferences, seminars, lectures and workshops on various topics and themes. Historically, this included a Venture Capital Conference and an Innovation Conference, and lectures.

InterTradeIrealnd also provides SMEs with funding advisory services, from funding workshops and clinics on the current funding options available, to the annual 'Seedcorn' competition, which tests the 'investor readiness' of early-stage businesses. As well as offering a total cash prize fund of circa €280,000, Seedcorn also gives short-listed enterprises the opportunity to pitch to potential investors.

13.6 The Credit Review Office

The Credit Review Office (www.creditreview.ie) is another government initiative set up to help SMEs, including sole traders and farmers, that have had an application for credit of up to €3 million declined or reduced by the participating banks, and who believe that they have a viable business proposition. Participating banks include AIB, Bank of Ireland, Permanent TSB and Ulster Bank. The Credit Review Office also examines cases where commercial borrowers think that the terms and conditions of their existing loan, or a new loan offer, are unfairly onerous or have been unreasonably changed to their detriment. This is a strictly confidential process between the business, the Credit Review Office and the relevant bank.

13.7 The SME Credit Guarantee Scheme

The SME Credit Guarantee Scheme is a government initiative that was set up to encourage additional lending to commercially viable SMEs which, under normal bank loan assessment criteria, are unable to obtain either new or additional facilities from their bank. The scheme offers state guarantees to banks on loans to SMEs of up to €1 million. Current participating banks are AIB, Bank of Ireland and Ulster Bank. Under the scheme, a 75% state guarantee of the facility's value is provided to banks against losses on qualifying loans to businesses that otherwise have difficulty getting credit owing to inadequacy of collateral or inadequacy of banks' understanding of the innovative nature of a business model or idea, market, sector or technology.

The SME pays a premium to the Government for the scheme, which is in addition to the interest paid to the lender. For the period June 2018 to June 2019, the premium will be 1%.

For more information, see https://dbei.gov.ie/en/What-We-Do/Supports-for-SMEs/Access-to-Finance/SME-Credit-Guarantee-Scheme/

13.8 The Ireland Strategic Investment Fund

In June 2013, the Irish Government announced the establishment of the Ireland Strategic Investment Fund (ISIF) which is an €8 billion sovereign development fund to invest in projects on a commercial basis in a "manner designed to support economic activity in Ireland". (The fund's predecessor was the National Pensions Reserve Fund (NPRF)). This unique mandate for the ISIF reflects a shift from the NPRF, being a sovereign wealth fund focused solely on wealth creation, to the ISIF being a sovereign development fund with a 'double bottom line' objective that will be measured by investment returns, economic impact and employment growth achieved.

The ISIF is one of the strategic funding partners of the SBCI, which is discussed in more detail in **Chapter 12**. As at 30 June 2017, the ISIF has committed €2.9 billion of capital in both direct investments and as a co-investor in funds that are professionally managed and which target innovating and growing sectors of the economy.

Examples of ISIF's investments include:
1. €75 million committed to the China Ireland Technology Growth Fund focusing on high-growth companies seeking access to the Irish and Chinese markets;
2. €10 million invested in medical device company Mainstay Medical to support the development and commercialisation of its products; and
3. a commitment to the Business Growth Fund (BGF), a new €250 million growth capital fund for investment in Irish SMEs, as detailed in **Chapter 11**, **Section 11.11.7**.

In addition to direct investments in transactions (where the ISIF is the sole investor), it has also made co-investments with other investors in a number of professionally managed credit and equity-type funds focused on investing in SMEs, including, for example:
• the Business Growth Fund (BGF);
• Frontline Ventures;
• Causeway Capital; and
• BMS Finance Ireland.

Although this is not a complete list of the funds in which the ISIF has invested, the funds listed are an example of the type of funds that are available to SMEs and in which the ISIF is a co-investor. Their co-investors can include, for example, domestic banks, pension funds and international investors. These funds are professionally managed by third-party fund managers, targeting investment in SMEs with the objective of achieving the fund's investment mandate which can, for example, have either a sector or alternative-lending focus.

13.8.1 The Business Growth Fund

As detailed in **Section 11.11.7**, a new development capital equity fund, backed by the ISIF, was launched in Q4 2017. According to the ISIF website, in November 2017 it made a "cornerstone commitment to a new growth capital fund with up to €250 million available for investments in Irish small and medium-sized companies".

The BGF is a UK venture capital firm and this fund offers SMEs initial investments of between €2 million and €10 million for a minority stake. In addition to the ISIF, other funders include AIB, Bank of Ireland and Ulster Bank. The new Irish fund is also backed by the BGF's existing investors, which include the funders of the UK BGF, i.e. Barclays, HSBC, Lloyds Banking Group, Royal Bank of Scotland and Standard Chartered.

A unique offering of the BGF is its offering of 'patient capital', which allows for long-term investments, unlike other private-equity firms, which typically seek a controlling stake in a business and an exit within five to seven years.

At the time of writing, the BGF has yet to complete an investment from this new fund.

13.8.1.1 SME Relevant Stage of Development for the Business Growth Fund

SMEs with strong management teams and annual revenues between €5 million and €100 million.

13.8.1.2 Types of Funding Provided

Minority equity stake investments. For further details, see www.bgf.co.uk

13.8.2 Frontline Ventures

Similarly, according to the ISIF website, the ISIF has made a €60 million commitment to Frontline Ventures ('Frontline'), a venture fund managed and focused on investing in leading early-stage companies. According to Frontline's website, "Frontline is an early-stage B2B venture capital firm powered by people – the ambitious founders we invest in, our strong networks of industry experts, and our own passionate team of ex-operators".

Similar to other venture capital funds, Frontline assists its investee companies by investing both time and money into building the relationships needed to fast-track a company's expansion, with a focus on the US market.

Frontline has completed investments in approximately 35 portfolio companies in Ireland, the UK, the US and Europe, across a diverse range of sectors, including Big Data, FinTech, e-commerce and cybersecurity to name a few.

13.8.2.1 SME Relevant Stage of Development for Frontline Ventures

Early- and seed-stage business-to-business (B2B) SMEs (i.e. those with business customers) with ambitious growth plans.

13.8.2.2 Types of Funding Provided

Equity stake investments. For further details, see www.frontline.vc

13.8.3 Causeway Capital

Causeway Capital (www.causewaycapital.eu) is a €60 million private equity fund that targets fast-growing SMEs in Ireland and the UK. The Causeway Capital Partners Fund, in which the ISIF is an investor, provides investments of up to €10 million to Irish SMEs with strong growth prospects, as well as overseas companies with the potential for growth in Ireland.

13.8.3.1 SME Relevant Stage of Development for Causeway Capital

According to Causeway Capital's website, it provides equity funding to established Irish and UK SMEs with ambitious management teams and strong growth prospects.

13.8.3.2 Type of Funding (Provided)

Equity funding between €2.5 million and €10 million.

13.8.4 BMS Finance Ireland

As discussed in **Chapter 12**, **Section 12.5**, BMS Finance (www.bms-finance. com) is a UK-based SME finance specialist (with operations in Ireland) that manages a €30 million debt fund aimed at SMEs offering growth capital to Irish companies for working capital, contract wins, capital expenditure, acquisitions and MBOs. BMS Finance Ireland is backed by investors, including the ISIF, and, according to market information, provides finance on a senior-secured basis, without the need for personal guarantees or personal security. Loan values ranging from €500,000 million to €5 million are considered, with the focus on loans from €1 million to €3 million.

BMS Finance Ireland is an alternative debt funder and primarily works with owner-managed businesses; it will also look at venture capital or private equity-backed businesses. The fund is sector-agnostic and, according to its website, has availed of a number of SME lending opportunities in business services, software, IT, media, healthcare and financial services.

13.8.4.1 SME Relevant Stage of Development for BMS Finance Ireland

Established SMEs in the growth phase that have demonstrated sales traction and good growth opportunities and that are either profitable or about to become so. BMS Finance does not lend to SMEs in either the property or biotech sectors.

13.8.4.2 Type of Funding Provided

BMS Finance Ireland provides loans ranging from €500,000 to €5 million for working capital, contract wins, capital expenditure, acquisitions and MBOs, on a senior-secured basis. According to BMS Finance's website, it does not "compete with traditional factoring, invoice discounting, commercial mortgages or other forms of specific asset based lending but rather [has] the ability to provide larger and more flexible cashflow lending through senior secured loans."

13.9 Industry-specific Government Supports

There are extensive industry-specific government and non-government agencies and supports available for SMEs operating in certain sectors of the economy. The Department of Business, Enterprise and Innovation maintains on its website a document detailing all supports available for entrepreneurs. The Department notes that the document "lists both State and non-State supports for entrepreneurs. It is not meant to be an exhaustive list of all supports. Instead, it is a living document that will allow amendments and additions." However, the document is a comprehensive overview of state supports, mentorship programmes, networks, and incubators (for early-stage companies), to name but a few. (See https://dbei.gov.ie/en/What-We-Do/ Business-Sectoral-Initiatives/Entrepreneurship-/Mapping-of-supports/.)

A summary of some of these supports is set out below.

13.9.1 An Bord Bia

The mission of An Bord Bia, the Irish Food Board (www.bordbia.ie) is to drive, in partnership with industry, the commercial success of world-class Irish food, drink and horticulture industries. To assist in achieving this, An Bord Bia offers and provides a number of SME supports through dedicated schemes including, for example, those set out in **Table 13.4** below, which are summarsied from the mapping of supports website referenced in **Section 13.9**.

TABLE 13.4: AN BORD BIA SUPPORTS AND ASSISTANCE

Bord Bia Vantage	Bord Bia Vantage is the online support centre for small food and drink businesses. Supports include market information, consumer insight, business and export development, as well as information on relevant industry events.
An Bord Bia Marketing Fellowship	This programme offers food and drink companies the opportunity to undertake research in export markets with a view to identifying opportunities and building relationships with potential customers.
Brand Forum	The Brand Forum provides quarterly events with expert speakers on branding from the food and drink industries worldwide. A series of workshops are provided on themes such as social media, media evaluation, food photography and styling.
Ascent Programme	The Ascent Programme provides a specific set of resources to support the development of companies with a turnover between €1 million and €20 million, and an ambition to proceed to their next phase of growth. These resources include targeted support on strategy, finance, pricing, management and technology. An Bord Bia partners with industry-leading mentors on this programme.

In.gredients Programme	An Bord Bia and KSG Catering have come together to form the 'In.gredients' programme, aimed at providing businesses with tailored support to assist them secure and grow business in some of the 110 outlets run by KSG Catering around Ireland.
FoodService Academy	Run by An Bord Bia and Musgrave MarketPlace, this programme aims to help 10 participating producers grow sales within the food service or out-of-home food markets.

13.9.2 Teagasc

Teagasc (www.teagasc.ie) is Ireland's agriculture and food development authority. Its mission is to support science-based innovation in the agri-food sector that will underpin profitability, competitiveness and sustainability. Teasgasc provides SMEs in the food and drink sectors advice, consultancy and training in a broad range of technical activities, including product and process development, pilot plant facilities (for food and crop producers), compliance with legislation and codes of practice, food safety, and quality management systems.

13.9.3 Bord Iascaigh Mhara

Bord Iascaigh Mhara (BIM) (www.bim.ie) is the support agency for the Irish seafood industry. It focuses on expanding the raw material base, adding value and developing efficient supply chains that deliver on the Government's Food Wise 2025 targets for seafood and creating sustainable employment. BIM supports the development of the Irish seafood industry by providing technical expertise, business support, funding and training, and by promoting responsible environmental practices. It manages schemes intended to support the Irish seafood industry, including those shown below in **Table 13.5**, which are summarsied from the mapping of supports website referenced in **Section 13.9**.

TABLE 13.5: BIM SUPPORT SCHEMES

Sustainable Fisheries Scheme	This scheme is specifically designed to assist all those directly involved, or soon to be involved, in implementing the landing obligation, including fishermen, organisations of fishermen, fishermen's co-operatives and processors.
Sustainable Aquaculture Scheme: Organic Aquaculture	This scheme supports conventional producers to move to organic production and participate in EU eco-management and audit schemes.
Sustainable Aquaculture Scheme: Capacity Building	This scheme promotes the sustainable growth of output, value and employment in the aquaculture sector.

Marine Tourism Vessel Safety Scheme	Grant aid is available for the purchase and installation of safety items for marine tourism vessels.
Inshore Fisheries Conservation Scheme: 'V-Notching' Support	This scheme provides for grant aid to implement local lobster 'v-notching' programmes.[2]
Fleet Safety Scheme	This scheme aims to improve the overall safety standards on board Irish fishing vessels through grant aid.
Enhanced Safety Scheme Training Scheme	This complements BIM's Basic Safety Training programme and the Fleet Safety Grant Aid Scheme (see above). It is intended to enhance survival prospects after man-overboard accidents at sea, and the search and rescue functions of the emergency services.

13.9.4 Fáilte Ireland

Fáilte Ireland (www.failteireland.ie) is Ireland's tourism development authority. It supports the tourism industry and works to sustain Ireland as a high-quality and competitive tourism destination. Fáilte Ireland provides a range of practical business supports to help tourism businesses better manage and market their products and services. It has a wide range of resources to help tourism businesses reach their full potential. Business supports include management tools, how-to guides and funding information, as well as specific advice on adventure tourism. For example, Fáilte Ireland's Mentor Programme is designed to provide specialist knowledge, skills, strategic guidance and insights, tailored to the specific challenges faced by tourism businesses. Practical advice is also provided in the areas of sales, marketing, digital marketing and enhancing online presence, revenue and channel management, managing festivals and business planning, with a focus upon the issues of seasonality, regionality and improving business capability.

Additionally, Fáilte Irealnd has developed a customised suite of supports focusing on the following key areas:
- training, including a calendar of supports;
- market diversification;
- competitiveness;
- Great Britain; and
- Brexit.

---

[2] A 'v-notch' is a mark on the tail flipper of a female lobster put there by a commercial lobsterman as a means to identify and protect a known breeder in the population from harvest.

13.9.5 Skillnet Ireland

Skillnet Ireland (www.skillnet.ie) supports and works with SMEs to address their current and future skills needs by providing funding to grow skills and sustain jobs. The objective of Skillnet Ireland is to maintain employee training and up-skilling, which are key elements in keeping Irish SMEs competitive. Skillnet Ireland allocates funding to groups of companies in the same region/sector that have similar training needs. Employer needs are addressed by focusing on skills that maintain businesses and protect jobs, as well as the enhancement of new skills to create new jobs. Supports include those set out below in **Table 13.6**.

TABLE 13.6: SKILLNET IRELAND SUPPORT SCHEMES

Training Networks Programme (TNP)	Businesses can join a Skillnet Ireland's training network to benefit from high-quality training that is subsidised, relevant to their needs, and delivered at a time and a location that suit.
Management Works Programme	A subsidised management development training and mentoring programme available to businesses in all sectors to assist them to achieve growth in terms of sales, output and employment.
Finuas Networks Programme	Subsidised training for businesses and employees in the international financial services sector. The main areas of training are in banking/asset financing, corporate treasury, investment management, aviation finance, securitisation, reinsurance, financial technology (FinTech) and related professional services.

13.10 Conclusion

An important lesson learned from the financial crisis was the lack of diversity of funders on the balance sheets of SMEs; they were too dependent on bank loans. As one CEO has remarked: "When our banks caught a cold, SMEs got pneumonia!" A common theme of the crisis was that when bank credit dried up there were few other types of funders available to SMEs to 'step in' and bridge the gap. Consequently, the Irish Government took action to alleviate the reliance of SMEs on the domestic banking system and to prevent this effect of the financial crisis from happening again. In addition to the equity and debt funding actions taken by the Government (as discussed in **Chapters 12** and **13**), a range of focused, government SME supports has also been made available to support the objective of having a diverse range of funders available to SMEs. These include both financial and non-financial supports, and can be identified according to SME size, sector, lifecycle stage, etc., using the online tool provided at www.support-ingsmes.ie. Industry-specific government supports may be available for certain SMEs, providing advice and guidance, a useful summary, or 'mapping', of which is available at www.dbei.gov.ie/en/what-we-do/business-sectoral-initiatives/entrepreneurship-/mapping-of-supports

AT A GLANCE: GOVERNMENT FUNDING AND SUPPORTS

What government supports are available for SMEs?	There is a range of supports, both financial and non-financial (e.g. advice), available to SMEs at all stages of the innovation lifecycle and these can be found at www.supportingsmes.ie
What are the benefits of government funding?	Benefits of government support include: • it helps bring another funder onto the company's balance sheet, thus reducing the risk of becoming overly reliant on a single source of funding; • there is no loss of control/shares; and • the SME has use of the funding for the period of the support.
How long does it take to raise?	This varies and depends on the government agency administrating the support. Like raising equity and debt finance, it is important, first, to be sure that the SME meets the qualifying criteria for the support and, secondly, that the SME has provided all the required information as stipulated by the agency. A key aspect of all government supports is the requirement for an up-to-date tax clearance certificate.

CHAPTER 14

OTHER POSSIBLE FUNDING SOURCES (FUNDING PILLAR 4)

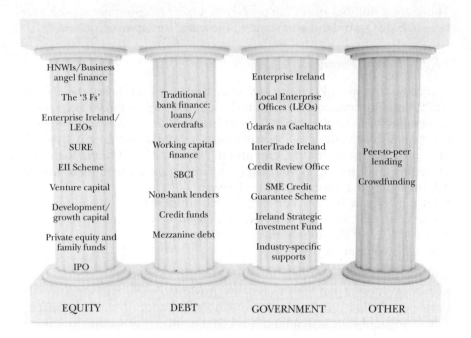

EQUITY	DEBT	GOVERNMENT	OTHER
HNWIs/Business angel finance		Enterprise Ireland	
The '3 Fs'	Traditional bank finance: loans/ overdrafts	Local Enterprise Offices (LEOs)	
Enterprise Ireland/ LEOs		Údarás na Gaeltachta	
SURE	Working capital finance	InterTrade Ireland	Peer-to-peer lending
EII Scheme	SBCI	Credit Review Office	
Venture capital	Non-bank lenders	SME Credit Guarantee Scheme	Crowdfunding
Development/ growth capital	Credit funds	Ireland Strategic Investment Fund	
Private equity and family funds	Mezzanine debt	Industry-specific supports	
IPO			

14.1 Introduction

As we have seen, conventionally, small and medium-sized enterprises (SMEs) have been funded by a combination of equity and debt finance, the former typically involving, for businesses in their infancy, equity investment from the '3 Fs', with the latter traditionally provided by the domestic banks. Such investments and loans require due diligence and risk assessment, by the equity investor and/or debt finance provider.

As outlined in **Chapter 12** on debt finance, a number of government initiatives have been undertaken to reduce SMEs' reliance on the domestic banks by the introduction of new, alternative lenders to the market. Added to this is the recent rise of 'peer-to-peer' (P2P) lending and crowdfunding from private and unconnected individuals directly to companies. Both of these funding sources have been driven by the reduction in credit available to SMEs following the financial crisis, the low rate of deposit interest available from the domestic banks, as well as the development of online peer-to-peer lending/crowdfunding services or platforms.

14.2 Peer-to-peer Lending

Peer-to-peer lending involves the lending of money by and to unrelated individuals (or 'peers') via online platforms without the use of a bank or other financial institution as an intermediary. Peer-to-peer lending is a relatively new concept in Ireland but has expanded quickly to provide finance to thousands of Irish SMEs, and for many SMEs has been the source of significant funding resources.

There are a number of online portals that offer peer-to-peer lending services to SMEs in Ireland and some of these are summarised below:

14.2.1 Linked Finance

According to Linked Finance (www.linkedfinance.com), it is Ireland's largest P2P lending company, connecting local businesses that need loans with a community of more than 18,000 individual lenders.[1] It uses technology to bring individual lending to SMEs at annual interest rates that vary from 6% to 17.5%, depending on the term and the grade assigned to the loan, with the higher grade having the lower interest rate. According to Linked Finance:

- businesses get a same-day credit decision;
- businesses can borrow between €5,000 to €250,000 (maximum) at a fixed rate of interest for a period of up to three years; and
- loans are repayable in monthly instalments by direct debit and there are no early repayment penalties.

Linked Finance enables people with savings to connect and lend to trustworthy businesses that wish to borrow. Any established and creditworthy business, whether it is a limited company, sole trader or business partnership, can apply for a loan on Linked Finance. According to Linked Finance's website, conditions include:

- A sole trader must be a permanent resident of Ireland.
- A partnership must have a permanent place of business in Ireland and at least half of its partners must be permanent residents of Ireland.
- If the business is a limited company, it must be registered with the Companies Registration Office (CRO), have filed accounts with the CRO (if required to do so) for at least the past two years and at least half of its directors must be Irish residents.
- The business must have been actively trading for at least the past two years.
- The business must meet the minimum credit risk and fraud criteria of Linked Finance.
- The business must not have any outstanding judgments for more than €250.

To avail of Linked Finance, an SME/sole trader/partnership must register as a borrower on the Linked Finance website and complete an online application form.

---

[1] As per https://linkedfinance.com (accessed September 2018).

Once the loan application is accepted and it goes live on the website, individual investors can 'bid' for the loan for which a time limit of 14 days is typically set. Once it is fully funded, the borrower is able to draw down the funds within 24 hours.

14.2.2 GRID Finance

SMEs can also apply for a business loan from GRID Finance (www.gridfinance.ie) on GRID's peer-to-business lending platform. Following a credit assessment completed by GRID's credit team, the loan is made available to investors (private individuals with an account with GRID Finance) who can choose to fund part of the loan.

Loans are repaid monthly (principal plus interest) to the investors, who are private individuals, at a rate of interest, which according to the GRID website varies between 0% and 15%. Investors can lend between €5 and up to 50% of the business loan being sought. The GRID team acts as the intermediary between both parties, facilitating not only the credit assessment of the business, but also the legally enforceable terms and conditions, as well as loan book management and administration throughout the term of the loan portfolio. GRID charges investors 15% on the interest income earned for the duration of the loan.

According to GRID Finance's website, the following loan facilities are available to businesses:
1. **Cash Advance Facility** A short-term finance solution that works with the business's existing credit/debit card machine used to debit customers' bank/credit card accounts who purchase goods/services using debit/credit cards. Businesses can borrow up to €500,000 over a maximum of 12 months. Repayments are made daily as a small percentage of future card sales until the loan has been repaid.
2. **Term Loan** A short- to medium-term finance solution designed for loans of up to €150,000 over a maximum of 36 months. Repayments are fixed and monthly.
3. **Invoice Finance Facility** Similar to an invoice discounting facility (see **Chapter 12, Section 12.3.4**) this GRID facility allows businesses to draw cash from the sales invoices raised with a percentage of the value advanced to the business.
4. **Leasing** A method of financing business equipment with the advantage that the full purchase price of the asset is not required up front. It allows businesses to conserve capital and pay for assets over time out of income with fixed repayments.

Similar to Linked Finance (see **Section 14.2.1**), businesses apply for finance online and submit required back-up, including financial statements and accounts, for approval. Once approved, GRID Finance will offer the loan as a lending opportunity available to its registered lenders.

A Note on Regulation

At the time of writing, P2P lending is not regulated as it does not (currently) fall within the remit of the Central Bank of Ireland. As a result, this may have possibly curtailed its growth and popularity among individual savers/investors. However, it is anticipated that the P2P finance sector will be regulated in the coming years. It is worth noting that GRID Finance voluntarily follows the UK regulatory framework as it is anticipated that the Irish framework will be similar, while Linked Finance has received full authorisation from the UK's Financial Conduct Authority.

14.2.3 Flender

Flender (www.flender.ie) is also a P2P lending platform that matches lenders with approved borrowers. It enables businesses and consumers to lend and borrow money through an app that links in with social media networks connections. While there are no lender's fees involved, unlike other P2P platforms, business borrowers pay a small fee based on completing a campaign successfully on the Flender platform.

According to the Flender website, its service is open to any business that wishes to secure funding and where a set of audited accounts is available. Though lenders can be resident anywhere in the world, business borrowers that create Flender campaigns need to be resident in Ireland. Any business that meets the affordability and credit-check requirements by Flender is eligible to launch a campaign on Flender.

In order to create a campaign, the borrower must meet the following requirements:
1. a sole trader must be a permanent resident of Ireland;
2. a partnership must have a permanent place of business in Ireland and at least half of its partners must be permanent residents of Ireland;
3. a limited company must be registered with the CRO;
4. it must have filed accounts with the CRO;
5. the business must have been actively trading for at least the past two years; and
6. it meets Flenders' minimum credit risk and fraud criteria.

The amount that a business wishes to borrow, the interest rate and repayment period are chosen by the business, with a limit of €150,000 per business. However, all borrowers are subject to affordability and credit checks to ensure that they are financially able to meet the loan repayments.

Lender interest rates vary, depending on the type of campaign and the rate the borrower is willing to pay.

A unique element of the Flender platform is that the borrowing business has control over who receives an invitation to participate in funding the campaign. Therefore, the business borrower controls the potential lenders. Once the campaign is approved by Flender, business owners can invite potential lenders from their existing social circles (including customers) to support the campaign via an app that links with the borrower's social media connections.

Businesses can promote campaigns either privately or publicly to their contacts using the email invite template provided, or through social networks or other online channels that the business may use. The campaign can be limited to followers of the business or its owner's online social profiles, or open it up to any viewer on Flenders' platform. Once a campaign is set up and live, the business receives a unique URL which can be used to send out invites and allow potential lenders to view the campaign page.

14.2.4 InvoiceFair

As discussed in **Chapter 12**, invoice discounting facilities allow SMEs to release cash tied up in invoices, with a percentage of the value advanced to the business. InvoiceFair (www.invoicefair.com) is an online invoice-trading marketplace that can help businesses release cash tied up in their debtors by selling invoices and getting paid immediately.

After the initial registration and on-boarding process, businesses can access funding by following the four steps outlined below to becoming a seller of invoices:
1. upload invoices for approval and set the parameters, i.e. what percentage of the invoice value is being sold and the minimum price acceptable for the invoices;
2. invoices are auctioned to approved buyers – when the auction ends the invoice is sold to the highest bidder;
3. funds are transferred from the buyer to the seller via the InvoiceFair segregated client account; and
4. when the invoice is paid by the customer into the InvoiceFair segregated client account by the debtor, the funds are distributed to the buyer. The unsold portion is distributed to the seller.

InvoiceFair charges a 1% transaction fee of the invoice value.

14.3 Crowdfunding

Crowdfunding is another form of P2P lending and an alternative funding source for businesses that involves attracting financial contributions from large numbers of Internet lenders. Businesses effectively launch fundraising campaigns through dedicated websites, inviting site users to become financial backers of their projects. Typically, a range of progressively more attractive (and novel) rewards may be offered to investors (e.g. a craft chocolate business might offer a box of premium chocolates for a €50 investment or a particular chocolate product named after an individual for a €500 investment). Additionally, some crowdfunding projects offer investors equity stakes in the business seeking funding. A report by CrowdfundingHub shows that in almost all European countries crowdfunding volumes are rising quickly, but large differences between countries remain.[2] The UK has the most mature alternative-finance industry when it comes to volume, as well as the ecosystem, where more than 10% of businesses are funded through alternative investment and this percentage is growing.

Irish SMEs have successfully used the crowdfunding model to develop their businesses. In 2013, the startup Galvanic became the first Irish company to fundraise $100,000 through the US crowdfunding website Kickstarter.com. Anecdotal evidence suggests that some business sectors will prove more appealing than others, and businesses would be advised to research this in advance of seeking such funding. More importantly and as noted above, there is currently no legislation in Ireland specifically dealing with crowdfunding, a fact that suggests caution and professional advice would be advisable before participation.

Those businesses that do decide to proceed with this model should further consider how the publicly visible aspect of this fundraising approach works and be prepared to invest time and energy into the fundraising campaign. A creative and intensive social media strategy will likely prove essential to gaining profile and traction among potential investors.

While success can deliver funds, raise the company's profile and potentially make it more appealing to business investors at its next stage of funding, it is important to note that a high percentage of business projects actually fail to reach their fundraising targets. The fundraising attempt will remain on the Internet, whether a success or failure, and could be easily searched by prospective investors in the future.

There are crowdfunding platforms particular to the Irish market including:
• www.sparkcrowdfunding.com
• www.kickstarter.com
• www.fundit.ie
• www.seedups.ie

14.3.1 Advantages and Disadvantages of Crowdfunding

For startups and certain types of small businesses, crowdfunding can be a low-risk way of raising funds and can be a stepping stone to raising other forms of capital. Importantly, business angel investors and venture capitalists (see **Chapter 11**) will gain confidence with promoters who have been successful in crowdfunding campaigns.

---

[2] See http://www.crowdfundinghub.eu/the-current-state-of-crowdfunding-in-europe/

However, crowdfunding also has its drawbacks, with high failure rates; a lot of crowdfunding projects fail to reach their fundraising goals. The industry in Ireland is not currently regulated and, as a result, professional advice should be taken before proceeding with a funding campaign. As with any form of raising finance, investors will assess the business plan, the track record and the people behind the business.

14.4 Conclusion

Increasingly, crowdfunding and P2P lending are sources of SME funding worldwide. Entrepreneurs and SMEs are using such funding as an additional and/or alternative source of finance to drive their business growth plans. However, as with raising finance from other sources, to be successful it takes planning and patience. Like all sources of finance, professional advice should be sought to assess whether this form of finance is suitable for the SME.

CHAPTER 15

THE IDEAL DEBT-TO-EQUITY FUNDING MIX: VIEWS OF AN SME FOUNDER, BANKER AND LATER-STAGE FUNDER

15.1 Introduction

When it comes to the financing of small and medium-sized enterprises (SMEs), venture capital tends to grab a lot of the headlines, such as announcements of new rounds of venture funding for young, vibrant startups. In comparison, debt finance can sometimes be seen as the poor relation of equity capital. In extreme cases, it can be seen, wrongly, as a last resort for SMEs that cannot raise equity capital.

The reality is that both sources of finance have a role in funding SMEs and complement each other. The timing, quantum and mix of both depend on the ambition of the SME, as well as its stage of development, growth trajectory, available assets that can be offered to a debt lender as security, along with its current and projected cash position.

For so-called 'lifestyle' businesses that start out with the sole ambition of becoming a steady source of income for their owners, the funding sources will most likely be equity from the owners, which may be augmented with debt finance as the business grows and scales. However, we have seen many SMEs that started out with this ambition and, as the company succeeds beyond the owners' initial expectations, their goals and ambitions also change. As a result, the sources of funding will also change to match this new ambition.

For fast-growing, scalable SMEs aiming to build a multi-million-euro company, venture capital can be an appropriate funding source. In fact, this is where venture capital works best, for example for SMEs with:
- unpredictable, weak, or non-existent cash flows; and/or
- lack of brand recognition or little or no track record as a business, but with a scalable product/service with a USP.

Venture capital works well for immature SMEs because, without predictable revenues/cash flows, it is going to be difficult for the business to pay back bank or other types of debt finance. Also, if it is uncertain that debt finance can be repaid without in turn impacting the viability of the business, it does not make any sense to add debt finance to the list of SME owner's anxieties.

An important intangible benefit of raising early-stage equity capital is that it adds credibility to the business plan and the owners behind it, which acts as an endorsement or stamp of approval that will assist the business in attracting new customers and key hires.

As the business grows and cash flows become more predictable in both their timing and quantum, a broader range of funding options will become available to the SME, including raising further equity or debt finance. Debt finance works best for SMEs where:
- there is strong and predictable cash flow;
- the SME and owners have the know-how, experience and credibility needed to grow the business; and
- there is no desire among the owners to give away any more equity.

However, holding on to equity is not just about maximising the pay-out on the sale of a business, it is also about maintaining control over its strategy and operations. For all SMEs, there will come a point when an equity capital injection is needed in order to fulfill growth opportunities, as ultimately debt funders will reach a lending limit dictated by a business's cash flows and security position.

But is there a 'correct' or ideal debt-to-equity mix?

As noted above, the composition of an SME's capital structure depends on its stage of development, growth trajectory, current and projected cash position and assets available to be offered as security to a lender. Other influential factors can include the company's industry sector, and the owners' appetite for giving up equity or raising debt finance, the availability of funding and the type of funding (equity, debt, etc.) at that particular point in time. Therefore, there is no single key metric that SMEs can target as the correct debt to equity ratio as they scale and grow. However, SMEs can look to capital structure trends within their industry, benchmarking themselves against their peers using the following three ratios/considerations:
- their debt/equity ratio;
- their net debt-to-EBITDA ratio; and
- their leverage (borrowing) policy.

15.2 The Debt-to-Equity Ratio

In order to maximise business value, SME business owners should try to find a financial/capital funding mix that minimises both the cost of capital and the risk of insolvency to the business itself. Put another way, this is the company's capital structure or 'capital stack'.

A company's capital structure can quickly be evaluated by calculating its debt-to-equity (or debt/equity) ratio as follows:

$$\frac{\text{Total liabilities}}{\text{Shareholders' equity}}$$

The debt/equity ratio is expressed as a percentage and it shows the proportion of equity and debt a company is using to finance its assets, and the extent to which shareholders' equity can fulfil obligations to creditors in the event of a business decline.

EXAMPLE 15.1: DEBT/EQUITY RATIO

The balance sheet for ABC Ltd shows total liabilities of €750,000 and total shareholders' equity of €250,000. Using the above formula, the debt to equity ratio for ABC can be calculated as:

Debt/equity = €750,000 ÷ €250,000 = €3 (or 300%).

This can be interpreted that ABC Ltd has €3 of debt for every €1 of equity and could be regarded as highly leveraged/geared with debt finance. A debt/equity ratio of 1 would mean that investors and creditors have an equal stake in the business. A lower debt/equity ratio usually implies a more financially stable business, while companies with a higher debt/equity ratio are considered more risky to creditors.

As noted in the example above, a low debt/equity ratio indicates lower risk, as debt holders have less claim on the company's assets, while a higher debt/equity ratio shows that a company has been financing its growth with debt and there may be a greater potential for financial distress if earnings do not exceed the cost of borrowed funds, with the assets of the company subject to a charge/lien by the company's debt finance lender.

The debt/equity ratio can help investors and lenders identify companies that are highly leveraged and that may pose an increased lending risk. To interpret the ratio meaningfully, investors/lenders compare a company's debt/equity ratio to the same ratio in prior financial years, to industry averages and/or to similar companies to gain a general indication of a company's equity/debt relationship.

As detailed above, when assessing a company's debt/equity ratio, it is useful to compare companies within the same industry rather than to look at the company in isolation, or attempt to compare companies from different industries, as there are industry factors that can influence the debt/equity ratio, i.e. the degree of stability in a business, the predictability of its cash flows, its ability to provide suitable assets as security, the interest rate charged, as well as legal or contractual restrictions on debt. For example, a company operating in an unpredictable business environment where a future downturn could impact its ability to repay lenders should have a low debt/equity ratio. Conversely, a company with long-term capital assets, such as buildings or equipment, and predictable cash flows can be more highly leveraged.

15.3 Net Debt-to-EBITDA Ratio

Another way of looking at an SME's capital structure is to calculate its net debt-to-EBITDA ratio (EBITDA being earnings before interest, tax, depreciation and amortisation). This is calculated as a company's debt less its cash/cash equivalents, divided by its EBITDA. The net debt-to-EBITDA ratio shows how many years it would take for the company to pay back its debt if both its net debt and EBITDA remain constant.

The lower the ratio the better; a net debt-to-EBITDA ratio shows two things:
1. whether the company has funded its growth by way of equity, retained earnings or a combination of both; and
2. whether the company has potential borrowing capacity.

Ratios higher than 4 or 5 may indicate that, in the event of a reduction in EBITDA (due to the loss of a key customer or reduced demand, etc.), the company will be less likely to be able to handle its debt burden, and thus less likely to be able to take on the additional debt required to grow the business.

As with the debt/equity ratio, discussed above, a company's net debt-to-EBITDA ratio should be compared to that of a benchmark or the industry average, and to the same ratio in prior financial years, in order to accurately assess and interpret the capital structure of a company.

15.4 Leverage (Borrowing) Policy

Banks will often review a business' net debt-to-EBITDA ratio in assessing its capacity for repaying a loan, and therefore certain SMEs will implement a leverage policy by setting a limit/cap on their borrowings at a certain level, which is calculated in terms of EBITDA. For example, a company may limit borrowings at three times its prior year (or current year) EBITDA; as the EBITDA grows, then additional borrowing capacity also becomes available.

Again, such leverage policies are driven by the ambition and risk appetite of the SMEs' owners, their industry sector, stage of development, etc. However, no matter how stringent or aggressive the policy, the ability to borrow at that level will ultimately be decided by the bank/lender.

15.5 The SME Founder's View (Justin Keatinge, Co-Founder Version 1)

Established in Dublin in 1996 by Justin Keatinge (CEO) and John Mullen, Version 1 has grown both organically and through strategic acquisition to be the market leader in IT services in the UK and Ireland. From having just two employees in 1996, by 2017 Version 1 had expanded to have 900 employees (40% of whom were UK-based), eight offices and annual revenues in excess of €100 million.

Up to 2014, Version 1 funded its growth from company-generated cash flow/retained earnings, with some bank debt to part-fund its acquisitions. In 2014, it raised €8 million in equity funding from the BDO Development Capital Fund (BDO DCF) to fund its acquisition growth. Following three further acquisitions and significant organic growth, Version 1 raised significant equity capital (circa €90 million) from the UK private equity firm Volpi Partners in March 2017.

How did you and co-founder John Mullen fund Version 1, initially and for its subsequent growth?

Justin Keatinge We bootstrapped it; we didn't raise any external funding until we raised equity funding from the BDO Development Capital Fund in 2014 and that was 18 years into the business. We only needed external funding for acquisitions and our first three or four acquisitions were with cash the company generated, along with some bank debt.

John and I started the company in 1996, so initially it was just the two of us and, because it is a consulting firm, the two of us were chargeable as consultants. As we accumulated cash in the business, we were able to hire another consultant and another consultant, and so on. I was constantly running spreadsheets on cash flow and thinking that I could hire another consultant every six weeks, as the cash flow allowed.

We had no external investment, no overdraft; we didn't even invest any equity. You hear about a lot of people starting their companies with personal investment, but we put in nothing. The objective was to raise the first sales invoice and to get it paid, which generates some cash for the directors as well as cash to start hiring staff.

Looking back on it, is there anything you would have done differently?

Justin Keatinge If I was doing it again now, and with the benefit of hindsight, I'd look to do things a lot faster, but that's only because of the knowledge that I have gained in the 20 years since, including a deep understanding of the industry. I don't think there is anything that we could have done differently because even if we had generated a pile of cash, we wouldn't have known what to do with it.

Both John and I were in our mid-twenties and we had both worked in an internal IT department for four to five years after finishing college. We had no idea what the IT industry was like, what consultancy was like, so we really had to learn it slowly. There was nothing we could have done differently as two young, green, naïve guys. If we wanted to start a similar business again and complete the 20-year journey in, say, five years (now that we know how the industry works), we'd start with a chunk of cash and hire IT delivery teams and sales people in advance of bringing in revenue, but it wouldn't have been the right thing to do back then.

Acquisitions have been very good for Version 1 and looking back we could have gone on the acquisition trail earlier if we had a bit more experience and knew how to do it, or if we brought someone in with experience in acquiring and integrating businesses. We could have, for example, commenced the acquisition strategy earlier; however, we would have needed to have raised funds earlier. When it came to expanding into the UK, we had two options: one was organic, the other was acquisition. We chose acquisition, which was the right choice, because organic expansion would have been too slow, but we were 15 years in business before we made that step. Early on we made some very small attempts to grow organically into the UK, but we really didn't know what we were doing and the early attempts failed and fizzled out. However, we didn't need to as there was enough business in Ireland to keep us growing at 30–50% per year.

At what stage then did you first bring funding into the business?

Justin Keatinge We set up Version 1 in 1996 and 18 years later, in 2014, we raised €8 million in equity capital from the BDO DCF.

What about before that? Did you take on any bank debt finance to fund the growth?

Justin Keatinge Our first acquisition in the UK, which we completed in 2013, was partly funded with circa €3 million in bank debt. Frankly, it was harder to raise €3 million back in 2013 than to raise €100 million in 2017!

Why did you decide on bank debt vs equity capital for that first acquisition? Was equity capital an option?

Justin Keatinge Equity capital was an option but we didn't want to give away equity as it is more expensive than debt. We had a very conservative leverage policy. The shareholders were all directors and we had never taken money off the table (i.e. sell some of our shareholding to private investors), so our risk appetite was low. We looked at what other companies were doing with regards to how much leverage they were putting in their businesses. In our industry, it seemed to be common to put up to 4 × EBITDA of debt into the business, but we had been through the downturn of 2008–2009 and knew that if bad things happened then EBITDA could go down, so we set a conservative debt policy of a 1 × EBITDA leverage limit. We never went above the 1 × EBITDA leverage limit as a result of the first couple of acquisitions we did. When we got the €3 million in bank debt finance for the first acquisition, that was well under the 1 × EBITDA leverage limit. Then, after a couple of further acquisitions, as we approached the 1 × EBITDA leverage limit level, we didn't want to breach our policy, so we then took in equity capital from the BDO DCF.

What are your positive or negative experiences from raising equity funding?

Justin Keatinge The successful rounds of funding we have done have been very positive. However, in 2012, we looked at raising private equity (PE) funding but, at a very late stage, pulled the plug on that, which was the right decision. At the time we thought we needed London-based PE experience on the board of the company to help us with growth by acquisition into the UK. We went a long way with one PE provider but because of differences in opinion we couldn't get the deal over the line. We then went on the UK acquisitions trail on our own without them. That was the only negative experience. We chose the wrong partner but, thankfully, we didn't do that deal. Five years later we did a very good PE deal, which was a structured as an MBO and I stepped down as CEO. In the interim, we raised the €8 million in equity capital from the BDO DCF and that was all very positive.

What would you advise companies are the advantages of equity vs debt?

Justin Keatinge The downside of giving away equity is it can be very expensive. Though your intention may be to create value by growing, you may be giving away a lot of value in doing so. The upside is that equity capital is low risk, so when you are raising money you need to figure out your risk appetite with regard to how much leverage you want to put into your business. At Version 1, we could easily have raised debt instead of equity finance at the time we took in the BDO DCF equity capital. As things played out, taking on the debt would have been better for us, would have been much more lucrative. But the equity approach was lower risk and it was the right decision at the time, and still the right decision, to take in equity and maintain a very low limit on leverage of 1 × EBITDA.

In terms of raising debt finance, a word of warning about bank covenants: debt can become a very expensive process if you breach covenants – you could lose the entire company. Though equity doesn't have this risk, the rewards for the investor are many multiples higher. Instead of a 5% return or similar for a debt provider, equity investors are looking for a 200–300% return. Again, it all comes down to your appetite for leverage and the risk associated with it compared to the lower risk but higher price of equity.

What would you see as the proper equity/debt funding mix for rapidly growing companies and what factors would influence that decision?

Justin Keatinge The industry standard for leverage is around 4 × EBITDA, which is a good place to start one's thinking. The banks may not even go that high, unless there is a PE investor as well, because the banks know that if there is a PE investor, they may look to put in more equity if covenants are breached. In our industry, it is starting at 4 × EBITDA and then increases or decreases from there, depending on your risk appetite. If you are a founder who has never taken any money off the table and have a valuable business, you may consider it reckless to leverage up to 4 × EBITDA because if you breach your covenants the bank may come in and sell your business. The leverage multiple can go up very quickly if there is a drop in EBITDA; it is really important to understand the details of covenants (there will typically be many) and to know what the industry standards are. We took what would generally be a very, very conservative multiple of 1 × EBITDA, whereas, as I've said, the top end of the industry standard is 4 × EBITDA. So, the right answer is probably, generally somewhere between 1 × EBITDA and 4 × EBITDA.

Depending on the type of business you are in, it may not require debt or equity investment. Version 1 was, and is, a services business, and a services business generally shouldn't need external equity or debt. All companies should be profitable to generate sufficient cash to achieve the growth the owners are targeting. In attempting to acquire companies, we came across a lot of companies with good annual revenues but with no profit, which meant that we could not acquire them. (They never generated any cash for their founders either.) Typically, we would buy companies that had between 5%–8% profit levels (EBITDA margin), whereas Version 1 had an EBITDA margin of 15%+. We would turn around these companies from making 5% to 15% EBITDA margin, just through improving efficiencies. A services business should be profitable enough to generate cash to fund growth, unless you are going to do an acquisition, or product development, or something extra that specifically requires cash. As a result, you need to have a good reason and business case for any debt or equity that you are looking to raise.

What advice would you give companies that are getting investor-ready?

Justin Keatinge There are three main things I would advise:
1. Having a really good set of metrics by which you run the business, a set of numbers that someone from outside the industry can be presented with and can understand, as well as being industry-specific so that they can compare metrics with other businesses in the industry where these are available. For example:
   - decent management metrics/key performance indicators (KPIs);
   - management reporting packs (i.e. profit/loss, balance sheet and cash flow); daily, weekly, monthly, quarterly stats on the performance of the business are vital.
2. Have good internal processes in place so that due diligence can be easily completed. For example:
   - all contracts, from customers to staff, are filed and stored safely together and accessible, and everything is also scanned and backed up electronically;
   - good documentation on everything from a share capital table through to the company's pension fund and insurance policies;

- similarly for the accounts: have good, consistent monthly and annual processes for managing the profit and loss account and the balance sheet so that they can be easily reviewed.
3. Budgeting: sophisticated investors will want to see that you have a good track record in budgeting and that in the last number of years (three years, say) you have been able to achieve your budgets. They will want to gain confidence that the company can set budgets and achieve them. If you can show that, they will have confidence in your future budget. PE investors, particularly, will always try to test and ask you to prove that what you say about the future is 'true', or least that it is highly probable. Many small businesses put very little effort into budgeting and forecasting. A wish and a desire to grow is very different from an actual budget for the next two to three years, combined with a sales pipeline, a plan and a strategy for how you are going to achieve it. It is then highly effective to back this up with documentary evidence of budgets actually achieved, of what you said you would do three years ago and what you have clearly delivered since, in Years 1, 2 and 3 respectively.

Would you challenge an owner entrepreneur if they said: "Equity is blood – I can never give away equity"?

Justin Keatinge If you never want to give away equity, you may be limiting your upside. If you give away minority equity, for example, selling 25% equity in your business, which then allows you to double in size instead of growing just 20%, then your remaining 75% has grown enormously compared to what it otherwise would have done.

If you look at the smartest businesses in the world, these are generally hot startups out of Silicon Valley. They will always sell a lot of equity at the start. The founders will end up after a couple of rounds of fundraising with, say, 10% of the equity, but the most successful companies will be valued in the billions and the founders will have 10% of billions, as opposed to 100% of very little if they hadn't brought in the equity investors.

To continue the example of Silicon Valley, when they bring in venture capitalists (VCs) they will bring in VCs with a huge amount of experience who have already backed companies to scale them to grow internationally. A start-up entrepreneur will be on a very slow learning curve compared to a VC, who has done it several times before and can introduce startups to other companies that have faced the same challenges in different industries. Though the smartest companies in the world are raising equity big time, most Irish companies have been very slow to do it. But if companies are not prepared to sell equity then they are putting the brakes on growth and are creating less value than they could otherwise have achieved.

15.6 The Banker's View (Andrew Graham)

Andrew Graham is Director, Corporate Banking at Bank of Ireland with responsibility for domestic leveraged acquisition finance, project finance and intermediary channels. Set out below are his personal views on what SMEs should contemplate when considering a bank lending application. His comments are his own and do not represent the views of Bank of Ireland.

What do you look for when assessing lending opportunities?

Andrew Graham The foremost consideration is repayment capacity. In considering this, a wider assessment of key influencing factors is taken into account. This would normally include: the quality and sustainability of the business model; strength and depth of the management team; the competitive landscape; addressable markets; and the historical and projected financial performance of the business.

In addition to this, thought is also given to what is normally referred to as a 'secondary way out', which essentially means that if the business does not perform in line with expectations, what mechanisms are available to both the company and the lender to work out the loan and ultimately repay it. This assessment also considers what security may be available to support the lending obligation.

Do you look at the security element in conjunction with the company's cash flows, or do you look at them as two separate propositions?

Andrew Graham As mentioned above, the security element is very much the secondary aspect to the assessment. So, even if there are strong, marketable and valuable assets from a security perspective, it shouldn't be the primary motivation in making an informed lending decision. Invariably, if you haven't assessed the capacity of the entity to repay the loan in the normal course, you're likely to end up in a workout scenario, which isn't good either for the borrower or for the bank. To my mind, this should hold true whether you are looking to lend to an SME, mid-corporate, large private or listed company.

Would the provision of personal guarantees help a lending proposition for a company that does not have that immediate repayment capacity?

Andrew Graham It depends! The first question it poses is why there is no immediate repayment capacity. If the company is actually generating cash but choosing to re-invest it back into the business to fund growth, then it is simply a matter of timing repayments rather than not (ever) having repayment capacity. If it is the latter, then perhaps taking on repayment obligations may not necessarily be the best option.

Generally, I would suggest that for larger SMEs, mid-corporates and PLCs, personal guarantees do not feature. However, for some smaller, recently established enterprises displaying moderate levels of cash generation, or that simply do not have any established track record, personal guarantees may be sought, or may assist in certain lending decisions.

In assessing smaller SMEs or start-up entities, the following factors often feature:
1. they are higher risk, given the size of the enterprise; or
2. the potential influence that an adverse macro-economic event could have on them; or
3. the level of financial information or supporting documentation isn't readily available to be assessed in relation to the reliability or sustainability of cash flows to service the debt.

In such cases, banks can at times default into looking for personal guarantees. Often, the bank is looking for a mechanism to lend but feels it necessary to ensure that the interests of the owner–manager or entrepreneur are aligned with the interests of the bank.

Do you see 'skin in the game' as an absolute requirement for a lending proposition?

Andrew Graham Certainly it is an important consideration. The key issue here is to ensure that all parties' interests are properly aligned. So, if trading and cash generation gets tough, as a lender you know that the business and management team you are backing are motivated to do all within their control to run the business to the best of their abilities.

What, in your view, is the correct debt-to-equity mix? Is there a formula that companies or entrepreneurs need to consider before they approach a bank for funding?

Andrew Graham This varies on a case-by-case and sector-by-sector basis and, unfortunately, there isn't a formula or rule book for this one. Entrepreneurs often know how much capital they need to invest into the business, but do not necessarily know whether it should all be debt, all equity, or a mixture of both.

From a debt perspective, lenders consider the 'equity cushion', which simply means how much higher-risk capital (equity) needs to be eroded from the business before the senior debt gets impacted. Usually, this is driven by either the amount of cash actually invested in the company or the underlying established enterprise value (EV) of the business. As market liquidity and the interest rate environment can change from time to time, business values also change and EVs can be considered either at a point in time or through a cycle-value range.

Given the different risk and pricing profiles evident between debt and equity, it is often beneficial to seek some advice. I would generally look to establish the business's ability to borrow debt, as it is usually the cheapest form of capital available. Finally, equity may be the most appropriate solution, and the choice as to which equity-funding partner to align with is important.

Are there sectors or industries to which it is more appealing for banks to lend?

Andrew Graham Not necessarily from a general lending perspective. There are certain sectors of the economy that can face tougher challenges from time to time. Perhaps they are in a more capital-intensive industry that operates based on high-volume throughput but low margins. That said, you still have good companies in tough sectors worthy of support. At a more macro level, any sector that provides an amenable market to prudently lend into will generally be appealing to banks. Finally, larger banks and institutions with capital and liquidity will also look to have a balanced portfolio of exposures covering many asset classes and markets. Ideally, lenders like markets that are relatively easy to understand and assess, capable of holding decent volumes of conventional debt and whose default characteristics are well established and known.

What is the current bank funding market like? How has it changed since the economic downturn?

Andrew Graham How has it changed since the crash? Quite fundamentally, in certain respects, and not that much in other ways. Some of the best learnings arising out of the economic downturn are the re-focus on the primacy of cash flows and the simple understanding that asset and property prices can go down as well as up.

Generally, both banks and borrowers remain more prudent and appropriately cautious in their assessment and appetite for debt. Regulation and governance around lending activities remain under a high, and increasing, level of scrutiny. The benefits associated with this include a more thorough understanding of risk appetite, a quantifiable level of exposure and a better understanding of the potential contagion effects through aggregated risk groups. None of this was properly known or established in the market previously.

Given the current low interest rate environment, there is a wide and varied selection of financing options available in the market. This is generally a positive factor for businesses that can differentiate the offerings and select the financing options and products most suitable for them.

How does a bank assess and set covenants?

Andrew Graham Bank covenants are a set of parameters agreed between the borrower and the bank, which it is understood that the business will perform to. In many ways, if a covenant is breached, this acts as a 'red flag'. This flag alerts the bank to the fact that the business is not performing to plan and that an agreed remediation plan may be necessary. Covenants are selected usually around key areas, including:

1. debt service cover ratio (DSCR) – the ratio of free cash flow to debt-servicing obligations;
2. maximum leverage – the maximum level of debt to EBITDA;
3. loan to value (LTV) – the ratio of marketable asset cover (usually property) to debt (usually expressed in a percentage form, e.g. 70% loan to value);
4. capital expenditure – the amount of cash the business can re-invest into its tangible assets;
5. dividends – how much cash can be extracted out of the business.

In setting covenant levels, consideration is given to the financial projections provided and which covenants are most appropriate, given the nature of the business and the strategy adopted by its owners. In setting the covenants, an open conversation between all parties should help establish a sensible set of covenants and a full understanding as to why they have been established.

Once set, it would be normal practice for the borrower to submit a covenant compliance certificate at agreed intervals and signed by a company director. The compliance certificate usually includes the various calculations underpinning the covenants.

Would a bank usually give some headroom on those covenants? Is there any flexibility with them?

Andrew Graham Absolutely. In all lending instances a bank should build headroom and flexibility into the covenants. In reality, businesses do not usually perform fully in line with projections over a three-to-five year timeframe. Outside influences impacting the business can throw up opportunities and threats that need to be reacted to. This sometimes means that the business may either under- or out-perform their projections, or simply deliver the same results over a different time horizon. The degree of flexibility built into the covenants should accommodate this and only lead to a covenant breach if performance is materially different from what was projected.

What tips would you offer SMEs looking to borrow funds from a bank?

Andrew Graham There are several things that SMEs should bear in mind when approaching a lender, including:

Be prepared Have a business plan, accounts and projections available to present. Know what quantum of debt is required, outline what the funds are to be used for and how the loan is to be repaid. The assistance of an advisor may be useful, but if you are going alone, research what rates and conditions are generally available.

Know your numbers Have a very, very good understanding of the year-on-year, monthly or quarterly historical performance of the business and the associated cash flows generated, and reflect this in a detailed information pack. One of the things banks will do is look at prior-year performance as a leading indicator of both the current and projected performance.

Full disclosure of all key facts Provide a full view and perspective of the business and your background. If pertinent information is omitted, it will subsequently come out and the fact that it wasn't initially disclosed will not count in your favour.

Build a relationship Build a relationship of trust with your bank. Even when you don't need anything immediately, by keeping them briefed on your business and strategy, there will be a corporate memory established that will benefit you in the future.

Assuming the company delivers on all of the above, how quickly could the company expect to get its lending?

Andrew Graham There are requirements on banks to respond to SMEs' credit applications within the prescribed timeframe set out by the Central Bank, which provide for banks to generally make an SME credit decision within 15 working days on receipt of all relevant information. (Interestingly, the Central Bank monitors bank funding liquidity to the SME market and publish updates on a regular basis.) When your approval is to hand, make sure to check there are no onerous conditions (conditions precedent, covenants or security items) that could delay or impede what you are looking to do. When lending to SMEs, banks generally have pre-scripted loan offer documents (with associated terms and conditions) that are filled out and issued centrally. Once the loan offer is signed, pre-conditions fulfilled and associated security taken, the loan is advanced.

15.7 The View of the Later-stage Funder (Orla O'Gorman, Euronext)

Orla O'Gorman is Head of Equity Listing Ireland at Euronext, the leading pan-European exchange in the eurozone, spanning Belgium, France, Ireland, The Netherlands, Portugal and the UK (see www.ise.ie or www.euronext.com). Orla is an experienced corporate financier, having worked on both the advisory and client side of corporate transactions with public and private companies across a diverse range of industry sectors. She has been involved in a wide variety of transactions including equity capital markets (IPOs, equity raisings), mergers and acquisitions (on both the buy and sell side), private equity, and restructuring. Orla is responsible for equity listings and the development and execution of #IPOready, a strategic financing programme designed to equip CEOs and CFOs with crucial skills in raising finance, getting their company investment-ready, investor relations, business management and scaling (www.ipoready.ie).

How would an SME owner know if their company is suited to a stock market listing?

Orla O'Gorman A company is suited to a stock market listing if it has a good story and investment case that can be brought to the market. The company needs to be, as one would say, 'a big user of capital'. I think there's no point in listing your company unless you want to access lots of capital over time because the reality is that when you're listing initially there is a lot of work to get your company listed on the stock market. Additionally, in comparison to other forms of capital, the process to obtain a stock-exchange listing can be more expensive and the real benefits only kick in when the company can go back to the market and raise subsequent capital very quickly, efficiently and cost effectively. For example, in January 2018, Total Produce plc went to the market and raised a further circa €145 million in a day. That's the market working efficiently.

There are several reasons why SME owners would list, the first of which is to access capital. Secondly, when you have shares that are publicly traded, it can bring other benefits; for example, if a company is acquiring another company, it can use its listed shares as consideration in the transaction, which can be helpful. This links back to the point about raising capital quickly and easily. If, for example, Total Produce plc was completing a large acquisition, it could have raised the money very quickly on the market or it could have issued shares as consideration, both of which would have facilitated the speed of the completed acquisition. Compare this to a private company trying to complete an acquisition while also raising the funding: it's trying to run two processes at the same time, both of which have an element of uncertainty.

Is a listing limited to bigger companies like Total Produce plc or is there a suitable exchange for scaling/earlier-stage companies?

Orla O'Gorman There are quite a lot of misconceptions about listing and the size a company needs to be to list. Obviously, there are certain obligations that go with being a listed company, in terms of reporting frequency and disclosures. However, there is no such thing as free capital and there are obligations associated with every type of capital, including both equity and debt. For example, if a company has raised venture capital or private equity, it is now in a relationship with, and has obligations to, those investors in terms of reporting and restrictions on what the company can and cannot do without the investors' agreement.

Similarly for a listed company, there is also that engagement with investors, though it is a much more defined, managed relationship. For example, a listed company would be expected to spend two weeks twice a year going to meet investors, along with formally reporting its financial results twice a year to those investors. Also, there are additional costs associated with being listed and I think for companies to have efficiencies around those costs (many of which are fixed, such as the admission document and the prospectus), they should be a certain size.

So does the company need to be a certain size?

Orla O'Gorman The benefit of a listing is to access significant capital to allow the company scale and grow quickly. For example, Kerry Group, when they originally listed in 1986, had a market cap of IR£9 million. Today, Kerry Group plc's market cap is circa €14 billion. Additionally, CRH Group plc, which had revenues of IR£25 million when it listed in 1986, has grown to €23 billion. So, the lesson from these two examples is to start small and then use the capital market to scale.

In March 2018, when Virtual Reality Education Holdings plc listed, their market cap was only €22 million. While it's gone well, they are at the smaller end of the scale for listed companies. Though I'm not suggesting that a smaller company cannot list, I think a company would need to have a market cap in the region of €25 to €50 million to really benefit from a listing. The reality is if you're a smaller company and you don't have a massive 'free float' [i.e. the proportion of shares that are in the hands of public investors] then there aren't that many shares available to be traded and therefore there is not going to be a lot of liquidity.

How much funding can be added through a listing?
An infinite amount?

Orla O'Gorman Yes, an infinite amount, but this is subject of course to trading performance and investors' appetite for the company's growth story, which will be reflected through the demand for its shares. For example, Virtual Reality Education Holdings plc raised €6.5 million in funding; and then there's AIB, which raised €3.4 billion in June 2017 following the sale by the Government of its 28.8% stake, so it can be any amount. I think that's the really significant thing about the public markets: with the quantum of capital available, the opportunities and potential outcomes are really massive, as demonstrated by both Kerry Group plc and CRH Group plc.

How does a company secure a stock exchange listing?

Orla O'Gorman Typically, the company achieves a listing (which is also know as an initial public offering (IPO)) by presenting its business case to investors for funding, who then decide to invest or not. IPOs involve the following three high-level actions:
1. the company puts an 'equity pitch' together in conjunction with its corporate and legal advisors;
2. the company then presents its equity pitch to potential investors seeking funding; and
3. the investors give feedback on whether they are willing to invest and if so, how much and at what valuation.

Euronext has prepared an IPO guide to give companies an overview of the IPO process.

Do SMEs have a choice of capital markets/exchanges from which to raise funding?

Orla O'Gorman There are two types of capital market, and companies have the ability to move between both:
• regulated markets; and
• multilateral trading facilities (MTFs).

An example of a regulated market is Euronext's main market, which is regulated by the EU, meaning that it must comply with EU Regulations. For example, to be listed on the main market, a company must have a three-year track record and 25% of its shares in public hands. These are absolute prerequisities.

The second type of market is the multilateral trading facility, which is exchange regulated. Examples are Euronext's Growth market, or AIM, "the London Stock Exchange's international market for smaller growing companies". SMEs are most likely to list on these markets; in fact, with much more flexibility, they're really designed for high-growth SMEs. There is no strict requirement for a three-year track record nor a minimum amount of shares to be held in public hands. Additionally, if the company is doing a transaction, it does not need shareholder approval if listed on these markets.

A company's choice of capital market for its listing can be interesting. For example, Dalata Hotel Group (Dalata) could have listed on either market: it was big enough to list on the regulated market because it had a three-year track record. However, its objective was to raise significant amounts of capital and complete a lot of acquisitions without the requirement to keep going back to shareholders for approval, so it initially listed on the Growth market. As a result it grew significantly by acquisition; when it got to a market cap of around €800 million, it then decided to move to the main securities market, which illustrates how SMEs have flexibility to move between markets as they scale.

What are the 'pros' and 'cons' of listing?

Orla O'Gorman The pros of listing include the ability to:
• raise money quickly;
• use the company's shares as consideration for acquiring other companies;
• use the company's shares to retain, reward and attract employees (this was a big positive for Applegreen in attracting key talent).

Additionally, there are other, intangible benefits of becoming a Plc, including profile, branding, stronger governance and better credit terms. However, there also new costs, including management's time for the company 'road show', going to meet investors at the publication of the company's annual report, which is an important document, providing both existing and potential investors with detailed information on the trading and financial position of the company.

It is worth noting, as well, that certain companies perceive being listed as having negative aspects, including being in the public eye, with an increased level of disclosures required, a little bit more attention, and with information about senior management salaries and benefits available publically, which not all business owners like. There's also a misconception among some business owners about loss of control. However, the reality is that investors don't have control of a listed company as they don't sit on its board. In fact, they don't *want* to be part of the senior management team or to be approving everything that you do; if they don't like what you're doing, they can 'leave' by selling their shares. Shareholders expect you as the management team to be in control and to grow and develop the business. So, from a day-to-day management perspective, you will actually have a lot more control of your business if you're a listed company than if you have received investment from a private equity firm.

Professional advisors are necessary to get a company listed. What do they cover?

Orla O'Gorman Professional advisors include financial, legal and stock-broking advisors, and all three are necessary to get a company listed. However, the cost is also something that business owners are mindful of. Structuring the listing is very important, including the amount of money to raise, the valuation, refining the company strategy and making it investment-ready. Good advisors are critical – choose them wisely.

What would professional advisors have specific input on?

Orla O'Gorman The advisors help a company get its investment business case right as well as the listing valuation, which is another very important aspect that requires professional advice because it is critical that the company lists at a realistic and open valuation. At the initial investor meetings, advisors will test the valuations and get a feel from the investors to assess if they would be interested in investing at this valuation level. This is really important. The other areas advisors are responsible for include preparing the admission document or the prospectus. Legal advisors will be involved in making sure that it's accurate and verified, and the accountants are responsible for ensuring that all the financial information is correct. Additionally, the working capital forecast is a key element as it says: "look, we have enough working capital to last us for 12 months".

While this is all really important work, what management and the board of directors need to remember is that the admission document/prospectus is what the investment decision is being made on, and so it must be accurate. All this checking and professional advice can be time-consuming, frustrating and costly, but it's actually for their protection; so that, in five years' time, say, if something goes wrong, somebody cannot come back and say 'Well, you said that and it wasn't true'. It's important for company directors to realise that this is an exercise in making sure that what goes out to the market is correct and that they, as directors, who are signing up to the document, can have the comfort that they need.

How important is the management team to securing investors?

Orla O'Gorman The management team is critical. You have to have the right management team in place and they have to be committed post-IPO. People invest in people and you absolutely need to have more than one person leading the company, though investors will want to see a visionary along with key supports from both a financial and operational perspective. It is very important that the CEO and the chief financial officer (CFO) tell the same story, though slightly differently, i.e. the CEO will describe the journey ahead for the company, while the CFO will detail this in numerical terms. They must be seen to support each other and show that they are a team, because investors will not want to invest in just one person. Ryanair do this brilliantly for their roadshow, they send out eight teams of two people. So the investors are seeing the head of operations and other business functions telling the Ryanair story. It's not just Michael O'Leary and Neil Sorahan all the time; they rotate the teams and the investors really feel they get a good view of the company and a consistent message.

What successful SME listings can you point to?

Orla O'Gorman A really interesting one is Applegreen, where the two founding shareholders, Bob Etchingham and Joe Barrett, between them owned 100% of the company. They looked at various different ways of funding the business's growth plan and concluded on an IPO because they felt it would give them ongoing access to capital, as well as some liquidity for their shares. With the profile and the branding, they really wanted to access the US market. As part of the IPO, they sold down 30% of their own holding. However, they had a big debate at the time regarding the listing price, which was slightly below their initial expectations. They openly tell the story how they debated this internally and focused on the fact that they would still own 70% post-listing. Let's not be greedy, they concluded – the listing price will always be the reference point.

If you review the Applegreen share price chart, it tells an incredible story of the growth of Applegreen and its share price. Applegreen listed in June 2015 at €3.80 per share, with circa 31% of the company sold to investors/the market. €70 million of the capital raised was invested in the company and €21.7 million was disposed of by the founding shareholders, resulting in them retaining 69% ownership of the company. Over time, as the share price went up, further investment was raised from the market. There was strong market demand, with investor sentiment strong along the lines of 'We really like the story and we'd like to purchase more shares'. So the shareholders sold down some 6 million more shares in September 2016, with the founding shareholders disposing of shares valued at €4.50 each (€27 million). Post the disposal, the shareholders owned circa 60% of the company. Then in October 2017, they raised another €47 million to fund acquisitions and the shareholders' ownership reduced to €55 million. In October 2018, the company raised a further €175 million at a price of €6.08 per share and the founders further reduced their holding to 41.4%.

This is a really good example of two guys who stuck with it, taking a lot of money out, raising extra money into the company, and with the value of what they hold going up all the time. It's the same if you look at Dalata, which is another good case study, whereby if you stick with the company one of the big benefits of an IPO is that you get to participate in the upside.

How is Applegreen using the funding raised from its listing?

Orla O'Gorman They are using the listing to expand Applegreen's forecourt presence both in the Irish and US markets. It took the company 15 years to establish 50 sites; they opened an additional 50 sites between September 2015 and October 2017. This is what the markets do; they allow you to raise money and grow very quickly if you're using them properly.

Is there a course SME owners/managers can attend on getting ready for listing?

Orla O'Gorman Yes, there is an IPO-ready course that SME owners and managers can attend to prepare for and learn about listing their company. The course is run by Euronext Dublin in conjunction with Enterprise Ireland and the Ireland Strategic Investment Fund. The key elements include:
- how to get your company investment-ready;
- the sources of finance that are available;
- tools to compare the different sources of finance and assess one versus another (what's the one source that suits you best); and
- what to expect from the fundraising process.

In order to get ready for the listing and the fundraising process, it's important to make sure you've got the right corporate structures in place, and have the simple things complete and ready, for example your share capital table. Is it correct and up to date, so that anyone who thinks they may have a share knows definitively if they do or they don't?

If you have good company governance, controls and a good board, and everything's up to date and in order, you're ready for a fund raise, whether you want to sell the entire company or whether you want to raise VC, private equity, or if you want to get a bank loan. It will all stand to you. There will be no surprises and you'll keep your advisors' fees down.

You mentioned a company's board. How important is it for an IPO?

Orla O'Gorman Yes, a company's board is critical. Pre-IPO, if a company can get some really good people onto its board, this will give a lot of credibility to the business growth story. And, as Gary McGann advised our IPO-ready candidates, boards are the cheapest advisors you'll ever get and it's really important to have the right board with the right experience, including international experience, if that's relevant to support you in getting the best from your business. Boards are really important to support a management team, but they are also very important for challenging management, to help them anticipate and appraise what's going on in the market and what's coming down the line.

Do you see more Irish companies list?

Orla O'Gorman Yes. There's a good pipeline; companies are beginning to think about it more. I think that per capita in Ireland there are a reasonable amount of listings but in other ways we don't have enough, and I question why we don't. I think that it's due in part to a deficit in awareness, with potential companies thinking that it's only for big companies, not for them.

It's not because Irish companies are not good enough; there are a lot of companies that could list; however, they choose to do different things and go different ways, including selling out. I think it is often a matter of a misalignment or mismatch between the ambitions and capabilities of the management team and the potential of the company. A company could be a perfect candidate for a stock market listing, but the CEO does not want to bring it. Or it can happen the other way around, where the management want a listing, but the company is not suitable. It's just about getting all of these variables lined up. But when it does work, it works really well. Although we have not had that many companies coming to the market in Ireland, most of the companies that have done so here have gone on to do very well – look at Kerry Group, CRH, Glanbia, etc. These aren't just good Irish companies; they are world-class companies.

A US investor has commented to me: "when you see a US company seeking a listing, they look like they're driving a Ferrari and you lift the bonnet there's some kind of crock underneath it. Whereas the Irish company looks like he's driving a banger and when you open up the bonnet you're really surprised." I think it's down to the psyche of the Irish; we are nearly apologising for ourselves. But there are some amazing companies listed on the Euronext Dublin and there's a lot of capital out there. For example, AIB held circa 1,400 investor meetings prior to the IPO, not just with

Bernard Byrne, but with all the teams and analysts around them. They did a really superb job of selling Ireland and the Irish story, warming investors globally to Ireland, which hasn't been unhelpful.

In March 2018, the Irish Stock Exchange became part of Euronext, the leading pan-European exchange in the eurozone, covering Belgium, France, Ireland, the Netherlands, Portugal and the UK. With 1,300 listed issuers, over 960 of whom are SMEs, this is an exciting development for Irish companies as Euronext Dublin markets can now offer access to a single pan-European order book with over 5,800 investors.

PART III

GETTING INVESTOR-READY

In Part III we build on the practical details provided in Part II to set out how a business can become investor-ready for equity, debt or government funding by discussing what details prospective investors (be they banks, equity funders or government) expect to see in a business plan. Some funders may request forms or questionnaires to be completed for assessment. However, it is likely that such forms will follow the elements of the business plan/information memorandum (detailed in **Chapter 11, Section 11.6**). **Chapter 17** gives some practical detail on how to prepare for and deliver an investor pitch, while **Chapter 18** summarises what to do and what not to do when raising funding.

CHAPTER 16

BUSINESS PLANNING FOR GROWTH

16.1 Introduction

"By failing to prepare, you are preparing to fail."

Benjamin Franklin

Every enterprise, irrespective of its size, needs a business plan. Few of us would get on an airplane if the pilot told us that the flight plan was (as is the case with some entrepreneurs' business growth plans) 'on the shelf' or would 'evolve organically'. Instead, we take our seats safe in the knowledge that the flight crew will navigate and continuously monitor progress against a clear plan and, where necessary, adjust and adapt to deal with any adverse conditions, such as turbulence, headwinds, etc. Just as airline pilots enter the destination co-ordinates into the cockpit system prior to take off, entrepreneurs must take time to plan the journey and path of their business to the next stage of its development and growth.

A well-designed business plan sets out the ideal path to growth while at the same time being flexible to respond to variances between the journey and the plan should unexpected and unplanned obstacles to growth emerge. **It is at this point that the plan needs to be updated for current business conditions.**

For many entrepreneurs, business planning may sound an unimaginative and almost mechanical requirement, an obligation that bears no relation to the excitement they feel as they set out their vision to grow their business. However, this need not and should not be the case. A business plan is not a telephone directory, there to be glanced at occasionally, most likely in the case of an emergency. A business plan should be a living document, familiar to management, and reviewed and updated regularly. If its plan sits on a shelf, ignored, as soon as it is completed, then there are likely to be real issues with how a business operates and grows. When seeking investment from investors, business owners should make potential investors feel comfortable about the company, its track record (if applicable) and growth prospects before they invest. The business growth plan is an essential part of building this confidence: it should be professionally prepared to meet the needs of the prospective investor. It should show the business from an investor's perspective and answer any concerns the potential investor may have, demonstrating that the business is 'investor-ready'. An investor-ready business plan will demonstrate to the potential investor that the company is expert in its industry and that it has a clear mission, with comprehensive and detailed business objectives and goals.

Prospective investors and funders of SMEs are all too familiar with the marked contrast between an entrepreneur's ability to vividly communicate in person their vision and plan for their business and the written business plan that, in the majority of cases, is a poor reflection of this. For reasons only known to themselves, many entrepreneurs are reluctant to commit their business vision to paper and to articulate it clearly in a detailed business plan. Additionally, those few who do very rarely monitor their progress against the plan.

Our recommendation to all such 'reluctant authors' is to think in terms of preparing a **growth** plan rather than a business plan. Entrepreneurs take a major risk by going into business in the first place. If they are seeking funding, one of the first challenges they will need to address is to be able to clearly, concisely and confidently describe their business's growth plan. Growth is the simple irrefutable fact that takes every company through its business lifecycle, and clarity around it is what every prospective investor expects, and growth is important for the survival of a business: if it does not grow, it is likely that its competitors will.

When asked about his or her plan for growth, an unprepared entrepreneur's answer is often of an 'organic/inevitable' kind. An example of this is the entrepreneur who, when asked how she would secure growth for her new company responded that she had just secured a very large customer, which would generate significant annual revenues. The growth "would simply come as a result". However, this particular entrepreneur did not have any idea of the profit (if any) that would be generated from this revenue growth, as well as the cash collection cycle invoicing her customers. It is all these elements that determine if, how and when an SME will grow and if such growth is sustainable.

So, all businesses, irrespective of their size, are advised to create a road map for growth, one that will guide them and their management team, and help reduce the risk that growth will simply not materialise. The road map can also help them find more growth opportunities and avoid common mistakes, such as failing to hire a key employee or investing in new technologies.

The first step is to invest time in outlining the plan for growth. However, rather than starting with where the company is now, an effective business-planning approach is to start at the end (where the company wants to be) and work back from there (see **Section 16.3**).

16.2 What Is 'Growth'?

Like individuals, every business is different, with different objectives, funding structures and at different stages in the business lifecycle. As a result, each business's growth objectives are different or at different stages or levels. The meaning of 'growth' varies from business to business, and depends on a number of different factors that need to be taken into account. Some clear signs of growth in the business will include:
- an increase in its revenues and profits;
- increasing customer numbers;
- improving gross margin percentages;
- a greater profit and cash balance at the end of the financial year;
- repayment of a loan, be it from a bank or a family member;
- completing an acquisition of another company; or
- securing new or further investment.

All of the above are credible growth objectives and can be the goal of a business's growth plan, but to achieve them the business will need the clarity of a well-written and structured growth plan, the key components or elements of which are set out below.

16.3 Start at the End, or the Ultimate Objective

It may seem counterintuitive, but the most important aspect of any serious growth plan is to set out its final objective. What defines success and what does success look and feel like? It can be any of the growth objectives set out above, or it can be broken down into smaller elements that make up the ultimate objective. **Example 16.1** below illustrates how a big goal can be achieved by degrees.

EXAMPLE 16.1: BREAKING THE OVERALL OBJECTIVE INTO SMALLER ELEMENTS

A successful Irish SME had an overriding growth objective of launching and selling its food products in the US market within a two-year period. Behind this major goal were several smaller objectives and plans, building blocks that, when put in place, one by one, assisted in developing the capacity to achieve the overall objective.

In this case, the smaller objectives included:
- speaking to other successful Irish SMEs that had experience of launching products in the US;
- selecting the initial US region in which to launch;
- meeting and assessing the correct distributors for the product and its target customers;
- getting Food and Drug Administration (FDA) approval for the product;
- setting up the US corporate entity;
- interviewing and recruiting staff for the US office.

The company's CEO had distilled and articulated the growth plan into specific tasks that were then included in the overall business plan itself, allocated to the team, and tracked and monitored on a regular basis. As a result, the product was successfully launched with a major US East Coast customer in advance of the original two-year timeframe, which had a very positive impact on revenues, profits and cash.

However, although this represented success in terms of the original growth plan, the CEO's response on being congratulated for what was considered a major achievement was: "It's only one customer and they are only an East Coast customer."

Already, a new plan was being drafted with the objective of leveraging this East Coast customer to gain access into customers with a nationwide US presence, which was achieved within a period of 18 months and funded by external investors who gained confidence from the US customer's demand for the product and the CEO's proven track record of winning the first major US customer.

This example illustrates two key points about business growth plans:
1. the value of reducing a major objective to a series of smaller, manageable steps; and
2. the shifting nature of the growth objective. Once a growth plan has been achieved, it is essentially redundant and needs to be updated and replaced with a new growth objective(s).

16.3.1 The Importance of Ongoing Business Planning for Investors and Funders

As well as being valuable for managing strategy, a written business growth plan reveals how a company would allocate the bank loan or investment it is seeking, which makes it a vital tool in attracting new funding. Ongoing business planning allows for benchmarking achievements against the original business objectives. A growth plan can be used as a tool to identify where the business is currently and in which direction it can grow. This will help the business take advantage of market opportunities, meet key targets and manage its priorities.

16.4 Set and Watch Your Objective Timeline

In growing a business, it is important to 'watch your timeline'. It is all very well writing down growth objectives in a business plan, but if a timeline or deadline is not set, despite the best intentions, it simply will not be achieved.

EXAMPLE 16.2: PUTTING A TIMEFRAME ON ACHIEVING OBJECTIVES

One Irish entrepreneur has set up a clock in the format shown below on the wall of her company's boardroom. She is the majority shareholder with the balance of shares held by the senior management team. Visitors to the boardroom often ask to what the clock represents.

730:00:00:09

Day : Hour : Min : Sec

The clock is ticking......

For this CEO and majority shareholder, her growth objective is to exit by selling her business within the next two years (i.e. 730 days) to a third party or the senior management team for a price in excess of €100 million. Everyone in her company is focused on this overriding goal and aware that their contribution is required to achieve it, as well as the fact that as fellow shareholders, they would share in the sale proceeds.

The growth plan that will maximise the value of the business is to be implemented by the time the clock completes its countdown.

As noted above, there can be numerous overall objectives to a growth plan: exit, trade sale, MBO, succession, securing more funding, a merger/acquisition or entering foreign markets. The most important requirement for a growth objective is that a realistic timeframe is set for achieving it and that this is adhered to.

16.5 Seven Key Elements in Developing a Growth Plan

As shown in **Figure 16.1**, for SMEs at all stages of development, a credible business plan will consider, contain and act upon seven key factors when planning for growth and maximising the company's value:
1. knowing the market;
2. understanding the business's strengths and weaknesses;
3. ensuring that the right people are in place to drive the business forward;
4. ensuring that the business has the right information for decision-making and monitoring the progress of the growth plan;
5. understanding and availing of external financial and non-financial supports, if required;
6. documenting and executing the growth plan incorporating the above; and
7. setting a realistic timeline for the business to achieve its goals.

Completing a growth plan that addresses all of these elements will assist a company to maximise value and achieve its growth objective.

FIGURE 16.1: ELEMENTS OF A CREDIBLE BUSINESS GROWTH PLAN

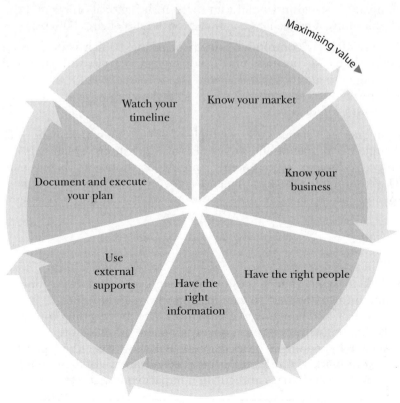

16.5.1 Know Your Market

Before starting on a growth plan, it is vital to have a thorough understanding of the business's current market and how it is expected to change and develop in the future. In this regard, useful questions companies should ask in preparing their business growth plans include:

- Where is our market now?
- Is it growing/retracting or stagnant?
- How will it evolve over the next three to five years?
- What are the trends and changes in business environmental factors such as technology, regulation, etc., that can/will impact the market in the short, medium and long term?
- What are the customers' needs both now and in the future?
- Where are the opportunities for growth? Is the projected organic growth rate sufficient for the business to achieve its growth objectives?
- Are there any acquisition opportunities to grow, e.g. by acquiring a competitor either domestically or internationally as a route to new markets?

One of the BDO Development Capital Fund's investee companies, Version 1, is an excellent example of how market knowledge and feedback can assist in shaping the growth plan.

EXAMPLE 16.3: KNOW YOUR MARKET

Version 1 is Ireland's largest and Europe's fastest-growing IT services company. Located in Dublin with three Irish regional offices and five UK locations, it has achieved annual growth rates of circa 30% p.a.

As part of their continuous growth planning (which is done on a quarterly basis), business unit heads engage directly with staff and customers to identify:
1. customer needs; and
2. growth opportunities.

Each quarter, Version 1 asks a sample of its customers (by rotation) to complete a simple online survey of 3 or 4 questions, which helps to ensure customer requirements and expectations are being met. The customer feedback has helped Version 1 identify new service lines to offer customers for future revenue growth and further investment.

PRACTICAL TIPS

- Talk to stakeholders (customers, employees, suppliers, funders and industry bodies) to gain insights into market trends.
- Research and benchmark competitors. Are they eroding your market share? Why? Is it price, quality, or some other factor?
- What is happening in other markets? Will these trends be replicated in your market? Can your business take advantage of these trends?
- How do/will changes in regulation impact your market?

16.5.2 *Know Your Business*

To objectively and coldly look at your business, you need to identify its strengths and weaknesses in terms of achieving the stated growth plan, as well as detailing the opportunities and threats that can either accelerate or impact that plan. This can be done by completing a SWOT analysis, setting out the business's strengths, **weaknesses**, **o**pportunities and **t**hreats. Once these are documented, actions can be taken to maximise strengths and opportunities while mitigating weaknesses and threats. **Example 16.4** below is based on our experience of one of BDO's clients, which successfully assessed the business's SWOT and adjusted its growth plan and key growth objective.

EXAMPLE 16.4: SWOT ANALYSIS – LOOKING AT YOUR BUSINESS OBJECTIVELY

A large professional services firm with a strong history of holding regular brainstorming sessions for its board and senior management team to challenge and test its objectives and business plan, engaged BDO as external facilitators for a series of these sessions, which were held off-site (to minimise distractions) and included key employees from each area, the board and senior management team.

The purpose of the sessions was to review what the firm did well, what it could do better and to explore opportunities and threats it was potentially facing. BDO's role was to challenge each area to assist the team in finalising their future growth plans.

From this engagement and analysis came the recognition that, in order to grow further, the firm needed to align with a larger international firm. **This became the company's key objective for its documented growth plan, with a related timeline and actions required for its achievement.** The firm aligned with an international professional services firm nine months later.

16.5.3 *Have the Right People*

The next factor to consider in planning for growth is whether the business has the right team of people 'on board' to drive it forward. In this context, useful questions businesses could ask include:
- Do we have the right team of people, in terms of experience, drive and enthusiasm, to achieve the growth plan?
- If yes, how does the business ensure that it retains the right people?
- Are there any gaps in skills?
- Are there succession management and planning issues that need to be addressed?

- Furthermore, are *you* the right person to be driving the business forward? (How many times have you seen a 'Dragon' on the TV show *Dragons' Den* comment that they would like to invest in the business but that the wrong person is CEO?)
- What can be learned from other companies or competitors that have put professional management teams in place to drive the business forward, for example Eason's or Gowans?

EXAMPLE 16.5: HAVE THE RIGHT PEOPLE

The founders and co-owners of a well-known Irish food company were looking for funding when the business had achieved strong profitability, annual revenues in the region of €10 million and export customers in Europe.

During the course of the funding discussions, they indicated their belief that, although they had led the company to achieve €10 million in turnover, they were not the people to bring it to the €20 million bracket. They wanted to bring in a professional management team and incentivise them with a share-incentive plan that would kick-in if the management team succeeded in achieving revenues and EBITDA of €20 million and 10% p.a. respectively in a period of five years.

By recognising that they needed assistance to achieve their growth objective and by incentivising a professional management team, the founders ensured they successfully achieved their plan.

PRACTICAL TIPS

- Continuously assess the team and make changes when necessary.
- Provide staff with regular assessments and feedback. Set new objectives for them and appraise their progress.
- Do not hesitate to make changes, as poor performance will impact on growth and hesitation to deal with it will undermine management's position with other staff members.
- Provide performance bonuses/incentive packages and share incentive plans to attract and retain the best people.

16.5.4 Have the Right Information

"In the business world, the rear-view mirror is always clearer than the windshield."

Warren Buffett

Irrespective of its stage of development, to monitor, adjust and achieve its growth plan, a business needs to have relevant and timely management information. Such information will vary from business to business, but should include such financial and non-financial information that will enable the business's owner or management team to determine and assess how it is performing compared to its budget and plan.

In this regard, useful questions businesses could ask to assess if they have relevant and timely management information and information systems include:
- Do we have relevant and timely information in terms of:
  o monthly/quarterly income statements compared to budget/plan with variances highlighted and explained;
  o actual monthly/quarterly cashflows compared to budget with variances highlighted and explained;
  o three-month rolling cash-flow projections?
- Are we also capturing key non-financial information to gauge real-time business performance in terms of key performance indicators (i.e. number of customers won/lost, percentage of customers fulfilled on time and right-first-time customer service levels)?

16.5.4.1 Key Performance Indicators

Key performance indicators (KPIs) are real-time financial and non-financial metrics used to measure business performance and progress and which business owners and managers should view as their 'dashboard' telling them, as the dashboard on a car does, how fast the business is going, what remaining resources it has, whether there are any issues to fix, etc.

KPIs should be numerical and detail key drivers for attaining the objectives of the business. They should:
- detail the results across the business and its business units;
- identify any areas for improvement;
- motivate and involve staff across all business units;
- be specifically aligned to the growth strategy, e.g. grow market share, profitability, customer satisfaction, etc.

Examples of KPIs include:
- weekly sales compared to budget/prior year;
- average sales price per unit;
- average sales value per transaction;
- customer retention and churn figures;
- production yield compared to target;
- minimum order values;
- cost of customer acquisition;
- working capital metrics;
- other KPIs specific to the business's industry.

16.5.4.2 What KPIs Should a Business Measure?

What gets measured gets changed. If something is not being measured then no one will know it needs changing, let alone influence how this is done.

A business's KPIs should be aligned to drivers specific to the company and its market sector. A low-cost, high-volume manufacturer and a high-cost, low-volume manufacturer may ostensibly produce the same thing (e.g. furniture, clothes), but would have very different business drivers and therefore KPIs because they are operating different business models in different markets. It is vital, therefore, to identify and understand the specific drivers of the business.

EXAMPLE 16.6: HAVE THE RIGHT INFORMATION (1)

A fresh produce company with a turnover of €7 million per year had two production sites, one in Ireland, the other in the UK. The output varies significantly between the sites, which resulted in lost orders when there was underproduction, and waste when overproduction. The company had poor and infrequent management information and no KPIs.

Following a review by external consultants (in this case it was BDO), a weekly KPI system was recommended and devised, based on production capacity and weekly targets. This enabled management to monitor actual weekly KPIs and to take corrective action if necessary. The monthly management accounts confirm the results and provide management with the information and confidence to make improved business decisions.

In having the right information at the right time, business owners and managers can make the right decisions. This enables them to accelerate production/service levels in times of real growth and to reduce costs, if required, in times of contraction.

Other key benefits of having accurate, timely information include:
• being able to forecast peaks and troughs in cash flow, thereby allowing for corrective action to be taken, e.g. accelerating cash collections, renegotiating payment terms with suppliers, etc.;
• communicating with stakeholders and lenders so that there are no 'surprises';
• reacting to margin reductions in terms of selling price or taking manufacturing yield-improvement actions if below target; and
• creating confidence with investors and funders that the business has a KPI dashboard to which it can respond to by taking corrective action as and when required.

EXAMPLE 16.7: HAVE THE RIGHT INFORMATION (2)

A manufacturing company with an annual turnover of €15 million produces and sells multiple products to Irish, UK and continental European markets. However, it only completes management accounts every six months, at the end of Quarter 2 and the year end. The year-end profit and loss account reveals that the company is only marginally profitable, despite the company generating significant profit in the first six months of the year. The business's owners did not understand why the cash balance was not growing, but in fact depleted.

Following a detailed review, it was discovered that the company is manufacturing certain products at a low/negative gross margin. The recommendation is to either cease production of certain loss-making products or increase prices to customers. In addition, management accounts now provide details of gross margin on a per-product basis and are prepared on a monthly basis.

Having the right information at the right time will help to minimise the risk of surprises in the company's financial reporting. Accordingly, this will play a very important role in achieving the business growth plan as well as instilling confidence in your stakeholders and potential investors.

16.5.5 Use External Supports

Achieving the growth objective for the business will require both financial and non-financial supports, the sources of which are discussed in detail in Part II of this book.

There are other external supports available, including networks and industry associations, which can provide access to potential new customers and contacts to assist SMEs achieve their growth plans. Examples of such agencies, associations and groups include:
- the Small Firms Association (SFA);
- the Irish Small and Medium Enterprise Association (ISME);
- Dublin Chamber of Commerce;
- Chambers Ireland;
- the Irish Exporters Association; and
- relevant industry bodies, e.g. the Irish Software Association, An Bord Bia, etc.

16.5.6 Document and Execute Your Plan

Once a business has decided on the elements of its growth plan as outlined above, it then needs to document, implement and review this plan in order to achieve its growth objective and maximise the business's value.

FIGURE 16.2: EXECUTING AND REVIEWING THE PLAN

- **Document** the growth plan and identify key actions, with responsibilities allocated across the team.
- **Implement** the actions by doing what you said you would do, driving momentum with early wins, seeking external supports where available and when required.
- **Review** progress against the plan: be flexible, adaptable and challenge yourself and your team.

Finally, it is important to enjoy success as and when it comes. We noted earlier that once one growth objective is achieved, another invariably follows. However, it is also important that, having planned and accomplished success, it is celebrated as it occurs. Creating and meeting milestones, and celebrating achievements along the way will help to build and maintain momentum. Put the growth objectives of the business at the top of the agenda for all key internal meetings, and as it comes to fruition, acknowledge and commend those who have made it a reality.

16.6 Financial Projections

The elements of the business growth plan as set above detail the business owner's vision for the business: the products/services it sells or will sell, its customers, how it compares with the competition, its key people, etc. However, the business growth plan is meaningless if the business does not justify investment financially in terms of bottom-line profits and is generating cash in the bank. The financial section of a business plan is one of its most essential components to have any chance of securing equity capital or obtaining debt finance.

Even if a business does not need financing, good business owners and managers will compile and maintain financial forecasts simply to be successful in growing the business. This final and key element of the plan sets out and explains how much investment the business needs to secure and accelerate its growth opportunities or, if at start-up stage, how much is required to get the business off the ground and keep it going. If seeking finance, the financial projections will show and demonstrate to the prospective investor:
- how much funding is required;
- how funds will be used and when;
- how the funds will assist to grow the business in terms of increased sales;
- if additional funds are required to fulfil an increased level of sales, e.g. to fund higher labour costs or additional working capital; and
- when and how the investor will get the investment back and the expected return.

The main purpose of the financial projections section of a business plan is two-fold:

1. to assist in securing investment from an equity funder (e.g. venture capitalist, angel investor, family member) or a debt funder. All prospective equity investors will want to see financial numbers showing that the business will grow, and how quickly, and that there is an exit strategy for them on the horizon, during which they can/will make a profit on their investment. Additionally, any debt funder will analyse these numbers to make sure the business can repay its loan.

2. to assist the business owner in understanding how the business will perform financially over the coming years. It is arguable that this second reason to compile financial projections is the more important.

Business owners and entrepreneurs should always be realistic when preparing financial projections. We have seen numerous business plans with 'hockey-stick' forecasts projected to shoot up like the end of a hockey stick at the point when the investment is received, which, unfortunately, are usually not credible.

One way to present a credible and realistic financial projections section for a business growth plan is to break the figures into components, e.g. by sales channel, by product/service, by customer or target market, and to provide realistic estimates for sales and the associated gross margins. For established businesses, this sales projection should correlate with the historical trading record, with detailed reasons set out for the investor for any significant variances, e.g. new customers secured or the launch of a new product.

Such explanations or clarification of assumptions enables prospective investors to assess and judge the reasonableness of the projections and, if necessary, apply flexibility/sensitivity analysis to the assumptions. For example: what if projected revenues are 20% less than budgeted, or gross margin is 1%–2% less than projected, or overheads are 10% higher than projected? For all such potential sensitivities, the business owner should have answers to either assure investors why that is unlikely to happen or, if it did, what actions can be taken to mitigate its effects so that the business is still profitable or breaks even. We recommend engaging corporate finance advisors to assist in the preparation of, and to 'road test', the financial projections.

16.6.1 Elements of the Financial Projections

There are four key elements to the financial projections section of a business growth plan:

1. financial projection key assumptions;
2. projected profit and loss/income statement;
3. balance sheet;
4. cash-flow projection;
5. sensitivity analysis.

16.6.1.1 Financial Projection Key Assumptions

For both new and existing businesses, entrepreneurs often make two basic assumptions about their financial projections:
1. they have a product or service customers want; and
2. the business owner can manufacture/provide and sell the goods/ services to customers profitably.

Investors, on the other hand, will want to see that business owners have done their homework and can support not only the two assumptions above, but can also show that other key assumptions underlying the financial projections have a valid basis and, where appropriate, assumptions are backed up with market research or other data. Making valid financial assumptions, and explaining them clearly, can make the difference between receiving funding or suffering rejection from lenders or investors. In our experience, the primary reason for approval or rejection relates to the unreasonableness and lack of a valid basis to the financial projections, culminating in the 'hockey-stick' approach previously outlined. It is essential that industry and competition research is diligently completed and referred to in the projections, with clear explanations as to why the business is/will be either exceeding or under-performing the current/projected market trends. The financial assumptions will be challenged and questioned by prospective investors, so it is important to have knowledgeable answers ready for these challenges.

16.6.1.2 Projected Profit and Loss/Income Statement

The key sections of the projected profit and loss/income statement are:
- revenues – this is the income earned by the business from the goods or services provided;
- gross margin – gross profit earned from revenues after deducting the direct cost of manufacturing or providing the goods/services;
- overhead expenses – all other expenses in running the business, i.e. rent, rates, equipment rentals, employee wages, accounting and legal fees, advertising, bank charges, insurance, office rent, telecommunications, etc.;
- EBITDA – earnings (gross margin) less overheads, but excluding interest, tax, depreciation and amortisiation;
- net profit – EBITDA less interest and tax costs, depreciation, amortisation charges.

16.6.1.3 Cash-flow Projection

The cash-flow projection will demonstrate to an equity investor or debt provider that the business is a good investment opportunity and it can repay the investment. The cash flow will detail how the invested funds will be expended, e.g. capital expenditure, sales and marketing spend, etc., and over what timeframe. It will demonstrate the expected cash receipts profile, including the company's working capital cycle. An area of focus for a prospective investor is the free cash flow, which, as discussed in **Chapter 11, Section 11.3**, calculates the rate at which EBITDA converts into cash.

16.6.1.4 Balance Sheet

A projected balance sheet contains assumptions about the specific projected scenarios set out in the projected profit and loss/income statement, along with assumptions on the timing of collection of certain assets (debtors, stock, etc.) and the liabilities (suppliers and finance providers) of the company along with any planned capital expenditure.

16.6.2 Risk Assessment

Alongside the financial forecasts, it is good practice to show that the management team have reviewed the risks that could potentially impact the business, and that the management team have looked at contingencies and mitigation to cover these. Potential risks can include:
- revenues being less than projected;
- possible competitor action, e.g. price reductions;
- staff – skills, availability and costs; and
- macro-environment risk, e.g. Brexit, particularly for businesses with a large portion of revenues derived from the UK market.

16.7 Conclusion

In summary, the growth plan for any business should include the following key elements:
- a clear picture of the business's current strengths, weaknesses, threats and opportunities;
- a vision for its main growth objective(s); and
- an action plan to achieve this objective, including who will do what and when.

It is vital that the right people are working in the business and on the same page, focused on its future.

An essential step in getting investor-ready is updating or preparing a business growth plan to outline to prospective investors the growth opportunities available to the business and how funding will assist unlock and accelerate these objectives. This, coupled with a sound knowledge of changes in the market and the business's SWOT (strengths, weaknesses, opportunities and threats), will instil confidence in a prospective investor and is an important first step in securing the funding required. The involvement of corporate finance advisors early on will assist in achieving an investor-ready business plan. The next chapters will outline how to pitch to investors and the dos and don'ts of raising funding.

CHAPTER 17

INVESTOR PITCHING

17.1 What are Investors and Funders Looking for in a Business?

By its very nature, investing in start-up businesses and SMEs is uncertain, and all investors and funders (including banks) will look for the same key strengths in any investment proposal. The greater those strengths, the more compelling the investment, and SMEs that can deliver convincingly on this will likely find no shortage of investors to fund their growth plans.

Banks, of course, can negate an investment risk somewhat by seeking security for their loans over the assets and/or shares of a company, and the elements of the business plan discussed in **Chapter 16** seek to address all of these. For the equity investor, however, there is no such luxury: an equity investment will rank *pari passu* with the founders' shares and carry the risk that if the company does not succeed and grow, it is unlikely that the investor will receive the return originally anticipated over the investment period.

There are seven key elements that all funders will seek and assess when considering a lending or investment opportunity. By addressing each of these key elements, the startup/SME owner, and indeed their professional advisors, will ensure that their investment proposition is robust and that their company has become, and will continue to be, investor-ready.

FIGURE 17.1: KEY ELEMENTS FOR ASSESSING AN SME
INVESTMENT OPPORTUNITY

17.1.1 The Market Opportunity

Starting at the centre of **Figure 17.1**, the most important aspect of an investment or lending opportunity in or to an SME business that all funders will want to understand is the current and potential size of the market opportunity for its product or service, be it a new or existing one.

To help inform potential investors/lenders to understand the market opportunity, SMEs should be able to detail with appropriate evidence (e.g. through market insight reports) the following:

- current market solutions or alternatives for the product/service;
- the differentiator or unique selling proposition (USP) that the company offers vis-a-vis other solutions currently available (faster, cheaper, better: how?);
- the existing market size in monetary terms;
- rates at which the market has been growing over the last three to five years and an assessment of whether the company has at least matched market growth rates;
- projected market growth rates over the next three to five years (according to industry bodies and/or market commentators such as An Bord Bia, Fáilte Ireland, Gartner, etc.);
- estimate of the SME's current market share and projected market share growth over the next three to five years.

EXAMPLE 17.1: THE MARKET OPPORTUNITY

A company in the ICT and software sector has developed its own software platform for its market segment, which is a distributive communication technology for the solution currently deployed in the market. It approaches an investment fund seeking an investment of €3 million in equity funding in order to drive a sales and marketing strategy to obtain customers in the US.

While the company has a circa 30% market share of the Irish market, there is a significant opportunity for it in the US market where a similar but less advanced technology is being deployed by a competitor. Industry reports project a five-year (compound annual) market growth rate of 25% per annum. The company estimates that if it achieves only 1% of this market growth rate, because of the size of the US market this will have a significant and materially positive impact on its revenues, profits and cash.

In comparison to the projected market-growth rates, the company's assessment of the opportunity for its product and its financial projections may appear reasonable and realistic, even conservative, to a prospective investor. This, along with other key elements of its business plan, such as the capability of the management, will be persuasive and reassuring.

17.1.2 Clear Strategy

A business seeking investment needs to have a clear understanding of the opportunity for growth and its strategy to achieve it. When asked about this, the CEO should be able to give a direct and clear response. However, many CEOs when asked to outline their strategy will give indefinite responses, often involving 'grey areas', assumptions and propositions that imply success is dependent on things outside of their control.

Remember: the investor is backing the reality of the business and its management team. The investor will want to be confident in the people in whom they are investing, and they will need to have the growth strategy clearly defined and thought out, including an assessment of likely reactions by customers and competitors. This will all help to build the investor's confidence.

17.1.3 Effective Management

It would be hard to overstate how important it is that a company seeking investment has an effective, experienced management team in place to execute its growth plan. (A warning to entrepreneurs: do not attempt to do everything yourself!)

A company should understand the strengths of the individuals making up its management team, how effective they will be in managing the business during its growth period, and how they will react if and when things do not go according to plan.

There should be an organisational chart for the business, which will help to highlight any gaps in expertise or experience, related in turn to a resource plan of how the company will address these gaps in time, i.e. as certain key milestones in the company's development are met.

Brief biographies of key staff are helpful for prospective investors to assess the strength and depth of the management team and any other critical roles. If it is planned to replace someone within its management team, then the prospective investor should be informed, in confidence if necessary. Again, this generates confidence that the business is being effectively managed and that difficult decisions can be taken to achieve its goals.

EXAMPLE 17.2: EFFECTIVE MANAGEMENT IN TOUGH SITUATIONS

A distribution company, which is a third-generation family business, is the subject of due diligence regarding a proposed €5 million equity investment. During the process, the queries relating to financial diligence are not progressing and the actions required of the financial controller are not being completed. Due to the time sensitivity of the queries, the CEO, at the behest of the owners, outsources the financial due diligence queries to an external corporate finance advisor. During discussions with the management team, it becomes apparent that there is broader dissatisfaction with the performance of the financial controller in the company, but that he has been allowed much leeway.

Matters come to a head when the CEO reveals that, while he shares these concerns, he has not wanted to address the issue as he "does not like confrontation", which then raises the even bigger question of whether the CEO is the right person for the role.

There will always be tough decisions to be made in situations that are far from ideal. A CEO, or management team, who does not recognise them and seek to either address them or ask for assistance when required will create unnecessary risks for the future success of the business.

17.1.4 Strong Governance

Corporate governance involves the rules, practices and procedures by which a company is directed and controlled. An investor will want to know that a potential investee company has the right checks and balances in place to ensure that the correct corporate decisions are made, recorded and effected.

An example of good corporate governance is a set of clear policies for the board of directors and the conduct of board meetings, including how often they are held, who they are chaired by and what regular items are included on the agenda.

Key governance issues a prospective investor will want to understand include financial governance matters such as the process for the preparation and review of monthly management accounts and the annual financial statements, as well as operational budgets and cash-flow forecasts.

Potential investors will also want assurance that the prospective investee company is compliant with all aspects of company law. Additionally, as a condition of their funding, investors may seek to amend/improve certain aspects of a company's governance, for example the introduction of an audit committee or a remuneration committee reporting to the board on their respective matters.[1]

17.1.5 Risks Identified

Every business, irrespective of its size or stage of development, has a weakness or core risk. Prospective investors expect there to be risks; it is when *they* have to point these risks out to the owners or managers of the business that their alarm bells start ringing.

---

[1] For more on strong corporate governance structures, policies and procedures, see David W. Duffy, *A Practical Guide to Corporate Governance* (Chartered Accountants Ireland, 2014) and for a guide for directors in complying with company law, David W. Duffy, *A Practical Guide for Company Directors* (Chartered Accountants Ireland, 2017).

It is important for prospective investee companies to be upfront with potential investors, clearly identifying their risks and potential weaknesses. Treat this as an opportunity to build investor confidence by also stating what actions are being taken to mitigate the impact of the risks identified.

For example, if there are gaps in the skills and experience of the management team, identify these and explain how it is proposed that these roles will be filled. If the company operates in the ICT sector and requires skilled software engineers, describe how it will attract and retain such highly sought-after staff, given that they are currently in huge demand. Be realistic: avoid trying to convince investors that such talent can be hired for less than the going market rate.

17.1.6 The Financial Model

The financial model for a prospective investee company should cover five-year financial projections incorporating a projected profit and loss account, balance sheet and cash-flow statement. The financial model should be integrated so that a change to a key assumption, e.g. pricing or sales quantities, in the profit and loss account flows through to the balance sheet and cash-flow analysis. It is helpful to provide to prospective investors the financial model in the form of an electronic spreadsheet, such as Microsoft Excel, so that the investors can assess and apply sensitivities to the assumptions with their own variables if required (see **Chapter 16** for further details).

The underlying assumptions of the financial model should be specified very clearly so that investors can understand the key drivers and enable them to be flexed either up or down, depending on the assumption. The model should be closely and realistically aligned to market growth rates (see **Section 17.1.1**); if it targets beating the market rate, there should be a very compelling reason for this. Have the model stress-tested for reasonableness by a financial advisor and incorporate any changes they recommend.

The financial model and the business growth plan (see **Chapter 16**) should show in detail how the investment sought will be used to grow the business in terms of its revenues, EBITDA and cash flow. Most importantly, the model should also show how the investor will be repaid over the investment term along with the associated return on their investment.

17.1.7 Commercial Risk-adjusted Return

In return for their funding, the investor or lender will seek a commercial risk-adjusted return determined by how robust and compelling the investment opportunity is and with reference to the key elements discussed in **Sections 17.1.1** to **17.1.6** above. In terms of bank funding, commercial risk-adjusted return will be determined by the cost of funds and repayment terms, as well as the level of security sought and the confidence with which the company's cash flows can be predicted.

For the equity investor, the percentage of equity will be determined by the pre-money valuation driven by the multiple usually applied to revenue or EBITDA. (See **Chapter 11, Section 11.3**. The multiple is that which is commonly applied in the sector in which the company trades.)

17.2 Potential Pitfalls in Accessing Finance

As financial advisors who work with entrepreneurs, we are often asked about potential pitfalls in the funding process and how best to avoid them. Experience shows that for the best chance of success there are four key pitfalls to avoid, and it is these areas on which you should focus to build the confidence of prospective lenders and investors.

FIGURE 17.2: POTENTIAL PITFALLS IN ACCESSING FINANCE

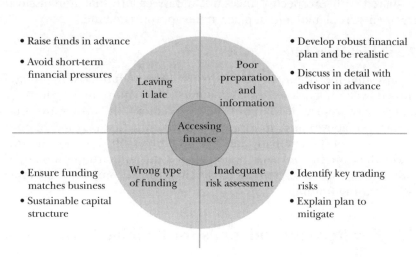

17.2.1 Poor Preparation and Information

The most common reason for an application for funding being declined is that it is poorly prepared and provides insufficient information. (Again, "fail to prepare, prepare to fail".) Lenders and investors require a robust growth business plan and a financial model with detailed assumptions and evidence to back them up. In most instances, it is worth involving an experienced financial advisor to assist critique plans and proposals in advance of submission, as well as providing guidance during the investment process.

17.2.2 Inadequate Risk Assessment

As discussed in **Section 17.1.5**, potential lenders and investors will expect prospective investee companies to be clear about their weaknesses (as well as their strengths), the risks the business faces and how it intends to mitigate those risks. Inadequate awareness of, or even obliviousness to, risk will not inspire investor confidence.

When endeavouring to access finance, companies should identify their trading risks or potential 'red flags', and assess what actions can be taken to mitigate these. Documenting and sharing this with lenders/investors will greatly improve the chances of obtaining funding.

17.2.3 The Wrong Type of Funding

It is very important that companies choose and pursue the correct type of funding to match the size, sector, ownership and structure, and as we have seen, its stage in the innovation/development lifecycle. Assess and identify the right funding partners for the company and ensure that the investment provides a sustainable capital structure going forward. (**Remember:** whatever the type of funding being sought, as business growth and innovation plans are shared with prospective investors, always ensure that non-disclosure agreements are signed and in place at the appropriate time.)

17.2.4 Leaving it Late

The investment process can be time-consuming, so fundraising should be planned well in advance of any immediate requirement. Short-term finance pressures can lead to hurried negotiations, the wrong investment partner (see above) and, most importantly, terms that may not be in the best interests of the company and its shareholders. It can also lead investors, lenders and indeed shareholders to ask the awkward question of why a CEO they are expected to trust has left it so late to commence the crucial work of raising funding.

17.3 Key Recommendations for Pitching to Investors

17.3.1 Be Prepared

Approaching and meeting investors unprepared is probably the single most common reason for entrepreneurs failing to secure investment capital. A typical professional investor and/or lender will consider up to 10 to 15 potential investment opportunities in a week. If your proposal does not comprehensively address all of the points set out above, chances are you will not get past 'first base' and your potential funder will move on to the next opportunity.

It cannot be over-emphasised how important it is to **rehearse** investor pitches. Due to lack of preparation, many otherwise capable entrepreneurs have either frozen or gone overboard when trying to explain their business opportunity and how it addresses a gap in the market. While clamming up due to nerves is understandable, and perhaps retrievable, there is nothing more off-putting for an investor than being told "I have a short presentation which I will bring you through for 10 minutes and then we will have a Q&A", only to find 30 minutes later that the pitch is still on the first slide!

17.3.2 Make a Good First Impression

Making a good, confident first impression on investors is crucial and having an effective pitch ready can mean the difference between a polite withdrawal of interest and a life-changing investment and support. Investors are, by definition, choosy about the projects and businesses they pick. Out of all the pitches they receive, they may pick two from 50 or three from 100. However, there is a common denominator among those to whom they respond 'Yes': they always choose opportunities that grab their attention and appeal to their imagination. Additionally, they can align with the owners and management team.

17.3.3 Avoid Jargon and Acronyms

Unless the target potential investor is known to be an expert on the prospective investee company's sector, it is generally advisable to avoid industry jargon in making a pitch. For the sector-agnostic investor, jargon is both unnecessary and off-putting. It can also lead to investor uncertainty as the presence of jargon and acronyms could create a sense that the pitch has not been honed for, and targeted specifically at, that lender or investor. As mentioned above, prospective investee companies should match the right type of funding and investors with their business and growth plans, and need to communicate this clearly to the investors chosen, i.e. *why* they have been approached.

17.3.4 Build Rapport

As we have seen, the most important factor for anyone considering an investment opportunity in a business is its key people. Investors look to invest in people they can get on with and who they trust are going to drive the business forward. In our experience, many otherwise laudable businesses get turned down for investment all the time because the wrong people are involved. A business growth opportunity can be solid, but without a committed and dedicated team behind it, investors will not get involved.

Though the stakes are high, it is important to be authentic when pitching to investors as they will want to get to know you and your team, and get a clear sense of what drives you. In responding to the pressure to make a good impression, business owners sometimes try to be something they are not, believing the investor will not notice. They do! It is vital to be yourself from the outset, not only because an act will be seen through quickly but because you are looking to build relationships that could last five or more years, through good times and possibly bad. Being yourself from the outset is the best way to future-proof this relationship.

17.3.5 Plan the Contents of the Pitch

An investor pitch should run to approximately 15 PowerPoint slides, and no more, which should allow the business owner, or whoever is making the pitch for the prospective investee company, to cover in high-level terms the items set out below, in a bullet-point format, with a maximum of four to five bullets per slide.

It is advisable to explain at the outset that the presentation will take 15 minutes, inviting questions and a fuller discussion at the end. If the potential investor asks questions during the presentation, this could be distracting, and confuse and negate its impact.

17.3.6 Pitch Content

17.3.6.1 Introduction and Background

The CEO should introduce himself or herself and others in the team (if present) and briefly explain each individual's background and experience. From the start try to engage the attention of the investor, capturing their imagination; for example demonstrating unique benefits and features using video, demos or product samples.

17.3.6.2 Current Problem – Market Opportunity – Proposed Solution

Describe the gap in the market that the prospective investee company will fill. Set out what the current problem is and how the product/service will solve this. Explain it in high-level terms so the investor can understand and appreciate it. Keep it concise and avoid going into too much detail. The investor will get the detail they need when carrying out due diligence on the company.

17.3.6.3 Target Markets

Market analysis is a key aspect of any pitch to investors as it sets the context for the subsequent presentation of the financial projections, including revenue growth rates. The market analysis should be broken down into three key areas:
1. the total addressable market (TAM);
2. the servicable addressable market (SAM), i.e. that part of the TAM within the business's initial, immediate reach; and
3. the servicable obtainable market (SOM), i.e. the management team's estimate of that part of the SAM that the company has the potential to capture, given the company's brand, product position, marketing capabilities, customer base and distribution channels.

The presentation of facts, figures and percentage growth rates, with references to credible market reports, will give assurance that the company has researched and analysed the market. For example, refer to markets in other, separate territories to gauge market reaction there to the launch or development of similar products or services.

17.3.6.4 Sales and Marketing Strategy (including Routes to Market)

The pitch or presentation to the investor should also outline clearly and concisely how the company currently reaches or proposes to reach its customers,

how it makes them aware of its product/service. Key questions to address and anticipate in this regard include:
- the cost of sales and marketing, including projected cost of customer acquisition (per customer);
- the proposed route to market and if a distributor, wholesaler or retailer is required, their likely margins; and
- any lead time required for accessing markets, e.g. securing regulatory approval, etc.

EXAMPLE 17.3: DISCLOSE ALL RELEVANT INFORMATION

A medical devices company had made what seemed to be a very compelling pitch for investment to fund the launch of its new, state-of-the-art product. The product had already received high levels of customer orders and projected revenue growth was significant. The CEO of the company was seeking funding to develop and start mass production, and also for a global sales and marketing campaign.

The pitch appeared very credible. However, in the follow-up discussion and review it transpired the company did not yet have the necessary Food and Drug Administration (FDA) approval to sell the product to potential customers in the United States, a process that could take a further 18 to 24 months to complete. The CEO immediately lost credibility as he had not been upfront about the fact that, despite having received customer orders in this key market, the product could not be sold in the US.

17.3.6.5 The Competition

Any investor pitch should also include details about the company's main competitors and how its key value proposition differentiates it from the competition. This, the company's unique selling proposition (USP), can involve several factors including price, quality, reliability, lead-time to market, improved performance, etc. Consider and explain to the investor your assessment of how competitors will react when a new product/service is launched or an extensive business growth plan announced. Are there measures that can be taken to defend the company's USP, e.g. protection of intellectual property by patents?

It is also important to be professional when discussing competitors and not to rubbish them or what they offer. Bear in mind that the investor may have an in-depth knowledge of the market and therefore the competition.

17.3.6.6 Business Model and Financial Projections

A slide of much interest to all investors will be the one showing how the prospective investee company will generate profits and cash. This should be a high-level slide containing the projected annual revenues, gross profit, overheads and EBITDA, summarising what is set out in the more detailed financial projections.

Current and previous financial years should be included for comparison, as well as providing the investor with a verbal explanation of the key drivers for the revenue growth and profitability.

The projections should relate back accurately to the slide about the target markets for the prospective investee company's product/service and to key assumptions about projected market penetration during the term of the investment.

As discussed in **Chapter 16**, avoid 'hockey-stick projections', i.e. projections that show results as flat for current and immediately forthcoming years but then somehow, magically, increasing steeply for future years. The actual results may well turn out this way and follow this pattern, but investors will want to see projections that are grounded in reality and based on experience and reasonable assumptions.

17.3.6.7 Management Team and Key Employees

As we have seen, investors invest in people first and companies second. Presentations to potential investors should provide detail about the key people in the company that will lead it and achieve the business growth opportunity. Talk about their track record, experience and ambition. If they are in the room, it is important that they speak also.

EXAMPLE 17.4: KEY EMPLOYEES

At a *Dragons' Den*-type presentation, we once experienced the CEO and finance director (FD) of a company pitching to five investors. The CEO spoke for the entire length of the pitch (including the financial slides) while the FD stood silently beside him. During the presentation, however, the FD became visibly agitated. He finally interrupted the CEO after the last slide was presented and before any investor questions could be asked. The FD informed the panel of investors that the key assumptions stated by the CEO were incorrect and offered to bring the panel through the correct information. Needless to say, this gave the panel a key insight into how this particular CEO operated.

Management teams always evolve and a team that was instrumental in growing a company from a standing start to where it is today is unlikely to be the same team that leads it to revenues of, say, €50 million. Be open with potential investors and share with them any analysis of the skills and experience the team may be missing to go to the next level and achieve the growth opportunity proposed, whether it is sales and marketing, technological, operational, financial management or even leadership. Let the investor know that you know what you do not know and bear in mind that this can be an opportunity for a value-added input from the professional investor, who is often well-connected with access to expertise and talent.

17.3.6.8 Funding Requirement and the 'Ask'

It is important to be clear about the monetary value of the investment being sought, i.e. the 'ask'. Specify what the investor will receive for their investment, i.e. the investment instrument, as set out in **Chapters 11 and 12**, whether it is equity (equity percentage), quasi equity, debt convertible loan note or otherwise, and provide detail about what the investment will be used for and when it will be spent. Always include a request for a small element for contingency to show realism that certain costs may be higher, though do keep it small thereby underlining confidence in the main financial projections.

Provide information on how much money has already been invested in the company, by whom, the ownership percentages, and how much more is needed to get it to the next level (being clear about what level that is). If there is an expectation that a further round of financing will be necessary, again make this clear and specify when.

17.3.6.9 The Investor's 'Exit'

Although this is the most important slide in the presentation, it is often not included or insufficiently detailed. All investors will want to know the company's strategy for repaying them; in other words, what and when is their 'exit'? The slide should set out how the company will pay back the investment plus the associated return, i.e. the cost of the investment on its due date. Investors will want to see that careful thought and diligence has been applied to their exit strategy as most will want to get out after the investment term.

In terms of bank funding, the projections should show sufficient cash (with an element of headroom, i.e. excess cash over the bank-loan repayments) being generated to fund the repayments.

If it is an equity investment, will the exit involve a redemption (a buyback by the company of the investor's shares) or is the plan to be acquired, or, as detailed in **Chapter 11**, listed on a stock exchange via an IPO, or something else?

EXAMPLE 17.5: CREDIBLE EXIT PLAN

When considering an investor's exit, it is important to be informed about the requirements of Irish company law and other possible legislative or regulatory restrictions. An Irish company once pitched on the basis that the equity investor's exit would be completed by a redemption at the end of the investment term. However, on a closer analysis, despite the company generating profits over the five-year investment term, it still had significant negative distributable reserves (i.e. accumulated losses, created in its early years of trading) and therefore would be prohibited by company law from redeeming the investor's shares.

17.4 Conclusion

In all cases, how entrepreneurs present about their businesses leaves an impression with investors, be it positive, negative or neutral. Business owners do not have to be masters at public speaking, but they do need to be genuine, inspiring and convincing, and this is achieved by telling a compelling story, listening, and responding to the audience.

As mentioned previously, investors invest in people, hence the importance of the investor pitch to be one that demonstrates a clear strategy and upside for the investment opportunity. Once you have an investor's attention, content is key and should include core data from the business growth plan, including the financial projections, how much investment is being sought, and details and quantification of the exit strategy and potential investor return.

Investors may ask some tough questions about the contents of the plan. If there are any such issues that can be anticipated, it may be beneficial for the business owner to raise them during the presentation or discussion, outlining what mitigating actions are being taken to overcome them. When asked tough questions, do not try to deflect; instead, tackle them head on. This is another chance to build investor confidence.

Having already discussed several of them in this part of the book, in the next and final chapter, we summarise and outline the 'dos and don'ts' of fundraising.

CHAPTER 18

THE DOS AND DON'TS OF RAISING FUNDING: A SUMMARY

18.1 Introduction

At some point in the development of every SME, it will most likely be required to embark on a fundraising journey. Make no mistake, the process can be daunting, stressful and protracted, if not all-consuming. It can also be something of a 'moment of truth' for many entrepreneurs. When raising funds, business owners are effectively showcasing their 'big idea' to the investment community, hoping the quality of the business concept and the management team driving it will attract and justify a substantial injection of funds from a third party. Of course, there will be challenges and setbacks but if the entrepreneur and management team really believe that their concept creates value and promises good growth potential, then they should embark on the fundraising journey with confidence and enthusiasm. There may be negative moments but our advice is:

Don't become disheartened, don't accept unfavourable terms and don't give up.

We noted before that potential investors will always look for particular company or promoter metrics to assess whether a prospective investee company merits further investigation. Anyone seeking investment in their company should have these metrics available on the 'tip of your tongue' at all times.

It is important to note also that the level of certainty or detail desired by investors can, in some cases, require a significant investment of time from entrepreneurs and business managers. While such requirements may not be avoided, they must be balanced against the need to ensure the business is still getting the attention it requires to perform at an optimum level. One way of doing this is to engage a professional advisor to manage the investment process.

Finally, it is useful to remember that, however isolated you may feel on this journey, you are not the first to undertake it. Many have gone before you and the following overview of fundraising 'dos and don'ts' are gleaned from both our good and bad experiences. Consider these insights a distillation of the advice brought together in this book. While they cannot guarantee success, if followed, we hope that they will allow you to remain focused on your company's goals and avoid the pitfalls, dead-ends and simple errors of judgement that the less well-prepared have fallen victim to in the past.

18.2 The Dos of Raising Funding

1. Have an experienced and capable management team	• A capable and experienced management team is just as important as the right leader. Their experience and track record of the team are hugely important. If there are gaps in the team, identify them upfront with a plan on how the gaps will be filled. • Ensure the team is balanced, whereby each member brings expertise to a different area and need of the business.
2. Prepare to succeed by learning from the fundraising experiences of other SMEs	• There is an enormous amount of information, resources and real-life experiences available to guide you on how to successfully raise funding. • Educate yourself on the fundamentals and maintain an open and critical mind, particularly when considering real-life examples of how other SMEs have succeeded and failed. • Understand why and how some companies have succeeded but, more importantly, find out about and talk to those who did not. What lessons can be applied to fundraising campaigns to ensure that such mistakes and missteps are not repeated?
3. Match your company with the right investor	• There is no point in a company pitching to, or even meeting with, an investor wanting a significant equity stake if the company is not prepared to give equity away. • Research potential investors to identify where there may be a potential fit and value-adding relationship. • Understand the investor's funding mandate and market focus. Research their investment history. Consider how you approached the target market for your own business and apply the same level of planning and scrutiny to finding the right investor. • Speak with other executives who have had dealings with the investor in the past and, in particular, seek out companies for whom the investment did not go as planned.

4. Weigh up and consider what else the investor has to offer	• Consider the potential investor as carefully as they are considering your company. Can the investor bring more than funding to your business? • Look for and ask about the 'value-add' in terms of introductions, advice and experience. Will the investor's history and experience complement the business and can they offer constructive insight to help the company achieve its plans and long-term goals?
5. Take time to prepare summary business information	• At an initial meeting, an investor will want to cover high-level information to understand the business, its products or services, and growth opportunities, and to assess whether to proceed to the next stage. • Prepare outline information in a slide deck (15 slides max.) about the business, its track record, market growth rates, competitors (see **Chapter 17**, **Section 17.3.5**). • This initial meeting is about building confidence. Begin by asking the investor how much time they have allocated for the meeting and complete the presentation with time to spare. • At the end of the meeting ask for feedback (even if the investor does not proceed, such feedback is invaluable). Is there a potential fit with the investor? What additional information can be provided to assist the investor complete an initial assessment decision? • Offer to host the next meeting at the company's premises. This is an opportunity to provide a demonstration of the company's products and services. Engage the investor in this way so that they get a sense of the value your concept will bring to the final customer.
6. Request and sign a non-disclosure agreement (NDA)	• If, after the initial meeting and presentation, the investor wants to proceed, request the completion of a non-disclosure, or confidentiality, agreement (NDA). • While it is likely that the investor will acknowledge the professionalism and importance of this request, at the same time be prepared to be flexible as to the terms of the agreement (see **Chapter 11**, **Section 11.6**). It is likely that the investor has a standard NDA that they use.

7. Know how much funding is required and how it will be spent	• It is important to have accurate figures for how much investment is required for the company, how it will be spent, on what and over what timeframe. An investor may disagree with the numbers, but will respect the planning (see **Chapter 16**, **Section 16.6**). • Be confident and definite, and avoid statements qualified by 'it depends'. Investors tend to be straight talkers. By responding in kind, you are already speaking their language (see **Chapter 16**, **Section 16.6**).
8. Know the numbers (historical and projected)	To show preparation and purpose, put the investor at ease: • As detailed in **Chapter 16**, prepare a five-year financial projection showing how the money will be invested and the contribution the investment will make. The projections should show how the investment will be repaid. Show historical numbers for the business as comparators. • Avoid 'hockey-stick' projected revenues and set out assumptions. Explain clearly any variances in the historical financials.
9. Back yourself	Having a financial stake in your own company projects confidence. Investors like to see that you and possibly others close to you have 'skin in the game'. It affirms that you believe the venture will be a success.
10. Engage professional corporate finance and tax advisors	• Meet with an experienced corporate finance advisor who can assist in the negotiations and help you to demonstrate an understanding of any complexities of your industry, e.g. seasonality of sales, longer payment terms or a large working capital requirement. Appropriate tax advice should also be considered as to how an investment will be structured to avoid any potential tax pitfalls. • Choose advisors with experience of representing both investee companies and investors, thereby knowing what is reasonable throughout the funding process. Their expert advice can also prevent tax or legal mistakes that can adversely impact subsequent funding rounds and investor exits.
11. Follow up in a timely manner	It is good practice, and again will build confidence, to follow up with investors in a timely manner after meetings and presentations, with soft copies of any information provided or additional information requested. Understand the investors' timeframes for a decision and respect them.

18.3 The Don'ts of Raising Funding

1. Don't get disheartened	• When determining how much money your business requires, don't let yourself become disheartened with any initial valuation provided by the investor that may contrast sharply with your valuation expectation. Understand the basis and differences with the investor's valuation, which may highlight areas of misunderstanding between you. • This is especially important if the business has not yet commenced trading. Any seed-round valuation is purely speculative, so stay confident and focused. Some equity dilution may be necessary to receive the funding required. • It may be possible that you will be asked to restructure the company and possibly dilute your equity stake in the business. If so, don't take this personally. • Try to evaluate the proposal as dispassionately as possible. Remember: the company is a separate entity from you, so try to come to a decision that best positions it to achieve its growth potential. • If the initial answer is a 'No', the investor may not have said no forever. Ask for feedback on areas in which improvements can be made in order to possibly revisit the opportunity with them at a future date.
2. Don't misunderstand the investor	• In order to secure funding, you may have to agree to some terms that you don't see as beneficial to the business. However, this may simply be the investor looking to protect their own interests. A certain degree of understanding is required at this stage. However, don't agree to any overly restrictive terms, especially in a seed round. As highlighted above, involve a corporate finance advisor to assist you in understanding the key terms. • One way to mitigate the long-term negative effect of such terms is to make sure they expire if the investor fails to participate in later rounds.
3. Don't disclose all your investment terms	Make sure your professional advisor is aware of your ideal terms prior to commencement of negotiations, but be careful not to detail all these terms in a first draft of the term sheet (see **Chapter 11**, **Section 11.6**). An investor may be willing to accept more favourable terms than you might expect so don't 'show your hand' too soon and don't sell yourself short.

4. Don't be afraid of criticism or challenges	• When dealing with savvy investors you can expect to receive 'constructive' criticism. • Investors can often be sceptical, highlighting potential weaknesses they see in financial projections assumptions, business plans and growth strategies. • Try to listen to these criticisms with an open mind and show appreciation for the ones that hold merit. Ultimately, however, don't be afraid to defend your business idea and your ability to create real future value for the investor. • Always thank investors for any feedback, whether you agree with it or not.
5. Don't become distracted	Raising finance can take a significant amount of time and resources in terms of preparing business plans, financial projections, etc. This can distract from the 'day job', resulting in poorer financial results and possible 'price chip', i.e. a sales-price reduction, when nearing completion of the investment process. To avoid this: • outsource the preparation of the business plan and financial projections to a professional corporate finance advisor; • let the corporate finance advisor progress discussions and only attend those meetings you are required to attend; • reschedule investor meetings if necessary for running the business. The investor will appreciate this and recognise it as a strength.
6. Don't put all your eggs in one basket!	• When raising capital, it is always beneficial to pitch to more than one potential investor. Having two sources of capital in the deal diversifies the risk if one investor decides not to proceed. It also creates competition on the terms, which may result in more favourable terms for your business. • Be measured and balanced, however, and don't tout the proposal around town as investors will not be willing to commit if they feel the opportunity is being oversold. • As discussed in **Chapter 11**, be careful and mindful of the exclusivity period on term sheets to ensure that these are as short as possible.
7. Don't send cold emails	Try to get introductions to investors through a trusted contact or, alternatively, pick up the phone to introduce yourself and your company. Don't send a cold email. Investors are inundated with random emails, which may be deleted.

8. Don't provide personal guarantees for company obligations unless absolutely necessary	A deal that requires the extension of a personal guarantee should be considered as a last resort. However, if all other options have been exhausted, make sure to involve a legal review and negotiate upfront the conditions upon which the guarantee will be either partially or totally released.
9. Don't disclose trade secrets/ know-how	As an investor will complete detailed due diligence, there is no need to disclose 'the secret sauce' until a term sheet is executed with the investor.

REVENUE OPINION ON TRADING STATUS OF CERTAIN INTELLECTUAL PROPERTY ACTIVITIES

Introduction

This appendix includes extracts from the Revenue Commissioners' published decisions in relation to the trading status of activities, i.e. whether the activities constitute a trade or not. It accompanies **Chapter 6**, Specified Intangible Asset Allowances, in particular **Section 6.3.2.1**. However, the concepts included here also have relevance to **Chapter 5**, The Knowledge Development Box, particularly **Section 5.3.2.1**.

The advanced opinions set out below, which have been provided by the Revenue Commissioners in the past, have given the companies that applied for the advanced ruling a level of comfort (but not a guarantee) that their operations will be considered by Revenue to be 'trading' should a review arise. The below cases were published by Revenue (with redactions to avoid disclosure of the taxpayers' identities) and have been reproduced here exactly as published. *Note*: Revenue's use of the term 'Case 1' is interchangeable with the term 'Case I' used elsewhere throughout this book.

Case number	Date received	Number of employees	Description of Activity	Opinion Given	Reason
6	March 2003	None	Company will be responsible for the group's global brand management activity, for which it will receive income from group companies and third parties.	Not Case 1	Under the new structure, the work involved in targeting, evaluating and negotiating contracts with suitable partners will be undertaken by other group companies. The company is carrying on investment activities from which royalties are derived. Case IV is the more appropriate classification.
8	March 2003	No additional employees	Company wants to treat (as an extension of its Case 1 trade) the income arising from licensing to a US subsidiary of the right to use an existing customer relationship.	Not Case 1	Unable to confirm Case 1 treatment. There is not sufficient ongoing work involved in maintaining the customer relationship for the exploitation of the customer base to be regarded as a trading activity.
15	August 2003	17–20 within two years	Company will: (1) license other group companies to use a proprietary system that will enable information to be delivered to clients over the internet. The Irish company owns the software, hardware and infrastructure; and (2) also provide a helpdesk and online sales in the provision of international media information.	(1) Not Case 1; (2) Case 1 confirmed.	(1) Unable to confirm Case 1 for this as the income flows from ownership of an asset rather than from being generated from activities undertaken by the company. The Irish company does not have full control and responsibility for the licensing and development of the system. All of the key decisions-makers in this area are located abroad and report to other group companies. (2) Case 1 confirmed for income from online sales and helpdesk functions as there will be sufficient activities in these areas to constitute a trade.

Case number	Date received	Number of employees	Description of Activity	Opinion Given	Reason
18	October 2003	None	The company is being established to develop, manufacture, market and sell a technological system.	No opinion given	It would not be appropriate to give an opinion on trading status. The strategic decisions and day-to-day management of the company will be carried out by a board of directors that will not be based in Ireland. The company does not have any senior personnel based in Ireland with the authority and skills to carry out the functions involved in the management of the R&D, and manufacture and sale of the company's products. The R&D phase of the operation would not be regarded as trading.
25	February 2004	Two to three	Irish company will license third parties to exploit trademarks in Europe and Asia. In the long term, the company also intends to expand its activities to include distribution and the provision of certain shared services for other group companies.	Case 1 confirmed	The company will be actively trading with the licences. Company employees are responsible for continuous monitoring and review of existing licences and licensees, seeking out potential new licensees, ensuring maintenance of brand image by driving and advising on marketing strategies.

Case number	Date received	Number of employees	Description of Activity	Opinion Given	Reason
26	February 2004	Outsourced initially	Established to protect and exploit the intellectual property (IP) of a non-resident.	Not Case 1	Unable to confirm that activities of the company constitute a Case I trade because it is not involved in the key activities giving rise to the income. None of the main players in the case are located in Ireland and the company's involvement is essentially passive. Case IV would apply if the company were resident in Ireland.
38	December 2004	50 initially, increasing to 350 by 2006	Operations centre to include sales, distribution, localisation, IP management and related support, and back office functions.	Case 1 confirmed	Case 1 confirmed on the basis that the activities of the company will be undertaken by personnel located in Ireland and that individuals with appropriate expertise and skills are employed by the company.
48	June 2005	415	Treatment of royalty income (as add-on to existing trade).	Case 1 confirmed	Case 1 confirmed on the basis that the royalty income represents only a small percentage of the profits of the company and cannot be separated from the trading income of the company.
49	June 2005	Seven, initially	The company is engaged in R&D with a view to patenting the resulting IP and granting licences for use of the IP developed. The company also intends to acquire existing patents from its parent company.	Case 1 confirmed	The proposed acquisition of patents would not of itself constitute a trading activity. However, it was agreed that if the company carries out all of the proposed R&D and licensing activities, then those activities would constitute a trade and income from the proposed activities would be taxable under Case 1.

Case number	Date received	Number of employees	Description of Activity	Opinion Given	Reason
58	December 2006	32 at present– 50–60 by 2007	Established company, whose activity consists of acquiring and developing pharmaceutical IP to commercialisation and earning profit by direct sales and licensing, proposes to establish new division to manage: (1) alliances with new pharma companies; (2) existing licences and negotiate new agreements for existing and new products.	Case 1 confirmed	Case 1 is confirmed on the basis that the level of the company's current activities and proposed expansion are such as to qualify to be taxable under Case 1.
60	January 2007	One part-time director	Company set up to exploit IP.	No opinion given	Unable to give advance opinion. From the information supplied it seems that the company is essentially passive. It does not appear to have the resources to actively manage the IP portfolio.
70	November 2007	Six initially, rising to 40 after four years	Company established to hold and develop IP rights.	Case 1 confirmed	Case 1 confirmed on the basis that the activities of the company will be undertaken by personnel located in Ireland and that individuals with appropriate expertise and skills are employed by the company.
71	November 2007	11	Company established to hold and develop IP rights.	Case 1 confirmed	Case 1 confirmed on the basis that the activities of the company will be undertaken by personnel located in Ireland and that individuals with appropriate expertise and skills are employed by the company.

Case number	Date received	Number of employees	Description of Activity	Opinion Given	Reason
76-643/2008	October 2008	15–20 initially, rising to 50–60 in 2009.	Company established to hold and develop IP rights.	Case 1 confirmed	Case 1 confirmed on the basis that the activities of the company will be undertaken by personnel located in Ireland and that individuals with appropriate expertise and skills are employed by the company.
116	January 2012	One	Company established to exploit the IP of an individual.	No opinion given	No opinion given as IP is an asset the mere ownership of which yields an income in its own right. The company would have to show that it has undertaken a high degree of activity in exploiting the IP. This is not a matter that can be agreed in advance.
124	May 2012	Not stated	Company established to carry out R&D and exploit the resulting IP by way of granting licences to use the IP.	Case 1 confirmed	Case 1 confirmed on the basis that the company will exploit IP by all means possible. A general manager, with the relevant expertise and skill, has been recruited to seek out potential opportunities for the exploitation of the IP product, licensing and development opportunities.
125	May 2012	Four	Company established to carry out R&D and exploit the resulting IP by way of granting licences to use the IP.	Case 1 confirmed	Case 1 confirmed on the basis that the company will actively enter into and conclude group financing transactions. The Irish directors have the necessary skills, qualifications, experience and authority to perform the day-to-day activities of the company.

Case number	Date received	Number of employees	Description of Activity	Opinion Given	Reason
126	June 2012	Not Stated	Company established to exploit group IP.	Case 1 confirmed	Case 1 confirmed on the basis that the board will actively manage and exploit the IP and the performance of licensees. The board will also be actively involved in the seeking out of new licensees.
129	July 2012	11 Initially	Company established to have overall responsibility for the manufacture and sale of group products, and to exploit the IP of both existing and newly generated IP.	Case 1 confirmed	Case 1 confirmed on the basis that the company has a sufficient number of employees with the relevant skills, expertise, experience and authority to carry on the proposed trading operations.
134	February 2013	25 Initially rising to 100	Company established to provide services to other group companies, including research and development and vendor management and purchasing support services.	Case 1 confirmed	Case 1 confirmed on the basis that the company has a sufficient number of employees with the relevant skills, expertise, experience and authority to carry on the proposed trading operations.
136	December 2012	23 by the end of 2013	Company established to develop and license software, and provide services and technical support to customers.	Case 1 confirmed	Case 1 confirmed on the basis that the company has a sufficient number of employees with the relevant skills, expertise, experience and authority to carry on the proposed trading operations.

Case number	Date received	Number of employees	Description of Activity	Opinion Given	Reason
140	May 2013	Existing company	An existing company intending to acquire and develop a portfolio of IP.	Case 1 confirmed	Case 1 confirmed on the basis that the company has a sufficient number of employees with the relevant skills, expertise, experience and authority to carry on the proposed trading operations.
142	June 2013	Not stated	Company established to exploit IP.	Not Case 1	The company is not considered to be carrying on a Case 1 trade as it would not be exploiting the IP to such a degree to be considered to be trading.
145	May 2013	Existing company	Existing company intending to exploit the IP of a group company.	Not Case 1	The company is not considered to be carrying on a Case 1 trade as it would not be exploiting IP to such a degree to be considered to be trading.
151	January 2014	Not stated	New company established to exploit, manage and develop IP of a group company.	Case 1 confirmed	Case 1 confirmed on the basis that the key management team of the company actively manage, develop, license and exploit IP acquired. The board will be responsible for developing the brand-enhancement strategy and setting strategic direction.
153	April 2014	25 Initially	The company will develop, manufacture and distribute software developed by it and other group companies.	Case 1 confirmed	Case 1 confirmed on the basis that the key management team of the company will have the skill, expertise and authority to carry on the relevant trading activities of the company.

INDEX